Routledge Revivals

Three Middle-English Versions of the Rule of St. Benet

Three Middle-English Versions of the Rule of St. Benet

Two Contemporary Rituals for the Ordination of Nuns

Dr. Ernst A. Kock

Routledge
Taylor & Francis Group
Routledge Revivals

First published in 1902 for The Early English Text Society
by Kegan Paul, Trench, Trübner & Co., Ltd.

This edition first published in 2018 by Routledge
2 Park Square, Milton Park, Abingdon, Oxon, OX14 4RN
and by Routledge
711 Third Avenue, New York, NY 10017

Routledge is an imprint of the Taylor & Francis Group, an informa business

A Library of Congress record exists under ISBN: 3029660

ISBN 13: 978-1-138-31066-7 (hbk)
ISBN 13: 978-1-138-31069-8 (pbk)
ISBN 13: 978-0-429-45928-3 (ebk)

BERLIN: ASHER & CO., 13, UNTER DEN LINDEN.
NEW YORK: C. SCRIBNER & CO.; LEYPOLDT & HOLT.
PHILADELPHIA: J. B. LIPPINCOTT & CO.

THREE MIDDLE-ENGLISH VERSIONS

OF THE

Rule of St. Benet

AND

TWO CONTEMPORARY RITUALS FOR THE ORDINATION OF NUNS.

EDITED,

WITH AN INTRODUCTION, NOTES, AND GLOSSARIES,

BY

DR. ERNST A. KOCK.

LONDON:
PUBLISHED FOR THE EARLY ENGLISH TEXT SOCIETY
BY KEGAN PAUL, TRENCH, TRÜBNER & CO., LIMITED,
PATERNOSTER HOUSE, CHARING-CROSS ROAD.
1902.

Original Series, No. 120.

RICHARD CLAY & SONS, LIMITED, LONDON & BUNGAY.

To Dr. F. J. Furnivall, Director of the Early English Text Society, Mr. A. Hughes-Hughes, of the British Museum, and Mr. A. Rogers, of the University Library, Cambridge, who have assisted me in this work, I here express my manifold obligations.

E. A. K.

Lund, in Sept. 1902.

CONTENTS.

INTRODUCTION.

§ 1. Of the Latin Rule of St. Benet, written about the year 516, the following Early English versions are known at the present day:

A. The so-called Common Version (West-Saxon), in several MSS.:

a. Cambridge, Corpus Christi College, 178, about the year 1000. Latin and English. The English text is edited by A. Schröer, in Bibliothek der angel-sächsischen Prosa, vol. ii, Kassel 1885–1888, pp. 9–77, the right-hand pages 79–91, p. 92, the right-hand pages 93–123, pp. 124–133. The Latin text is accounted for in the footnotes of the edition mentioned under *D* (see below); the Latin chapter headings are printed in full, *ib.*, pp. 8, 10, 11.

b. Oxford, Corpus Christi College, 197, about the year 1000. Latin and English. The English text is accounted for in the introduction and footnotes of the Kassel edition (see above); the prologue is printed in full, *ib.*, pp. 1–6. The Latin text is accounted for in the footnotes of the edition mentioned under *D* (see below).

c. British Museum, Cotton Tiberius A. 3, leaves 103, 104, from the beginning of the 11th century. Contains only the fourth chapter. Latin and English. The English text collated by G. Caro in Englische Studien, vol. xxiv, pp. 161–176 (1898).

d. Durham Cathedral Library, B. 4. 24, leaves 98 ff., from the middle of the 11th century. Latin and English. The English text collated by G. Caro (cf. above).

e. British Museum, Cotton Titus A. 4, from the end of the 11th century. Latin and English. The English text is accounted for in the introduction and footnotes of the Kassel edition (see above). The Latin text is accounted for in the footnotes of the edition mentioned under *D* (see below); the 62nd chapter is printed in full, *ib.*, pp. 124, 126.

f. British Museum, Cotton Faustina A. 10, about the year 1100. English only. Accounted for in the Kassel edition (see above). The chapter headings and the first chapter are printed in full, *ib.*, pp. 6–8, 134–141.

All these MSS. are "masculine," *i. e.* they refer to monks, not nuns. But various pronouns, etc., erroneously left in the feminine, show that the said MSS. go back to a version written for nuns. This version, again, is supposed to originate in a translation made, about the year 960, by the abbot ÆTHELWOLD and probably, like its Latin original, intended for monks.

B. The Wells Version, "masculine," in a fragmentary MS. (loose leaves) belonging to the Chapter of Wells, Somersetshire, from the beginning of the 11th century. Contains the greater part of chapters 50–64 (65). Latin and English (West-Saxon). The English text is printed in the Kassel edition (see above) on the left-hand pages 78–90, 94–122. The Latin text is accounted for in the footnotes of the left-hand pages 102–136 in the edition mentioned under *D* (see below).

C. The Interlinear Version, "masculine," in Cotton Tiberius A. 3 (see above, *A c*), leaves 105 ff., from the beginning of the 11th century. Latin and English (Kentish—West-Saxon). Edited by H. LOGEMAN, E. E. T. S. 90. London 1888.

D. The Winteney Version, "feminine," in British Museum, Cotton Claudius D. 3, from the beginning of the 13th century. Latin and English (Hampshire). Edited, with the Latin text to the left, the English to the right, by A. SCHRÖER. Halle 1888.

E. The Northern Prose Version, in the beginning "masculine," then "feminine" (with some masculine forms left; see § 6), in British Museum, Lansdowne 378, from the beginning of the 15th century. English (with Latin catchwords). Printed here for the first time.

F. The Northern Metrical Version, "feminine," in British Museum, Cotton Vespasian A. 25, from the former part of the 15th century; bearing a more southerly stamp. English (with Latin catchwords). Printed, with a few hundred errors, by K. BÖDDEKER in Englische Studien, vol. ii, pp. 61–93 (1879). Discussed, without collation, by F. HOLTHAUSEN in Anglia, vol. xiv, pp. 302–308 (1892). Collated, insufficiently, by E. KÖLBING in Engl. Stud., vol. xxiii, pp. 284–286 (1897). Reprinted here.

G. The CAXTON Abstract, "for men and wymmen," in Cambridge University Library, printed volume AB. 4. 64, from the end of the 15th century. Reprinted here.

§ 2. Closely connected, in import, with the 58th chapter of the rule (de disciplina suscipiendarum sororum) is *þe furme how A Nouice sall be made*, following in the Lansdowne MS. (§ 1, *E*) immediately on the rule, and written in a contemporary hand. Printed here, so far as I know, for the first time.

An analogous appendage, somewhat longer on account of several Latin prayers being given in full, is found after the other Northern Version (§ 1, *F*). It is written in a contemporary, if not the same, hand, save the heading, *The Method of makeing a Nunn*, which is of a later date. Printed, with numerous errors and inaccuracies, by W. Maskell, Monumenta Ritualia Ecclesiae Anglicanae, vol. iii, pp. 360–363 (second edition, Oxford 1882). Reprinted here.

[Two other rituals, more than half a century younger, out of the Lansdowne MS. 388, and Cambridge University Library, Mm. 3. 13, are printed by the Surtees Society, vol. 61 (Durham, etc., 1875), and by Maskell (see above), pp. 333–359.]

§ 3. Still less than the Common Version (§ 1, *A*) is the Northern Prose Version (§ 1, *E*) a verbal translation of the Latin text. Certainly the different parts of the rule are, on the whole, rehearsed in the usual order (cf. Logeman's edition, pp. vii–xiv, and Schröer's edition of the Winteney Version), the chief exceptions being that the greater part of ch. xiii, about week-day services, and the whole of ch. xviii, with its detailed directions, "quo ordine psalmi dicendi sunt," are omitted, the end of ch. xiii is put in the place of ch. xviii (on p. 18 read xiii for xviii !), and ch. lxii is placed before lxi. But in details, numerous alterations have been made. The majority of these are intentional modifications, partly due to "the grete change in that religion and the length" (Caxton's Abstract, p. 137, l. 12); see for instance the notes on 2/13, 3/31–4/1, 7/3, 32, 13/21, 15/29, 18/30–33, 19/31, 38/39, 39/34. But there are also cases of misapprehension or inadvertency on the part of either the paraphrast or some transcriber, *e. g.* the *sexe salmis*, p. 17, l. 10, instead of the Latin "sexagesimus sextus psalmus." Of the originator of the version we know nothing. In an indirect manner, however, his existence is constantly brought before the reader's mind. The chapters begin with *in this sentence spekis sain benet*, or some similar turn, and end with an added short prayer, being, as it were, an echo out of the spiritual children's hearts.

That we have no original, but a transcript, before us is sufficiently proved by the nature of the errors. I need only refer to (the notes on) 14/2, 43/18, 45/4. (The same holds good of the other Northern texts. See *e. g.* Metr. Vers. ll. 159–160, 1775–1778, Lansd. Ritual 142/14–15.)

In the opening sections of this sober rule there are some attempts at poetical diction:

Yef þu wil to þat rengne cume,
do þe dedis of godis sune, 2/26–27,

þat wid tunge lezis noht,
bot sothfastnes in his þoht, 2/33–34,

Lord, of us es it noht,
bot til þi name ioy es broht, 3/8–9,

Yef we þe painis of helle will fle,
and cum till ioy þat ay sall be,
  þanne full-fille we his wille.
Loke þat ȝe renne suiþe,
yef ȝe will to þe lange liue.
  þare may help þe here to. 3/31—4/1,

þan sal þi hert liht be,
in godis trouht yef þu it se, 4/7–8,

chasti þaim fra iuil wne,
als þe fadir dos his sune, 6/13,

þan he for oþir sal ancewer swa,
full riht az he at ga,
  And mende him in dede.
þe mare he mendis his cuuent,
Till mare ioy sall he be sent,
  til god at take his mede, 7/12–15,

haly lescun bliþelike here;
And clene uresun for to lere, 9/6–7,

leue þe wille of yure fles,
sua sal ye yure sinnes les, 9/8–9, etc.

§ 4. Whether induced by such poetical passages in extant English versions, or inspired by the moral elevation of the ancient Father's lore, another follower of his in the North turned the whole rule into English verse. The author enlarges on passages of ethical value, *e. g.* the prologue, whereas the minute directions about hymns and lessons, etc., for the various hours of devotion, occupying ten chapters (ix–xviii) in the Latin rule, are disposed of in not so many lines (1137 ff.). Totally missing are chapters xxi (de decanis monasterii), lx (de religiosis mulieribus quæ voluerint in monasterio habitare), lxi (de sanctimonialibus peregrinis), and lxii (de sacerdotibus monasterii). The remainder are treated of in the following order (one might say disorder): i–viii, xix–xx, xxii–xxx, lxv, xxxi–xxxii, xxxv, xlv–xlvii, xxxix–xl, xxxiii–xxxiv, xxxvi–xxxviii, xli–xliv, xlviii–lix, lxiii–

lxiv, lxviii–lxx, lxvii, lxvi, lxxi–lxxiii. Occasionally there is "easy vigour" in the lines:

> *To lay on þam þat vnder hir er* (are)
> *No euyer* (heavier) *band þan þay may ber,*
> *þat whils scho rubes a-way þe rust,*
> *þe vessel fal not al to dust,* ll. 2273–76.

But there are also such pitiful rhymes as:

> *In tym of winter, in Descember,*
> *Fro þe kalandes* (first) *of Nouember,*
> *Vn-to þe pase* (Easter) . . , ll. 1121–23.

§ 5. The metre is essentially the same as that of Genesis and Exodus, HAMPOLE's Pricke of Conscience, etc., described by R. MORRIS in E. E. T. S. 7, pp. xxxix–xlii, *i. e.* iambic bimeter ⏑ — | ⏑ — | ⏑ — | ⏑ —:

> *þe súth/fast réule / of sánt / Benétt,* l. 6,

regularly varying with — | ⏑ — | ⏑ — | ⏑ —:

> *Áls | sant Bé|net hís | ordánd,* l. 2,
> *Rýn | we súld | whyls wé | haue dáy,* l. 87,

and liable to several modifications, particularly the exchange of ⏑ — for ⏑ ⏑ —, or the slurring over of a short unstressed syllable (*-er*, *-el*, *-en*, *-ir*, *-yr*, etc., or a final vowel before another vowel) so as to make the apparent ⏑ ⏑ — sound like ⏑ —:

> *To þe býd|ynges óf | þi mó|der fré,* l. 26,
> *To cúm | in án|y gude cóm|pany,* l. 1028,
> *Ne súff|er hym ín | þam háfe | no stéde,* l. 150,
> *Túrn | fro éu|il and séke | to gúde,* l. 109,
> *And gíf | vs fúll|y all fólk | in-fére,* l. 233,
> *With sór|ow of sýn | we súld | him séke,* l. 1185.

The accent varies, of course, in numerous words of French origin, also in compounds, in words in *-and*, *-er*, *-est*, *-ing*, *-y*, etc. The final *e* in *ane*, *liue*, etc., is silent. So is mostly the vowel in the inflectional endings *-es*, *-is*, etc., not seldom even in *-ses*, *-cis*, *-ches*, and similar combinations, so that, e. g., *nouices* 1209, 1535, *nouysces* 2088, *teches* 636, are metrically on a par with (the plural) *nouece* 2361, *rais* (3 sg.) 1068, *tech* (3 sg.) 1284. Cf. ll. 120, 742, 798, 860, 939, 970, 1156, 1400, 1530, 2011, 2012, and others. However, both words like *teches*, and such as *childes*, *clothes*, *flodes*, *gestes*, *harmes*, etc., are also used for — | ⏑. In a good many instances the original shape of the lines has been altered through the substitution of younger and shorter forms, or through some omission, transposition, or other corruption. Cf. ll. 86, 160, 249, 446, 508, 783, 908, 936, 942, 957, 1211, 1269, 1365, 1452, 1458, 1589, 1619, 1661, 1843, 1931, 2151, 2180, 2434, 2484, 2498, where the restitution of the original structure seems to lie more or less close at hand. Lines of only six syllables, where the cause of the abnormity seems more open to guesses—later shortening of a form? accidental omission of some word? original juxtaposition of two stress-syllables?—are 779, 1463, 1721, 2074, 2183. In some lines not included in the above list, a shortening like *awin* > *awn* (cf. 2074) may have taken place, *e. g.* 540.

The original rhymes are disturbed or destroyed in ll. 159–160, 555, 1153, 1518, 1600, 1843. Spelling with *e* for *i*: 266, 267, 458, 505, 1521, 1592; *o* for original *a*: 1961.

Instances of alliteration are frequent, from the first line, *All þat wyll lely lyue in land*, to the last *Vnto þat lif our lord vs lede!*

§ 6. In the Prose Version, the prologue and the two first chapters are "masculine," *i. e.* they use *son* (*fili*), *mastir*, *fadir*, *munkis* (*monachorum*), *abot* (*abbas*), where the Metrical Version has *doghter* (*filia*), *maystress* (*magistre*), *moder*, *men or wemen* (*religionis*), *priores* (*priorissa*). But in chapter iii *þabes* steps in with *sororibus* and all. In the continuation there are only occasional traces of manly sway: *hym* 22/12, *hys* 25/9, *what man he is* 25/23, *spiritel fadir* 34/9, and, rather confusingly, *hym-selfe*, *He* 40/6.

The Metrical Version keeps all men out, except that the place of the *senex sapiens matura* as gate-keeper is filled by a *witti old man* (ch. lxvi). Passages like ll. 497 ff. can scarcely be called exceptions. *Priours* in l. *319 is surely a mere slip made by the scribe.

§ 7. CAXTON'S rule is a meagre "compendious abstracte," which leaves out the prologue and ch. i, xliv, xlvii, l–li, lvii, lxv, lxxiii, deals very summarily with ch. viii–xviii, xxi–xxx, xxxix–xli, lx–lxii, and fuses ch. xlii into vi, ch. lxiv into ii–iii, thus really accounting only for: ii–vii, xix–xx, xxxi–xxxviii (xlii), xliii, xlv–xlvi, xlviii–xlix, lii–lvi, lviii–lix, lxiii (lxiv), lxvi–lxxii.

§ 8. Several editions of the Latin Rule and commentaries on the same are mentioned by LOGEMAN (§ 1, *C*), pp. xxvi ff. I will refer the reader also to L. TRAUBE, Textgeschichte der Regula S. Benedicti, in Abh. d. hist. Cl. der kgl. Bayerischen Akad. d. Wissensch., vol. xxi, sect. 3, pp. 599–773 (1898), to G. J. AUNGIER, The History and Antiquities of Syon Monastery, London 1840, and particularly to Lina Eckenstein, Woman under Monasticism, Cambridge 1896, a book full of interesting information, although containing some linguistic and bibliographical errors. (An amusing instance is the comment on Metr. Vers. l. 410, containing the word *trauel*, to labour, to toil: "the prioress shall not favour any one nun by letting her travel more than the rest.")

For convenience' sake I here give a short survey of the matters dealt with in our texts.

(† means: some part of)	Latin Rule.	Prose V.	Metr. V.	Caxton.
	CHAP.	PAGE.	PAGE.	PAGE.
A. Prologue	Prologus	1–4	48–54	—
Different kinds of monks and nuns... ...	I	4	55–56	—
B. Superior; his or her election and duties	II, †LXIII, LXIV	5–7, 41, 42–43	56–62, 110–113	119–120, 121
consulting the convent	III	7–8	62–63	120
Functionaries—	XXI	20	—	127
specially:				
subprioress	†XXI, LXV	20, 43–44	85–87	—
cellaress	XXXI	24	87–88	127–128
sacristan, caretakers	XXXII	24–25	88–89	128–129
conductor of the divine service	†XLVII	32	—	—
infirmary attendants	†XXXVI	27	94	130
gate-keeper	LXVI	44	115–116	137
mass-priests, etc. ...	†LX	39–40	—	—
Order of the congregation; mutual reverence and love	LXIII, †LXXI	41, 46	110	137, 139
C. A good life—	IV	8–9	63–66	121–122
specially:				
obedience	V, LXXI	9–10, 46	66–68, 116–117	122–123, 139
to over-hard commands	LXVIII	45	113	138
silence	VI, †XXXVIII, †LXII	10–11, 27, 29	68–69, 97	123–124
humility	VII	11–15	69–78	124–126
poverty, *i.e.* community of property	XXXIII–XXXIV, †LV	25, 36	93	129, 134–135
letters and gifts ...	LIV	36	104	134
regularity	XLIII	30	97–98	131
industry	XLVIII	32–33	99–100	132
particular strictness and devotion during Lent	XLIX	33	100–101	132–133
D. Divine offices (rituals), etc.	VIII–XX	15–19	78–81	126–127
Collation; last part of the day	XLII	29–30	96–97	—
Regularity and strict observance ...	†XLIII, XLVII	30, 32	91, 97–98	131
Use of oratory ...	LII	34–35	101–102	133
Rehearsal of the rule	†LVIII, †LXVI	38, 44	107	135–136, 138

(† means: some part of)	Latin Rule.	Prose V.	Metr. V.	Caxton.
E. Dormitories	XXII	20	81	127
Food, meals	XXXV–XLI, †XLIII	25–29, 30	89–90, 91–93, 94–96	129–131
the abbess' kitchen and table	†LIII, LVI	35, 37	105–106	135
Clothing	LV	36–37	104–105	134–135
Brethren or sisters out at work or travelling	L–LI, LXVII	34, 44–45	101, 114–115	138
Skilled workers ...	LVII	37	106	—
Visitors	LIII	35–36	102–103	133–134
F. Punishments and atonements	XXIII–XXX, XLIII, XLIV–XLVI, †LXXI, etc.	20–23, 30, 31–32, 46	81–85, 90–91, 98–99	127, 131–132, 139
Unauthorised correction	LXX	45–46	114	139
Undue intercession ...	LXIX	45	(114)	138–139
G. Admission and ordination of				
such as wish to be monks or nuns ...	LVIII	37–39, Rituals	106–109, Rituals	135–137
children offered to God's service ...	LIX	39	109	137
monks or nuns from other convents ...	LXI	40–41	—	137
priests	LX	39–40	—	137
such as wish to be priests or deacons	LXII	40	—	137
H. Conclusion	LXXII–LXXIII	46–47	117–118	139–140.

§ 9. The Lansdowne MS. 378, vellum, 8vo, contains 46 numbered leaves. On the first page, left blank by the scribe, is fixed a scrap of paper with the title: *The Rule of St Benet & an Exposition of it. The forme of entring a Nouice.* The lower (blank) part of the first leaf is cut off. Each of pp. 1 b–45 b contains 23–27 (usually 26) lines, p. 46 a, where the "forme" ends, only 14 lines. On the last page is written in a late hand: Const. fol. 46.

The book is ornamented: 1. with large red initials placed at the beginning of lines and occupying the height of two, sometimes 3–5 lines (rendered in my print by extra large capitals); 2. with smaller red initials placed anywhere at the beginning of sentences or clauses (rendered in my print by ordinary capitals); 3. with small red characters (rendered by fat letters); 4. with red strokes in or across various black letters (not specially indicated by me); 5. through the prolongation upwards of the staves of several letters in most top-lines, these letters being, moreover, adorned with black and red strokes, tags, and arabesques, and thus more or less resembling capitals (in my print appearing as ordinary small letters).

In some instances chemical reagents had to be resorted to for the deciphering of words which were almost obliterated. (The Vespasian MS., on the other hand, is well preserved.)

An English catchword at the bottom of the page occurs only once: *charite*, leaf 7, back. The blank between this word and the last full line on the page answers to the height of about five lines.

§ 10. In the Cotton volume, Vespasian A. 25, 8vo, are united some blank paper leaves and 205 inscribed and numbered paper and vellum leaves of different ages. On the second page of the first leaf there is a table of contents (in a late hand) including 10 different headings. Some of the pieces are printed (or reprinted) by K. BÖDDEKER under the title Englische Lieder und Balladen aus dem 16. Jahrhun dert, in Jahrbuch für roman. u. engl. Spr. u. Literatur, N. F., vol. ii, pp. 81–105 (with a detailed table of contents, pp. 82–85), 210-239, 347–367, vol. iii, pp. 92–129 (1875–76). The 8th and 9th of the said headings are: *St Bennets Instructions In English verse* and *The Method of Ordaining a Nunn.* The corresponding texts occupy leaves 66–119 (according to an older, partly incorrect, pagination: 76–128) and 120–124 (129–133). Of these leaves, 66 and 71, 72 and 77, 78 and 83, and so forth (thus not all, as BÖDDEKER states), are of vellum. Between are inserted gatherings of four paper leaves (67–70, 73–76, 79–82, etc.), only that leaf 118 is also of vellum.

Our MS. (*i.e.* our part of the volume) is ornamented in much the same way as the Lansdowne MS. In the "Method" the English text (with some short Latin expressions) is underlined in red ink.

The characters are somewhat smaller and appear to be a little younger than those in the Lansdowne MS.

§ 11. The printed 8vo volume AB. 4. 64 in Cambridge University Library contains, on towards 150 leaves, three different treatises, of which the first is called "Orologium sapiencie," the second, "xii. prouffytes of tribulacyon," the third is our text. The rule occupies 2½ sheets (signed aa, bb, cc,) or 20 leaves. On the last page, however, there is a kind of index to the whole book and some information about the printing:

¶ Thus endeth this present boke composed of diuerse fruytfull

ghostly maters . . . .
. . . .

¶ The thyrde treatise sheweth the holy rule of saynt Benet whiche is right necessary to be knowen to al men & wym*m*en of Religyon that vnderstonde no laten / whiche sheweth xxxiij. poyntes to be obserued /

¶ Emprynted at Westmynstre by desiryng of certeyn worshipfull persones ·.·

§ 12. The characters ď, ħ, ƚƚ, ñ, r̕ (mostly practically equivalent to d, h, ll, n, r), ȝ (equivalent to either gh or þ), and z (meaning the same as gh or þ, once put in the place of s, 38/2, once for x, 6/14, footnote) are retained in my texts, save the ñ of the Caxton print, which is rendered by n*n*. For γ I print y or þ, according to its signification. Initial ff and ss are rendered by F and S, the apparent h and c in Ihũ, Ihc̃, by e and s, the & c', & c^w (and so on) of the Latin quotations simply by &c., γ^e, γ^i, by þe, etc. Often it can hardly be decided whether a certain character is meant for a capital or for a small letter. In each case I rendered it as I thought convenient, thus not claiming consistency in so unimportant a point. Expansions are printed in italics. For: a chesoun, vn to, under stande, I put: a-chesoun, vn-to, under-stande, etc. (the hyphens thus always being my own). In Introduction, Notes, and Glossaries, I mostly disregard such differences as ħ and h, vn-to and vnto, and so forth.

For the punctuation in the Northern texts I am solely responsible, the reader thus being at liberty to rearrange the stops wherever he thinks the words or clauses should be otherwise connected. In the Caxton print I retain all the slanting strokes (/). Some of the full stops and colons are converted into minor stops. Besides I add a good many commas and a few other punctuative marks.

Emendations are, according to the latest practise of the Society, greatly introduced into the text itself, the footnotes then accounting for what is actually to be found in the MSS. and the old print.

The Roman figures above the sections or in the margin refer to the chapters of the Latin rule (§§ 3, 8). The sign / in the notes to the Northern texts indicates the end of a line.

Those parts of the top-lines on pp. 1–140 which aim at stating the contents of each text page, are added by Dr. Furnivall.

ABBREVIATIONS.

imp. = imperative mood.
M.V. = the Northern Metrical Version.
O.E. = Old English (often practically = Old Northumbrian, or Old Anglian).
O.F. = Old French (including Norman-French).
O.I., O.Scand. = Old Icelandic, Old Scandinavian.
postpos. = in postposition.
pp. = past participle.
ppr. = present participle.
pt. = past tense.
pt.-pr. = past tense (in *-d*, *-de*) with the sense of present (§ 127).
P.V. = the Northern Prose Version.
sb. = substantive.
sbj. = subjunctive mood.
sup. = superlative.
W.T. = West Teutonic.
* (before a figure) = see footnote.

Other abbreviations will cause no difficulty.

Figures like 1/14, 15, 4/4, refer to page and line in the prose texts, figures like 1, 14, 182, to line in the Metrical Version.

SURVEY OF THE PHONOLOGY OF THE NORTHERN TEXTS.

A. STRESSED VOWELS IN WORDS OF TEUTONIC (LATIN, ETC.) ORIGIN.

§ 13. W.T. i, ī = O.E. i, io; (4) u.

1. *i*: *drink*, *fisch*, *hir*, *is*, *lig* lie, *þidir*, *will*, *writen*; *milke*, *siluer*; *blis*, *siþin*. Likewise (O.Scand., Latin, etc.): *ill*, *sister*, *skill*, *witerli*; *blys*, *bisschop*, *schrift*, *sikir*.—*y*: *drynk*, *hyr*, *whyder*, *wyll*, *wrytyn*; *blys*, *syþin*; *skyll*, *ymbrindays* (a fast).

2. To vowel-length [ī] points the spelling *syen* (*syne*, *sine*) adv. then. The verb *lif*, live, rhymes only with *gif*(*e*).

3. *e* [close]: *besy*, *þeder*, *wretyn*; *sethin*; *weterly*, *seker*. These are words with the first syllable open. Note. Often unstressed: *es*, *her*, *sen* conj. since, *wele* will. Forms due to loss of stress could afterwards be used also in accentuated position. The words *biriele* (O.E. *byrȝels*) 584, *elder* (Teut. **aldiz-*) 2206, *wirchep*(*e*) 1165, 1950, are accentuated ⏑ — (like *wessel* 1502, etc.) so as to rhyme with *wele* [ĕ] well, *err* [ĕ] are, *kepe* [ē] keep, respectively. Cf. § 73,2, end.

4. *u*, *ou* [of disputable value; cf. Luick, Sarrazin, Morsbach, Heuser (Engl. Stud. xxvii); I henceforth employ the symbol ɯ for long or short close vowel-sounds of the o-, u-group]: *wuke wouke* week.

§ 14. W.T. ī, i = O.E. ī, īo, ēo, ē.

1. *i* [ī]: *bide, life, rise, þi* thy, *time, stize* ladder, *wise*; *bi* by, *siþe* times, *suiþe* much; *bringe, childe, finde, behinde.* Likewise: *slike* such; *pine, pipe, schriue.*—*ie*: *obied* abide, *lie* (encroachingly) to lie.—*y*: *obyde, lyf, ryse, thy, tyme, wyse*; *by, syþe* times, *bryng, fynd, ly*; *pyne.*—*ye*: *pyen.*—*yi*: *wyis.*

2. The vowel is shortened in: *fift, fiftene, fyftyd, liht* easy, *lyghtly.* O.Scand.: *titter* rather.

The alternation of *er* and *ar* in words with *rd* or *rn* after the vowel (cf. §§ 16,2, 18,2, 44,2, with § 15,3) seems most easily explained through the assumption of M.E. shortening (at least to some extent) of the vowel before r + certain consonants. Thus short (or half-long): *hird* shepherd.

3. *e* [ē]: *betwene, stegh* ladder.—*ey*: *bitweyn.*

4. Short vowel: *wemen*; *herde* shepherd (cf. 2). Note. Unstressed: *be* by. Cf. *þe* *19/34.

5. *o*: *woman women.*

§ 15. W.T. e = O.E. e, eo, ea; (5) o, ō.

1. *e*: *bel, help, heuen,* heaven, *nek, reknyng, self, sex, seuin, welth, wheþer.* Likewise: *omell* between, *semtembir.*

2. Long vowel [ę̄]: *bede* prayer, *bere* to bear, *breke* break, *ere* (rhyme: *bere*) are, *ete* eat, *gete* (cf. § 100, no. 65, also 64) get, *scere* cut, *speke, wele* weal, *wreke* punishment.—*ey*: *steyl* steal. Cf. *þeis* these.

The adv. *euen* (*euyn,* etc.) constantly rhymes with *heuen.* But the spellings *eueyn heueyn* point to vowel-length. For words in *-est,* see § 100, no. 63.

3. *e* > *a*: *fer* far, *fare* further, *hert hart* heart, *smerte* smart, *werk wark, werld* world. Likewise: *wer war* worse. Cf. §§ 16,2, 19,3, 44,2, 72,3, and the cases in which an a-sound is expressed with an *e* before r, §§ 17,1, 18,2 (74,1).

4. *i*: *briht, hight* (encroachingly) promised, *riht, whider* whether. —*y*: *fyght* (beside *feght,* which rhymes with *night*), *whyder* whether.

5. *o, u* [u]: *world, worth wrz*; *wor* (cf. 3) worse.

6. For e + ȝ, see § 63.

§ 16. W.T. ē, e = O.E. ē, ēo.

1. *e* [ē]: *here* adv., *hete* (encroachingly) promise, *lete* he let, *mede* meed; *he, me, þe, we, ȝe*; *felde* field, *yelde.* Likewise: *sere* various.

2. *e* > *a*: *herd* flock, *lernyng* teaching, *ȝerne* eagerly, *ȝernyng ȝarnyng* yearning.

3. *i*: *hir-fra* from this, *wirchep.*

§ 17. W.T. a = O.E. a, æ, ǫ (eǫ).

1. *a* : *after*, *fast*, *harmyd*, *lagh* laugh, *lam* lamb, *latter* later, *þanc*, *þan* than, then, *waisse* (§ 69,3) wash, *whan* when, *warm*, *wat(t)er*. Likewise : *gabbing*, *happin*, *kast*, *want* ; *abbot*, *angel*, *anger* anchorite, *candel*.—*e* (before r ; cf. § 15,3) : *hermyt* harmed.—Cf. under 2.

2. Long vowel : *are*, *fare*, *glade* gladden, *late*, *make*, *name*, *shame*, *spare*, *tale*, *ȝate* gate. Likewise : *gate* way, *scaþe* injury, *takin tane* taken.—*ai* : *aile* ale, *fair* journey, *laite* late, *maide* made, *taile* ; *þus-gaite* thus.—*aie* : *aier* are.—*ay* : *layte* late, *mayde* made, *nayme*, *spayr* ; *þusgayt* thus, *tayn* taken.—Cf. § 63.

haue (always a main-verb when at the end of a verse) rhymes only with *craue* and *saue* (about 20 times).

A tendency to lengthening of the vowel in words like *all*, *call*, *stall*, known from other Northern texts, is reflected in the occasional spellings *stayle stale*. In *salme saulm*, the spelling may be (partly) influenced through *sauter* Psalter.

Forms like *sparde spaird*, with *rd* after the vowel (cf. § 14,2), but answering to an inf. with ā + single cons., seem to waver under the double influence of sound-law and analogy. Cf. § 100, no. 20.

3. *e* : *efter*, *togeder*, *þen*, *wesch* wash, *when* ; *keste*, *setirday*. Note. Through loss of stress, or by mistake : *women* 567, where we had expected *woman*.

4. *i* : *togidir*.

5. (M.V.) *o* [ǫ] : *tone* taken.

6. Short : *mony*, *os* as, *wos* was.

§ 18. W.T. ā, a = O.E. ā, ǭ.

1. *a* [ā, partly approaching to ǭ] : *slape* sleep, *þare* there, *ware* were, *whare* where (also *slepe*, *þer*, etc., § 21); *ga gane* go(ne), *sla* slay, *swa* so, *wha(m)* who(m); *alde* old, *bald* bold, *cald* cold, *fande* try, *halde* hold, *lande*, *lang*, *sande* gift, *stande*, *tald*. Likewise : *wane* number, *fa* few, *fra* from, *fang* get, *wrang* wrong ; *cal-* cabbage.—*aa* : *caald* cold ; *faa* few.—*ai* : *þair* there, *whaire* where, *whaim* whom, *fainding* temptation.—*ay* : *gay gayn* go(ne), *slay*, *saynd* messenger.—*au* (cf. § 74,3) : *cauld* cold, *faunde* try.

(*fendyng* in l. *148 is apparently due to the temptation of the following *fend*. *þer* in l. 1153 is a younger substitution ; cf. § 21.)

2. The vowel is shortened (cf. 14,2) in : *hard*, *-ward*, *warn*. —*e* (cf. § 15,3) : *herd hert* hard, *wern* warn.

Likewise with short vowel : *latte lat* let (cf. § 21,2).

3. (M.V.) *o* [ǭ] : *wor* were, *whor* where, *go gone*, *so*, *who(m)*, *old*, *bold*, *holde*, *told*.

Note. Shortened and dropped in: *also als as*.

§ 19. W.T. a = O.E. e.

1. *e*: *bed*, *hell*, *let* hinder, *mel* (rhyme: *tell*) speak, *heuy*, *men*, *nesch* (*neis* § 69,3) soft, *rest* repose, *þeneke* (*þencke*?) think, *wrechid* wretched. Likewise: *beri* beat, *eggyng*, *gest*; *belt*.

2. Long vowel [ę̄]: *dere* injure, *here* praise, *mete* meat, *stede* stead, *suere* swear, *were* wear.

3. *e* > *a*: *ger gar* make, *mare* mar, *merk* mark, *tery tary*.

4. *i*: *brind* burnt, *might*, *night*, *think*, *wrich* wretch.—*y*: *myght*, *nyght*, *ryst* repose, *thynk*.

§ 20. W.T. a = O.E. ęa.

1. *e* [ę̄]: *mere* mare, *teris* tears.

2. Short vowel (cf. § 14,2): *ȝerd* yard.

§ 21. W.T. ā, a = O.E. ē.

1. *e* [ē]: *dede* deed, *drede* dread, *euin* evening, *grete* weep, *leche* leech, *mete* suitable, *nehe* approach, *nere* near, *rede* read, advice, *schepe*, *slepe* (cf. § 18), *speche* speech, *þer* there, *wede* weed, garment, *wend* weened, *ȝere* year; *elde* age, *ende*, *english*, *hende* hands, *sende*, *strengh* strengthen, *weld* wield, *wend* go.—*ee*: *reed* advice.

Cf. § 100, no. 36, 50.

2. The vowel is shortened in: *dredde* dreaded, *redde* pp. read, *next*.—Uncertain is *lete let* to let (cf. § 18,2, end).

3. *i*: *ingles* English.

§ 22. W.T. ā = O.Scand. ę̄.

1. *e* [ę̄]: *sete* seat. 2. *a*: *rad* afraid.

§ 23. W.T. a = O.E. o. *ǫ*: *of* (*o*, *ǫffe*), *on*, *opon*.

§ 24. W.T. ā, a = O.E. ō.

1. *o* [ɯ]: *done*, *moneth*, *oþer*, *sone* soon.—*o*, *u*: *soth suth* truth.

2. The vowel is shortened in: *soft*, *broght*, *thoght*.

§ 25. W.T. o = O.E. o.

1. *o* [o, ɯ]: *god* God, *folk*, *rotyn* rotten, *wroght*. Likewise: *crosse*.—*o*, *ou*, *u*: *doghter doughtir*, *com cum*, *forth furth*.—(*w*): *wrht* wrought.

2. Long vowel: *before*, *dore*, *hope*, *loue* praise, *note* business.

§ 26. W.T. (O.Scand., Lat.) ō, o = O.E. ō.

1. *o* [ɯ]: *do*, *dome*, *flod*, *flore*, *inoh*, *mode* mood, *rodis* rood's, *stode*; *bone* prayer, *skole* school.—*oe*: *doe* do.—*oy*: *doy* do; cf. *oi* in *loises* lose, *moises* Moses.—*o*, *oo*, *ou*, *ow*, *u*: *none noon noune* noon, *done down* done, *bihoues bose b(ih)us* behoves, *boke buke* book, *gode gude* good, *loke luke* look, *sone sune* soon, *toke tuke* took.—*o*, *ue*: *proue pruefe*.—*u*: *bute* remedy, *rute* root.

2. The vowel is shortened in: *shod*; also (cf. 14,2) in: *bord* board, *born*, *corn*, *word* (rhyme: *hurd*).—*forþe furde* bring about, *hurd* treasure up.

§ 27. W.T. ō = O.E. œ̄.

1. *e* [ē]: *bete* amend, *deme* deem, *fede* feed, *fele* feel, *fete* feet, *hede* heed, *kene* bold, *kepe* keep, *mete* to meet, *seke* seek, *seme* seem, *spede* speed, *swete* sweet, *to-queme* agreeably. Likewise: *sleze* skilful. —*ee*: *feet*.

2. The vowel is shortened in: *rek* care.

§ 28. W.T. ō = O.E. œ̄ > e. *i*: *blis(se)* to bless.

For W.T. ō final, see § 30.

§ 29. W.T. u = O.E. u.

u [ɯ]: *full*, *kun* know. Likewise: *mun* will; *butter*, *nunn*.—*u*, *o*: *drunkin dronken-*, *sum[m]ir somer*, *sun son* son, *þurȝ thoro* through. Likewise: *munk monk*.—*o*: *dom* dumb.

wne wone, dwell, which in the North. Psalter rhymes with *mone*, shall, does not occur here as rhyme-word. Beside *obouen*, we find the contracted form *oboun obown*. For *obufe* and *lufe*, see § 100, no. 116.

§ 30. W.T. ū, ō final, u = O.E. ū.

1. *u* [ɯ]: *ful* foul; *schuldir*, *ȝung*.—*u*, *ou*, *ow*, *o*: *abute about abowte*, *dune doun down*, *huse hous howse*, *ut out owte*, *withuten -outen -owtin*; *hu how*, *þu þou þow*, *cuþe couth* could, known, *muþe moth*, *bun bown(yd)* bound, *fun(den) fon* found, *murn mourn*, *tunge tong*. Likewise: *true trou trow* believe, *trouz troht* belief.—*ou*, *ow*: *loud*, *loute lowte* bow, *toun town*, *now*. Likewise: *bown* ready.—*o*: *pond* pound.

bow (once *bew*; perhaps a mere slip; yet cf. § 79) § 62,2.

2. The vowel is shortened in: *buxum*, *curs* curse. Note. Often unstressed: *bott*, *us*.

§ 31. W.T. u = O.E. y (i).

1. *i*: *iuel*, *birs* behoves, *fil* fill, *-kin* kind, *mikil*, *mirth*, *sin*, *think* seems, *wirk* to work. Likewise: *bigg* build, *lift*; *kirk*, *kichin*, *kiln*, *miln* mill.—*y*: *dyn* din, *-kyn* kind, *mykil*, *myrth*, *syn*, *thynk* seem, *wyrk* to work; *bygg*, *kychin*, etc.

2. *e*: *euil*, *mekil*, *mery*. Likewise: *kechin*.

3. *u* (*w*), *o* [ɯ]: *wrm worm*, *work* to work.

§ 32. W.T. ū, u = O.E. ȳ (ī).

1. *i* [ī]: *fire*, *kind*; (encroachingly) *bie* buy, *ȝing* young. Likewise: *pride*.—*y*: *kynde*; *by* buy, *ȝyng*, *pryde*.

2. The vowel is shortened in: *filth, hid hyd* pp., *kide* pp. made known.

§ 33. W.T. eu, e + ụ, etc., ii + vowel = O.E. ēo, īo.

1. *e* [ē]: *bede* offer, *chese* choose, *dere* dear, *dreze* endure, *fle* flee, *lese* lose, *leuer* rather, *meke* meek, *tene* injury; *knes* knees, *tres* beams; *fe* property, *se* see; *held* pt.; *be, fende* foe, *fre, frende, sche, þre, yede* went. Likewise: *preste* priest.—*ee*: *knees, see, freend.*—*ei*: *kneis.*

2. The vowel is shortened in: *frenschep, fell*; *deuel.*

3. *i*: *þifte* theft. Note. Often unstressed: *bi by* to be.

4. *o*: *scho* she.

§ 34. W.T. eu = O.E. ē, ī. *i, y*: *liht lyght* sb.

§ 35. W.T. eu = O.Scand. ȳ. *i* [ī]: *tine* lose.

§ 36. W.T. eu + ụ = O.E. ēow, īow.

1. *eu* [ẹɯ, ɯ]: *breu-* brew-, *neu, reuþe* ruth.—*ew*: *brew-, new, rew* cause regret, *trew* true.

2. *u, ou, ow, o* [ɯ]: *yu ȝou yow, yure ȝour ȝor, four fourt fortt.*

§ 37. W.T. ai = O.E. ā; (2) a.

1. *a* [ā]: *a ane* one, *are* ere, *arely* early, *baþe* both, *claþe* clothe (O.E. *clāðian*), *gaste* Ghost, *haly* holy, *lauerd* Lord, *ma mare* more, *rase* rose, *stane* stone.—*ai*: *aire* ere, *airly* early, *daile* part, *haite* promise.—*ay ayn* a, one, *ilkay* each, *ayrly.*

The pron. *þa þai þay þo* (3) they, those (gen. *þar þair*, obj. *þam þaim þaym*, etc.) reflects both native sound-development and Scand. influence (§ 38).

(*ey* in *alleyn* *2257, rhyming with *tayn*, is accidental.)

2. The vowel is short in: *ask, clad* pp., *halows.* Note. Unstressed: *an a* indef. art.

3. (Mostly in M.V.) *o* [ǭ]: *o one* one, *both, gost, holi, lo, mo more, or* ere, *sore, stone, wo* woe. Likewise: *lone* loan.

4. The vowel is shortened in: *lord* (§ 14,2, § 100, no. 108), *noght nott not, oght, ony.*

§ 38. W.T. ai = O.Scand. ei, ē.

1. *ai* (*ay, aie*) > *a* [ā]: *ai ay* ever, *baine bayne* ready, willing, *graid grayde grathly* prepared, direct, straight, *graue* steward, *laite layte* seek, *naie* no, *raik rayk* wander, *raise rayse* raise.

2. *e* [ē]: *hel* sound, *þer* their, *þer* these.—*ei*: *þeir* their, *þeir* these.

3. *i* [ī]: *þire* these.

§ 39. W.T. ai = O.E. ǣ, ē.

1. *e* [long vowel; cf. § 100]: *clene* clean, *clethe* clothe (O.E.

clǣðan), *dele* deal, *-hede* -hood, *hele* heal, health, *hete* heat, *lede* to lead, *lene* lend, *lere* teach, learn, *lest* least, *leue* to leave, *rech* reach, *se* sea, *swete* to sweat, *tech* teach.—*ei* : *leire* learn.

2. The vowel is shortened in : *cled* clad, *clensid* cleansed, *euer*, *flesch* (*fleis*, § 69,3), *left* led pp., *les lesse* less.

§ 40. W.T. ai = O.E. ǣ > æ.

a : *fat*, *last* inf. Cf. § 63.

§ 41. W.T. ai + u̯, ā + u̯ = O.E. āw.

1. *au* : *slau* slow, *saule* soul ; *knau* know.—*aw* : *raw* row, ? *law* pile up, *slaw*, *sawle* ; *knaw*, *sawn* sown.

2. *a* [ā] : *sal* soul

Cf. *ouþer owþer oþer or* either, or, *nouþer nowder noþer nourę nor* neither, nor.

§ 42. W.T. ai + u̯ = O.E. ǣw.

ew [ęɯ, ɯ] : *slewth* sloth.

§ 43. W.T. au = O.E. (ēo) ēa.

e [ę̄] : *bete* beat, *brede* bread, *chepe* sb. purchase, *dede* death, *ere* ear, *grete* great, *heued hede* head, *lede* sb. lead, *lesyng* falsehood. For *leue*, permission, see § 100, no. 66.—*ee* : *eere* ear.

§ 44. W.T. au = O.E. ē.

1. *e* [ē] *eghen ezin* § 62,3, *eke* increase, *ethy* easy, *hegh* § 62,3, *here* hear, *les* loosen, *nede* need, *yeme* care, keep.

2. *e* > *a* : *herd harde* heard. Cf. § 17,2, end.

3. *i* [ī] : *high*. Cf. *die dy* die.

4. The vowel is shortened in : *hight hyght* height.

§ 45. Teut. au in words of Scand. origin.

ai (*ay*) > *a* [ā] : *hay* (O.I. *hey* ; the O.E. *hēȝ* would have developed in accordance with § 44), *layne lanande* conceal, -ing (O.I. *leyna*), *unait unat* useless, idle (O.I. *úneytr*). As appears from a comparison between this paragraph and § 63, there is no p h o n e t i c hindrance to explain *lay* 13/15 as identic with the O.I. poetical *leygr*, "flame" (whereas O.E. *lēȝ* would have given *leze* or the like, § 44) ; cf. however Notes.

The verb *die*, supposed to be of Scand. origin, is not analogous to the above group ; cf. § 44,3.

Other words : *lowsid* released (O.I. *lǫuss lauss*, loose) ; *þoȝ* though.

§ 46. W.T. au + u̯ = O.E. ēaw.

ew [ęɯ, ɯ] : *schew* show, *schrew*, *thews* manners.

B. UNSTRESSED VOWELS.

§ 47. Occasional notes on words and syllables with fluctuating stress have been given under A. On Romance words see chiefly under E. Here only a few remarks.

Of the unstressed syllables *ir*, *is*, and *er*, *es* (cf. § 5), the former are much more common in P.V., the latter, in M.V. The spellings *ys* (*askys*, *godys*, *terys*, etc.) and *ur* (*chantur*, *chapitur*, *sobur*, *sisturs*) are not frequent, *yr* (*ouyr*) and *ar* (*ayþar*) are rare, *or* *941 is probably a slip (like *goton* Caxt. 130/15). Alternate *-i*, *-e*, *-y* also in *meri mere mery*. Note the svarabhakti in *bownyd* bound, *eryd* earth, *seryf* serve, *telfete* twelfth, *werangus* wrongous.

Unstressed *be-*, *bi-* are commoner than *by-*. Unstressed *a-* (*ai-*), *e-*, *i-*, *in-*, *o-* alternate in *abide obide*, *again* (*aigain*) *igain ogain*, *apon opon*, *away oway*, *emang imang inmang omang*, etc.

The vowel of the def. art. is dropped in *tabbes* the abbess, etc. For *tapostil* we find *ta postil*, which has the appearance of an aphetic form of the noun with a fuller form of the indef. art.; also with *a* twice: *ta apostil*.

C. SEMI-CONSONANTS.

§ 48. W.T. i̯ § 66.—W.T. u̯ = O.E. w.

1. *u* [u̯] (P.V.): *sua* so, *suere*, *tua* two, *tuelue*.—*w*: *warn*, *win*, *witnes*, *write*; (mostly in M.V.) *swa*, *swere*, *two*, *twelf*.

2. Confused with *wh*: *where whor* were, *whit* for *with*, *whitnes* witness, *whreþid* made angry.

3. Confused with *v* (cf. § 55,3): *vun* come.

4. After a stressed vowel, see §§ 33, 36, 41, 42, 46.

5. Dropped (cf. 4): *sa so*, *telfete* twelfth, *lap* wrap. Likewise: *laite* seek. Cf. *werangus* (*wrang* + *wis*).

D. CONSONANTS IN WORDS OF TEUTONIC (LATIN, ETC.) ORIGIN.

§ 49. W.T. s = O.E. s (also voiced).

s [also voiced]: *answer*, *chese* choose, *wise*, *chosen* (encroachingly).—*c*: *ancewer*, *wice*. Likewise: *decem ber*.—*sc*: *anscewer*; *Descember*. Cf. *blisce blisced* bless(ed), and § 84.—*ss*: *chossin*.

Doubled in: *als-sua als-so* also.

For sk, see § 69.

§ 50. W.T. r, z = O.E. r.

r: *briht*, *rinne*, *thrid third*, *thirld*, *thurgh thrugh*; *here* hear, *here* praise.

Supplanted by *s*, § 49.

§ 51. W.T. l = O.E. l.

1. *l*: *worldly*; *alswa also als* also, as.

2. Dropped: *wordly*; *as.* Perhaps *suik* 31/32 and *sich* 2008 are both erroneous.

§ 52. W.T. m = O.E. m.

Usually *m*. In endings it became *n* and was dropped; cf. § 53.

§ 53. W.T. n = O.E. n.

1. *n*: *ane one* one, a, *nane none* none, no, *mine* my, *þine* thy (all these mostly independent, or immediately before the initial vowel of the qualified noun); *euin* evening, *opon* upon, *on*, *-redin* -red (hatred, kindred), *seuin*.

Joined to the following word: *a noþer* another, *na noþir* no other. Doubled: *an noþer*.

2. Dropped: *a o* one, a, *na no* none, no, *mi my* my, *þi thy* thy (all these mostly before cons.); *a* and (here perhaps only a slip), *opo* upon; finally in most inflectional endings except strong pp. (§ 124).

§ 54. W.T. *η* = O.E. *η*.

1. *n* [*η*]: *groching* [-i*η*g], *ingles, lang, think.*

2. Dental: *lentin* Lent, *grochin.*

§ 55. W.T. f, ƀ = O.E. f, v.

These are confused both as to their phonetic distinction and as to mode of writing.

1. *f*: *fadir, gifte, stifly, twelft*; *lafe* loaf, *life* sb., *staf* stick. To judge from 2, it is not certain that the *f* of the last words always represents an unvoiced sound. On the other hand, more or less distinct unvoicing may partly be represented by spellings like *haf* to have, *lif* to live, *gif* to give,—varying with *hafe, life, gife* and those given under 2. Distinct appear cases like *life* [līv] sb., rhyming with *schriue*, after the analogy of the inflected forms (2). Further examples: *obufe, lufe, þarf* is needed, *unlefful* not permissible. Likewise: *pruefe* to rest.—*ff*: *offe* (at the end of a clause; usually *of*), *giffe* if; also *liffe* to live, *giffis giffyn.*

2. *u*: *euen, giue* to give, *giue* if, *haue, heued* head, *lauerd, liue* to live, *obouen* above, *steuen* voice, *tweluemonez*; also *laue* (rhyme: *saue*) loaf, *liue* (rhyme: *fyue*) sb. life, after the inflected forms, as: *liuis* life's, *liues* lives. Likewise: *heuin* avenge, *proue* to test.

3. Confused with *w* (cf. § 48,3): *ewyn hewyn* even, *prow* to prove, test.

4. Assimilated or dropped: *wymmen women, leful* permissible,

bihus bus behoves, *had, has, hed* head, *lord, o* of, *oboun obown* above, *tuelmoneth* twelvemonth, *þar* is necessary.

§ 56. W.T. ƀ, b = O.E. b.

1. *b*: *band.* Likewise: *abbot abot.*

2. Dropped: *dom* dumb, *lams* lambs.

§ 57. W.T. or Lat. p = O.E. p.

1. *p*: *appil, shep* sheep, *spare.*

2. *m* (through a kind of assimilation): *semtembir.*

§ 58. W.T. þ = O.E. þ, ð.

1. þ [þ, ð]: *muþe* mouth, *whreþid* made angry, *yuþe*; *þar* there, *þe, þu*; *erþe*; *bliþelike, broþir, claþis* clothes, *forþe* bring about, *forþermare, noþer* neither, *oþer, siþin* afterwards.—*th*: *forth, moneth, moth* mouth, *slewth* sloth, *wrath* angry, *wreth* make angry, *ȝouth*; *the, with*; *erth*; *bathes* baths, *blithly, clathis, nother* neither, *other, sithen, worthy.*—*ht* (cf. § 62,1, end): *forht* forth, *trouht troht* belief.—*tht*: *ertht* earth.—*ȝ, z*: *forȝe forz* forth, *-monez* -month, *muz* mouth, *trouz* belief, *wraze* angry, *wrez* make angry, *yuȝhed* youth, *ȝer* these, *ȝur ȝurh* through; *clazing.*

2. *t*: *hight* height, *sight, þifte* theft; pronouns and adverbs with initial þ, when the preceding word ends in s, t, d: *tam, tar, te, tu,* etc.; *sal tu* shalt thou; *whit* § 48,2.—*tt*: *fortt* fourth, *neyntt* ninth.

3. *d*: *clad* cloth, *forde* forth, *wid* with; *eryd* earth; *furde* bring about, *noder* neither, *oder* other, *wheder.*

4. Assimilated or dropped: *clad cled* pp., *close* clothes, *noure nor* nor, *or, sine sen* then, since.

For *wirchep*, see § 70.

§ 59. Teut. ð = O.Scand. ð.

1. þ, *th, z*: *graiþe* procure, *grath* ready, direct, *hundrez* hundred.

2. *d*: *graid* ready.

§ 60. W.T. ð, d = O.E. d (t).

1. *d* (*dd*): *fadir, girdid, godspel, hard, harmyd, hider, word, endid endydde, bownyd, funden, hend* hands, *standand* ppr., *wend* go.

2. *t*: *hermyt* harmed, *endit* ended, *rasit* raised, *standant* ppr., *hent* seized, *lent* (pt. of *lene* lend), *schent* ruined, *sent, went* pt.; isolated forms: *went* inf. go, *hert* hard.

3. Assimilated or dropped: *an in* and, *ancewer* answer, *bown* bound (*vnbun* unbound), *fun* found, *gospel, blisse blisce blis* to bless.

For *fren(s)chep*, see § 70.

§ 61. W.T. t = O.E. t.

1. *t*: *hert* heart, *it, take.*

Joined to the following word : *þe tane* (for *þet ane*) the one, *þe toþer* the other. (*þe tyme* *148/20 for *þe yme*, the hymn, is probably due solely to *þe tyme* in the preceding line.)

2. *d* : *id yd* it.

3. Confused with *th* (cf. § 58,2): *herth* heart. Cf. also § 93,3.

4. Dropped : *best, last* ; accidentally, possibly reflecting a careless pronunciation : *brihnes* brightness, *lighlike* lightly, *rihuisnes* justice, *scrif* shrift.

§ 62. Teut. medial or final χ, hw, ȝ = O.E. or O.Scand. χ (velar), χ́ (palatal), ȝ, ȝ́.

1. *h* [χ]: *ahte* ought, *ahtend* 8th, *broht* brought, *dohtir*, *liht* sb., *niht* night, *noht* nought, not.—*gh* : *aght* ought, *aght* eight, *broght*, *doghter*, *feght* fight, *lagh laghter* laugh(ter), *light* sb., *night*, *noght*.—*ȝh* : *aȝht* ought.—ȝ, *z* : *doȝtir*, *fezte*.—*h* and *t* transposed (cf. § 58,1): *broth* brought, *lyth* sb. light, *nith* night.

2. *h* [χ], ȝ (*z*, *ȝh*, *gh*) > back vowel, disappears : a. *ah aȝh aȝ az aw* ought ; *aȝen azen auen aune awin awn ahen* own, *daw* dawn, *draȝe draze draw drahe* draw, *gainsaȝe* gainsaying, *laus law* law(s), *saz saw* pt. saw ; *aze aw ahe* awe, *felaze felow felahe felascap* fellow (-ship), *laȝis law* low(ers) ; cf. *fag*[*n*]*is* fawn 43/27.—b. *þoȝ þoz* though, *lowe* flame.—c. *ȝouth yuþe* youth, *bow* to bow.—d. *þurȝe þurz thurgh thoro þur* (*ȝur*) through ; *folow folu* follow, *halow* hallow, *halows* saints, *sorow* sorrow.

The spirant is dropped also in : *not* (cf. 1).

3. ȝ (*gh*, *z*) [palatal] > front vowel, disappears : a. *hi hy* hie, *stize stegh* ladder.—b. *negh nehe* approach, *heȝe hez hegh heyes hee he high hyes hi* high, heighten(s), *ezin eghen eye ehin ehe ee* eye(s). —c. § 63.—d. *foliz filiȝ folihe* follow, *haliz* hallow, *haliȝes* saints, *herberz herber* to lodge, *tary*, *hali* holy, *meri* merry, *inoh* enough, *mirth*. Cf. *beri* to beat (O.I. *berja*).

4. *th* : *thurth* through.

5. The spirant + s > *x* : *waxe* grow ; *buxum*.

§ 63. O.E. ȝ́ (§ 62) with a preceding e, æ (§§ 15, 17, 40).

ai (*ay*, *ayi*) > *a* [ā] : *allways allwase* always, *again agayn ogans* again(st), *dai day*, *fain fayn*, *fair farest* fair(est), *lais* he lays, *lay* inf. (encroachingly), *lay* pt., *mai may*, *maydyn madyn* maiden, *maine mayne mayine* main, *said sais sayand sayng*, *slayn* ; *ayþar aþer* either. Likewise : *gaine gayne* profit, *play*.

§ 64. W.T. initial χ = O.E. h.

1. *h* : *has*, *hegh*, *her*, *heuy*, *hir* their, *heuyn* heaven ; *behoues*.

2. Dropped (assimilated): *lafe* loaf, *lauerd*, *lady*, *lagh* laugh, *nek* neck; *it*, *ass* have, *egh* high, *eghnes* highness, *er* her, *euy* heavy, *ire* their; *bus* behoves; cf. *þaue* they have; *bakkows* bakehouse.

Excrescent: *hare* ere, *heuyn hewyn* even, *hus* us. Cf. § 83.

§ 65. W.T. initial hw = O.E. hw.

1. *wh* [hu̯]: *wham* whom, *what*, *when*, *while*.

2. *w* [u̯]: *waim* whom, *wat*, *wen*, *wilis* whilst.

3. *qu* [ku̯]: *quat* what.—*qw*: *qwen*, *qwil* while.

§ 66. W.T. initial ȝ, i̯ = O.E. ʒ́.

1. *ȝ* [ʒ́] (mostly M.V.): *ȝapli* keenly, *ȝate* gate, *ȝe*, *ȝelde*, *ȝeme* keep, *ȝere*, *ȝet*, *ȝung*.—*y* (P.V.): *ye*, *yef*, *yelde*, *yeme*, *yer*, *yet*, *yung*.

2. Dropped: *if*.

§ 67. Teut. ȝ, g = O.E. or O.Scand. g, ǵ.

1. *g*: *begin* (after pt. *begane*), *gadir*, *girdid*, *glad*, *go*, *gold*, *greting* weeping; *-ing* (*groching*, etc.); *lang*, *thing*; *gabbing*, *gate*, *ger* make, *gerne* eagerly (beside *ȝerne*, § 66), *gest*, *gete* get, *gete* keep, *gifte*, *giue* give, *giue* if.

2. *k*: *kissink*, *thynk* thing.

3. Dropped: *lentin* Lent, *-in* (*grochin*).

§ 68. W.T. k = O.E. k, ḱ (> tš).

1. *k*: *bak* back, *ilk* each, *kald* called, *ken* know, *kide* made known, *knaw* know, *kun* know, *kyng* king, *like* adj., vb., *make*, *rike* rich, *seke* seek, *swilk* such, *think*. Likewise: *slik* such, *take*; *kirk* church.—*c*: *bac* back, *cald* called, *claþe* clothe, *couth* known, *cune* know, *ic* I, *þanc*, *þinc* seem.—*ck*: *þincke* think.—(*x*): *bytuix*.

(*thyngyng* *42/33 is a blunder.)

2. *ch* [tš]: *chese* choose (encroachingly: *chosen*), *child*, *leche* leech, *speche* speech, *tech* teach; ? *sich* such (no Northern form). Likewise: *kichin* kitchen.—*sch*: *scheke* cheek; *schosin*. Cf. § 95.

3. Dropped: *I*, *-ly*, *ma* (*mase*, *maide*) make; *ta* (*tan ton*) take.

§ 69. Teut. or Lat. sk = O.E. or O.Scand. sk, sḱ.

1. *sk*: *ask*; *skill*, *sklaunder* slander, *skole* school.—*sc*: *sclaunder*, *scole*, *scripture*.

2. *sch* [š]: *flesch*, *nesch* soft, *schall*, *schame*, *schep*, *scher* cut, *schilde* to shield, *wesch* wash; *schort*, *schrift*, *schriue*.—*ssch*: *bisschop*.—*ssh*: *flessh*.—*sh*: *english*, *shal*, *shame*, *shep*, *shod*.—*sc*: *scere*, *scifte*, *scorn*; *scort*, *scrift*, *scriue*.—Cf. § 70.

3. *s*: *fles* flesh, *sep* sheep, *silde* to shield (these only in P.V.); *ingles* (once O.E. *englis*) English, *sal* shall, *suld* should.—Palatal pronunciation seems to be specially marked (in P.V.) through the spellings *is*, *iss*: *fleis*, *neis* soft, *waisse* wash.

§ 70. O.E. sḱ and a preceding þ (§ 58), d (§ 60).

ch, *sch* [tš > š]: *wirchep* worship; *frenchep frenschep* friendship.

E. VOWELS IN WORDS OF ROMANCE ORIGIN.

(Some side-forms in these paragraphs are not, or need not be, due to English sound-development, as they occur already in O.F. The signs ′ and ˘ denote stress or want of stress.)

§ 71. O.F. i, ī.

1. *i*, in a syllable which has a. remained stressed: *riche, simpil*; b. become stressed: *litter, relígioun, ríches*; c. remained unstressed: *sĭlence*; d. become unstressed: *perĭl, seruĭs*. Cf. *spirt spirit*.—*y*: *ryche, punўst, perўl, seruўs, latўn*.

2. The vowel is long in: *crie, fine, vile, desíre, decípill, mercí, seruíce, signifí, sprite, strife*.—*y*: *cry, vyl* vile, *gyde* guide, *mercy, seruyse, stryf*.—*ii*: *multeplii, singnefiis*. Cf. *propirtarij*.

3. *e* [close]: *préson, relĕgion, seruĕs, perĕl*.

4. Long vowel [close]: *gede* guide, *eremete* (rhyme: *perfite*) hermit, *chastese* (rhyme: *wise*), *seruese* (rhyme: *wịse*), *sprete* spirit.

For *euaungelest*, cf. § 100, no. 93.

§ 72. O.F. e, ẽ.

1. *e*: a. *abbésse, drésse* direct, *létter, mes(se)* mass, *assént, reuerénce, siléncе*; b. *lésson, pénance, tréspas*; c. *ĕntent, lĕsson, pĕnance, sĕsoun*; d. *abbĕs, richĕs*.

2. Lengthened: *feste* feast.—*ee*: *feeste*.

3. *e* > *a* (before r): *ermitis armitis* hermits, *certayne sărtayn* certain, *maruayl* marvel, *peril parel, serue sarue, seruice săruyse*.

a: *presánd* gift, *reuerance, antente* (O.F. rarely *a*-).

4. *i*: *litters* letters, *trispas, orĭsoun*.—*y*: *ynke*.

Further in § 78.

§ 73. O.F. ē, ee, ie, etc.

1. *e* [long vowel]: [ē] *avisé, charité, degré, breue* brief, *chef* chief, *clere, feris* belongs, *greue* grieve, *manére, pepil* people, *prophete* (rhyme: *bĕte*), *quere* choir, *releue, repreue* reprove, *soppére*; [ę̄] *lele* loyal, *mene* middle, *sele* seal, *-tene* (abs-, con-, main-tain).—*ee*: *gree* step; *leel* loyal.—*ey*: *-teyn* -tain.—For *requered*, cf. § 100, no. 57.

2. Shortened, when losing stress: *asemblĕ, prophĕt, soppĕr, manĕr, matĕr, priuĕlike* privily. With new stress: *prophétt prophét* (rhyme: *set*).

Thus the last word affords a good example of the fluctuations in accent, quantity and quality: O.F. and M.E. stressed ē > unstressed ē, e, ę (ə), with poetic re-accentuation > stressed ę (occasionally ę̄).

3. *a*: *preuăly* privily.

§ 74. O.F. a, ā.

1. *a*, in a syllable which has a. remained stressed: *abbásse, damne, principáll*; b. become stressed: *látyn, tráuel* labour; c. remained unstressed: *chăstese, părtie, trăuaile* labour; d. become unstressed: *penănce.*—*herdy* (M.V., once) should probably be placed here; cf. § 15,3. P.V. has *hardy*, O.F. *hardi* and *herdi*.

2. *a* [ā]: *blame, case, chaste, dame, hast* haste, *place, state, tast, waste*; *chápiter, chástese* chastise.—*ai*: *chaiste* chaste, *plais* place, *staite, waist* waste; *chaipitur, chaistese.*—*ay*: *blaym, daym* dame; *chaypitur.*—*madăum* 2210 is written with the abbreviation-mark which I in other cases have expanded as *au*; cf. 3.

Half-long or uncertain appears the stressed vowel before *r* + consonant: *reward*, § 100, no. 20, *depart depairt depayrt* divide.

3. *au* > *a* [ā]: *chaumber, daunger, ensaumpil ensawmpil ensampil, euaungelest, graunte grante, laumpe, maunde* foot-washing, *penance, remnaunt remanant, sclaunder sclandir, seruaund seruand* servant. Cf. the cases in which an ā-sound is expressed with *au*, § 18,1 (§ 74,2).

§ 75. O.F. o.

1. *o*: *acorde, order, propir, torch*; *amónesce, fólis* follies, *óffice*; *fŏrest*; *comfŏrt, recŏrd* agreement.

2. Long vowel [ǭ]: *close, cote, fole* fool, *restore.*—*oo*: *fool.*

§ 76. O.F. ou, ō > u, ū.

1. *u* [ɯ]: *acumbird.*—*u* (*eu*, cf. § 79), *ou*, *o*: *curs cours, gruche greuching groch, suffer soffer, super sopper, guuerne gouerne, cumpany company, glutunie glotony, cŭntrè cŏntresse.*—*ou*, *o*: *soume* sum, *touch, furme form, ŏurel* oriel.—*o*: *couir* heal, *scorid* scurged, *trofils* trifles; *lessŏn, resŏn.*

2. Long vowel: *anure* worship, *aure* worship, *pronunce.*—*dute doute dowte, hure houre owre* hour, *religiun -oun -own -on, labur -our -ore, resun -oun -on, cunsel counsel consel.*—*toumbe, cownte, prowe* profit, *towel.*—*lessóns.*

§ 77. O.F. ü, ṻ.

1, *u* [ɯ]: *hurt, custúm, púnych pŭnest, iŭgement.*—*u*, *o*: *studie stody, sugetes sogetes.*

2. Long vowel: *armur* armour, *cure, excuse, refuse, mesure, remue* remove, *rudely, vse, uertú.*

§ 78. O.F. ai, aī, ei, eī, partly alternating with, or contracted into, simple vowels (*a*, *e*).

1. *ai* (*ay*) > *a* in a syllable which has a. remained stressed [ā]:

abbái abbáy, *certáyne certáne*, *couáyt* covet, *counsáile cunsále* counsel, *faile fayle falled* (§ 99) fail(ed), *faith fath*, *lai lay* law, *ordáin ordán*, *praise prayse prase*, *puruáie -uáyde*, *sainte sant*, *-saive -ceaue -saue* -ceive, *segerstane* sacristan, *souerain -ayn -ane*, *straite strate* strict, narrow, *trauaile -ayle* labour, *tuaile* cloth, *vaile vayle vale* veil; b. become stressed: *máistres máystres mástres*, *máynten*, *práier práyer práer*; c. remained unstressed [ā > a]: *frăitur* refectory, *lăiser lăser* leisure, *măistres* mistress, *măinè* household, *măynteyn*; *văssel*; d. become unstressed: *abbăy abbăis abbă* abbey(s), *certăyn certăn*, *couăite*, *maruăyl*, *puruăyd*.

2. *e* [ę̄]: *encrese*, *ese* ease, *frelty*, *pese* peace, *plese* please, *trete* treat, *venys* "pardons."—*ei*: *veine* pardon.—*ey*: *conseyue*, *dedeyn* disdain, *obey*, *verrey* true.

3. Unstressed: *mĕnȝè* household, *couĕt*, *curtĕsly*, *counsĕl*, *puruĕd* purveyed, *trauĕl* labour, *towĕl* cloth.

4. (M.V.) *o* [§ 37,3]: *segerstone* sacristan.

§ 79. O.F. eü, ev.

eu, *ew*, [ęɯ, ɯ]: *reule rewle*; *eschew*.—*ou*: *rowle*.—*u*: *duly*.

§ 80. O.F. au.

1. *au*: *auter* altar, *caus*, *claus*, *faute*, *sauf* safe, *sauter* Psalter. —*aw*: *awter*, *bawmes*, *fawte*, *sawter*.

2. *a* [ā]: *safe*, *saue*.

§ 81. O.F. oi, oĭ, üi.

1. *oi* [oį, ɯį] (P.V.): *cloister*, *noise*; *aioingne* enjoin, *croice* cross, *noi* annoy, *pointe*, *voice*.—*oy* (final in both versions): *ioy*; *(a)noy*, *poynte*, *stroy*.—*vi* (P.V.): *invinis* enjoins, *vinemens* ointments.

2. *o* [long vowel] (mostly M.V.): *chose* choice, *closter*, *nose* noise; *aiont* together, *ponte*, *voce*.

3. *u*: *frute* fruit, *nuse* hurts.

§ 82. O.F. *povre*, poor, appears as *pouer pore* (rhyme: *dore*) *pure*.

F. CONSONANTS IN WORDS OF ROMANCE ORIGIN.

§ 83. O.F. h.

1. *h* [partly silent]: *habete*, *hardy*, *honest*, *honour*, *houre*.

2. Dropped (as often in O.F.) also in writing: *abit*, *aires ayres* heirs, *deseret* disinherit, *eremete* hermit, *onest*, *onur*, *our* hour.

Excrescent: *hordand* ordained. Cf. Lat. *hymnus*, O.F. *ymne*, M.E. *hym yme ymne*.

§ 84. O.F. s etc. (*ss*, *sc*, *c*, *z*).

s [also voiced]: *benysoun*, *counsel*, *finise*, *leson*, *peris* perish, *punest riches*, *-sa(i)ue* -ceive, *seruis seruyse* (rhyme: *wise*), *verse*, *vose* voice.—*c* (*ce*): *benecun*, *councel*, *degrece* sg. degree, *perceaue*, *puruyance*, *recaiue*, *seruice*, *sience*, *verce*, *voice*.—*ss*: *lesson*.—*sc*: *amonesce* admonish, *discipil*, *lescun*, *nouysces*, *punysce*, *stresce* stress.—*sch*: *leschun*, *nurischis* nourishes.—*ch*: *benichun*, *chanch* (rhymes: *sufferáns*, *repentáns*), *puruyanch*, *rechaive* receive, *punych* punish.—Once *z*: *uiltez* "vilenesses."

§ 85. O.F. r, l remain: *sprite spirit spirt*; *abil abill*.

§ 86. O.F. m remains; once *n*: *inpair*.

§ 87. O.F. n.

1. *n*: *confort*, *perfourn*, *ymne*. 2. *m*: *comfort*.

3. Dropped: *hym yme* hymn, *solemply*.

§ 88. O.F. ń.

1. *gn*: *digne* worthy, *regne* kingdom, *signe* sign, *signifi*.—*ngn*: *dingne*, *rengne*, *singne*, *singnefiis*. Cf. *aioingne* enjoin.

2. *n*: *sinis* signs.

§ 89. O.F. f (*ph*).

1. *f*: *faith*, *professe* vow, *profete* prophet, *profite* to profit, *strife*, *suffer*.—*ph*: *prophet* prophet, *prophet* profit.

2. *u* [cf. § 55]: *prouese prouesse* vow, *souerand* (twice) suffering.

§ 90. O.F. v.

1. *v*: *avise* advise, *verset* versicle, *vessel*, *vile*, *visit*.—*u*: *auis*, *uil* evil, *serue*, *souerain*, *striue*, *uerset*.—*f* [cf. § 55]: *seryf* serve, *sofferayne sufferayne sufferaine sufferane*.

2. Confused with *w*: *awise* advise, *werset*, *wessell*, *wil wils* evil(s), *wisit*.

Cf. §§ 79, 82.

§ 91. O.F. p remains.—O.F. *b*.

1. *b*: *numbir*. 2. Assimilated: *nummer*.

§ 92. O.F. ṷ; gṷ.

1. *u*: *quaintelike* prudently, *quere* choir, *quit* free.—*w*: *qwere*; *reward* regard, *wait*, *warant*, *warest* healed, *waste*.

2. *g*: *gyde* guide.

§ 93. O.F. t.

1. *t*: *comfort*, *diseret* disinherit, *-mentis* -ments.

2. *d*: *comfŏrd*, *deserўd*, *presand* present.

3. *th*: *comforth cumforth*. Cf. § 61,3.

4. Dropped: *-mens* (*cumande-*, *iuge-*).

§ 94. O.F. d.

1. *d*: *cumandemens* commandments.

2. *t* : *cumantemens.*

3. *th* : *faith.*

4. Assimilated : *mellid* mingled. Cf. *immonesis* 43/22.

Excrescent : *ordaind* to ordain.

§ 95. O.F. tš (*ch*).

ch [tš] : *chalese, chapiter, charge, chastisyng, eschew, gruch, prechis, rich, riches.*—*sch* : *schapiter, schar, schastisyng.* Cf. § 68,2.

§ 96. O.F. dš (*j, g*).

1. *i* [dš] : *iangler* chatterer, *ioy, iolyose* jealous, *iugement* judgment, *soietes* subjects.—*g* : *sogetes, vengance* vengeance, *charge.*

2. Unvoiced [tš] : *chanch* change, *charch* charge, *larch* large.

3. Dropped : *invinis* enjoins, *scorid* scourged.

§ 97. O.F. k (*c, q*).

1. *k* : *katel, sklaunder.*—*c* : *case, catchid* taken, *sclaunder.*—*q* : *aquaintance, quantite, question, quit.*

2. *g* : *segerstane* sacristan.

§ 98. O.F. g.

1. *g* : *gardin, glotony, gouerne, grant.*

2. Unvoiced : *clotony, neccligence.*

For gu̯, see § 92.

§ 99. General remark. The consonant is written double after a long vowel in : *contresse* (rhyme : *lese* loose) 303, *plasses* 252, *wisses* directs 1073, *fullyng* fouling 1266, *falled* (original rhyme *counsailed*; possibly, but not necessarily, a slip) 1517, *prudde* proude 20/12, etc.

INDEX OF RHYMES.

§ 100. 1. *-ai, -ay* [ā] : *abbay* 1453, 2164, 2198, 2402, *aray* 1454, 1473, *array* 2099, *ay* 654, 2415, 2440, *day* 69, 222, 352, 1474, 1726, 2386, 2416, etc., *lay* inf. 2149, *may* 221, 340, etc., *play* 2385, *pray* 653, 2163, etc., *puruay* 1388, *sai* 1725, *say* 339, 1550, 1755, 2100, 2150, 2401, etc., *þai* 351, 2197, etc., *þay* 1549, 1756, *way* 70, 1387, 2439, etc.

2. *-abil(l)* : *abill* 2228, *acceptabil* 722, *stabil* 721, 2227.

-*ac*, see no. 4, -*acc* no. 24.

3. *-ade, -aid(e), -ayd(e)* [ād] : *glade* inf. 1797, *graide* 1714, *grayd(e)* 1767, 2087, *layde* pp. 1547, *mayde* pp. 1798, *paide* 532, 685, 715, 1638, *payd(e)* 1311, 2000, *prayde* pt. 1097, *puruayde* 1799, 1862,

1999, 2088. *said(e)* 531, 686, 716, 1098, 1312, 1548, 1637, 1713, 1768, *sayd(e)* 1800, 1861.

-afe, see no. 28, *-ai* no. 1, *-aid(e)* no. 3, *-ail(e)* no. 7.

4. *-ac* : *bac* 606, *lac* 605.

5. *-ak(e)* [āk] : *make* 591, 1879, 1927, etc. *sake* 37, 238, 592, 1928, 2344, etc., *slake* 2343, *tak(e)* 38, 237, 1880, etc.

6. *-akes* : *forsakes* 282, 821, *takes* 281, 822.

7. *-ail(e)*, *-ayle* [āl] : *aile* sb. 1605, *assayle* 239, *avayle* 496, *cownsaile* 2242, *daile* 2045, *faile* 240, 1537, *fayle* 495, 2241, *haile* 2046, *taile* 1606, *trauayle* 556 (cf. Note), 1538.—Note. *counsell* 555, for original *counsa(i)le*. Similarly *counseld* 1518, for original *counsa(i)led*, rhyming with *falled* = *failed*.

8. *-ald* [āld > ǫld] : *ald* 526, 1674, *bald* 525, 2109, *-hald* 1673, 2039, *tald* 2040, 2110.—*bold* 1961, for original *bald*, rhyming with *hald*. Cf. no. 102.

9. *-all* : *all* 246, 476, 559, 2212, 2442, etc., *call* 189, 517, etc., *fall* 190, 320, 1944, etc. *principall* (*pren-*) 319, 2211, 2441, *sall* 245, 475, etc., *small* 518, 560, 1943.

-alled, see no. 7, Note.

10. *-als* : *als* also 299, *fals* 300.

11. *-am(e)*, *-aym(e)* [ām] : *blaym* 1776, *ham* 1310, *name* 374, 1649, *nayme* 1368, *same* 373, 1309, 1367, 1650. *schame* 1775.

12. *-amyd*, *-aymyd* : *blaymyd* 1227, 2357. *s(c)hamyd* 1228, 2358.

-anch, see no. 17.

13. *-an(e)* [an] : *can* 1099, *kan* 1503, 1754, *man* 207, 1100, 1305, etc., *þan* 208, 1009, 1032, 1504, 1753, etc., *wane* won 1306, *woman* 1010, 1031.

14. *-ane*, *-ain(e)*, *-ayn(e)*, *-ayine* [ān] : *allayn* 769, *ayn* 788, *agayne* 276, *ogayn(e)* 32, 98, 313, 723, 1004, 2142, etc., *baine* 261, *bayne* 349, 541, 1180, etc., *certayne* 2013, 2041, *sertane* 1003, *sartayn* 574, *fayn(e)* 97, 2067, *gaine* inf. 226, *gayn* 787, *gane* 2035, *ilkane* 89, 1231, *ilkayn* 2132, *layn(e)* 990, 1179, *maine* 225, *mayn(e)* 275, 613, etc., *mayine* 2141, *nane* 1471, *payn(e)* 614, 941, 2036, etc. *playn(e)* 314, 2014, 2042, etc., *segerstane* 1472, *slayn* 942, 1382, *souerane* 350, *sufferane -aine -ayn(e)* 542, 262, 31, 1381, 2068, etc., *tayn(e)* (*-tayne*) taken 90, 770, 1232, 2131, *trayne* 989, *vayn* 573, 724.—*alleyn* *2257, meant for *allayn*, rhyming with *tayn*.

15. *-and(e)* [ānd] : *alweldand* 202, 1144, *band* 2082, *command* 1788, *cumand* 1089, *fande* 1613, *hand(e)* 470, 1358, 1508, 1764, 2187, 2319, *land* 1, 2320, *lifand* 1046, *offerand* 2188, *ordand* 2,

sande 1614, *seruand* 1507, 2314, *stand* 201, 469, 1045, 1090, 1143, 1763, 1787, 2081, 2313, *wande* 1357.

16. *-ang* [ãŋg]: *emang* 1191, 2139, *omang* 2247, *fang* 2023, *gang* 642, 1723, 1851, 2129, etc., *lang* 1192, 2024, 2130, *-sang* 1724, 1852, *strang* 568, 1607, *wrang* 567, 641, 1608, 2140, 2248, etc.

17. *-ans*, *-anch* [ans]: *chanch* 1363, 1656, 1774, *puruyanch* 1364, *repentans*, 1773 312, *sufferans* 1655.

18. *-are*, *-ere* [ar]: *fare* further 311, *were* worse 312.

19. *-ar(e)*, *-air(e)*, *-ayr* [ār]: *air(e)* *hare* ere [456, 2327, 1207, *bewar* 882, 1750, *fair fare* sb. 2384, 308, vb. 1789, *fair* adj. 1603, *gar* vb. 1749, *inpair* 1604, *lare* 397, 1208, *mare* 398, 410. *-mair* 2328, *schar* 881, *snare* 957, *spare* 409, 455, *þair* 307, 958, 1790, 2383.—Note. *þer* 1153, for original *þa(i)r*, rhyming with *mayr*.

20. *-ard*, *-erd*, *-arde*, *-aird* [§ 17,2 end]: *afterward* 242, *fraward* 384, *hard* 241, *herd* 383, *reward(e)* 417, 1059, 1497, 2251, *spaird* 1060, *sparde* 418, 1498, 2252.

21. *-arkes*, *-erkes* [arks]: *clerkes* 858, *warkes* 857.

22. *-art(e)*, *-ert* [art]: *gart* pp. 544, *gert* pp. 1630, *harte* heart 543, *hert* heart 1629.

23. *-as(e)*, *-ass*: *ass* has 2404, *has* 1527, *hase* 2043, *pas* 995, 1351, 1528, 2403, *was* 996, 1352, 2044.

24. *-ase*, *ais(e)*, *-ayse*, *-ace* [ās]: *abbais* 1632, *case* 1375, *dais* 2302, *days* 199, 2077, *grace* 951, 1464, 2070, *palays* 134, *place* 952, 1739, 2069, 2096, *plase* 1463, *prase* 975, *prays(e)* 173, 393, 1461, *rase* pt. 1376, *raise* inf. 1065, *rayse* 59, *sais* 332, 394, 534, 708, 837, 976, 1066, 1631, 2301, etc., *says(e)* 60, 94, 133, 164, 200, 1462, etc., *space* 1740, 2095, *wais* (*-wais*) 331, 838, 2078, etc., *ways* (*-ways*) 163, 174, 533, 707, *-wase* 93.

25. *-ast*, *-aist* [ăst]: *last* 183, *fast* 184, 1708, *past* 1707.—The same *past* 2116, *tast* 2115, 1610, 1677, 1265, *mast* 1609, 1678, *wast* 1266, *waist* 2284, *hast* 2283.

26. *-ate*, *-aite*, *-ayt(e)* [āt]: *algate* 1777, 2413, *couayt* 2472, *hate* 1600, 2004, 2269, *late* adv. 1599, 1778, *laite* 2270, *layte* 2424, *layte* to search 709, *straite* 710, *wate* know 2003, *wayt* wait 2471, *ȝate* 2414, 2423.

27. *-ath* [āþ]: *bath* both 1334, *scath* 979, 1333, *wrath* angry 980.

28. *-aue*, *-afe*, *-aiue*, *-ayue* [āv]: *craue* 211, 766, etc. *haue* 46, 212, 765, 1015, etc. *laue* loaf 1581, *persaiue* 443, *raue* 362, *safe* vb. 1016, *saue* 45, 361, 1582, etc. *wayue* 444.

29. *-aues*: *craues* 586, *haues* 585.

30. *-aul(e)*: *paul(e)* 170, 486, 1829, *saul(e)* 169, etc.

31. *-aw* [au]: *aw* 327, 460, etc., *daw* 1135, *draw* 640, 1296, *knaw* 1035, 1136, 1256, etc., *law* 328, 775, 1036, etc., *raw* 1255, *saw* 459, 639, 776, 1295, etc.

32. *-awn(e)* [aun]: *awn(e)* 403, 999, 1616, 1930, *knawn* 404, etc.

-ay, see no. 1, *-ayd(e)* no. 3, *ayine* no. 14, *-ayle* no. 7, *-aym(e)* no. 11, *-aymyd* no. 12, *-ayn(e)* no. 14, *-ayse* no. 24, *-ayt(e)* no. 26, *-ayue* no. 28.

33. *-e* [ē]: *avisè* 2294, *be* 25, 181, 333, 359, 1021, 2008, 2086, 2243, 2293, etc., *cuntrè* 2007, etc., *degrè* 182, etc., *ee* 402, *entrè* 870, 2085, *fe* 360, *fle* 755, 869, etc., *fre* 26, etc., *he* 756, etc., *me* 695, 1005, etc., *menȝè* 2244, *se* 401, 696, etc., *-te* 334, 676, 1006, etc., *þe* 1022, etc., *thre* 675, etc.

34. *-ech* and *-echis*: *tech*, teach, rhymes with *lech* [lētš] 1283, 1687, *techis* with *prechis* 192.

35. *-ed(e)*: *bede* bed 1201, *clede* pp. 1202, *cled* 2006, *led* pp. 2118, *lede* pt. 1952, 2497, *red* pp. 2117, *rede* pp. 1951, 2498, *sted* pp. placed 2005.

36. *-ede* [ēd, ę̄d]: *mede* meed, 128, 371, 562, 1184, 2056, etc.; *dede* deed, 41, 72, 78, 123, 180, 372, 1081, 1337, etc., *drede* dread 124, 464, 494, etc., *rede* read, advice 463, 493, 561, 624, *wede* weed, 1338; *fede* feed 2055, *hede* heed 71, 77, 179, etc., *spede* speed 42, 127, 623, 1082; *bede* offer 1183, etc. The stressed vowel in these words corresponds to W.T. ē, ā, ō, eu, O.E. ē, ēo.—They rhyme also with words which in O.E. had *i*-mutation of W.T. au, ai. Thus the same *mede* 335, 355, *dede* 204, 581, *drede* 274, 1359, *rede* 1127, *fede* 1570, *hede* 231, *bede* 1286, 1994, 2037, rhyme with *nede* 582, 1128, 1285, 1360, 1569, 1593, 1993, 2038, *-hede* -hood 1594, *lede* to lead 203, 232, 273, 336, 356.—*rede* also rhymes with *dede* (W.T. au) death 914, 950, *dede* dead 1372, *stede* (W.T. a) place 149.

37. *-edes*, *-edis* [cf. 36]: *dedes* deeds 391, *-bedes* -bids 392.—The same *dedes* 2114, *dedis* 2427, *nedes* needs 2113, *nedis* 2428.—*bedes* prayers 1827, *stedes* places 1828.

ee, see no. 33.

38. *-eft*: *eft* 1132, 1486, 2029. *left* 1131, etc.

39. *-eke* [ēk, ę̄k]: *seke* seek 741, 778, 1085, 1315, etc.; *seke* sick 1446, 1643, 1660, *scheke* cheek 971, *meke* 742, 777, 972, 982, 1086, 1316, 1445, 1644, 1659, etc.; *eke* 981. The stressed vowel in these words corresponds to W.T. ō, eu, and au (+ palatal), O.E. ē, ēo.—*breke* break 1955, *speke* 749, 1956, *wreke* 750.

40. *-el(e)*, *-ell*: *angel* 879, *cel* 306, *dwel(l)* 228, 305, 450, 661,

680, 1645, 2017, 2105, etc., *fell* 1501, 2398, *hell* 227, 679, 2460, *mel* 1736, *omell* 488, *sel* 2018, 2106, *-spel(l)* 487, 662, 1646, *tell* 449, 880, 1735, 2397, 2459, etc., *wessel* 1502.—*wele*, well, rhymes with *fell* 185, with *biriele* (§ 13,3, Note) 584, with *fele* [ē] feel 1383; in other instances with words mentioned under no. 41.

41. *-ele*, *-eyl* [ę̄l]: *dele* sb. 2001, vb. 2510, *lele* loyal, lawful 2147, 2315, 2509, *sele* seal 2148, *steyl* 569, *wele* 570, 2002, 2316; cf. no. 40, end.

-eld, see no. 7, Note.

42. *-eld(e)* [ēld]: *eld* 1092, 2260, *feld(e)* 467, 596, 1091, 1182, *weld(e)* 501, 1181, *ȝeld(e)* 468, 502, 595, 2259.

-ell, see no 7, Note, and no. 40.

43. *-el(e)s*: *angels* 1164, *beles* 1759, *cels* 1539, *dwels* 177, 1271, *els*, 451, 743, 802, 1272, 1760, *ourels* 1540, *tel(e)s* 178, 452, 744, 801, 1163.

44. *-elue*: *ourselue* 1026, *twelue* 1025.

45. *-eme* [ēm]: *seme* 1583, 2410, *ȝeme* 1584, 2409.

46. *-ember*: *Descember* 1121, *Nouember* 1122.

47. *-emys* [ēms]: *demys* 714, *semys* 713.

48. *-en*: *ken* 10, 79, 258, 472, 552, 1030, 1033, etc., *men* 9, 80, etc., *þen* 1029, 2025, etc., *women* 257, 471, 551, 1034, 2026.

49. *-ene*, *-eyn* [ēn]: *bedene* 844, 1479, 1706, 1772, 2171, *bene* 1223, 1977, *betwene* 2034, *bitweyn* 473, *clene* 843, 1417, 1480, 1978, 2172, *maynteyn* 1418, *mene* to mean 1587, 1705, *sene* 474, 1224, 1588, 1771, 2033, 2400, etc., *tene* injury 2399.

-ence, see no. 51.

50. *-end(e)*. Words with old vowel-length due to contraction, like *fend(e)* foe 148, 1369, *frend(e)* 758, 1902, 2374, and the Romance *contened* contained 757, rhyme with *end* 44, 56, 147, *lend* dwell 1370, *wend(e)* go 43, 55, 1901, 2373, which had W.T. a. Such words—*end* 933, 1910, *hend(e)* hands 790, 1431, 2262, *lend(e)* 1237, 1909, 2103, *send* 1289, pp. 1276, *wend(e)* 804, 934, 2104—also rhyme with the Romance words *(a)mend* 1238, 1275, 1290, 1662, *descend* 803, *spend* 1661, 2261, pp. 789, 1432. The verb *kend* taught, knew, known (with Teut. nn) 198, 321, 365, 1020, 1406, 1964 rhymes both with the last two categories, *end* 322, *hend* 1963, *(a)mend* 197, 366, 1405, and with *wend* thought 1019 (W.T. ā, O.E. ē).

51. *-ens*, *-ence*: *presens* 1918, *silence* 1917.

52. *-ent*: *assent* 36, 153, 375, 1905, etc., *auisement* 2121, *couent* 284, 1496, etc., *entent* *(in-)* 161, 376, 717, 1150, 2122, 2389, etc.,

hent seized 1331, *obidient* 154, 283, *present* 1149, *schent* ruined 1332, *sent* 162, 718, etc., *tent* heed 35, 1495, etc., *went* 1906, 2390.

53. *-entes*: *rentes* 1488, *vestmentes* 1477.

54. *-ep(e)* [ēp]: *kepe* 61, 291, 1166, 1779, 1846, 1949. *schep* 292, *slepe* 62, 1780, 1845, *wirchep(e)* 1165, 1950.

55. *-er*, *err*: *elder* 2206, *err* are 2205.

56. *-er(e)* [ēr, ȩr]: *cher* cheer 1064, 1511, *clere* clear 113, 213, 405, 664, 1881, 2138, etc., *dere* dear(ly) 152, 379, 2137, *infere* together 233, 1210, 1729, *her(e)* to hear 67, 76, 81, 114, 663, 1782, *here* adv. 15, 24, 214, 248, 954, etc., *lere* learn 16, 23, 82, 234, 247, 343, 380, 406, 432, 1063, 1209, 1302, 1304, 1701, 1834, 2089, 2361, *maner(e)* 68, 75, 431, 953, etc., *nere* near, 1991, 2063, *power(e)* 151, 344, 1303, 1817, 2064, 2443, *quere* choir 1781, 1818, *sere* various 1512, 1992, 2090, 2444, *sopper(e)* 1730, *were* sbj. 1301, *ȝer(e)* 1702, 1833, 1882, 2362. These words have O.E. or O.Scand. ē, or are of Romance origin.—*fere* frighten 278 rhymes with *dere* harm 277.—*dere* harm 768, 1214, *ber(e)* to bear 571, 760, 767, 1213, 2274, 2329, 2469, *er(e)* are 572, 759, 2273, 2330, 2470, *ger* gear 1623, 2429, *wer* to wear 1624, 2430.

-erce, see no. 58.

57. *-erde* [cf. § 17,2, end]: *lerde* 1054, *requerde* 1053.

-ere [ar], see no. 18, *-erkes* no. 21, *err* no. 55.

58. *-erse*, *-erce* [ers]: *reherce* 1140, 1965, *verce* 1966, *verse* 1139.

59. *-er(e)s* [ērs, ȩrs]: *heres* 354, 1188, 1700, *leres* 353, 1187, 1193, 1699, 2300, *maners* 2299, *prayers* 1194.—*beres* 347, *deres* 2392, *eres* 348, 2391.

-ert [art], see no. 22.

60. *-es(e)*, *-ess*: *dress* direct 219, *es* is 33, 48, 141, 396, 1240, 1280, 1361, 2209, 2364, etc., *les(e)* less 601, 1239, etc., *mastres* 2210, 2363, *-nes* 34, 47, 142, 220, 395, 602, etc., *priores(e)* 1279, 1362, etc. —*sese*, cease, rhyming with *mese* mass 1811, was probably pronounced with short vowel. See no. 90.

61. *-es(e)*, *-esse* [ēs, ȩs]: *chese* choose 91, 1108, *contresse* 303, *degrese* 1107, *lese* lose 92, 304. See no. 91.—*disese* 1847, *encres* 1940, *ese* 1975, *pesė* 1939, *plese* 1848, 1976.

62. *-esch*: *flesch* 874, *nesch* soft 873.

63. *-est* [ĕst]: *arrest* 297, *best* 298, *brest* burst 2280, *forest* 2279, *degest* 1126, *gest* guest 1926, *prest* ready 1925, *rest* 1125. See no. 93.

64. *-et(e)*, *-ett*: *Benett* 6, 251, 318, *let* hinder 1974, *lete* sb. 2317, *prophet* 1018 (cf. no. 65, and § 73,2, end), *set* 1017, pp. 1973, *sett* 5,

252, 317, 2318.—*forgete* inf. rhymes with *sett* pp. 1895 (cf. no. 65).

65. -*ete* [ēt, ę̄t]: *bete* mend 997, 1810, *fete* feet 1809, 2134, *hete* promise 2133, *prophete* 998. See no. 95.—*bete* beat 1920, *ete* eat 1250, 1568, 1670, 1695, 1721, -*gete* (cf. no. 64) -get 1669, 1680, 1722, 2380, *grete* great 442, 579, 1509, 1709, 1919, 2379, etc., *mete* meat 580, 1249, 1510, 1567, 1679, 1696, 1792, etc., *sete* seat 1791, *swete* to sweat 1710, *trete* to treat 441.

66. -*eue* [ēv, ę̄v]: *greve* grieve 883, 1981, 2353, *leue* permission 884, etc.

67. -*eued*, -*euyde* [ę̄v(e)d]: *heued* head 421, *leuyde* left 422.

68. -*euen*, -*eu(e)yn*, -*ewyn* [§ 15, 2]: *euen* even 119, *euyn* 490, 807, 1189, 2477, *heueyn* 249, *hewyn* 1104, *heuen* heaven 120, 130, 138, *heuyn* 250, 489, 795, 808, 1103, 1190, 2478, *steuen* voice 129, 137.

-*ew*, see no. 98, -*ews* no. 121.

69. -*ext*: *next* 1841, *sext* 1842.

70. -*i*, -*y* [ī]: *I* 99, 116, 210, *bi* prep. 1260, *bodi* 810, *chasty* 2355, *cry* 115, *dy* 616, *enmy* 1589, *envy* 1415, *foly* 2356, *hi* 1551, *ly* lie 1220, -*ly* adv. 615, 1416, 1552, *mercy* 209, -*ny* 1259, 1590, *signifi* 809, -*ty* adj. 100, *þi* 53, *why* 1219, *worthy* 54, and many more.

71. -*ide* [id]: *dide* 1001, *hide* pp. 839, 1002, *kide* 840.

72. -*id(e)*, -*ied* [īd]: *ascried* 1641, *bide* wait 1794, 1889, *chastid* 1642, 1793, *chide* 1378, *pride* 1377, *side* 2157, *tide* 1890, 2158.

73. -*if(e)*, -*yf* [īf]: *lif(e)* sb. 230, 806, 1891, 2180 ?, 2464, 2486, *lyf* 101, *strif(e)* 805, 2463, 2485, *stryf* 102, *wife* 229, 1892, 2179.

-*if(e)* [īv], see no. 96, 97.

74. -*ift*: *schrift* 988, *swift* 987.

75. -*ight*, -*yght* [iχt]: *flight* 1942, *fyght* 40, *hight* 786, 897, etc., *hyght* 65, *lyght* 66, 1212, 1728, *might* 223, *myght* 19, 538, etc., *night* 537, 898, *nyght* 20, 39, 1124, 1211, 1938, etc., *right* 1123, 1727, 1937, 1941, etc., *ryght* 224, 617, etc., *sight* 618, 785, etc.—*night* rhymes with *feght* 267.

76. -*ike* [īk]: *inlike* 408, 1576, *rike* 2238, *slike* 407, 1575, 2237.

77. -*il*, -*ill*, -*yll*: *fil* 1602, -*fil(l)* 215, 683, etc., -*fyll* 29, 377, *hyll* 135, *il(l)* 108, 1072, etc., *skil(l)* 845, 851, *skyll* 51, *stil(l)* 107, 888, 1071, etc., *til(l)* 285, 684, 887, etc., -*til(l)* 136, 216, 378, 491, 1601, 1960, *tyll* 52, -*tyll* 30, *vigil* 1959, *wil(l)* 286, 846, 852, etc., *wyll* 492.

78. -*ile* [īl]: *file* defile 860, *vile* 859.

79. -*ild(e)*, -*yld(e)* [īld]: *child(e)* 792, 1069, 2268, *myld* 1070, 2267, *schylde* 791.

*

-*ill*, see no. 77.

80. -*ym* [im]: *hym* 674, *lym* 673.

81. -*ims*: *lims* 1936, *pilgrims* 1935.

82. -*in*, -*yn*: *begin* (*bi-*, *by-*) 168, 176, 244, 1681, etc., -*gyn* 1281, *blin* 1682, *complin* 1746, *dyn* 1666, *in* 1665, etc., -*in* 139, etc., *min* 175, *myn* 1241, 1745, *ryn* 1766, *sin* 167, 437, 1242, *syn* 63, 140, 1282, *thin* 428, *win* 243, 427, 1765, *wyn* 64, 438, etc.

83. -*ine*, -*yne* [īn]: *fine* 855, *pyne* 856.

84. -*ind*(*e*), -*ynd* [īnd]: *behinde* 399, *blind* 400, *mynd* 1235, *pynd* 1236.

85. -*ing*, -*yng* [ĭŋg]: *bryng* 669, 2060, *kyng* 288, 2476, *ryng* 2196, *sing* 1159, etc., *thing* (*þing*) 301, 520, 527, 2195, 2475, etc., *thyng* 86, 287, etc., *ȝing* 519, 528, 650, 658, etc., numerous verbal nouns in -*ing*, -*yng* 85, 302, 649, 657, 670, 1160, 2059, etc.

86. -*inges*, -*ynges*: *likinges* 829, *thinges* 830, *thynges* 761, *vnderlynges* 762.

87. -*ink* [iŋk]: *drink* 1597, *think* 1598.

88. -*ire* [īr]: *desire* 590, 955, *fire* 956, *ire* 589.

89. -*irk*(*e*), -*yrk*: *irk* 236, *kirk*(*e*) 235, 260, etc., *kyrk* 12, 27, 193, *wirk*(*e*) 194, 259, etc., *wyrk* 11, 28.

90. -*is*(*e*): *perise* 1300, *þis* 1299.—*peris* rhymes with *es* 505.

91. -*ise*, -*yse* [-īs]: *avise* 521, 1076, *avyse* 57, *awise* 2108, *despise* 439, *rise* 440, 454, 603, 1075, 1403, 2107, 1865, *ryse* (-*ryse*) 21, 58, *seruyse* (*sar-*) 604, 877, 1554, 1762, 1866, *thrise* 1404, 2152, *twise* 453, 1579, 1628, *wise* (-*wise*) sb., adj. 522, 878, 1553, 1580, 1627, 1761, 2151, etc., *wyse* 22.—*wise* rhymes also with *chastese* 458, *seruese* 1521, and (as a verb) with *blis* 1120.

92. -*isses*: *blisses* 902, *misses* 901.

93. -*ist*, -*yst* [ĭst]: *crist* 912, 1954, *list* 1307, *myst* 1308, *pup*(*p*)-*list* 911, 1546, 1953, *wist* 1545.—With *crist* rhymes also *euaungelest* 1592.

94. -*it*(*e*), -*ytt*: *fit* 871, *flit* 1412, 1483, *it* 1438, *sit* 1251, 1731, 1795, *wit*(*e*) 465, 1252, 1437, 1484, *wytt* 73, *writ* 466, 872, 1732, *wrytt* 74, *ȝit* 1411, 1796.

95. -*ite* [īt]: *delite* 854; 1117, 2489, *perfite* (*par-*) 853, 1118, 2490.—With *perfite* rhymes also *eremete* 266.

96. -*if*(*e*) [§§ 13, 55]: *gif*(*e*) 511, 1178, 1884, 2193, 2483, *lif* vb. 512, etc.

97. -*iue*, -*yue*, -*if* [īv]: *fyue* 2083, *lif* sb. 628, *liue* sb. 2084, *shriue* 627.

98. *-o, -ou, -ow, -u*; *-ew* [ǭ—ɯ; ęɯ; cf. §13,4]: *go* 1347, 1983, *fro* 1408, 1984, *so* 255, 1348, 1407, *þo* those 256. These words had ā in O.E. (O.Scand.).—Such ā-words, *so* 1229, *also* 1171, 2154, 2388, *mo* 2499, rhyme also with the ō-words *do* 1172, *-to* 1230, 2153, 2387, 2500.—*do* 8, 103, 272, 316, etc., *to* (*-to*) 7, etc.—The ū-group: *bew* (for *bow*) 966, *bow* 2445, *now* 1824, *prow* advantage 2446, *trow* vb. 1823, *þou* 965; *iesu* 1116.—*eschew* 1115, *new* 2321, *trew* 2322.

99. *-ode, -ude* [ɯd]: *gode* good 50, *gude* 109, 279, 294, 587, etc. *mode* 49, etc.

100. *-oght* [oχt]: *broght* 2166, *noght* 445, 482, 608, 726, 2165, etc., *thoght* 143, 481, 607, 725, 832, 849, etc., *wroght* 144, 446, 831, 850, etc.

101. *-oke, -ouke, -uke* [ɯk]: *boke* 131, 263, *buke* 269, 687, 1096, 1872, 2492, *loke* 132, 264, *luke* 688, 1095, 1500, 1871, 2491, *wouke* 270, 1499.

102. *-old* [ǭld]: *old* 2203, *told* 2204. Cf. no. 8.

103. *-om(e), -um* [ɯm]: *cum* 1024, 1217, *custum* 1113, *sum* 1218, *-sum* 1023, 1114.—The same *cum* 499, 1267, 1836, 2245, *-dom(e)* 500, 1268, 2246, *-dome* 1835.

104. *-on(e), -oun(e), -own, -un* [ǭn—ɯn]: *allon* 158, 172, 290, *gon(e)* 1349, 2111, *ilkon* 157, 1386, 1481, *lone* loan 330, *none* pron. 187, 289, 329, 2199, *on* one 2119, *segerstone* 1385, *stone* 188, *ton(e)* 171, 1350, 1482, 2112, 2120, 2200. These words had ā (a, ai) in O.E. (O.Scand., O.F.), and the only connection between them and the following group is the rhyme *none* pron. 1757, *done* 1758.—*done* pp. 711, 931, 1439, 1773, 1849, 2382, *sone* soon 932, 1440, 1774, *bone* prayer 2381, *none* noon 712, 1850. These had ō in O.E. or O.Scand. The last substantive is also spelt *noun* 1077 and rhymes with *foune* few 1088.—The ū-group: *bown* bound 699, *bown* ready 967, 1145, 2143, *vnbun* freed 508, *doun(e)* down 800, 2169, 2192, *down* 1525, 1741, *fun* found 507, *toun* 1987, *towne* 345; *encheson* occasion 2341, *persoun* 1996, *reson* 536, 2342, *seson* 1899, *sesoun(e)* 1995, 2508, numerous words in *-ioun(e)* 3, 4, 346, 535, 799, 968, 1900, 1988, 2144, 2170, 2191, 2507, *-iown* 700, 1742, *-isoun(e)* 1146, 1526, etc.

105. *-oun(e)s, -owns* [ɯns]: *meditacioun(e)s* 1129, 1911, *orisouns* 1130, *orisowns* 1912.

106. *-ong, -ung* [ɯŋg]: *tung* 105, 740, 2184, *tong* 1052, *ȝung* 739, 2183, *ȝong* 106, 1051.

107. *-or(e), -our(e)* [ǭr—ɯr]: *mor* 1288, *sore* 1287. The same *more* 2487 rhymes with *before* 2488; and *fore* 1342, with *restore*

1341.—*dore* 1448, 1808, *flore* 1807, *pore* 1447.—*honour(e)* 651, 1867, *labore* 1839, *myrour* 893, *oure* hour 1840, 1868, *sauiour* 894, *sucoure* 652.

108. *-ord(e)*, *-urd* [ǫrd—uːrd]: *lord* 118, 415, 728, 1170, *acord(e)* 117, etc.—*hurd* treasure up 1747, *word* 1748.

109. *-orn*: *born* 1855, *beforn* 625, 1856, *lorn* 1455, *morn* 593, 626, 1456, *-sworn* 594.

110. *-our(e)s* [uːrs]: *confessours* 2495, *doctours* 2496, *oures* hours 1863, *laboures* 1864.

111. *-os(e)* [ǭs]: *chose* pp. 1389, sb. 2240, *depose* 1390, 2239.

112. *-osen*: *chosen* 2219, *losen* ? 2220.

113. *-ote* [ǭt]: *cote* coat 2012, *note* business 2011.

-ou, see no. 98, *-oue* no. 116, *-oues* no. 117, *-ouke* no. 101, *-oun(e)* no. 104, *-oun(e)s* no. 105, *-our(e)* no. 107.

114. *-oute*, *-ute* [uːt]: *bute* remedy 2285, *doute* 1492, *loute* 2216, *oboute* 326, 1491, 2215, *rute* 2286, *withoute* 325.

115. *-outh* [uːþ]: *couth* 13, *ȝouth* 14.

116. *-oue*, *-uf(e)*, *-uefe* [uːv]: *luf(e)* has only one word with O.E. u to rhyme with: *obufe* 1040. In all other instances the rhyme-words are *behoue* (*bi-*) 83, 566, 665, 826, 2213, 2474, *pruefe* 2253, and *reproue* 600.—*bihoue* 2079, *proue* 2080.

117. *-oues*, *-ufes* [uːvs]: *lufes* 890, *proues* 889, *reproues* 389, *behoues* 390.

-ow, see no. 98, *-own* no. 104, *-owns* no. 105.

118. *-oy* (oi̯): *noy* 145, *stroy* 146.

-u, see no. 98, *-ude* no. 99, *-uefe*, *-uf(e)* no. 116, *-uke* no. 101, *-um* no. 103, *-un* [long vowel] no. 104.

119. *-un*: *kun* 18, 461, *sun* son 462, *vun* won 17.

-ung, see no. 106, *-urd* no. 108.

120. *-us*: *Jesus* 121, 693, 875, 947, *þus* 206, 694, 935, *vs* 122, 205, 876, 936, 948.—*contrarius* 2291, *suspecius* 2292.

121. *-use*; *-ews* [uːs, e̯uːs]: *excuse* 368, 1056, 1222, 1494, 2435, *nuse* hurts 752, *refuse* 367, 1493, 2502, *vse* 1055, 1221, 1751, 2436, 2501.—*s(c)hrews* 429, 1426, *shews* 430, *thews* 1425.

122. *-used* [uːsd]: *excused* 1802, *vsed* 1801.

123. *-ust* [uːst]: *dust* 2276, *rust* 2275.

-ute, see no. 114, *-y* etc., see *-i* etc.

A FEW NOTES ON

INFLECTION AND SYNTAX

(referring to the Northern texts, except where Caxton is expressly mentioned; cf. K. Böddeker's treatise in Engl. Stud., vol. ii, pp. 358 ff., on a par with his text).

Nouns.

§ 101. The plural usually ends in *-es* (*-is, -ys*) or *-s* (*-se, -sse*). Plurals in *-en* (*-in*): *eghen ehin, erin* (P.V.). In *-er* (*-ir*): *childer -ir.* (In *-ern*: *childern*, Caxt.) With mutation only: *feet, hend* (besides *handes*), *men*; cf. *women, wymmen.* Like the sg.: a. *maner* (beside *-s*), *moneth* (beside *-s*), *paire, schep, siþe* times, *þing* (beside *-es*), *vessel* (M.V.; P.V. has *vassels*), *ȝere*; b. *mekenes, mese* messes, dishes, *nouece* (beside *nouices*). Once, 2383, occurs *sister* for the usual *sisters.* (*saynd* *1643 is incorrect.)

The spirant is voiced in inflected forms of *life, bath*, etc.

§ 102. The gen. usually ends in *-es* (*-is, -ys*) or *-s.* The gen. is like the nom. (cf. O. Knapp, in Engl. Stud. xxxi, pp. 20-77) in: a. *broþir, fader* (P.V. has *fadirs*), *moder, sister, awter, god* (beside *-es*), *man* (beside *manes, mannis*), *hel, saule, -kyn* (beside *-kins*), *ȝere, cuuent, lady, souerayn* (beside *-ans*), *prophet, crist* (usually *-es*); b. *abbes, priores.* Plural gen.: a. *eghen, moneth, winter*; b. *noues.*

§ 103. Co-ordination of gen. and *of*-phrase: *þabbesse kychin and of hir gestis* 35/27.

§ 104. Dative: *musterd it þabbesse* showed it to the abbess 36/9 (cf. *muster to þabbes hir sekenes* 45/15). Similarly: *gif ensaumpil mor & lese* give example to greater and smaller 916, *sal þe elder loute* shall bow to the seniors 2216, *multeplii þe* multiply unto thee 7/6.

§ 105. Apposition: *nun nouece* 147/13; Caxt. *mounkes strangers* 137/9, *broder portar* 137/35, *childern nouyces* 127/26.

Adjectives.

§ 106. *All þe hale* all the, the whole 2376. Double comparative: *more largelier* Caxt. 131/30. Superl. + *of all other* Caxt. 125/21.

Articles.

§ 107. Definite article used in: *þe ded(e)* death 9/2, 12/17, 914, *þe lentin* Lent 33/1 (*lentin* 33/6), *te super* supper 28/8, *þe heuyn* heaven 808 (*heuyn* 814).

§ 108. No article in: *And abbes ses* and the abbess sees 43/35, *sua az abot at be* so ought an abbot (the abbot) to be 5/13, 6/11, *calde in cuuent* reckoned amongst the convent 38/35, *halde reul* keep the rule 6/4, *til endyng* till the end 13/6 (*til þending* 14/20), *in world* in the world 996, *in oþir stede* in another place 3/11, *ne . . þing* not . . a thing, nothing (cf. Fr. *ne . . rien*) 39/10.—Caxt. *at gate* at the gate 137/32, *at last oryson* at the last orison 138/10.

Numerals.

§ 109. Cardinals: *ane* (*one*), *twa* (*two*) *twane tuinne* (*twine*), *þre thrin*, *four*, *fyue*, *sex*, *seuin*, *ten*, *tuelue* (*twelf*), *fiftene*, *tuenty*, *hundrez*.

Ordinals: *first*, (*t*)*oþer secund*, *þridde third*, *ferþe* (*ferde*) *fourt*, *fift*, *sext*, *seuind seuent*, *ahtend ayht*, *nihend neyntt*, *tende tent*, *ellofte* (Caxt. *enleuenth*), *telfete twelft*, *fyftyd* 50th, *sextid þe secunde* 62nd, *hundred seuintende* 117th.

Pronouns and Pronominal Adjectives.

§ 110. Personal: *I* (*i*, seldom *ic*), *me*, *we*, *us* (*hus*); *þou* (*þu*, *tu*), *þe*, *ȝe*, *ȝou*; *he*, *his*, *him*; *sche scho so*, *hir her*; *it* (*id*); *þai* (*day*), *þair* (*tayre*, *thar*) *þeir ire hir* (Caxt. *her*), *þam* (*taim*, Caxt. *theim*, *hem*).

§ 111. *It* for modern *there*: *Yef it be an þat* if there is one who 25/14.

§ 112. Reflective: *myself meself*, *ourself* (*-selue*) *usself*; *þiself*; *himself*, *hirself* (*-selu*), *itself*; *þamself*. Besides: *him*, *hir*, *þam*, etc.

§ 113. Possessive adjectives: *mine mi*, *our*; *þine þi*, *ȝour*. Poss. pron.: *ȝoures*; *his*, *hirs*; *þaris*.

§ 114. Demonstrative: a. *þis* this, *þas þos þes* (*þeis*, Caxt. *theys*) *þis þise* (Caxt. *thyes*, *thys*) *þer* (*ȝer*, *þeir*) *þir* these. b. *þat* that, *þa* (*þai*) *þo* those; old instrum.: *þe* (before comparatives), *þi* (in *for þi*); cf. the def. art.

§ 115. Interrogative: a. *wha who*, *whas*, *wham whom*, *what* (*wot*) *quat*; old instrum.: *whi* (in *for whi*). b. *whilk*. c. *wheþer*.

§ 116. Relative: a. *þat* (see Gloss., practically: "whose" 24/33). b. *wha* (*who*) whoever, *whas* whose, *wham* (*waim*, *whom*) whom, *what*. c. *who þat*, *wham þat*, Caxt. *who that euer*. d. *wha sua* (*who so*), *what so*, *what* (adj.) . . *so*, *whatkyn* . . *so*; *wha sa euir* (*who so ever*). e. *wha sam*, *what sam*, *what* (adj.) . . *sam*, *what sum*; Caxt. *who som euer what som euer*. f. *whilk* which, who; *whilk* (adj.) . . *sua*; *whilke sam*; *þe whilk*. g. *als*. h. *at*.

§ 117. *Who*, *who so*, are distinctly plural in cases like 1443, 2005, 2007. *That* represents two different cases in co-ordinate clauses, Caxt. 122/33.

§ 118. Relative omitted: 4/24, 6/17, 7/9, 9/33, 501, 1752, etc.; as subject: 4/16, 8/20, 11/21, 130, 1531.

§ 119. Indefinite: *ane on* (Caxt. *oo*) one, a person, some, *many ayn* many a one, *all* (*aller* of all), *any ony* any, any one, *ayþar* either, *baþe both*, *euery* (Caxt.) every one, *ilka ilkon euer-ilkane*, etc., *ilkman*, *man* (P.V.) and the plural *men* (M.V.) "one," *naman noman*, *nan non no*, *nathing nothing*, *noght* nothing, *oþer*, etc., another, the other, each other (Caxt. "other things"), *ohte oght* aught, *sum*, *sumþing*.

VERBS.

§ 120. Inflection: a. ind. pr. sg. 1: —; 2, 3: *-es* (*-is*, *-ys*, *-ice*), *-s* (*-se*); pl. 1, 2: —; 3: *-es* (*-is*), *-s*, or —; pt. weak: *-ed* (*-id*, *-yd*), *-d*, *-it* (*-yt*), *-t* (*-te*); strong: —. b. sbj.: —. c. imp. sg.: —; pl. *-es* (*-is*), *-s*, sometimes —. d. inf.: — (silent *-e*). e. ppr.: *-and*, seldom *-yng*; pp. weak: *-ed*, etc. (cf. above); strong: *-en* (*-in*, *-yn*), *-n* (*-ne*), —.

Pr. pl. 3 (ind. and sbj.) of *be* and *do* has sometimes the ending *-n*. (Caxt. has the pl. *commen* come, *goone* go, *dyden* did.) Once occurs the imp. sg. *sais*, 142/23.

§ 121. Pres. 3 sg. in *-s* for *-ses*: *rais* 1068 (beside *rases*) raises, *stablis* establishes, *suffes* 1824 (cf. *sufficis*), *trespasse* 31/36 (beside *-passis*), *witnes* bears witness. Similarly: *tech* = *teches* 1284.

§ 122. Past tense or past partic. in *-t*, *-d* (*-te*, *-de*), for *-ted*, *-ded*: *arrest* stopped, *cumfort* comforted, *degest* digested, *directe* directed, *dyght* prepared, *flit* removed, *gete* kept, *graunt* (beside *-tid*) granted, *hent* seized, *hurt*, *keste* cast, *list* pleased, *lyght* lit, *myst* missed, *past* (beside *passid*), *put*, *schent* ruined, *sent*, *set*, *visit* visited, *went*; *amend* (beside *-did*), *cumand* commanded, *send* sent, *spend*(*e*) spent, *suspend* suspended; *clad*, *dredde* dreaded, *hid*, *kide* told, *led*, *spede* advanced. (Caxt. *correct* corrected, *distribute*, *suspecte*, *translate*, *gyrde* girt).

§ 123. Pres. partic. in *-yng*: *thynkyng* 42/33, *sayng* 42/34, *grofelyng* 147/40, *ianglyng* chattering 1780.

§ 124. Table of strong verbs (as far as they occur outside of the pres.).

I.	*druie*	——	*driuin*
	rise	*rase*	——
	write	——	*writen wretyn.*
II.	*chese*	*chays*	*chosen chose*
	lese	——	*lorn*
	bede offer	——	(Caxt. *boden*, commanded). Cf. below.
III.	*begin*	*begane*	——
	bind	——	*bownyd bown bun*

	drinke	——	(*drunkin*, adj.)
	find	——	*funden fun fon*
	ring	——	*rungen*
	sing	——	*songen sung*
	win	*wane*	*run.*
IV.	*bere*	*bar*	*born*
	breke	——	*brokin*
	scere (*scher*)	——	*scorn*
	speke	*spac*	——
	cume come	*cume come*	*cumen.*
V.	*bid*	*bad*	*forbed* forbidden. Cf. below.
	ete	——	*etin*
	gete	(*for*)*gat*	*getyn*
	giue	*gafe*	*geuen gifin*
	lig lie ly	*lay*	——
	se	*saz saw*	*sene.*
VI.	*slay sla*	——	*slayn*
	stande	*stode*	——
	take ta	*toke tuke*	*takin tayn ton* (Caxt. *taken*, also *take*)
	swer	——	(*for*)*sworn.*
VII.	*fall*	*fell*	*fallen*
	hald hold	*held*	*halden*
	haite hete	*hizte*	*hight*
	lat (*latte*) *let*	*lete*	*let*
	knaw	——	*knawn.*

The verbs *bede* II and *bid* V are greatly confused. The pp. of *rede*, advise, read, is *red* (*redde*, Caxt. also *rad*).

§ 125. Irregular weak verbs: *by* buy, *boght*; *biteche* beteach, *bitaht*; *bring*, *broght*; *sel*, *salde*; *tel*, *tald told*; *think* appears; *wirk*, *wrht wroght*.

§ 126. "Anomalous" verbs.

inf.	—	pr.	*ah aw* (Caxt. *owe owen*)	pt.	*ahte aght* ought.
,,	*cune kun*	,,	*can*	,,	*cuþe* (Caxt. *cowde*)
,,	—	,,	*may*	,,	*myght*
,,	—	,,	*mun* will	,,	*munde*
,,	—	,,	*shal sal*	,,	*sulde* (Caxt. *shulde*)
,,	—	,,	*þarf þar* is needed	,,	—
,,	*wit*	,,	*wate wote wit wyte*	,,	*wist*
inf.	*wil*	pr.	*will wele* (Caxt. *woll*)	pt.	*wald wold.*
inf.	*do* (pl. 3 also *done*)	pt.	*did dyde*	pp.	*don*
,,	*ga go*	,,	*yede* [*went*]	,,	*gane gone.*

The verb *be* (*bi*, *by*). a. pr. ind. sg. 1: *am*, *is*, *es*; 2: *es*, *ert*; 3: *is*, *es*, *bese* (shall be); pl.: *ere*, *err*, *are* (*aier*), *es*, *be* (Caxt. *er*, *arn*, *is*, *be*, *ben*). b. pr. sbj.: *be*, pl. also *bene*. c. pr. imp. sg.: *be*; pl.: *be*, *bes*. d. pt. ind. sg.: *was*, *wos*; ind. pl. and sbj.: *were*, *ware*, *w*(*h*)*or*. e. pp.: *ben*.

§ 127. The first group of the verbs in § 126 are the old (Teutonic) præterito-præsentia. There are also some of later date (English). Just as the Teut. *aih* and *skal*, thus the M.E. *ahte* and *sulde* came to assume the signification of the present tense. *birde* and *byhouid*, two other expressions for the idea of obligation or propriety, are used in our texts as equivalents to *bird* and *byhouis*. MURRAY gives quotations like *Me byrd be blyth þat sycht to se*, Barbour, St. Martha 152, but speaks of *bird(e)* and *behoved* (*byhod*) simply as "Pa. t." (past tense), thus not noting the peculiarity of the usage. In my glossary I mark the younger (weak) præterito-præsentia with a *pt.-pr.*

§ 128. Omission of the verb *be* before a participle (or adj.) co-ordinated with a preceding verb which has the same subject: *þus for hir werk scho may haue mede, And þai dampned* (be damned) *for þair mysdede* 372. *For els sum wold take no kepe, Bot oþer ianglyng* (be chattering) *or els slepe* 1780. *So þat none do oþer disese, But ilkon paid* (be satisfied) *oþer to plese* 1848. *So þat þai be seruyd at ese, And ilkman redy* (be ready) *þam to plese* 1976. *shal haue grete rewarde & crowned* (be crowned) *in heuen* Caxt. 128/8. Cf. § 138.

Somewhat different, in so far as the subject is repeated, is this sentence: *þat non of þam sal oþer dyng, Ne none herdy* (be bold), *oder to greue* 2353. The possibility of unintentional omission is not excluded. Such an interpretation may seem still more natural in the following: *Who tentes to trofils & wil not rede And þai ouertayn with þat dede* 1878.

§ 129. A few constructions.

a. Change of mood (sbj. + *and* + ind.): 2071–73, 2083–84.

b. *es to do* is to be done 515; simil. 549, 1043, 1179, Caxt. 126/19. *ger gestes kepe* cause guests to be held 1949.

c. *when sho is geuyn in mynde*, the modern turn for Lat. *dum ei suggeritur* 43/19. Cf. 43/17.

PARTICLES.

§ 130. Redundancy of prepositions: *In hir pouste loke þat þare be nane vtrage in* 42/20. *In þe price . . loke þare be na cuuaitise inne* 37/25. *Tyl þe nedful sal sho meke hir for* 25/27. [No uncommon construction, but often misunderstood, *e. g.* by J. ULLMANN, Engl. Stud. vii, p. 435 (1884). Hampole's *Of alle þeise poyntes I thenke of sey* needs no emendation.]

§ 131. The conj. *þat* introducing quasi-independent exhortative or admonitory sentences: *First þat þu* (first thou shouldst) *aske of hym* 1/9. *Yef ani faute be funden in þaim, þat it be* (let it be) *sone mendid* 6/16. 7/31, 9/2, 31, 20/24, etc.

§ 132. Omission of the conj. *þat*: 1/21, 2/11, 5/,20 10/31, 12/23, etc.—Repetition § 141.

§ 133. Double negations: 4/3, 23, etc.

Word-order.

§ 134. Subject and verb: *For þi he giuis us respit* 3/18. *Efter þe ferþe Respun, þabbes sal byggynne þis ymne* 16/34. 30/19, 25, 37/32, 40/34.

Reverse: *sal ȝe noht be for-getin* 2/14. *hauid tay na bettir mede* 12/13. *And salle ye cume* 47/26.—*o niht ras I* 18/3. 20/23, 31/4, 35/10.

§ 135. Noun and adjunct. *þe sufferans may þu noht wite of god her witerlike* 3/20. *winde þe tuaile þar-a-bowte of þauter* 39/8. *Or be ensampil to vnderstand Of þam*, etc., or (what is) to be understood from example of those, etc., 1045. *The mesure salbe of þer drink Set efter* . . 1597.—*Of priores who takes þe name* 374 (cf. Spec. of Early Engl., ed. Morris and Skeat, part ii, p. 70, l. 26).

§ 136. "Introducing" word in the middle of the clause or sentence: *entre þat ere* who are to (shall) enter 2/31. *And al obseruaunce þat syne for-sakes* and who afterwards, etc., 282. *All vnto þam þat es nede* all that is necessary to them 2038. *Godis uoice þat ȝe here* that ye may hear God's voice 1/23. *his wille þat ȝe may do* 2/6. 2/22, 24, 3/2. *in godis trouht yef þu it se* if thou seest it in the trust in God 4/8. 4/12, 6/34. *als hir maistiresse þoz scho ware* as though she were her mistress 10/8. 11/27. *Il or gude wheder it be* 868. 273, 494, etc. *To say for dred, or wirk, oght wrang* for fear of saying or doing anything wrong 2432. *Whils þai wer furth how it befell* how it happened whilst they were away 2398.

§ 137. Correlative conjunctions: *Bot if þai oþer swink or swete In hay or corn* unless they toil or sweat in either hay or corn 1709. *Vnto him-self & oþer bath* both to himself and others 1334 (common).

Structure of Sentences. Congruency. Shortness. Redundancy.

§ 138. In P.V. there is often a certain conciseness, abruptness, or rusticity of style; see *e.g.* 9/26–27, 10/17–18, 14/17-18, 20/31–33, 21/4, 38/7–9, 11–12, 35, 39/29–31. Additions like the following would appear somewhat naive, if occurring in a modern text: *sua sais sain benet* 2/16, *sua az abot at be* 5/13. Similarly 8/14, 9/12, 10/26?, 35/34, 1889–90, etc.

Abrupt change of person or number: 1/20–22 (*we* . . *yure*), 2/20–22 (*we* . . *ye* . . *tu*), 8/12–14 (*ye* . . *yure* . . *ti* . . *ye*), 10/26–27 (*tu* . . *yu*), 25/9–10 (*nan* . . *þair* . . *hys* . . *tair*), 32/28 (*þai* . . *ye*),

33/32–33 (*ye . . ye . . we*), 37/12–13 (*þai . . sho*), 501–502 (*þai . . his*), 697–698 (*þai . . he*), 733–734 (*we . . his*), 928–929 (*þai . . our*), 2385–87 (*on . . scho . . þai*, rather confusing), etc. Frequent are constructions like: *an þat delitis tam* one who takes delight 25/14, *illkon þat . . er* each one who is, all who are 17. Caxt. 120/35–36, 124/31–32, 35–36.

The nouns *schep* 1314 and *writ* 2040 are followed by the pron. *he*. In both cases (thus not in the latter alone, as Böddeker means), the idea of personality (the sinner, the prophet) prevails (constructio ad sensum).

§ 139. Nom. used as the "indifferent" case in which an idea is introduced, before it has fallen under the influence of any particular word: *te sistirs þat ere in labur . . , þabbes sal cumaunde þaim* 34/14. *that another that nede hath / that pite is shewid vppon hym* Caxt. 129/19. Cf. *þat es best, halde þar-to* let her hold to that which is best 7/23.

§ 140. Proleptic pronouns: *Mikyl walde he fle pride, þe prophete* 11/12. *Sho sal haue þam enbreuid, alle þingis þat fallis til þe hus* 24/34. *þat it es inoh, twane maner of potage* 27/33. *gif it þam, þe entre* 37/33. *halde it welle, all þat man cumandis hir* 38/18. 37/11, 39/12. Caxt. 132/3.

§ 141. Repetition: *þat ta þat sal ga til laburs, þat tay may haue þe morning* 15/30. *So þat . . þat* 45–47. *that . . þat* Caxt. 139/23. Cf. § 130.

§ 142. Constructions resembling the Lat. Ablativus absolutus and Participium conjunctum (in Caxton): *þe which exercisid and doon* (que cum fuerint . . adimpleta) 122/32. *all thynges set aside* (relictis omnibus) 131/16. *the whiche had* (and when that has been had) 134/19. *after the blessyng yeuen* (has been given) 130/29.

§ 143. Anacoluthons (possibly not original): 830–833, Caxt. 119/10.

I. THE NORTHERN PROSE VERSION

OF

The Rule of St. Benet.

(*Lansdowne MS.* 378, *British Museum.*)

Asculta, o fili ! [leaf 1, back]

Prologue.

Son, Herkyn þe co*m*maundementis of þe mast*ir*, & lay to þe eere of thy herte, & gladly take And spedily fulfil þe warny*ng* of þe meke fad*ir*, þat þu mai turne a-gayne to hy*m* by þe labur of obedience, fra whame þu had gane by þe slewth of inobedience. Tharfore my worde be now directe to the, þat forsakis thy awne lustis & takis þe ryg*h*t stra*ng* & doghty arm*ur* of obedience to seryf our lorde Iesu criste, þe verrey kyng. First þat þu aske of hy*m* wid besy prayer alle gude thing þat þu begy*ns* to do to be p*er*fytely endid ; þat he, þat hase vochyd safe to cownte vs i*n* þe nu*m*mer of hys sons, be not greuyd ony tyme be our euyl dedis. Sa, for sot*h*, it is to obey hy*m* at al tyme for hys aune gudis þat ere in vs, þat he, as a wrat*h* fader, not alanly diseret vs os not hys sons, Bot also os a dredful lord, wrathid thoro o*ur* euyl dedys, betake vs to p*er*petual payne os ful wykkyd seruandis, whylk wald not folow hy*m* to blis.

In order to return to God, whom we have deserted through disobedience, we must, invoking God's help, serve Him in obedience.

primum capitulum. Exurgamus ergo. [leaf 2]

In þis first sentence bidis us sain benet þat we be wakande, and bidis we sal rise, þat es of ure sinne, als it es writen, and þat yure ehin be opin, and yure herte[s], til godis brih[t]nes, Godis uoice þat ȝe here and under-stande

Thus we must rise out of our sins, be attentive and energetic,

3. MS. þ^e; similarly p. 12, l. 32, p. 13, ll. 9, 36, etc. 16. MS. o^r. 19. *primum;* one of the downstrokes required to make *-mum* is missing.—After *capitulum,* and in several places on the seven first pages, the sign ·:· is used instead of a plain stop. 22. MS. *yures herte;* cf. p. 2, l. 2. 23. MS. *brihnes.*—MS. *under. c. / stande.* At the end of several lines on the nine first leaves (but never afterwards) some strokes, sometimes apparently forming real letters or words, are added simply in order to give to the lines their full length.

it, als it sais: "Hodie si uocem eius—Yef ye þe uoice of god herd o day, yure hertis ware noht hard; it mu*n*de ma þam neis;" Als haly writ says: "Qui habet aures audiendi, audiat—þat erin hauis, herkins wat þe haly spirt sais in haly writ." wat sais he? "Cumis to me, I sal yu lere þe dute of god, his wille þat ȝe may do. Rennes fast do wilis ye haue liht, þat þe mirkenes o ded our-take þe noht." þe haly spirt bidis us þat we trou his reed, þat we may cum to þe lif and se þe dais of godis sune in ioye wid-uten ende. "yef þu wiƚƚ haue þat ioy, gete þi tunge, þu speke na scaþe, and tine lippis fra iuel. Turne þe fra iuil & do þe gode, þat ti lif folihe þaim. wen þat ȝe þus do, þan sal min ezin be on ȝow. Til ȝure praier sa[l] I here, sal ȝe noht be for-getin. Or þat ȝe calle to me, I sal saie: I es here." My suete sistirs, I saie to †yu: es na sueter uoice þan of iesu; sua sais sain benet. God al-mihti kenne us þe rihte gate til endeles ioy. Amen.

careful in our speech,

[† leaf 2, bk.]

Sec*un*d*u*m capitulum. Succinctis ergo fide.

and lead a life according to the precepts of Holy Scripture

IN þis sentence mustirs sain benet us hu we sal lede ure lif, and sais þat we sal belt us wid chastiment, riht trouz þat ye haue wid gode dede, þat tu belte þine lendis sua, and þat tine fete be shod in riht gate, Als þe gospel tellis, in his tretes þat þu ga, til his rengne þat þu may cume, þare hise frendis sal euir be, þat here hauis wele wroht. Yef þu wil to þat rengne cume, do þe dedis of godis sune; þu sal [be] þidir broht. we aske þe, laue*r*d, þurz þe muz of þe p*ro*fete, Wha in þi tabernakil sal wne. "An wha sal wne wid þe in þe muntain þat es sua briht?" Laue*r*d, þan we haue askid þe, þe ancewer of þe sal we here: þe riht þid*ir* at cume þai sal haue, entre þat ere wid-uten sinne; þat rihtuis es of dede and rihtuis of speche in his hert of alle þing; þat wid tunge lezis noht, bot sothfastnes in his þoht; þat euil dos til nan, ne rep*ro*ues na man of þaire mis-dede. He dos aƚƚ to noht þe sinne þat wnis in

and the example of Christ.

3. MS. *aur/res.* 4. Between *erin* and *hauis* there is a blank large enough for about five letters; it seems to have been left thus by the scribe. 7. MS. *mirken/nes.* 13. MS. *sa.* 27. MS. *sal þidit.*

his þoht and quites him †at te nede. Lauerd, we prai þe þat we may serue sua, in þi tabernakil þat we may wne. Amen.

[† leaf 3]

Tercium capitulum. Ergo preparanda.

IN þis sentence sais sain benet til þa þat luuis god & dutes hym: yef þu findis ani god in þe, til god sal þe louing be, a[n]d grace til him giue, of whame we haue al þe gude; als þe prophete sais: "Non nobis domine—Lord, of us es it noht, bot til þi name ioy es broht"; Als sain paul sais: "Lauerd, of me haue I noht, bot þu sende it me." In oþir stede sais he: "In god sal man be glad and loue him in dede." And heris wat ure lauerd sais in þe gospel: "Qui audit—Wha sam heris my word and dos it in werke, Til þe wyis man sembils he, þat fundes his hus opon þe stan fra þe water and te flod; for þi ne failed it noht, for it [was] wrht o-pon þe harde stane." þus kennis ure lauerd us his werkis, at folu his cumandementis. For þi he giuis us respit, þat we sal mende ure sinne and siþin to þe ioy be sent; Als þe postil sais ȝur godes word: "An nescitis—þe sufferans may þu noht wite of god her witer-like, þat he to þe hauis don?" Als ure lauerd sais: †"Of þe sinfull will I noht þe dede, bot þat tay turne and liue." wen we aske þe, lauerd, wha in þi tabernakill sall wone, and we here þi cumandement, and dos te werkis þat fallis þar-to, þan sall we be ayris in þi ioye. lord, for þi mercy þu gif us grace þare at be. Amen.

For what good we do, glory be to God alone,

who is the true foundation.

It is through God's long-suffering that we have the chance of mending our ways.

[† leaf 3, bk.]

Capitulum IIII. Monachorum.

IN þis sentence bidis us sain benet þat we make ure hertis redy, and ure bodis als-sua, in mekenes, yef we will wone wid god. þan ure force es gane us fra, we pray ure lauerd be ure help for his mikill miht. Yef we þe painis of helle will fle, and cum till ioy þat ay sall be, þanne full-fille we his wille. Loke þat ȝe renne suiþe, yef

Thus, once more, let us invoke God's help, and be up and doing.

1. MS. *praiþe.* 4. The Latin catch-words *Ergo preparanda* are placed in the right margin; they properly belong to l. 27. 7. MS. *ad.* The same slip was made in p. 6, l. 12, and p. 9, l. 29, in which latter place, however, *ad* was immediately crossed out, and *and* was added. 14. MS. *se m bils.* 16. MS. *it wrht.* 20. MS. *nescitits.* 27. *Monachorum* properly belongs to p. 4, l. 14.

St. Benet has established a school for the service of God, strict, yet comforting.

ȝe wiƚƚ to þe lange liue. þare may help þe here to. þus sais sain benet: Mi scole wil i stablis to godis seruise. Greue þing wiƚƚ i noht stablis, na noht þat wrange es, bot a stresce will I make in mendnis of ȝoure sinne, And for to yeme charite, þat þer nan iuil lares by-gynne, Bot þat haly kirke ȝow lokis. Loke þu folow þi do*m*num in haly religiun; þan sall þi charge be liht; þan sal þi hert liht be, in godis trouht yef þu it se. In mikiƚƚ suetnes may þu renne, wen þu can knau god and [† leaf 4] †his cumandement. þan sall tu euir mare wone wid him in þat suete felazscap. þat here liuis in clene scrift and in paine, þai sall haue part wid him. Lauer*d*, þu grante it us sua, til þi ioy þat we ga. Amen.

I.

Quartu*m* vero gen*us*.

This refers only to such monks (and nuns) as live in convents under a rule.

Foure maner of Munkis es in religiun, sais sain benet. þe first maner þan er þa in cuuent es gadird for to liue in godis pais, vndir reul of dicipline, and a abbot ouir þam. þe toþir maner þan ere ermitis and reclusis, godis wille bi þam ane at do. þe ermitis and þe reclusis þat liuis sua, kenning bi-hus þam haue for to fezte wid þare miht a-gain þe deuil and a-gain þar sinne. þanane byhouis þam fezte þam ane, at god es tar best help. þe þridde er þa þat in na reul will ga, na hauis na kenning. Als es o þaim at saie als þe gold þu may se, þat semis gode and es noht: wen it es forht broht, þan es it als þe lede. Bi-fore þe werld er þai semande, and fals-like liues, and tines þaire mede, And leris o-gain god of þar abit. þai er unwise; þai desaiue þam-self and oþir baþe. þe ferde maner er wel werre, þat nouþer wiƚƚ wone, bot gange fra stede til stede wil þai, noure wone lange. [† leaf 4, bk.] †þair auen wille wiƚƚ þai do. Glutunie luue þai. better es to be stille þan for to speke of þair lif. Sain benet sais: now wil I blinne to speke of þaim, for it ne helpis noht, & speke of

Hermits fight their battle alone.

Certain monks (living apart) follow no rule.

Others roam about the country in a disgraceful fashion.

2. MS. *wilistablis.* 3. MS. *sta = blis.* 6. *domnum?* the *d* is defective, and resembles an *o*; no contraction mark is distinguishable. 8. Between *yef* and *þu* there are a couple of indistinct strokes slanting like the two first of a *w*. Possibly the scribe was about to write *we* instead of *þu*. 10. MS. *felazhap* (thus *h* for *sc*). 14. The catch-words properly belong to l. 28. 24. *þaim*, *i* above the line.—*at*, MS. *þat*.

þa þat liuis in godis ordir. þat we wid þaim may ga, god gif it us. Amen.

II.

Abbas qui *pre*sse.

IN þis sentence mustirs sain benet wat man az at be abot. þe abot ah fo[r] to wite what his name singnefiis and whi he beris þe curun. He [ah] at mustir gode dedis and wel rede and singe in haly kirke, Gode a-saumpil til oþir at giue for to liue riht. þe name of þe abot bitakins fadir of maine. For he sal be in haly kirke in godis stede for to lere his munkis wisdom and charite. He ah na þing at cumande bot þat he may haue warant at god. Rihtuis ah he at be, and of charite, Als haly writ sais, wis of speche, Of gode cunsaile at þe nede; sua az abot at be. He sal lere his cuuent þe riht gate, in godis troht þat þai be. Euer sal be in his þoht þat his munkis be wel lered, þat þai dute god. þe abot sal be blamid if þe cuuent mis-ga. þa þat ere of ille dedis, he †az at chasti þam. þan saƚƚ he be quit at þe iugement, And saie wid þe *prophete*: "Lau*er*d, I ne hid noht in me þe reht-uisnes of þe. I bad þai sulde it gete. Summe hauid me in despit, wen I lered þaim, And did þaire azen wille." þanne sais saine benet of þaim þat ere unbuxum ogain god, þat þai saƚƚ to paine ga. lau*er*d de-fende us þar-fra. Amen.

The superior of a convent should be like a father: teach through words and deeds; be at once just and kind, wise, [† leaf 5] and strict;

Ergo cu*m* aliquis suscipit.

Sain benet spekis yet of þa þat saƚƚ be abotis: Gode a-saumpil sal he giue, Of twine maner at lere his discipilis in religiun in halynes at seiue god: baþe in word and dede, baþe to þe simplis and tiƚƚ þe harde of hart. His dedis az at be suilke als he cumandis til oþir. He bidis þai saƚƚ nan euil do. Yef he kennis gode tiƚƚ oþir, and him-self dos noht sua, God refusis him; Als haly writ sais: "Quare tu enarras &c.—Whi telles tu mi rih[t]uisnes wid þi muz, and dos it noht? Dicipline þu hatid, and keste mine wordis obac; þare for-gat tu þe. In þi broþir ehe þu ses a stra, And noht a balke in þin azen." þabot az at loue nane mare †þan oþ[i]r for his heze kinredin, bot he be

act up to his own commandments; love all alike, [† leaf 5, bk.]

4. MS. *ar*, for *az* or *ah*. 5. MS. *fo;* cf. p. 6, l. 18. 6. MS. *He at*. 26. MS. *lers*. 32. MS. *rihuisnes*. 36. MS. *oþr;* cf. p. 7, l. 26.—*be* omitted and then added above the line.

except on good grounds; buxum and religius bot ilkain oþir broþir. For nede he may do an bi-fore an[o]þer for reuerance, yef he ne wiłł noht ilkain in his ordir, als he takis. Baþe yung and alde sałł halde reul; til a god haue we tan. Alle sal be louid eftir an in haly religiun, bot if þai bettir do; For þai az at be louid euin-like in charite, ilkain als tay ere. shrive them; Scrif[t] sal he do on þaim, þare sinnis for to les. Lauerd, þu giue us sua at do, þat we may cume to þi regne. Amen.

In doctrina sua nam*que*.

chastise each one according to his disposition, Sain benet sais þat abot az at lere his cuuent, als sain pol bidis: Blame þat mis-do, a[n]d do þam liue riht; chasti þaim fra iuil wne, als þe fadir dos his sune. þa þat ere fraward and recles, Lede þaim þe straiter. þa þat er buxum and meke, þai sałł haue cumfort. Yef ani faute without delay; be funden in þaim, þat it be sone mendid. He sałł vmbe-þinke hym of þe prest of sylo, þe ire of god com to, fo[r] he ne chastid noht hise childir, bot lete þaim in þaire wille. þe gode sall he chasty wid word and amonesce þaim. þat er prude and kene, þai sałł be chastid wid [† leaf 6] wand. For it is writen †þat man sałł chasti þaim: "Percute filium &c.—Smite þi sune wid þi wand, and make him meke, and deliuir his saul fra paine." Lau*er*d, þu deliuer us fra paine. Amen.

Meminisse.

ever remember his great responsibility, Ay, sais sain benet, þabot az at þinke þat, wat his name es. þe mare he hauis in pouste, þe mare hauis he at yelde. Abot az at be wis; greueus þing es hym bi-taht: þe sauls for to gete, And mony þing for to wite. Wid summe sal tu faire speke, and summe gete wid chastiment & haue þam under wand, and lere þaim ilkain eftir þar maner wid resun. þan þar þe noht be calanged of þe cuuent þat es undir þe, þat es giuin [þe] at yeme. *þurȝ þe dute þat þai haue þe ioy of god, may þai ler at serue

2. MS. *anþer*. 6. *at*, MS. *þai*. 7. MS. *Scrif*. 12. MS. *ad*. 14. *straiter*? The fifth character, at the end of a line, is blurred; possibly *strat/ter* (cf. p. 2, ll. 3, 7, footnotes). 15. MS. *buxum*. 16. *þat*, MS. *þai*. 18. MS. *fo*. 33 MS. *giuin at*; cf. p. 7, l. 2, and p. 41, l. 15.

him to will. For nan erþelike pouste az he at for-gete þe sauls þat es bitaht him at yeme. þe tresur of god er þai. Resun sal he yelde to god of þaim. Yef þu be of litil uresun, be of riht trouz, and here what haly boke sais: "Primu*m* querite regnu*m* dei—First sal tu seke godis rengne and his rihtuisnes, þan saƚƚ þing multeplii þe." He þat made þis salme sais: †"wha sua liuis riht, þai sal haue na ned. Nichil de-esse—Na þing sal faile þaim þat wil luue god." þabot az at under-stande of þe sauls he hauis at yeme, þat he sall yelde resun of þaim. Loke þe numbir of his cuuent: Als well az he to yeme þaim als his azen saul, yef he wil be sauf. þan he for oþir sal ancewer swa, fuƚƚ riht az he at ga, And mende him in dede. þe mare he mendis his cuuent, Till mare ioy saƚƚ he be sent, til god at take his mede. Lau*er*d, giue us sua at liue, þat we may yelde þe resun for us-self at þe day of dome. Amen. Qui uiuis & regnas.

seeking first the righteousness of God.

[† leaf 6, bk.]

The superior shall yield account of each soul entrusted to him.

III.

De adsc[i]endis ad consiliu*m* sororib*us*.—Quociens aliqua.

Sain benet mustirs in þis sentence Hu þabes sal take hir cunsale. Scho saƚƚ calle þe cuuent to-gidir and muster þaim þe nede, and loke whilke sais best resun, and proue þair wit sua. þan ilkain hauis said þair auis, þat es best, halde þar-to. Sua bidis haly writ, þat alle be cald til cunsaile, yung and alde, in hali religiun; For ofte sendis god resun til þe yunge þat a-noþ[i]r ne can noht. þat aƚƚ consentis †to sal nan gain-saie, bot halde it in obedience. Als te decipill es at his maister cumandement, Als sal þabes consent til þaire cunsale þat resun es. Alle sal folihe þe maister of þe reule, baþe yung and alde. þat nan folu þair ahen wille, ne nan bere þaim sua heze, þat tay striue ogain þair abes. Yef any sal take discipline, gruching sal sho make nane, bot halde þe cumande-

In matters of general importance, the abbess should consult her whole convent. What is most reasonable should be decided on and strictly adhered to, meekness and obedience being required from all.

[† leaf 7]

1. MS. *er þe like.* 18. MS. *adscendis.—Quociens aliqua* fills up the blank at the end of Chapter II, thus apparently preceding the heading of the next chapter. 20. *þis*, MS. *his;* cf. the beginnings of most chapters.—*þabes*, MS. *þabas* with an *c* over the second *a*. 26. MS. *a noþr.*

ment. þe dedis of þabbesse sal be in þe dute of god, for sho [sal] be set til resun of aƚƚ hir iugemens and of al hir dedis bi-for god, þat es rihtuis of iugement. þar es p*r*iue cunsale be at do, þe alde sal sho calle þar-to; Als haly writ bidis: "Om*n*ia fac cum consilio—Alle þing do wid cunsale, and eftir þe dede sal þe noht mis-like." Lau*er*d, we pray þe þat we may suilke cunsal take, þat we may do þi wille. Amen.

In private matters the seniors only need be consulted.

IV.

Que sunt in-strumenta bonor*um* op*er*u*m*. — In p*r*imis d*omi*n*u*m.

Summary of a good life. Love and numerous virtues,

IN þis sentence spekis sain benet, and mustirs til his cuuent what þaire god dedis ah at be. First sal ye luue god wid al yure herte and wid al yure saul and wid al yure uertu, And ti prome als ti-self; sua ah ye at do. Man [†]ah ye noht at sla; na to licherie ga; Na til þifte; Na cuuatus; Ne bere fals witnes, bot onur alle men; & do til na man bot als tu walde man did to þe; And leue þin ahen wille, and foliz godis wil; and halde þe in chastite, and iuil langingis do away; luue fasting; þe pouir help bi-for þe ga; þat ere nakid claþe; wisit þat er seke; þe dede winde and til eryd bringe; Sahtil þat ere wraze; And uncuþe be wid þe dedis of þe werld; luue god ouir alle þing. when þu es in ire, heuin þe noht; þar-of cumis ille ending. Halde na feluni in þi harte; Ne giue na fals pes; Charite felle þu noht; Iuil for iuil sal tu noht do, Ne wrang to na man; Til god uengance fallis it. Yef ani do yu wrang, ye sal take it in pacience, Als hali boke cumandis. Ye sal luue yure enemis & striue noht ogain þam, ne banne þam noht, bot blisce þam and suffir iugement. Ye ne sal noht be prude in herte; Ne ete our-mikil; Ne drinc ouir-mikil; Mesurlike slepe; Ne be noht slau, Ne gruchande; In god al yure trouz, and ful of [†]charite; And yef ye finde ani gode in yu, tiƚƚ god sal þe louing be, and grace til him giue. ye sal dute

[† leaf 7, bk.]

like obedience and chastity,

charity,

moderation,

[† leaf 8]

2. MS. *sho be.* 5. MS. *Omnis.* 9. MS. *Quo.—In primis dominum,* cf. the footnote on *Quociens aliqua,* p. 7, l. 18. 16. MS. *Na cuua'us* twice. 19. MS. *þein.* 22. MS. *þe dedis of* twice.

domis-day And te fir of helle; And haue god trouz til þe lif þat lastes ay; And ilke day þat ye þinke o-pon þe ded; And haue bi-fore yu þat god in alle stedis may se; wicke þohtis do oway þat to yu cume, and bide þaim ga forz, and quite yu wid scrift; And gete yure muþes fra unait wordis; haly lescun bliþelike here; And clene uresun for to lere; wid teris and wid sizing knau yure sinne, sua sal ye amende yu o-gain god; leue þe wille of yure fles, sua sal ye yure sinnes les. þat yure abes cumandis yu, sal ye do, and be not þar-o-gain, Als ure lau*er*d bad his deciplis; his cumandement do noht oway; luues chastite and kaste pride oway; loke ye do sua. þe alde men sal ye onur, þe yunge luue in god; And pray for yure enmis; and for-giue þaim þaire fautes þat mis-do ogain yu. yef ye be wrad þan þe sune rises, make pes are it ga to rest. þat ye ne falle in na mis-hope, bot in godis trouz to liue. þis is þentendement of haly kirke for to wirke godis wille; †þan sal it come be-for us at þe day of dome; he giuis us ure mede. God giue us þat ilke mede þat he hizte til hise freendis, þat nan eye may se, ne erin here, ne herte forz telle, what god hauis graid til þa þ*at* luues him. [L]uues haly kirke and yure cloister; þanne may ye do godis wille. [L]au*er*d, giue us sua þir cu*m*andemens at do, þat we may cum to þi ioy! Amen.

hope, prayer and repentance, are repeatedly enjoined.

[† leaf 8, bk.]

V.

IN þis sentence spekis sain benet of obedience, what it is at saie. [þ]at es te firste mekenes: wid-uten duelling til þat man bidis yu do. [M]eke bi-houis yu be for þe luue of god, for he mekid him for yu. [M]eke yu to godis seruise in hali kirke and do yure miht þar-to, þat ye may fle þe fir of helle and cum til heuin-rike; þare es faire at be. [þ]at yure abes cumandes yu at do, þat ye do it suiftlike; als god cumandis: "Ob auditu &c.—[þ]urz þe wordis ye here o me, þan ah ye at be meke"; als yure maistiresse leris yu, als it sais: "Qui uos audit—

Obedience should be prompt,

15. MS. *sunerises.* 22 ff. On this page several rubrics were never entered in the blanks left for them. On the preceding pages the usual red strokes in the black letters are entirely wanting. 26. MS. *este.*

wha sam heris yu, þan heris me." for þi sal ye understande þaim: þat of mekenes wil lere, þai sal here þe cumandemens, and do als man bidis þam. ye sal leue ✝yure ahen propir wiƚƚ, and do oþir mens. þoz ye be in labur, and yure maistires cumande yu at do a-noþir þing, ye sal laie it dune, & do þat scho bidis; þan er ye buxum under reule. ilkain sal take discipline at oþir, als hir mastiresse þoz scho ware, in þe dute of god. ye sal wne yu til strate gate, for þe luue of god; Als ure laue*r*d sais: "Angustia &c.—Straite gatis toke I me for to giue yu a-saumpil at liue." ye ne sal noht liue i*n* yure ahen wille, bot giue yu til mekenes. ye sal do oþer mens wille, yef ye wil cu*m* to god. þa þat wil liue in cuuent, þai sal haue maistiresse ou*ir* þam for to yeme þaim, þat tay foliz þe wordis of god, als he sais: "Non veni &c.—I ne come not in-til erþe for to do mi wille, bot my fadirs þat me sent." þat es godis wille, þat ye foliz yure ordir, and luue til yure prome, and do wi*th*-uten gruching þat yu es cumandid. þe mekenes þurz god ye can, als he sais hi*m*-self: "Qui uos audit—þat heris in yu, þai here me." For þi bi-houis þe decipils do þe mekenes, als þai haue tane to; þat es godis wille. þoz þu gruche, þe cumandement sal be haldin. And yef þu gruches & dos þat ilke þi*n*g, god es noht paid þar-of; ✝for he ses ty herte, & for ty hauis þou no mede of þat þing þat tu dos gruchande; for þi sal tu quite þe wid scrift; ye, it *bi-cimis yu. laue*r*d gif us sua meke at be, þat we may halde ure ordir, and syne cume til þe ioy þat lastes ay. Amen.

regardless of individual [✝ leaf 9] convenience or inclinations, and cheerful. [✝ leaf 9, bk.]

VI.

Sain benet spekis in þis sentence of silence, how ȝe sal it halde. he bidis þat ȝe do als þe p*r*oph*e*te sais: "kepe ȝour tunge, it sp[e]ke no scaþe, & ȝour lippis fra iuil, & kepe ȝow fro dedly synne." for þi sal ȝe seldin speke, for ȝe sal speke nan unat, ne vse yow noht þar-to. & i*n* oþir stede es writen: "Mors & uita &c.—In þe pointe of þe tunge es lif & ded." loke wheþer ȝe wil take to. þe maistires aw at speke for to lere hyr dicipils wisdom. þe decipils sal here þar lesson & understand it.

Silence saves from many a sin. The disciple should listen.

20. *yu*, MS. *me*. 26. *bi-cimis*, see Notes. 31. MS. *spke*.

VII.

yet

Of mekenes spekis sain benet in þis sentence, & sais [Meekness,] w*ith* hali script*ur*e: "Omnis qui se exaltat &c.— þa þat heyés þam, þai sal be mekid; & þai þat mekes þam sal be heyed." vre lord saide þat it es p*r*ide in þaim þat hyes þaim. Til mekenes he bides yu se, & say als þe p*r*ophe*te* saide, when he spac til ure laue*r*d w*ith* muþe: "Do*m*ine, no*n* e*st* &c.—laue*r*d, my hart es not heyid in me, ne min eyen. Mikil o me ne held I noht to praise me-self. yef I leuid at se to mekenes & heyid me, My laue*r*d munde do †to my saul als þe barne þat is done [† leaf 10] fra his modir milke ouir-arlike." Mikyl walde he fle pride, þe p*r*ophe*te*, als hali writ sais. Yef ye wyl be hezid, lokes þat ye be meke, And make yure stize to he [like Jacob's ladder,] heuin wid yure gode dedis, þat iacob saz slapande: he saz gode wid his angels cume dune and vp in þe stede þare he lay. yef ye wil se to mekenes, þare sal ye be hezed, [leads to heaven.] and gang vp wid þat stize. þat bitakins, þan þai com dune, ye sal be lazed, yef ye be prude; and tan þai yede vp, þat ye sal be hezed, yef ye to mekenes can se. þe stize betakins vre lif here. þe stize hauis tua tres, bitakins [Its stalks are our body and soul; its rungs, our good deeds.] þe body and te saul, ayþar at helpe oþir. þe stelis by-tuixe bitakins oure gude dedis, þat sal bere vs vp to god. þe tres betakins mekenes to goddis seruise and vnder discipline. Laue*r*d, we prai þe for þi misericorde þat we mai sua yeme þis reul o mekenes, In þe felazscap of þin angels þat we may be. amen. Qui viuis & *regnas* de*us* pe*r* *omnia secula*.

Sain B*enet* sais þat te dedis of mekenes ere ful suete; [Meekness implies: 1. the fear of God,] sua kennis he us; And sais þat ye sal haue firste þe dute of god, þat ye liue sua, þat ye be noght for-getil and fle evil dedis, And tat ye recorde wel þe cumantemens of god. Loke þat ye fle sinne, †yef ye wile cume to þe [† lf. 10, bk.] ioy of heuin fra þe pines of helle; þat yure wyl be euir at gete yu fra scaþe; þat ye gete yu fra iuil þohtes, yure tunges fra iuil speche, yure eyen, yure hend, yure fete fra vnait gate, fra iuil wylle; And scere o-way al þe langing of yure fleis. God ses al yure þoght and al yure dedis.

3. *scripture, i* above the line. 31. The first *þat*, MS. þa[t].

þe angel þat here yemis yu dos hym at wit aƚƚ yure dedis; sua sais te p*ro*ph*ete*. Alle yure þohtes may he se; And whyder þai wyl lede yu, resun sal ye yelde of þam. for þi ah ye at gete yu fra iuil þohtes, þat ye may cume to þe ioy of heuin. god gyf it us! ame*n*.

and the giving up of one's own wishes

Of propir wyl spekis sain benet; and ye saƚƚ do it als god bidis i*n* haly writ and sais: "Et a voluntatibus—Turne yu fra yure wille and gete yu fra iuil; þan may ye liue in pais." Of yure ahen wylle sall ye blinne, al þat wil do yu sinne; Als it is wrytyn: "Sunt vie que—þe rihte gate, it es til þe lyf þat lastes ay." þa gates sal ye fle þat wicke men gas to heƚƚ by. for þi ar þai rotyn þat folyzed wicke wylle; hauid tay na bettir mede. sua sal yure antente be, þat god may se al yure wylle; Als te p*ro*ph*ete* sais. He sais: "aƚƚ his langing es by-fore god." for þi †es gude þat ye doe o-way yure wicke dedis & þohtes; þe dede is set to chasti þaim. for witte ye wele þat god may se baþe iuil and gude; es noght hyd be-fore hym. God lokis ut of heuin i*n*-tyl erþe tyƚƚ hise at visit þaim, and lokes yef man askys hy*m* ohte. For þi lokys þat ye do wel, þat yure angel may do yure nedis to god of al þat ye haue nede. And getes yu wel, yure fautes be noght musterd by-fore god. Lau*er*d, þu do vs sua at liue, þat we may deliuir vs of al vre fautes, And siþin to ioy cume. Ame*n*.

[† leaf 11]

2. and desires;

Þe toþir maner o mekenes is, sais sain benet, For to hate yure ahen p*ro*pir wyl, And fulfil noght yure langing, bot do godis wylle, and his desire fulfille; Als him-selfe sais: "Non veni &c.—I ne cume noght for to do my wille, bot my fadirs þ*at* me sent." And i*n* odyr stede sais he: "Volu*n*tas habet &c.—Wille he hauide paine at do, at haue þe curune þat lastes ay, als it was hys wille." Lau*er*d, we pray þe þat we may sua halde þis mekenes, þat we may do þi wille. ame*n*.

3. obedience to the superior;

Of þe þridde maner o mekenes spekys sain benet to þa in his reul wyl be, And bidis þat ye sal be meke vnder yure abbes and do godis seruise; Als ta-postil saide of godis sune, þat he was meke riht tyl þe ded. God giue vs þat †we may sua be. amen.

[† lf. 11, bk.]

3. *yu*, MS. *ye* (or þe).

4. patience and perseverance

Of þe ferþe maner o mekenes spekys sain benet, hu ye sal meke yu of þingis þat yu þinc es igainis yu, þat fallis to yure ordir. yef ma*n* dos yu ani wrang, ye sal take it in pacience, and noħt fle þar-fore, ne leue yure gode dede; Als haly boke sais: "Qui pe*r*seue*r*auerit &c.—Wha sua wel wirkis til endyng, þai sal be sauf of alle þing"; Als þe p*ro*phe*te* sais: "Confortetur &c.—ye sal haue cumfort i*n* yure hertis of god." For þi sal ye be of pacience, for þe luue of god, of þi*n*g þat es o-ganis yure fleis; Als te p*ro*phe*te* sais to god: "Laue*r*d, we ere ilke day, for þe luue of þe, i*n* þe dute of dede als te shep þat ere driuin to ded, for we folih þe; bliþelike we suffir it, for we sal haue mede of þe"; Als haly writ sais: "Probasti nos &c.—Laue*r*d, þu prouis vs here als te siluir þat es brind; þu did vs in þe lay and noy opon vre bak." for we sulde lere vnder maistires hu we sulde liue; Als te letter sais: "Inposuisti &c.—Ouir vs hauis þu don men," þi wylle at fulfille. þa þat ere vnbuxum, þai sal be done to paine. Of þaim spekis sain paul, and sais þat tay ere fals. þai caste þair mantil and rennis a-mise. þat bytakins, þai sal liue here bot †a while. Alle be blisced þat weris taim. God giue vs sua meke at be, and sua his wille at do, þat we his ioy cum to. amen.

for the love of God;

[† leaf 12]

5. unreserved shrift;

Of þe fifte maner o mekenes spekis sain benet for to lere hys sistirs hu þai salle scriue þaim to þair abbes, baþe nunne and sistir. Loke þat ye be buxum and scriue yu of alle þe sinnis þat ye haue don; Als haly writ bidis yu: "Reuela d*omi*no &c.—Must*ir* til god al þi gate, & he sal make it i*n* pes." And i*n* odir stede sais he: "Confitemini &c.—Knaus to god al yure sinne, for he es of mercy and gude at al nede." yet sais þe p*ro*phe*te*: "Delictu*m* meum &c.—Laue*r*d, I mustird þe myne dedis, I ne hid tam noħt and alle my herte." þa*n* ye do þus, þan sale yure sinnes be for-gyvin. Laue*r*d giue vs grace sua for to muster vre dedis, þat we may til his ioy cu*m*. ame*n*.

6. self-depreciation and readiness to do menial work,

Sain B*enet* spekis of þe sexte de-grece of mekenes Til his sistirs, and sais þat ilkain sal halde þaim-selfe lest of alle odir. And al þingis þat ma*n* bidis yu do, þat ye do it mekely, þat resunnabil es. þu sal þinke i*n* þi herte þat tu es vndinge to gode dede; Als þe p*ro*phe*te* saide:

[† lf. 12, bk.]

"Ad nichilu*m* &c.—Til na þing es I made †bot for to doe godis wylle. ic is like tyl a mere þat beris þat ma*n* lais on hir bak." In what dede sam ye be, loke þat yure þoht and ȝure herte [be] to god almihten. Laue*r*d, we praie þe, what sam we do, þat we to þe be broħt. ame*n*.

7. thinking one-self the lowest of the low;

Sain benet spekis yet til his sistirs of þe seuind degrece o mekenes, and bidis þat ye sal meke yu ilka in-til oþir, baþe mare & lesse, And saie als te p*ro*ph*et*e saide: "Ego sum &c. Ic es wrmis and na man, And ut-castyng o men. First was ic hezed, and siþin lazed þur scrifte, and ouir-cumin." sua sal ye do, & tanne mai ye sai w*it*h þe p*ro*ph*et*e: "Bonum michi &c.—Laue*r*d, god it es to me þat þu mekyd me to lere þine cumandemens." God giue vs sua his cumandemens at lere, þat we may cume til his mekenes. Ame*n*.

8. compliance with the precepts of rule and superior;

Of þe ahtend maner o mekenes spekis sain benet til his cuuent, and bidis þat ye sal do als te reul sais, And als it cumandis, And meke vnder þare maistres i*n* alle þaire dedis. Laue*r*d, ye giue vs at halde þis mekenes til þending. ame*n*.

[† leaf 13]
9. refraining from much talk

Sain benet spekis til his cuuent of þe nihend degrece o mekenes, And biddis †þat ye ne sal noġħt vse yu tyl mekil speche. for hali writ spekis þare-of, and sais þat nama*n* may mikil speke, bot yef þare be sinne i-mang, Na naman wil p*ra*yse þaim þat es of mikil speche; Ofte speke þai wrang. Laue*r*d, þu giue vs sua vre silence to yeme, þat we may serue þe to-queme, in yuþe and i*n* elde. ame*n*.

10. and laughter;

Of þe tende maner o mekenes spekis sain benet til his cuuent, And bidis þat ye ne sal noġħt be oui*r*-lazand; and þinkes what þe p*ro*ph*et*e sais: "Stultus i*n* risu &c.—þe fool turnes hys þoġħt i*n*-til lazter, and helpis noht." Laue*r*d, we pray þe þis resun be halden witħ vs, and send vs þi wit. AMeN.

11. gentleness, conciseness, and prudence in speech;

Sain benet spekis yet til his cuuent Of þe ellofte maner of mekenes, And biddis þat ye sal mekely speke when ye speke, & wid-vten lazter, and o fa wordis & stabil, and speke wiselike. þan þu sal speke to þi felahe,

2. *ic*, MS. *it;* similarly 9 and 10. 4. MS. *herte to;* cf. p. 38, l. 7. 9. *wrmis*, see Glossary.—MS. *naman.*

crie noght o-pon hir, bot faire aske þin erand, als haly boke sais: "Sapiens verbis &c.—þe wyse man musters hym wid fa wordis & welle sitande." Lauerd, we pray þe Of þis maner þat we may be. Amen.

[leaf 13, bk.]

Saint benet spekis in þis sentence Of þe telfete maner o mekenes, And bidis þat ye sal meke yure herte til alle men, baþe to mare & les. In what labur sam ye be, þoz ye be in þe kirke, Ouþir in þe garde, Ouþir in gate, Ouþir in felde, ouþir what labur sam ye do, þat ye haue yure heuidis enclind to þerþe, And þeneke on yure synnys for to mende þaim, And tat ye be als rad als ye saz þe iugiment of god, And þinke what þe puplicane saide, when he laide hym by-hinde þe dore, Als te gospel telles: "Domine, non sum dignus &c.—Lauerd, I ne is noght digne at lifte mine ezin til heuin for mine sinnes." loke what þe prophete sais til oure lauerd in haly writ: "Incuruatus sum &c.—Ic is lazed and mekid til alle þat mine ezin se." When ye haue fulfild þis al, þire mekenes, þan sal ye cume til perfite charite, til þe ioy þat god hauis graid til mannis sunis. Lauerd, graunt it vs, þat we may sua þir mekenes halde, þat we to þi ioy may cume. amen. Qui viuis &c.

12. lowliness in carriage.

VIII.

IN þe tyme of wintir, þat es fra þe *Kalandis* of nouembir til þe paskys, als it is forlokyd wyd resun, þanne sal ye ryse at þe aztend time †of þe nyght, þat it be litil ouir mid-nyght; þan es tyme at rise, als it is set, til godis seruise; And siþin, þe space eftir matins, til sauters and til haly lescuns at here. þat es hele of þa þat ere in sekenes, þat es at say in sinne. And fra þe paskis til þe *Kalandis* of nouembir sal þe tyme be sua set, þat tare be lytil entirual, þat ta þat sal ga til laburs, þat tay may haue þe morning in þe begining of þe lyth to þair labur.

At the nocturnal divine offices, during hours [† leaf 14] varying according to the season,

IX.

IN þe tyme of wintir, þan sal þe first vers be at matins: "Deus, in adiutorium"; And in þe toþer tyme þris þis vers: "Domine, labia mea aperies"; at þe

certain rituals should be gone through,

10. MS. *heuid is enclin do.*—*þe/neke,* originally *þencke*? 28. The first *in* is above the line.—MS. *þt/þat.*

different in winter

þridde tyme aiont wid þe "glo*r*ia patri"; and siþin efter þe nihend-ferþe salme wid þe antefe*n* ouþir wid-vten; and syþin efter þe ymne; And tare-eftyr sexe salmis wid þe antefens. Wen þai ere said and te verset, þabbasse saie þe benecun; þan sal alle site, And nym þre lescuns, red o-pon þe lettrun, & by-tuixe þe lescuns þre respuns; and eftir þe þridde respun þe vers wid þe "*glo*r*i*a p*at*ri," standande alle for þe onur of the haly trinite. þe boke of þe halizes sal be red, baþe of þe newe lay & of þalde testament, and te exposiciuns of þaim Of oure fore-fadirs þat ware in stabil trouz. Eftir þe þre lescuns wid þe respuns, Oþir sexe salmis sungen wid all*eluia*. And eftir salbe redde þe lescun of þa-postils wid gude deuocion, and te vers, and siþin þe letanie "Kyrie*leison*." And sua †finise matins.

[† leaf 14, bk.]

X.

and summer,

FRa þe paskis til þe k*alandis* of noue*m*bir sal be halden a quantite of þe salmis, als is said bi-fore; for þe nihtis er scorte als mikil, þat te þre lescunis be noght red, bot an for þa þre of þalde testament, wid a scort respun; Bot al þe toþir finist, als it sais by-fore, þat na nyħt be lesse saide þan tuelue salmis, vt-takyn þe þridde and te nihende-ferþe salme.

XI.

on Sundays

IN þe sunendais es for to ryse arliker, And halde yure mesur o waking; þat es þat ye syng þe sexe salmes and te vers, als is ordainde by-fore, sitande alle wid ordir, and foure lescuns red wid respuns, als es ordainde, and eftir þe "glo*r*ia patri"; þan sal alle stande for þe reuerence; And efter oþir sexe salmis wid þe antefens, als by-fore, wid þe werset; And efter oþir foure lescuns wid þe resp*uns*, wid þat ilke ordir by-fore; And tare-eftir þre cantikils of þe p*r*ophe*t*is, als te abes stablis, and songen wid "all*eluia*"; siþin þe verset, and te abes te ben*icun*; And siþin foure lescuns red of þe new lay wid þat ilke ordir by-fore. Efter þe ferþe Re*spun*, þabbes sal by-gynne þis ymne: "Te d*eum* laudamus." When it is finist, þanne sal þabbes by-ginne a lescun of þe †gospel wid honur and

[† leaf 15]

24. *ye syng* twice.

wyd þe dute of god; þan sal alle stande. when it is red, þe oþ*ir* sal say amen; And tabbesse by-ginne: "Te decet laus"; And giue þe benicun, and biginne matins. þis ordir sal be haldin euin-like opon þe sundais als wel i*n* sum*ir* als in winter, bot if it sua be, þat ye rise ouir-late; þan may ye make lesse lescun; bot loke þat it be-time yu noht. Loke þat it be endid wid al þat fallis þar-to. And yef it fallis yu ani time, On waim þe for-getilnes es on-long sal man take ame*n*dis for þat faute i*n* þe kirke.

(special directions being given for the case of accidental late rising),

XII.

At matins on þe feste-dais, First sal ye saie sexe salmis wid-vten antefens, And siþin þe fyfty*d* salme wid "all*eluia*." wen þai ar said, þe hundred seuintende and þe sextid þe secunde, siþin þe benichune, and a leschun red of þa apocalips wid gude deuocion, & te respun, and te ymne ambrosine, and te u*er*set, and te antefen of þe gospel, & te letanie, and sent forz.

on feast days,

XIV.

IN þe haly dais al sal be als we haue bi-fore saide id on þe sundais, Bot þat te salmis and te antefens and te lescuns be saide als †fallis to þe day. Bot te vse bi-fore be haldi*n*.

and on saints' days,

[† lf. 15, bk.]

XV.

Fra þe paskis til þe witsundai salle "all*eluia*" be saide wid-vten entirual als wel at te salmis als at te respuns. And fra þe witsunday til þe lentyn sal it ilke niħt be saide wid þe sexe last salmis of te noct*ur*ne. Ilke sunday wid-uten lentin sal þe cantikils be said wid "alle*luia*," Matins, Prime, Vndrin, Midday, Noon; Al be saide wid "all*eluia*"; Bot te respuns noht Bot fra þe paskis til þe witsunday.

employing the 'Halleluiah' more or less frequently.

XVI.

Als te p*ro*ph*ete* sais: "Sepcies i*n* die laude*m* dixi tibi—Seuin siþe o-po day saie I louing to þe." Whilke haly seuin syþe er þa þat sal be ful-fild wid vs o þis maner, yef we folih þe vris of god: Of Matins, Of prime, of Vndrin, Of Midday, Of noon, Of euensang, Of

For the day services

16. *forz; z* has a peculiar shape, reminding of the sign for *and*.

[† leaf 16]

cumplin. Of þes times sais he: "seuin syþe o-þo day saie I louing to þe." Til þa þat rysis o night and wakis Sais vre lau*er*d: "My frende, o niht ras I for yu and wakid." For þi sal ye giue louing til hy*m*, in þe iugime*n*t of hys riht†visnes, at matins, at prime, at vndern, At midday, at noon, at euensang, at cu*m*plin; And o nith ryse for to loue hy*m*.

XVII.

there are similar directions: 2. prime, 3. undern, 4. mid-day, 5. noon, 6. evensong,

Now haue we deuisid þe ordir of þe salmis on þe niht, at matins. Loke we now tyl þe vris þat folihis. At prime þre salmis ilkain by þam ane. Þe ymne of þis ilke vre sal be saide efter þis verse: "Deus i*n* adiutoriu*m* meu*m*," Are ye beginne te salme. when þe þre salmis ere saide, a lescun sal be red, and siþin þe vers, And "Kyrye*leison*," and finist þe hure. Vndern, Midday, Noon wid þat ilke ordir be sungen, þat is, wid vers, wid ymnis þat fallis to þaim, þre salmis, and lescuns, and vers, and "Kyrye*leison*"; And sua finise þe vres. Þe salmis sal be su*n*g wid antefens, yef þe cuuent be mikil; And yef þai be fa, saie it plane forde. Bot euensang sal be saide wid foure salmes And te Antefens, And efter þe salmis A lescun, & siþin þe respun, and siþin þe ymne and te verset, þe cantikyl of þe gospel, and te letanie, And syþin þe "Pater noster." O þis maner sal þe vris be sent forde.

[† lf. 16, bk.] 7. compline.

Cumplin †sal be saide wid þre salmis wid-vten antefens, & siþin þe ymne þat fallis þar-to, A lescun, and te verset, & siþin "Kyrye*leison*," and te benicun, and sent forde þe vris til god.

XVIII.

The 'Pater noster' should be said aloud, to stop outsiders' slander, and to impress more forcibly

Sain B*enet* cumandis þat tis þing be haldi*n*, þat yure "Pater n*oste*r" be saide hezelike at matins and at euinsang, for þe sclandir þat hauis ben of religiun þat cuþe not *noħt þaire "pater n*oster*." Ilkain ah at quite þam of þis vice. Alle ah at cune þair "Pater n*oste*r" þat in religiun wil be als god cumandis. for ye sal vmbeþinke yu what resun fallis to þis vers, when ye it saie: "Et dimitte nobis debita n*ost*ra, sicut & nos dimittimus

6. *And*, MS. *At*. 31. *not noht*, evidently wrong, possibly for *not all*. 31, 32. *ah at*, MS. *ahat to*; cf. p. 22, l. 11 and footnote.

debitorib*us* no*st*ris." þan prai we þus: "Laue*r*d, þu for-giue vs ure sinnis, als we for-giue þaim þaire fautes þat hauis mis-don a-gain vs." When ye here þis vers at matins, ye sal for-giue alle men þaire trespas for þe loue o gode. And als-sua at euinsang sal ȝe for-giue. for þi wil sain benet þat it be saide hezlike, for alle wrezis sal be for-giuin. Laue*r*d giue vs sua at liue, & sua at for-giue, þat we may ga þe riħt gate til heuin. Ame*n*.

the duty of forgiving-ness.

XIX.

IN þis sentence tellis sain benet hu ye sal do yure office, when ye cume i*n*-to þe kyrke. Ye sal true þat god may se in alle stedis baþe vyl & gude. Ye az at say yure seruise als ye stode by-fore god, wyd als gude deuocyon, And think wat te p*r*oph*e*te saide: "Seruite d*omi*no &c. —Ye sal serue god wyd ahe, & here hym wyd dowte." And i*n* oþir stede sais he: "Psallite—ye sal singe god wyslike"; Als haly write sais: "In co*n*spec*tu* &c.—Laue*r*d, I sing to þe in þe siħt of þin angels to loue þe." loke ye do yure seruise als ye stode by-fore god almihti. And lokis, when ye sing, þat yure herte acorde wid yure voice; þan sing ye riħt. Laue*r*d, þu giue vs sua vre seruise at do, to þe felazscap of angels þat we may cu*m*.

[† leaf 17]

In all divine service the presence of God should be remembered.

The heart should accord with the voice.

XX.

Sain benet spekis in þis sentence til hys cuuent, and kennys þam how þai sal make þair prayer to god & wid what reuerence. When ye wyl aske any thing at a ryche ma*n* in ertħt, ye aske ful mekelike yure erande. wyd mekil mare deuociun ahte ye þanne at pray to god, of whaim þat al þe gude cumis. yure antente sal be þat ye ne sal noġħt be herde for yure many wordis; bot scort vrisun, †and wyd deuocion, and wyd terys of herte; for þi sal yure vrisun be breue & clene, Bot yef it sua bi-tide, þat any falle in mis-trouz; þa*n* sal scho pray gerne to god. Bot te cuuent vrisun sal be breue, þat ere in stedfast trouz. Laue*r*d, we prai þe þat we may suilke vrisun make, þat it be to þi wil. AmeN.

Prayers should be reverent, short, and pure.

[† lf. 17, bk.]

34. *þi*, MS. *þe*.

XXI.

In large convents certain functionaries should be appointed, able, trustworthy, pure in life, loyal.

IN þis sentence spekys sain B*enet* of þa þat sal be in officis, and bidis, yef þe cuuent be mikil, þat tay sal be chossin þat sal þe officis yeme, And by-kenne it taim þat best can serue god & te cuuent; als tabbesse cumandis taim sal þai do. Þabbes ah at set nan þar-to bot þat scho is sikir offe, þoz þai be noht þe ordenest, bot þat tay be of clene lif and leel. Yef any waxe prude i*n* hir office, man sal byd hyr amend hyr Ane tyme, and anoþir tyme, And þe þirdde tyme. Yef þai wil noħt amende sua, man sal do þam ut of þair bayly, And do anoþir in hir stede, þat man ses es dingne. Sain benet cumandis, yef priuresse be prudde, þat man sal do sua wid hir. Lau*er*d, þu giue vs sua vre office at do and resun at yelde, þat we may cume til ioy †þat lastes ay. Amen.

Whoever grows proud is to be replaced after the third refusal to amend.

(Cf. p. 44, ll. 6 ff.)

[† leaf 18]

XXII.

Dormitory regulations.

Sain B*enet* spekys here, and kennis yu hu ye sal slape ilkain in bedde by þam ane, al wid ordir, als tabbesse lokys taym. Yef yt sua may be, alle sal lie i*n* a hus, þat ilkain wite of oþir. Yef þe hus be ouyr-litel, su*m*me sal lie i*n* a-noþir huse, ten ouþir tuenty. Bot te eldest be wyd þam for to yeme þaim. & þat ye haue liħt al þe nyħt brinnande. Ye sal lie clad and beltyd. Knyvys sal ye haue nane by yure bed, nouþ*ir* gret ne smal. Whe*n* þe bel ringis, þat ye be redy, and ilkain help oþir, and ga in-to þe kyrke til godys seruise. Þe nouice beddis sal be þat nane þaire may nehe oþir; By-tuix þalde þai sal lie. Man sal wakin þaim faire til godis seruise. Lau*er*d giue vs sua for to lie and sua for to rise, þat we may haue þe ioy þat lastes ay. Amen.

All shall sleep clad and belted.

Novices shall lie between old folk.

XXIII.

Punishment gradation:

IN þis sentence leris sain B*enet* hys cuuent hu þaire fautes sal be amendid. Yef any be of grete herte and wyl noħt be buxum, ouþir prud, ouþir ani greuching make aigain haly religiun, ouþir þe cumandeme*n*t †hauis in despit, þa þat ere of suilke dedis, Priuelike man sal amoneste þam, þat tay amende þaim. yef þay wyl noħt

[† lf. 18, bk.]

1. privy admonition,

amende sua, þai sal be broħt by-fore þe cuuent and tare amende hir faute. Yef sho wyl not yet amende, sho sal be cursyd. yef sho be a fole & ful of iuil, and mas na force of þe cursing, sho sal be berid ful wel, and do hir a-mende it sua. Lau*er*de schilde vs fra þat cursing; and yef ani þar-inne be, god for his grace bringe þam vte. AmeN.

2. open admonition and atonement, 3. excommunication, 4. beating.

XXIV.

IN þis sentence mustirs sain B*enet* Hu man sal do wid þaim þat es in sentence, & bidis þ*at* man sal do þaim efter þaire faute es. Yef þe faute be litil, þai sal make þe cuuent at wite and a-ioingne hir þar-eftir. Wylys sho is in sentence, sho ne sal noħt be in cuuent, til it be amendid, In kirke ne salme beginne ne antefin, lescun nan rede. sho sal [ete] when alle hauis etin. Yef þai ete at midday, sho salle ete at noon; yef þai ete at noon, sho sal ete at euin, als te ordir sais, til sho haue am*en*did hir faute. Lau*er*d giue vs sua vre scrifte at do, þat we may hys rengne cu*m* to.

The punishment should be measured by the fault: be lighter, as partial seclusion,

XXV.

Sain B*enet* spekys in þis sentence til þa þat ere fallen in greuer faute, †Hu þai sal amende. þai ne sal noht cum in þe kirke, na in fraitur, Bot yef þabbesse cumande hir. Nan sal comun wid hir, Bot an þat es set til hir. Wid greting sal sho do, and wyd reuþe of herte, þe penance þat es laid on hir; sua salle hir fautes be mendid. for sain paul sais þat þai þat dos wicke dedis, þat tay giue þam-selfe til þe deuil. for þi ah þai at be chastid, þat te saule ga noħt til helle. And ta þat ere in cursing, þai ah at dreze þaire penance wid reuþe of herte and be sari of þair dede, þat te deuil haue na pouste ouir þaim. sho sal ete al-ane suilke als tabes cumandis hir; nan sal blisse hir mete. Lau*er*d for his gr*a*ce, he silde vs fra suilke paine. Ame*n*.

or heavier, [† leaf 19] as excommunication.

XXVI.

Sain benet sais i*n* þis sentence: yef any sistir ouþir broþir of þordir be sua hardi at comun wid hir, wid-vten cumandement of þabbes, wid speche, ouþir ani

Unauthorized communion with one excommunicated brings

4. *hir*, MS. *it;* cf. p. 25, l. 16. 14. MS. *sal when.*

the same punishment.

erand sendis til hir, suil[ke] sentence sal sho haue. Lau*er*d for his grace, he gete vs fra þat sen[ten]ce and fra alle oþir.

XXVII.

The abbess should be [† lf. 19, bk.] lovingly concerned about the one sick in sin,

IN al maner, sais sain benet, sal þabbesse ta yeme of þa þat mis-dose; for þe hale hauis †na mister o miri, Bot te seke hauis mister. For þi sal sho do als te wyse miri dos, þat wyl hele þe seke. Priuelike sal sho sende an ordane nunne til hir þat es in sentence at comforth̄ hir, and for to turne hir wylle til amendeme*n*t and til mekenes, and for to moneste hir þat sho haue reuþe in herte of hir misdedis and rih̄t trouz; Als sain paul þapostil sais: "Mikil charite mustirs he." al ah at prai for hym. On alle maner sal þabbes entirmete hir Al maner of sentence at muster til hir sep, þat nan be tint. for wyte sho wel sho hauis vnder-tan þe saules at gede, And noh̄t at striue o-gain þaim. Bot sho sal haue dute of þat vre lau*er*d saide wyd þe p*ro*ph*et*e til þe hirdis of haly kirke: "Quod crassum videbatis &c.—Þat fat ere, sal ye ta; þat ere febyl let ga." Þis is at vnder-stande, þat so ne sal noh̄t entirmete hir sua mikil of þa þat ere strang and hale als of þa þat ere febyl and seke. O þis maner sal þabbesse folize þe saumpyl of Ies*u*, þe gude herde, þat lefte in þe munte ane wane of a hundrez sep, and yede at seke þis ane þ*at* was want. When he hauid funden it, sa fain he was; he toke it on his haly schuldirs and broh̄t it til þoþir. Þis is at vnderstande †þat he lefte in heuin þe felascap of angels and com in-til erþe at laite þe man þat was tint; sua mekyl pyte hauid he of hym, þ*at* he þurz his haly grace by-com man & bar manes kinde til þe felazscap of angels til paradis, where-in Adam fel for hys synne. Lau*er*d, for þi merci giue vs grace sua at wirke, þat we til þat felazscap may cume.

and act like a good shepherd,

like Jesus, to the straying sheep.

[† leaf 20]

XXVIII.

If the said modes of correction,

SAin b*enet* sais: yef any be tane ofte in faute, and sho be cursid, and wyl noh̄t yet ame*n*de, wyd smerte beting sal sho be chastyd. Yef sho wyl noh̄t o

1. MS. *suil*, for *suilke*, or *suilk*, or possibly *suik*; cf. p. 31, l. 32. 2. MS. *sence*. 11. MS. *ahat*.

þis maner a-mende, bot wid pride defende hir dede, þan sal þabbes do als te sleze miri: wen sho hauis laid hir plaisters and hir vinemens wid faire wordis and te medicinis of haly writ, and cursid hyr, & berid, And may noħt helpe do hir best, þabbes & al þe cuuent sal pray for hir to god, þat he make hyr hale. Yef sho may noht be hale of þat maner, sho sal be done oute of þair felahscap; Als te apostil sais: "Auferte malum &c.—Do a-way þe wycke fra yu." And in oþir stede sais he: "Infidelis &c. —yef so be vnleel, do hyr A-way." for a wicke shep may spille al þe flok. Lauerd, yef it be þi wille, þu †gete vs fra þis sentence.

as well as united prayers, prove inefficient, there remains only 5. expulsion.

[† lf. 20, bk.]

XXIX.

IN þis sentence sais sain Benet þat wha sam es þurz þaire dedis don out of þe kirke and wil cum i-gain, At te begining sal sho haite a-mendement of hir faute warfore sho was don ut; þanne sal so be recaiuid, And don at te laste ende for to loke hir mekenes. Yef sho gas ut a-noþir tyme, þris shal sho be recaiuid sua; bot siþin wite sho wel es tare na cuming a-gain. Lauerd for his grace defend vs fra þis vice.

An expelled member can be re-admitted twice.

XXX.

Þis sais sain benet, þat ta þat ere of elde and vnderstandis, þai sal haue þaire mesur; & for þi þe barnis þat ere yunge, þat vnderstandis noht what paine fallis til cursing, when þai misdo, wid fasting ouþir wid smerte beriing sal þai be chastid; þar-þurz sal þai be helid. Lauerd, for yure pite ye gete vs fra sinne, baþe yunge & alde.

Excommunication is not applicable to children.

XXXI.

IN þis sentence sais sain benet þat te celeresse sal be chosin of þe cuuent, þat sho be meke, and sobur, and noht of mekil mete, ne prude, ne noius, ne wrangdoande, ne latte, ne wastande, Bot god dutande; Of al þis †sal ye ta yeme. Wid-vten þe cumandement of þabbes sal sho na þing do. Þat sho cumandis hir sal sho do,

To the functionaries (ch. xxi) belongs the cellaress, on whose qualifications and service [† leaf 21] special claims are laid,

19. *es tare*, MS. *eftare.*

bot sho sal [noht] noy hir sistirs. Par auenture yef ani man askis hir ohte þat es a-gain resun, sho sal noħt for þi haue þam in despit, ne mis-ancewer þam, Bot mekelike saie naie of þaire ful asking. Ouir al thing sal sho gete hir saul & þincke what ta apostil sais: "Qui b*ene* &c.—wha sua seruis wel, mede by-fore god sal he haue." Of þe seke, and of þe barnis, And of gestys, and of þe pouir sal sho take yeme eftir hir miħt. For wite ye wel þat sho sal yelde resun o domes-day of alle hir dedis. Þe vassels þat fallis til hir mester sal sho yeme als onestelike als te vassels þat ere halized obute þauter. for-getil ah sho noht to be, Ne ouir-mikil haue, Ne ouir-mikil waste of þat fallis to þe huse, Bot alle þingis do wid mesur, als tabbes cumandis hir. Ouir þat sho be buxum. And when sho hauis noħt at giue, þat sho anscewer þaim faire, als hali writ bidis: "Sermo bon*us* &c.—Gode speche es better þan grete gifte"; And do þat tabbes cumandis hir; and tat sho defendis, do it noħt. Sho sal graiþe þe cuuent mete wid-vten greuching and wid-vten duelling, þat tay be noħt sclaundird; And þincke what vre †lau*erd* sais in þe gospel of þaim þat sclandirs ani of his barnis: "him ware wel bettir," he sais, "þat a milnestane ware a-bute his hals i*n* þe deppest of þe se." Yef þe cuuent be mikil, þe celeresse sal haue a felaze at helpe hir, þat sho wid gode wil may do hir labur þat es bitaħt hir, þat sho may do i*n* time þat sho ah for to do, þat nan be wre[t]hid ne noid i*n* godis hus. Lau*er*d, for þi merci giue hir sua hir office at do, þat so may haue þanc o god and of þe cuuent.

and on whom great responsibility falls;

[† lf. 21, bk.]

also an assistant to relieve her, if the convent is large;

XXXII.

and persons who, under the supervision of the abbess, act as care-takers,

In þis sentence cumandis sain B*enet* þat tabbesse sal ta yeme of alle þing þat fallis til þe hus, and of vstilem*en*t and oþir þingis sal sho puruaie o lif and ded þat so be sikir, and cumande til ilkain þat sho ses ned at do. Sho sal haue þam enbreuid, alle þingis þat fallis til þe hus, for to wite what sho recauis and what sho giuis, when sho sal remue þat ere in officis. yef ani haue ille

1. MS. *sal noy.* 19. MS. *greuehing.* 26. MS. *wrehid.* 32. *sho*, MS. *mo.*

wroħt wid þe þing þat was bitaħt þaim at yeme, sho sal be apreuid; yef sho wil noħt mend, þe iugiment sal sho suffir. Lauerd, for þi merci giue vs wel at yeme þis sentence And alle þe oþir. Amen.

and are responsible for their trust.

XXXIII.

Of propirte spekis sain *Benet*, and sais þat of alle oþir vices sal man fle þis, þat nan be sua hardy, þat tay o-way do ne giue na þing wid-vten leue of þabbesse, ne þat nane haue þing in propirte, boke ne tabils, ne nan oþir þing; for nan may haue þair aħen body at hys wylle ne at tair pouste. þai sal haue alle þingis at tabbes þat tay haue nede of. þai sal haue na thing bot þat tabbesse deliuirs taim. þat ane hauis sal be comun til alle; Als haly boke cumandis: nan sal calle þat tay haue þair azen. Yef it be an þat delitis tam in þis vice, And wil not do it, Man sal saie til hir an time, and a-noþir time, and te þridde. Yef so wil noht amende sua, Man sal do hir amende on oþir maner. Lauerd, for þi pite defende vs fra þis vice. Amen.

[leaf 22]

Individual property is not allowed; everything should be had in common,

XXXIV.

IN þis sentence cumandis sain *Benet* þat tabbes sal do als ta-postils did at te beginning of cristiante: þai departid þair þing til þa þat hauid nede. "þai departid," als hali writ sais, "til ilkain, als tay hauid ned." sua salle þabbes do. sho salle noħt loke what man he es and of what kinredin, Bot te sekenes of ilkain, and do þam efter þat tay haue ned. til god sal sho yelde grace, and noħt be sari of †hir gifte þat so hauis giuin til þa þat hauis mare nede þan sho. Tyl þe nedful sal sho meke hir for in ire sekenes, And noħt bere hir heze for þe helpe þat god hauis lent hir; And o this maner sal al liue in pais. Ouir al þing sal þai loke þe wicke þat ere imangis þaim; and yef þare be ani funden, wid smerte beriing sal þai be amendid. Lauerd, for þi merci giue vs miht at fle al iuils. Amen.

distributed according to each one's need.

[† lf. 22, bk.]

XXXV.

IN þis sentence bidis sain *Benet* þat ye sal serue sua, þat nan be quit of þe seruise of þe kichin. Bot yef þai be acumbird wid sekenes ouþir wid odir laburs; for

Kitchen service is obligatory, with certain exceptions.

2. MS. *aperuid*.

Those serving should keep everything clean

[† leaf 23]

and in good order,

have provisionary light meals,

and go through certain ceremonies at the weekly change.

man sal haue grete mede for þat seruise. Til þa þat ere febil sal ye finde helpe and cumforth̄, þat tay ne serue noh̄t wid ouir-mikil noye. Al sal haue comfort eftir þat þe cuuent is mikil, and efter þai ere *in* ese to serue. Yef þe cuuent be mikil, þe celeresse sal be quit of þe seruise of þe kichin, And ta þat ere acumbird wid laburs. þis oþir sal serue al wid luue. þa þat ere out of þaire wuke sal opo þe set*ir*day ma þe maunde, and waisse þe tuailis þat tay sal wipe þaire hend opon and taire fete. þa þat ga ut of þe wuke, and te toþir þat cumis in, sal waisse þe oþir fete at te †maunde. þe vassels þat tay serue wid, sal þai ta yeme to, & yelde þame til þe celeresse clene and hale; and sho sal loke what sho yeldis & what sho recaiuis. þa þat serue o þe kichin sal miste bi-fore þe mikil mete bred, butter, þat tay may serue wid-vten gruching and wid-vten noy. And so þat gas vt of þe wuke, and so þat cumis in, sal recaiue þe benichun at morne at matins. Sho þat gas ut sal say þis vers þris by-for þauter, and al þe cuuent eftir: "Benedictus es." þan so hase rechaiuid þe benichun, þan sal þe toþir, þat sal serue eftir hir, cume by-fore þauter and saie þis vers þris, and alle þe cuuent eftir: "Deus, in adiutoriu*m*"; And siþin rechaiue þe benichun, þat god giue hir grace at serue þaim to pay. Laue*r*d, for þi grace giue vs sua at serue, þat we may [haue] vre mede of þe.

XXXVI.

Special care and kindness should be bestowed on the sick,

[† lf. 23, bk.]

Of þe seke spekis sain benet in þis sentence, And cumandis ouir al þing þat man sal ta yeme of þaim, þat tay be serued als it ware god him-selfe. For he sal say on domis-day: "I was seke, ye visit; þat ye did til an of myne, ye did it me." Bot tay sal recaiue *in* þe onur of god þe seruise þat man dos tam; þai ne sal noht þurz þair surfait noy þaire sistirs þat seruis tam. Bot †yef it sua be, þat taire iuil be sua mikil, man sal suffir þaim þe mare and be of pacience, for of þaim sal man haue grete mede of god. þabbesse tal ta yeme of þe seke þat tay haue na defaute. A hus sal þai haue bi þam ane. And tat so þat sal serue þam dute gode, and do hir miht for to

2. *cumforth*, *r* above the line, *t* apparently expuncted. 24. MS. *may vre;* cf. p. 37, l. 4.

serue þam wel and wid luue. þai sal haue at ete alle timis þat tay haue mist*er* of; bot til þe hale, þat mai wel ete, and til þe yunge sal ma*n* giue latter. þe seke þat ere febil sal man giue fleis at ete at couir þam wid-al. þabbes sal do hir antente to þe seke, þ*at* tay haue na defaute for þe forgetilnes of þe celeresse and of þe fermerier; For sho sal a-mende al at tay misdo. Lau*er*d, for þi merci gete vs fra alle iuils of body & sal. Amen.

who shall be allowed meat,

XXXVII.

Of þe alde & of þe barnis spekis sain benet in þis sentence, And sais þat taire elde prais þat man sal giue þam charite, als te reule es set to þaire mete; bot mikil pite birs man haue, þat tay sal ete ar þe oþir.

also on the old, and on children.

XXXVIII.

IN þis sentence cumandis sain benet þat te lescun sal noht faile at mete. O þis maner sal þis be stabilist, þat nan ta þe boke at †rede bot sho þat sal rede al þe wuke; sho sal begi*n*ne o-po þe sunday. sho sal cum by-fore þauter o þe sunday efter þe messe and say þris þis verse, and al þe cuuent eftir: "D*omi*ne, labia mea ape*r*ies," And recaiue þe benediccion, þat gete hir fra pride. þai sal halde silence at te borde, þat na uoice be herde bot of hir þat redis. þa þat serue sal ta yeme til þam þat etes, þat tay haue na defaute of þat tay sal haue, wharfore þai make na noise. Yef * wil aske ani thing, sho salle make sinis and noght speke. Nane sal speke of na demande in þe lescun, whar-of noise may rise. Bot tabbesse, yef sho wille, sho may breuelike, a sentence for to amende. sho þat sal rede sal miste ay litil, be-fore sho rede, þat sho ne be not ou*ir*-mikil engreuid. Ye sal ordain nane for to rede bot þat can do þe ofice, þat may pai al þat it heris. Lau*er*d, for his grace, he giue vs sua for to rede and singe, þat we may pai hy*m* and al þat vs heris.

During meals one sister, [† leaf 24] conforming to certain rules, should read aloud; the others should be silent, making signs if they want any-thing.

XXXIX.

Of þe mesur of þe mete spekis sain benet in þis sentence, And sais þat it es inoh, twane maner of

Regulations about food: meat,

23. The subject (*ani*, or the like) is omitted. 26. Possibly the verb *speke* is omitted before or after *breuelike*.

soup, [† lf. 24, bk.] fruit, bread; more during hard work, but always with moderation; no meat of quadrupeds except for the sick.

potage al þe wuke in þe tweluemonez, what tyme sam ye ete, at midday ouþir at none, þat tay þat may †noght ete of þe tane, lat þaim ete of þe toþir. þir tua mese sal þai ilke day haue. Yef þai haue whar-of, þe þridde may þai haue of frute ouþir of oþirkin felazscap. A lafe of brede mesurde es inoh o day baþe at none and at euyn. Yef þai sal supe, þe celeres sal take þe þridde parti of þe lafe & laie it by-fore þam at te super. Yef tabbes ses þai haue mikil trauaile, yef scho wil, scho may mende þam; Bot gete þar be nane owtrage, þat nane be costiue, ne nane oþir wil, þurz surfait o mete. for na þing es als mikil igain cristen men als gluterie; sua sais vre lord: "Videte &c.—Loke yure hertis be noghħt noyd þurz gluterie o mete ne drinke." Til barnis sal man noħt giue sua mikil als til þalde for to gete mesur ouir al. Of þe beste þat beris foure fete sal nane ete bot ta þat ere seke and febil. Lauerd, for þi merci giue vs sua mesur-like at ete, þat we alle wils o bodi & saul mai fle.

XL.

The measure of drink may vary; [† leaf 25] those who cannot forbear, are allowed a 'hemina.' All should be moderate and contented.

IN þis sentence spekis sain *Benet* Of þe mesur o drink, and sais þat ilke man hauis p*ro*pir gifte o god in al maner; And for þi stabelis sain B*enet* wit*h* mikil doute þe mesur of oþir mens liflade. Na-for-þi, for þe febilnes †of þa þat may noht for-bere, hauis he for-lokid til ilkain a mesur of wyne of þe day, Ouþir suilke als tabbesse may furde; þe mesur es callid eminan; þai ne mai noħt haue bot mesurlike anis þar-of. þa þat may be of abstine*ns*, mede of god sal þai haue. Yef þa*m* by-houid mare ouþir for trauaile ouþir for hete, In þe forloking of þabbesse sal it be. Bot sho sal loke þat þai ne be not ouir-ful ne drunkin. We rede þat wyne, ne na drinke þat wil make man drunkin, ne feris noħt til men of religiun. for þi þat te tyme is sua þat ye ne mai noħt al for-bere, for þi co*n*sentis sain B*enet* þat ye drinke ay litil, bot noħt sua mikil þat ye be ful; for ou*ir*-mikil drinke dose man ofte do folie. Yef it be ani þat dar noħt drinke hir mesur, þai sal grace god and gruche noħt. Ouir alle þinges loke ye

1. MS. *sain.* 4. MS. *þrid de.* 11. MS. *þinges.*

ne be noħt gruchande of na þing. Lau*er*d, for þi pite gete vs fra gruching and fra ouir-mikil drinke, sua þat we mai haue þi grace.

XLI.

Regulations about meals after Easter, [† lf. 25, bk.] in summer, in winter, during Lent.

IN þis sentence sais sain B*enet* þat ye sal ete twise of þe day ilke day fra þe haly paskis til þe witsunday; and siþin til þe †hali rodis dai i*n* semtemb*ir*, Al þe wukis in þe su*m*mir, sal ye faste ilke wuke tua dais, þe wedenisdai and te fryday, bot yef ye haue mikil trauaile, ouþir feeste-day, ouþir it be mikil hete; þan relesses sain B*enet* yu þe fasting of þa tua dais, Als tabbesse forlokis. sua sal sho ordain and a-tempir al hir þingis, þat þe saulis of hir disciplis mai sauf be; And at tay do wid-vtyn gruching þat tay sal do. Fra þe haly rodes day til þe lentyn sal ye fast ilk day, bot if it be for heze feste. Fra þe beginning of lentyn til þe paskis sal ye ete eftir euensang, bot it sal be sua, þat yu ne þarf na candil, bot al be don by day alle tyme, baþe whe*n* ye faste and when ye ete tuis. sua sal þe time be sett. Lau*er*d, for þi grace giue vs sua at be of discreciun baþe of fastyng and of mete, þat we mai be sauf.

XLII.

After the last meal follows collation— [† leaf 26] on fasting-days it is after even-song— and then compline, where-after speaking is forbidden.

Of silence eftir cumplin spekis sain B*enet* in þis sentence, and bidis þat ye sal do yu payne at halde silence eftir cu*m*plin. yef þe cuuent etis tuise, Als tite as tay rise fra þe supere, þan sal þai site wid ordir in þe cloistir. when colaciun ri*n*gis, þan salle alle asembil i*n* þe chapitir. an †sal rede þe lescun of þe halizis, ouþir of haly writ, for to comforth þaim þat it heris. In þat tyme sal ye noħt rede þe boke of þe kingis, for nan vnait sal be herde þat tyme for þa þat ere of febil þoħt; In oþir tyme mai it be red. yef it be fasting day, þai sal haue gode entirual, And when colaciun ringis, Alle þat þe belle heris ga til *to colaciun; And siþin eftir at cumplin; siþin be nan sua hardy to speke. yef ani es tan wid-al, þat hauis broki*n* silence eftir cumplin, smerte correccion salle man take of hir. yef gestis cume, and tabbesse cumandis at

7. *summir;* one of the four downstrokes required to make *-mi-* is missing. 32. *to*, for *te* (= *þe*)? or redundant (= *til*)?

speke, þat tare be nane vtrage. Lau*er*d, for þi merci giue vs miħt at halde þis sentence als sain B*enet* cumandis.

XLIII.

Punishments for those who do not regularly attend canonical and meal hours.

IN þis sentence spekis sain B*enet* of þa þat cumis late til þair seruise o god and til þe borde. Als tite als te belle es herde, ilkain sal leue þe werke þat es in þaire hende, and rinne hastelike til þe ure of god, þat na man may telle foly to þam. For na þing sal man leue þe seruise o god. þa þat cumis noħt at te begining of matins by-fore þe "gl*or*ia p*at*ri" of þe "Venite," sal noħt ga i*n*-til þaire stalle, bot sho sal ga til þe grece by-fore þe †autir, þat tabbes mai se and al þe cuuent; þare sal sho be til þabbes giue hir leue at gange in-til hir stalle. And for þi wil sain B*enet* þat ta þat cume late ga til þe grece, þat tay haue shame of þair faute and sua salle be amendid. for suilke mai it be þat duellis, þat þai wil slape, Ouþir þinke vnait, wha*n* þat þe deuil mai finde a-chesun in þam; for þi shal sho ga to þe grece for to ame*n*de hir faute, þat sho amende hir siþin forward. At te huris als-sua, yef sho ne cumis noħt by-fore þe "gl*or*ia p*at*ri" of þe first salme, sho sal ga to þe grece and cum noħt in hir stalle, are þabes cumande hir; Bot sho sal haue nane oþir penance for þat faute. At te verse by-fore þe mete sal alle be asembild at te borde; sho þat is noħt tar-at, for hir neccligence man sal say til hir ane tyme, and a-noþir tyme. Yef sho wylle noht a-mende, sho ne sal noħt ete wyd þe cuuent, bot by hir ane, and þarne hyr part of þe drinke, suilke als te oþ*ir* haue, til sho haue amendid hir faute. Als-suilke sal sho haue þat es fra þe vers eftir þe mete; for þi es it forlokid, þat ta þat er noħt at te vers sal ga til þe grece bi-fore †þe dese at say hir verse and aske leue at ete; siþin mai sho ga at ete in hir ordir. Nan sal ete ne drink bot at te tyme þat oþir ete, bot yef it be wyd leue. Yef þabbesse offirs ani þing til ani of hir sisturs and sho refuse it, when sho walde haue it, man salle noġt giue it hir, Til sho haue amendid hir faute. Lau*er*d, for þi grace giue vs sua at yeme þis sentence and al þe oþir, þat we til þe ioy of paradise mai cume. AmeN.

[† lf. 26, bk.]

Unrepentant offenders shall eat by themselves.

[† leaf 27]

A thing once offered by the abbess, but refused, is not at disposal afterwards.

6. MS. *þeure.*

XLIV.

Atonement to be made by such as are excommunicated for grave faults. The offender shall lie before the church-door as the convent walks in and out.

IN þis sentence kennis sain Be*net* vs what amendement þai sal do þat es in cursing, þat es don owte of þe kirke for greue faute and owte of þe fraitur. At ilke owre, when þe belle ringis, sal sho lie by-fore þe kirke dore til alle þe cuuent be cumen in, And siþin rise vp and obied wid-vten þe kirke dore to þe vre be sungen. When þe cuuent cumes forz owte of þe kirke, sho sal lie dun agayne by-fore þe dore til þai be passid. þus sal sho do ilke day til þabbesse bidde hir leue. When sho sal be asoilid, sho sal cume *in*-til þe chapitir and take hir veine by-fore þabbesse and crie hir merci. Whe*n* þabes asoiles hir, sho sal falle til hir fete, & siþin by-twixe tua and tua o knees, and take †hir veine. þan salle sho site þar þabbes cumandis hir, bot noħt in hir ordir; bot sho ne salle noħt by-ginne in kirke antefin ne Resp*un*, ne rede lescun, Bot yef þabbes cumande hir. Eftir "Benedicamus" at ilke vre sal sho take hir veine on knes, whare sum sho standes i*n* þe quer. þis sal sho do ay til þabbes cuma*n*de hir at leue of þat penance. sho þat es done owte of þe fraitur for lesse faute, In þe kirke sal sho amende o þis maner: At ilke vre, when þai say "Kiriel*eison*," sal sho take hir veine by-fore þe auter at te grece, & ligge þare til þe "Benedicamus" be saide. sua sal sho do til þabbes asoile hir, And recaiue þe benecun. Laue*r*d, for þi pite giue vs sua at mende vre fautis, þat we may haue þi benicun. Ame*n*.

When forgiven, she shall fall at the abbess' feet.

[† lf. 27, bk.]

For lighter faults,

she shall lie at the altar-steps till absolved.

XLV.

Atonements for those who have made mistakes in their divine service,

Sain benet cumandis in þis sentence þat ta þat faile in þe kirke at te mi*n*ning of þe salmes, Ouþir of þe Respuns, Ouþir Antefens, Ouþir lescuns, At te erþe sal sho take hir veine by-fore þam al. yef sho wil noħt do it, Greuer correccion sal ma*n* take of hir, for sho walde noht w*ith* mekenes amende hir faute. þe barnis sal man chasty wid wande for suik mis-dede. †Laue*r*d, yef it be þi wil, giue vs welle at halde þis sentence.

[† leaf 28]

XLVI.

or have not been careful during their work.

Sain Be*net* sais: þa þat ere in laburs, In kichin ouþir in calgard, in gard ouþir wid-vten, in ani labur, and sho trespasse, Tinis þingis ouþir brekis, yef sho misdo, o þis maner sal sho amende: sho sal cum in-til þe chapitir bi-fore alle þe cuuent and take al hir veine, And knaw hir faute wid hir azen wille. Yef sho hydes it, and a-noþir sais hir owte, Greuer correccion sal man take of hir þan sho hauid mustird it wid hir azen wille. Yef it be *pri*ue sinne þat wille a-noy þe saul, sho sal ga *pri*uelike til þabbesse and schriue hir, Ouþir til a preste þat kan hele hir of hir sinne. Lau*er*d for his grace giue vs sua at schriue vs, and sua at mend vre sinne, þat we til his rengne mai ga.

XLVII.

On the abbess falls the duty of maintaining the regularity of the worship hours.

Sain B*enet* cumandis in þis sentence þat þabbes sal take gude yeme þat þe vris of godis seruise be finist rigħt baþe day and niht. Ouþir sho hir-selfe sal finise þam, Ouþir set a nunn in hir stede þat wil ententiuelike do þe office o god. Þe salmes and te antefens sal þai biginne eftir hir wid ordir. Nane sal be don til þat office bot þat may singe and †rede welle, þat alle þat heris be edefied þ*er*-of. sho þat þabbes cumandis þis office, wid mekenes sal sho do it, And stabelike wid-vten pride, And wid þe dowte of god. Lau*er*d, for þi merci giue vs sua for to singe and rede, þat we mai do þi wille.

[† lf. 28, bk.]

XLVIII.

Idleness injures the soul; manual labour and study should, according to the season, fill up the intervals between worship and rest.

Of þe trauaile spekis sain B*enet* in þis sentence, and sais þat vnait sete es il to þe saule. For þi salle ye trauaile times, And in þe times at lescuns, als it es ordaind. Fra þe paskis til þe Mihelmesse, when matins es done til heze vndirn sal ye wirke, ilke day when time es, þat es nede to do. Fra vndirn to midday at lescuns. Eftir midday, when þai haue etin, sal ye reste in yure bedde alle wid sile*n*ce. Yef any wille þat tyme loke lescun, loke þat sho rede sua, þat sho ne noy noħt þe oþir. Noon sal be rungen by tyme, And siþin wirke til euensang. Yef þai haue mikil at do, corn at gadir and oþir laburs at do, þai salle noħt gruche for þi; for þan liue ye rigħt, yef ye liue wid þe labur of yure hende, Als haly me*n* did bi-fore yu, & ta-postils; bot mesurlike sal ye wirke for þa þat ere febil.

Fra þe feeste of þe Mihthel til þe lentin, when prime is sungen til vndern salle †ye studie in lescuns. fra vndern til noon salle ye wirke suilke as ye haue at do. When noon ringis, ilkain sal lay downe þat es in þaire hende, and ga til þe kirke; And eftir mete til lescuns ouþir salmes. In lentin, fra p*r*ime til heze vndern sal ye entende yure lescun, And syþin wirke til noon. At te bigining of lentyn sal be broght in-til þe chapitur alle þe bokis, and ilkain take þaris & rede it ouir. þabbesse sal loke a simpil nunne ouþ*ir* tua for to ga imangis taim atte timis þat tay sal saie for to loke þat nane site vnait, And for to loke wilke attendis mare til vnait þan til hir lescun. þa þat ere funden suilke, for þi þat tay do iuil til þamselfe and til oþir als-sua, þai sal be warnid ane tyme, and a-noþir time. Yef sho wil noht a-mende, Man sal take suilke amendis of hir, þat te oþir be warnid þurz hir. At te timis þat es set efter euensang til lescuns, þa þat ere acumbird wid laburs sal noht studie on þe sundais, ne on þe oþ*ir* feste-dais, Bot toþir alle at lescuns. Yef it be ani þat mai noht studie ne rede, Oþir labur sal þai do, þat tay ne sitte noht al dom. þa þat ere noht i*n* ese, man sal giue þaim sum þing at do, þat tay ne sitte noht vnait, Ne þat tay ne be noght †ou*ir*-mikil greuid wid trauaile; þabbes sal loke þaire sekenes. Laue*r*d for his pite giue vs sua to wirk, and sua vre lescuns at vnderstande, þat we at te ende til heuin be broght. Amen.

[† leaf 29]

During Lent much reading—

as far as possible—

[† lf. 29, bk.]

XLIX.

IN þis sentence kennis vs sain Benet how we sal gete þe tyme of lentin. Alle timis of þe yer, he sais, sulde we wid rihte halde þe liflade o lentin, bot faa it es þat te vertu mai haue. And forþ*ir* cumandis he þat we sal in lentin gete vre lif in alle þing, þat we mai amende vre fautes of oþir times in þe dais of lentin. þan may ye sauflike liue, yef ye gete yu fra alle ille vices, And yef we do vre entente til vresun wid teris And til lescuns wid reuþe of herte and wid abstinens. In þa dais sal we here sumþing of godis seruise mare þan we do an noþir tyme,

and special care, devotion, and abstinence are required.

14. MS. *and til* twice. 30. *forþir*, "further," originally *for þi*, "therefore," Lat. "ideo." The *i* was written above the line and easily changed into the abbreviation-mark for *ir*.

Yet nothing [† leaf 30] should be done without the superior's knowledge.

And priue vresuns, and o mare mesur of mete and drinke. Ilkain salle, wid þaire ahen gude wille, Offir sum þing to god mare þan þai es cumandid, wid þe ioy of þe haly sprite; þat es, ye draze yu mare fra mete and drinke, & fra slepe, and fra speche, And fra gabbingis, þat ye mai haly paskis o-byde wid ioy of spiritel langing. bot ilkain salle mustir til þabbesse what ye wille offir to god, †wid yure azen wil, of vresuns; for yef ye ne do it wid leue of yure spiritel fadir, ye ne sal haue na mede þar-offe, bot turne yu to vanite. For þi sal ye do als tabbesse cumandis yu at do. Laue*r*d, for þi merci giue vs sua þis haly lentyn at yeme, þat we mai wid ioy of þe hali spirit hali paskis obide.

L.

Sisters working far away from the church should observe the hours of worship as well as they can.

IN þis sentence cumandis sain B*enet* þ*at* te sistirs þat ere in labur fer fra þe kirke, and mai noħt cume in time til þaire vris, þabbes sal cumaunde þaim o þis maner, þat whare sam þai wirke, þat tay do godis seruise And taire veinis in þe dute o god. And als-sua þa þ*at* aier by þe gate, þai ne sal noħt leue þe vris þ*at* ere stablist, bot sua als tay mai, sai þaim And yelde god his seruise. He giue vs for his grace, þat we mai yelde þe seruise þat we ah til hym.

LI.

Those out for the day must accept no food.

Sain B*enet* spekis of þa þat ere sent owte ani erand and sal cum o-gain þat ilke day, þat tay ne be noħt sua hardy at ete owte, þoz man pray þaim, Bot yef þabbes giue þaim leue; yef þai do, þai sal be cursid. Laue*r*d for þi, yef it be his wille, he kepe vs fra cursing.

LII.

The oratory should be [† lf. 30, bk.] used only for prayers.

IN þis sentence cumandis sain B*enet* þat þe ortorie be nane oþir þing þan it es †cald. Of na þing sal it serue bot for to aure, man to god, inne. When þe vris of god es done, þanne sal alle ga forħ and make reueren*ce* to god. Yef any wille dwelle for to make p*ri*ue vrisun, sho ne sal make noise for to sturbe þe oþir, Bot simpelike gange in and make hir vresun wid teris and wid reuþe of herte, And noht wid heze voice. Þa þat wil noht do, þai ne sal noht dwelle eftir in þe kirke for to noy þe oþir.

Private devotion should be quiet.

Lau*er*d for his pite giue vs sua for to cuntaine vs in þe kirke, þat nane be desturbid for vs.

LIII.

IN þis sentence cumandis sain *Benet* þat te gestis þat cumis to yu be als faire kald als it ware god hym-selfe. for he salle say at te day of dome: "Hospes fui &c.—I was geste, and ye recaiuid me." Alle sal man comunlike recaiue, And men of religiun and pilgrims. Als tit als te gestis cume, þe p*r*iuresse ouþir a-no*þir* nunne sal gange againis tam wid luue & charite. Yef it be sistir, first sal þai anure to-gidir and siþin kis; bot bi-fore þe vre sal þai noht basse for þenticement of þe deuil. Allekin mekenes sal man muster til þe gestis. Ilkain, when þai ga and when þai cume, sal *alure to-gidir ouþir wid þe heuidis ou*þir* †wid al þe bodi, and Iesu crist sal aure þam. Whe*n* þai ere rechaiuid and aurid, þabbesse sal sitte wid þaim, ou*þir* a-noþir nunne, wilke sam sho cumandis, þat can speke wid þaim o godis lay for to comfort þaim and speke of man-hed. Þe fasti*ng* sal þabbesse breke for þe gestis sake, yef sho wiłł, Bot yef þe fasting be for hez feste, þat sho ne may nan gate breke; bot toþer sal foliz þe reule o fasting. Þabbesse sal giue þe gestis water til þaire hende, And waisse þaire feet, And alle þe cuuent wid hir. And siþin sal þai sai verse: "Suscepim*us*, de*us* &c.—Lau*er*d, we haue recaiuid þi merci I-middis ti tempil." And ay ta yeme of þe pouir and of þe pilegrimis, for þai er kald godis men, And to þe rike als-sua baþe for aze & for honur. Þabbesse kychin and of hir gestis sal be bi it ane, þat te gestis þat cume noy noħt te cuuent. In þat kichin sal tua sistirs serue, þat tay may do þe office þat apendis þar-to. Yef þai haue mikil at do, man sal finde þam helpe; And when þai haue lesse at do, ga til oþir laburs, whare sua man cumandis þam. Þe howse to þe gestis sal man biteche a sistir at yeme þat dowtis god; sho sal puruay þat tare be beddis inne; sua sal godis howse be ordaind. Wid þe gestis salle †nane speke bot þai þat hauis leue. Yef ani sistir metis þam, mekelike sal

Guests should be received charitably

and humbly,

[† leaf 31]

yet without breaking of the rule,

and arrangements be made accordingly.

[† lf. 31, bk.]

13. *alure*, probably corrupt; see Notes. 16. *wilke*, *i* omitted and then added above the line.

sho aske þair benicun and siþin passe forz, yef sho hauis na leue for to speke wid þam. Laue*r*d for his grace giue vs sua for to herberz his gestis, þat we may herber wid hi*m* in þe ioy of heuin. AmeN.

LIV.

Letters and gifts can be accepted and disposed of only at the discretion of the abbess.

IN þis sentence cumandis sain *Benet* þ*at* nane be sua hardy at recaiue lettirs ne erand þat cumis fra þair frendis, ne fra nane oþir man, ne noħt recaiue giftis bot þurz þe leue of þabbesse. Yef hir be sente ani þing fra hir frende, sho sal noħt recaiue it, ar sho haue leue & musterd it þabbesse. Yef sho giuis hir leue at recaiue it, In þabbes pouste salle it be at giue whare hir þinke. Bot wrez hir noht þat te þing es sent to; And yef þabbesse giuis it til a-noþir, loke þat sho ne wrez hir noħt þat te þing es sent to, wharefore þe deuil finde a-chesun in hir; yef sho dos, þe reul of discipline sal sho fele. Laue*r*d giue vs sua at yeme þis sentence and al oþ*ir*, þ*at* te deuil fi*n*de nan achesun i*n* vs.

LV.

Regulations about clothing. [† leaf 32]

OF þair claþing spekis sain *Benet* in þis sentence, and sais þat man sal * clazing †til ilkain eftir þat tay ere, and eftir þe te*m*pra*n*ce es of þe cuntre. In caald cuntre es nede of warmer hend. þis sal be forlokid þurz þabbes. Of þe culur of þe clad, na of þe mikilnes, sal nane speke, bot take suilke als man may finde in þe cuntre and of liħt chepe bie. þabbesse sal loke þat tay be riħt mesurd. When þai ta þe newe, þan salle þai yelde þalde for to giue to þe pure. Tuinne paire claþis sal ilkain haue for to scifte and for to waisse; yef þai haue mare, it sal be scorn. þair beddis sal þabbes ofte ripe, þat tay ne haue na p*ro*pirte. Yef sho findis ani þing wid-vten hir leue, wid greue discipline sal it be amendid; And for þi þat it es vice of propirte, sal it be scorn als þifte. þabbes sal giue til ilk-ain als tay haue nede. þabbes sal ta yeme of þis sentence of þe dedis of þe apostils, þat sho depart til ilkain als tay haue mist*er*. Sua sal þabbes ta yeme of þe

(Cf. ch. xxxiii and xxxiv.)

19. A verb seems to be omitted, possibly *giue* or *puruay*. 32. MS. *ilk ani*, for *ilk-ain* or *ilk-ane*.

sekenes of þe nedful, And noħt to þe wikke wille of þenuius. In alle hir iugement sal sho umbe-þinke hir what mede sho sal haue at god. Lauer*d* giue vs sua at do, þat we may haue owre mede of hym. AmeN.

LVI.

Sain B*enet* sais þat te Abbes bord sal be ay wid gestis and wid pilegrimis. When sho hauis nane gestis, sho sal take wilke of hir sistirs sam sho wille; bot þat sho leue in þe fraitur an ordene nunne ouþir tua þe ordir for to gete. Lauer*d* giue vs welle at gete oure ordir.

[leaf 32, bk.]

At the abbess' table there should always be guests, or else some sisters.

LVII.

Yef þare be any þat can any labur, wid mekenes sal þai it do, als sain B*enet* cumandis, þat tabbes cumaundis taim at do. gyf þai auantis taim of þair werke, for þi þat sho þinke sho dose gude tille þe howse, sho sal be don owte of hir mist*er*, til sho haue amendid hir faute, yef sho wille noħt be buxum til þat þe abbes cumandis hir at do. Yef any makis any þinge þat sal be salde, Loke what it is wrz, þat ye ne sette na felun price þar-on. And ȝe vmbe-þinke yu of ananie & of sapher his wife, þat salde þaire lande in þe tyme of þa apostils; þai helde a partie of þe price, and a-noþir partie broħt by-fore þa apostils; and sain petir was parcaiuid of þe tricherie, and askid þam why þai made p*r*opirte of þat þai †hauid done in comun; And tai felle baþe dede downe. Mikil dowte birde þam haue þat dose in þing þat fallis til hali kirke, þat taire sauls suffir na dede, als te cors dose here. In þe price of þe þing þat ȝe salle selle, loke þare be na cuuaitise inne; bot bettir chepe sal ye selle þan þe men of þe werld dose, þat god may be payde of yure sale. He giue vs for his grace þat we may sua wirke and sua selle, þat he be payde þar-of.

If a sister is skilful at some work, she must do it humbly

and disinterestedly.

[† leaf 33]

LVIII.

When any wymmen of þe sekil, sais sain B*enet*, cu*m*mis at aske þordir, man salle noghħt ligh[t]-like gif it tam, þe entre, bot man sal do als ta-postil sais:

Reception as a nun should be granted only after long waiting

1. *wikke*, MS. *wilke*. 32. *cummis;* instead of the four downstrokes required to make *mi* there are five; the same inaccuracy occurs p. 40, l. 25.—MS. *lighlike*.

"proue þaire hertis, yef þai be to god." yef sho be stabil in hir asking, And haitis for to suffir alle þe uiltez þat man wille put hir to, Efter þe fifte day sal sho be recaiuid in-til þe howse, And don in-til þe celle *with* þe nouicis.

and preparation;

þare sal sho studie and ete and slape. suilk yeming sal sho haue, þat te saule be turnid to god allemihtye; And ta yeme to hir for to loke yef þe spirte be to god, and yef

[† lf. 33, bk.]

sho dose hir entente to godis seruise, And buxum, †and of suffrance. Man salle muster hir harde þinges and smerte, þe riħt gate to god. Yef sho euir haitis stabilnes, eftir tua wukis sal hir be red þis reule of þordir, And saye to hir: "þis es þe rihte gate whare-inne þu salle life. Yef þu may halde it, cum inne; and yef þu ne may, ga forz al deliuir." Yef sho obidis yet, when sho is prouid o many maners, þan sal man rede hir þe reule, þat sho may wite witerli whar-to sho salle halde hir. And at te tuelmonethes ende, when sho hauis herde þe reule þris, yef sho haitis for to halde it welle, aħ þat man cumandis hir, þanne saħ sho be recaiuid i-mang þe cuuent. bot witte sho

for there should be no going out again, after she has made her vow, under solemn ceremonies,

welle, fra þat day forward may sho noħt gange owte, Ne þe life of þe reule fle, ne caste it fra hir nek; For sho hauid bi-fore laiser for to gange owte. When sho saħ make hir professe, In þe Kirke bi-fore þame alle sal sho haite stabilnes and buxumnes, by-fore god and alle his haliȝes. þat sho euir-mare brekis þat cuuenant, witte sho welle þat god sal damne hir witħ-owtyn ende. þis þing

[† leaf 34]

salle sho write *with* hir awne hande; And †yef sho canne noht write, pray ane of hir sistirs; Bot sho hir-selfe sal make þe singne of þe croice, and lay it on þauter, And siþin say þis verse: "Suscipe me &c.—Lauerd, þu recaiue me, and I sal liue als te wordes es of þe; þat es myne entent, þat I confundid be noħt." at þis verse sal alle þe cuuent ansewere hir þris; and siþin "Gloria patri" at te laste. When sho es blissed, Fra þat time forward sal sho be

and given up the world.

calde in cuuent. Yef sho hauis ani katel, parte it i-mang þe pouir, Ouþir make offrand til þe kirke, þat sho ne halde na þing by-hinde; For fra þat day forward sal sho haue na pouste of hir Awne body. Hir clathis þat sho broħ sal man restore þe kirke *with*-alle, þat sho fra þat day forward haue na wille at gange owte of þe kirke þurȝe enticeme*n*t of þe deuil. Þe bref of hir professe sal sho noħt haue, bot in þe kirke sal be gete. Laue*r*d for his grace giue vs herte and wille i*n* owre ordir to duelle.

LIX.

When any riche ma*n* of þe sekil, sais sain B*enet*, Offirs his doȝtir til god and til haly kirke, And þe childe be yunge, þat it ne kan noht aske þe peticiun, hir frendis †sal aske for hir. And when þai offir hir hande, þai salle winde þe tuaile þar-a-bowte of þauter. And tanne sal þai suere þat þai ne sal neu*ir* mare, ne na man þurz þaim, o na maner giue þing to þe childe, ne sende, whare-þurz þat þe childe haue wille to p*ro*pirte. Bot yef þai wille ani almus do til þe kirke, do it al opinlike, þat þai wil giue. Yef it be lande, and þai wil halde it þaim-selfe, þai sal make chartir, and yelde ilke ȝere þe ferme þat þai may liue w*ith*-alle. And sua sal ȝe do wid alle þe þing þat fallis propirlie til þe child, þat na þing bi-leue w*ith* hir frende, whare-þurz þat sho haue wil til p*ro*pirte; Sain B*enet* hauis te sperance of þoþir. And on þis ilke maner sal þe pure man childe be offird: simpelie make þaire peticiun, and bi-fore whitnes offir þaire childir. Laue*r*d for his grace giue þat we may wel gyde þe offerande þat owre fre*n*dis made of vs.

For the reception of children into the church, certain ceremonies and conditions are prescribed.

[† lf. 34, bk.]

LX.

Yef ani preste, sais *sain* B*enet*, prais ȝerne for to be recaiuid i*n*-til þordir, ȝe ne sal noġht hastelie graunt it hym. Bot yef he duellis in his asking & †prayis ȝerne, Man sal muster him alle þe disciplines of þe reule, þat he salle yeme w*ith*-owtyn reles; þat it be done als it is writi*n*, And say til hym: "Amice, ad quid venisti—Frende, wharto es þu cumen?" Bot toȝ-wheþir sal þe howse be grauntid him, And recaiue benicun, and singe his messe, yef þabbes cumandis him. And yef it sua bitimis, þat he ne wyl noġht lere na sience, þe reule of discipline sal he fele; for he sulde giue oþir ensampil of mekenes. Yef þar be ani labur at do i*n* þe kirke, Of him sal man ta yeme what he dose, when he is entird in; And noġht for þat he es preste and þai haue done him reuer-

Priests should not be received into the order except after due consideration.

[† leaf 35]

They must obey like the rest.

25. MS. & / *and.*

Similarly in the case of clerks.

ence, be vnbuxum. Yef any clerke desiris to ordir, o þat ilke maner at be i*n* felaȝscap, þai sal be done in mene stede, O þis maner, yef þai haite for to holde þe reule of discipline and stabil dwelling.

LXII.

To be priests or deacons only such should be ordained as prove [† lf. 35, bk.] worthy.

Yef þabbes prais for preste ouþir for dekin at be ordainde til hym-selfe, He sal loke, þat þai be dingne þ*er*-to at be preste. He salle fle pride & leue alle ille vices, ar he be preste. And þat †he do na þing bot þat man cumandis him to do; And yef he do, he sal be vndir þe reule of discipline. Ne þat he for-gete noħt þe ordir þat he hauis tane, na þe reule of obedience ne of discipline, And euir aua*n*ce hy*m* in godis seruise, And þinke þat he ne come noħt to þe kirke, bot til godis seruise. And yef þe cuuent wille, & þabes consentis þar-to, þai mai auance hym for þe godenes of his life. Loke þat he neuir-þe-later halde þe reule of stabilnes baþe in and owte in gudenes. And if he oþ*ir*gate dose, and wil noħt be buxum, bott rebel, *whilk man salle repreue hym ofte. Yef he wil nogħt sua amende, Man salle muster hym til þe bisschope. Yef he ne may do him amende, Man sal muster his fautes alle opinlie, and do him owte of þe kirke, yef he be prowde, þat he wil nogħt be buxum vnder þe reule of haly kirke.

If they are illoyal,

they should be corrected and expelled.

LXI.

Visiting nuns may, on certain conditions, be allowed, or asked, [† leaf 36] to stay for good,

IN þis sentence leris sain B*enet* vs, how we sal recaiue þe vncunyng nunnis þat cu*m*mis owte of fer landis. Yef sho wille als geste wne in þe kirke, and folow þe custume als sho findes, †And noy nan þat langes to þe kyrke wi*th* hir surfait, bot simpelike recaiue þat sho findis, sho salle be recaiuid ay to whilis þat sho wille dwelle. Yef sho mustirs ani resun & wi*th* luue, þabbes sal quaintelike drahe hir to hir, and þanc gode þat hir sent. yef sho wille þar stabilnes make, loke þat wille be noħt refusid. And als-sua, yef man may persaue, to whilis þat sho es geste, þat sho es surfaitus & il maner, Man sal nogħt felaȝ-scap witħ hir, bott faire and swetelike latte hir ga, þat

18. *whilk* appears entirely out of place; cf. Notes. 25. *cummis*, cf. p. 37, l. 32, footnote.—MS. *ferlandis.* 31. MS. *þane.*

to*þir* haue na shame of hir. Yef sho be of gude maner, Man sal noħt abide hir asking for to duelle, Bott man sal prai hir at dwelle, þat þe to*þir* mai be amendid þurȝ þe sampil of hir; For in alle stedis may man serue god. Yef þabbes ses hir life be suilke, sho may do hir in heȝer stede, if sho wille, þan hir ordir askis. Bot loke þe abbes þat sho knaw hir wel þat sho sal halde in þe kirke, Ouȝir ȝurh hir abbes ouþir þurȝ hir lettirs. For hali write cumandis þat þu sal do to na man bot als þu walde man did to þe. Lau*er*d giue vs welle at gete þis cuma†ndement And alle þoþir.

even take a high position in the convent.

[† lf. 36, bk.]

LXIII.

IN þis sentence cumandis sain B*enet* þat ilkain be w*ith* order als þai cume in, And als tabbes stablis þaim eftir þat þair lif es. þabbes sal noħt greue þe cuuent, þoȝ þai be giuin hir at yeme, Ne deliuir pouste haue nane for to giue of þe þing þat es stablist in comun, Bott vmbe-þinke hir þat sho sal yelde resun of alle hir iugement til god. als tay ar ordainde, þat tay be stablist and gang in comun. þai ne salle noħt tine þaire ordir for yuȝhed; For samuel and daniel, when þai where barnis, þai demid þe alde men. alle sal be als þai cume in-til þordir, bot ta þat tabbes heȝis ouþ*ir* laȝis for a-chesun. sho þat cumis at te secunde owre of þe day sal be done w*ith* hir þat cumis at þe first, O what elde sam sho be. Til þe barnis salle man halde discipline. þe yung salle onur þalde, and þe alde salle lufe þe yunge. Nane sal calle oþir by þaire name, bot þe priures sal calle þaim hir "sistirs." þabbesse, for sho es in godis stede, sal be callid "dame," noħt for þe heȝnes þat sho es abbes, bot for þe onur of god. Loke þat sho †do sua, þat sho be dingne at recaiue þat onur. When ane metis a-noþir, þe yunger sal noħt sitte bi hir, bot sho haue leue; for hali writ cumandis, þe yunger sal onur þelder. þe barnis sal þinke on þaire ordir w*ith* discipline in kirke and i*n* fraitur; w*ith*-outyn and w*ith*-in, i*n* alle stedis, sal þai haue geting & chastiing. Lau*er*d, for þi m*er*cy giue vs welle at halde þis sentence and euir þi wille do. AmeN.

The sisters should occupy a certain order according to seniority in the convent and the just provision of the abbess.

Reverence and love should be shown in appellations and deeds.

[† leaf 37]

Children should keep their order and be kept in order.

3. MS. The second þe twice. 9. MS. *na / man.*

LXIV.

The election of the abbess. Her qualifications,

Sain Be*net* leris vs in þis sentence, how we sal chese vre abbesse. Suilk resun, he sais, sal man loke at þe lecciun, þat sho be ordene and þat al þe cuuent consentis to w*it*h þe dute of god. Sho þat þe haler partie of þe cuuent chesis, þurȝ gude life and wisdom sal sho be chosin. Yef it sua be, þat alle þe cuuent chesis ane þat wil consent til þaire vices, þe abbotis þat es þare, and þe folke of þe cuntre, sal defende þat tat felun lecciun be noħt forth broth. Bott suilk sal þai take þat can guuerne godis howse and dingne es þar-to. [† lf. 37, bk.] And witte þai wel, †þai sal haue gude mede, if þai do it for þe lufe of god, And sinne, yef þai leue.

responsibility, and duties,

Þe abbes, when sho es ordainde, sho salle vmbeþinke hir what charge sho hase recaiuid, And þat sho sal yelde resun of alle. witte sho wele þat mare bi-houis hir studie for to auance hir cuuent, þa*n* maistri for to haue. sho aȝħt at be wise in goddis law, þat sho draȝe til witnes baþe to þe new law and til þe alde testament. Chaste aȝħt sho at be, and sobir, & ful of pite, And euir heȝe þe misericorde of god ouir hir iugeme*nt*, þat god do þat ilke w*it*h hir. Ille vices salle sho hate, and luue hir sistirs. In hir pouste loke þat þare be nane vtrage in, Ne þat sho ne chaste nan sa fellike, þat þai fle ne falle i*n* wra*n*g trouȝ. Þabbesse salle gete hir welle hir-fra, And euir haue hir aȝen misdede bi-fore hir siħt. Sho salle noħt suffir þe *beli pipe be brokin; þat whe*n* sho seis ani of hir sistirs be chargid w*it*h sinne, sho salle noħt greue hir sua mikil, þat sho fle a-way, bot sho salle be besy more to be luuid þan to be dredde. [† leaf 38] sho sal †nott be trubellus, nor angri, nor ou*ir*-obstinate, nor iolyose, nor ou*ir*-suspiciose, for þan sal sho neu*ir* haue reste. sho sal be wice & discrete in hir co*m*ma*n*dment*is*, þat þai be ouþ*ir* efter godde or efter þe worlde. sho salle discerne and temper þe werkis whilk sho i*n*vinis to be done,

as taught by Scripture

thynkyng a-pon þe discrecion of sainte Iacob sayng i*n* þis wise: "If I sulde make my herdis to labur to mikil in walkyng, þai sal alle die on one day."

and good examples.

Therfore sho sal take þir and odir ma examples of discrecion, þe moder of vertues, and temp*ir* and dispone

25. *beli pipe*, see Notes. 26. *greue hir* omitted and then added above the line. 33. MS. *thyngyng*.

aƚƚ thingis sa, þat hir demena*n*ce be swylke, þat sisters þat er strang and of gude lyuyng may desire and lufe it, & thay þat er febil may bere it; and namli þat sho kepe þis present reule i*n* aƚƚ thingis, that when sho hase welle done hir ministracion, sho may here þe worde of oure lorde whilk þe gude seruande harde, þat gafe corne to his seruandis i*n* his tyme: "Amen dico vobis &c.—For soth̄ I say to ȝow, godde saƚƚ sett hy*m* ouir aƚƚ his thi*ngis*."

LXV.

Sothly, ofte-timis it happins þat be †þe ordinance of þe p*r*ioresse greuus sklaunders rysis in monesterys, whils þ*er* be su*m* bownyd w*ith* þe wikkid sprete of pride, thinkis thame-selfe als gude os thayre abbes, And takis a-po*n* thame tyranry, and nurischis sclaunders, and makis dissensiones i*n* þe co*n*uente, And nameli i*n* tha places where þe p*r*ioresse es ordande of þe same sist*ir*, or of þe abbesse, whilk hase made be-fore þe abbas. Whilk inco*n*ueniens it es ethy to co*n*seyue; for þe prioresse is geuin a mater to be prowd i*n* þe begynny*n*g of hyr ordinance, when sho is geuy*n* in mynde be hir awne thoghtis þat sho is lowsid owte of þe power of hir abbesse, be-cause þe same pe*r*sones made hir p*r*ioresse whilk ordanid þe abbas be-fore. Thoro þat er raysid i*m*monesis, strifis, bakbyty*ngis*, haterede, dissensiones, And werangus ordina*n*sis. And when þe abbas and þe prioresse er of co*n*trary opynion, both̄ thayre awne saules bus nedly be in pe*r*el in þat dissensione, And thay alswa þat er vnder thame and fag[n]is both̄ pa*r*tis fallis i*n*-to grete pe*r*el; whilk pe*r*el fallis chefly opon thayme þat hauis made †thame-selfe þe autors of chesyng of þe p*r*ioresse. For þi hauis sain B*enet* forlokid þat tabbes sal chese whilke sam sho wille, for to halde pese and charite. Yef hir orda*n*ment es in buxumnes, alle þingis þat fallis to þe kirke sal be als tabes cumandis, þat an ne be noh̄t prude of þat es getyn til comun. Yef þe cuuent askis resonabillike and in mekenes, And ábbes sese it es nede, þai sal make p*r*iuresse, þat sho

[† lf. 38, bk.]

The appointment of a prioress may give rise to much mischief,

[† leaf 39]

unless left entirely at the abbess' discretion.

2. *lufe* omitted and then added above the line. 18. *prowd*, MS. *previd* ("tried"). 22. *immonesis*, for *immondesis*. 27. MS. *fagis*. 31. MS. *ordannent*.

The prioress must be submissive;

otherwise she is liable to correction

and deposal.

[† lf. 39, bk.]

The abbess, however, should be led by no impure motives.

be chosin þurȝ þe cunsaile of þa þat dut*is* god. When þe priuresse es ordainde, w*ith* mikil reuerence sal sho do þat tabbesse cuma*n*dis hir, þat sho do na þing a-gain hyr wille na a-gain hir cumaundeme*n*t. for þe mare þat sho est heȝid ouir toþir; þe mare aȝħ sho at halde þe cumandeme*n*t of þe reule. And if sho be of ille vicis and prowde, ouþ*ir* man may finde þat sho hauis þe haly reule i*n* dispite, sho sal be repreuid foure siþe w*ith* worde. Yef sho wil noħt amende, þe reule of discipline sal sho fele. Yef sho wil noħt amende sua, sho sal be don owte, and a-noþ*ir*, þat es dingne, be don in hir stede. Yef sho wil noħt be buxum in cuuent, sho sal be done owte of þe kirke til sho wil amende. †þabbesse sal vmbe-þinke hir þat sho sal yelde resun on domes-day of alle hir iugement*is*, And loke þat þe lowe of envie and hateredin ne brenne noħt hir herte. Laue*r*d for his mercy defende vs fra envie & hateredin.

LXVI.

One sister should act as gate-keeper.

If possible, well, offices, and garden should be inside the enclosure.

The rule should be frequently rehearsed.

[† leaf 40]

At þe ȝate, sais sain B*enet*, sal man do a sister þat can wisdome, And can recaiue & ȝelde answer; þat sho be stabil of worde and dede. by-side þe ȝate sal sho haue chaumber, þat þai þat cum to þe ȝate, alle timis finde hir redi and speke witħ þaim. Als tite as ony smitis on þe ȝate, Ouþir pouir crie, sho sal grace god and w*ith* buxumnes hastelie ancewer þam and do þaire erand. Yef sho hauis mister of help, man sal finde hir helpe at þe ȝate. Yef þe howse may forþe it sua, þan sal it be stablist o þis maner, þat þe water, & þe milne, and bakehuse, and breuhuse, and calgard, and al þat ȝe haue mister of, þat al be w*ith*-in þe gard, þat ȝe ne haue na nede at sende owte; for þat es noħt gude to þe saule. þis reule sal ofte be redde imang þe cuuent, þat nane ascuse þam of þis þing þat þai ne do it. Laue*r*d for †his pite giue vs sua at vnderstande þis reule, and siþin for to wirke, þat we may cum til þe life þat lastis ay. god gif it vs.

LXVII.

Rules with regard to those who have to go outside the convent.

IN þis sentence cumandis sain B*enet* þat whilk sister sua man sendis owte any erand, sal take þe benicun are þai ga, And cumande hir in þe vrisun of þabbes And of alle hir sistirs; And at ilke vre of þe day þat [tai] prai for þa þat er vte. Þat day þat sho cumis hame, sal sho recaiue þe benicun at ilke ure Of þat þai haue misdon *with* siħt, ouþir *with* *iois, ouþir *with* speche, ouþ*ir* ani ivil dedis. Þai sal noħt telle til þe toþir alle þat þai haue sene vte & herd, for þat es ay mikil vice. Yef any dose, þe correccion of þe reule sal sho suffir. And þ*at* ilke sal sho suffir þat gase owte of þe cloister, labur for to do, be it neuir sua litel, *with*-owtin leue of þabbes. Lau*er*d for * gete vs, þat we ne do ne saie þing þat til destruciun fallis.

LXVIII.

Even hard or impossible injunctions should be received in humility and patience.

Yef man cumandis, sais sain B*enet*, ani þing at do, and it be greue, and sho may noħt do it, sho sal recaiue þe cu†mandement softelie and wid mekenes. yef sho ses þat þe charge of þe cumandem*ent* ouir-gase hir force, wħit mekenes sal sho muster to þabbes hir sekenes, and noħt *with* pride, na *with* gain-saȝe. When sho hauis musterd hir firmite, yef þe cumandement of þabbes haldis forȝe, witte sho wele þat it es hir prowe til þe saule; sho sal recaiue it in obedience in þe trouȝe of goddis lay. Lau*er*d, he giue vs mekenes, for his merci, als he cumandis.

[† lf. 40, bk.]

LXIX.

No improper intercession is allowed;

Mikil aȝ ye at fle þis, sais sain B*enet*, þat nane defende ne warne oþir for nane achesun, ne for sibredin, ne for na oþir aquaintance; for mikil blame þan may cu*m* þerof. Yef ani trespassis þis cumandem*ent*, greuelike sal it be amendid. Lau*er*d defende vs fra alle achesun of sclandir.

LXX.

nor yet unauthorized corrections.

IN þis sentence cumandis sain B*enet* þat a-chesunn*ir* sal be defendid in haly kirke, als it es ordainde and stablist, þat nane be sua hardy for to curse oþir, ne discipline, bot sho þat þabbes giuis þe pouste. Þa þat †tresspassis, by-fore þam alle salle þai be chastid, sua þat þe

[† leaf 41]

1. MS. *þat prai.* 4. *iois* ("joys"), corrupt for *erin* or the like. 9. Here a phrase like *his grace* (p. 39, l. 21, etc.), *his mercy* (p. 44, l. 16, etc.), *his pite* (p. 44, l. 31, etc.), is missing.

oþir haue dute þ*er*of. til þe barnis sal man halde discipline ententiuelike, Til þai be o fiftene winter elde. Alle sal do þat to þam w*ith* mesur and w*ith* resun. Yef ani sistir w*ith*-outen þe cumandeme*n*t of þabbes dose þe barnis ani owterage, þe reule of disclipine sal þai fele; for haly write cu*m*mandis þat þu sal do to na noþir bot als þu walde man did to þe. Lau*er*d for his pite giue vs weħ at halde his cumandemens.

LXXI.

The juniors, however, with due preference given to the abbess and prioress, should obey their seniors, and, if they have displeased them,

Sain B*enet* cumandis in þis sentence þ*a*t al sal make obediens, and noħt alane to þabbes, bot ilkane to oþir. þurȝ þe life of obediens may ye cum to heuin. þabbes and þe priuresse sal cumande til þa þat es vnder þaim; þat na p*ri*ue cumandement be hid in þaim. þe yunger sal meke þaim til þelder w*ith* mikil charite. Yef any es funden w*ith* fawte, be it neuir so litel, witħ þabbes, ouþir w*ith* p*ri*uresse, ouþir w*ith* ony oþir, sho sal acline to þerþe. Yef sho haue whreþid ani of †hir sistirs, o what man*er* sam it be, hastelike w*ith*-vten dwellyng sal sho falle to her fete and aske hir for-gifnes, and crie hir merci, And ligge þare til sho for-giue it hir and giue hir her benicun. Sho þat at þis amendme*n*t hauis an despite, and wille noħt do it, Of hir body sal man take amendement. Yef sho be rebel þar-again, vte of þe kirke sal sho be putt. Lau*er*d for his merci giue vs sua obediens and mekenes at halde, and rebel at fle, þat we may cum til þe ioy þat ay sal be.

[† lf. 41, bk.]

readily and humbly ask their forgiveness.

LXXII.

Now, of the two kinds of life,

Of tua maner in a lif spekis sain B*enet* in þis sentence, And sais þat the ille lif, þat es ful of wille, it departis man fra god and ledis ma*n* til þe pinis of helle, And a-noþir lif, þat es gude, þat departis man fra helle and ledis man to god almihti. þis gude life sal ye lere w*ith* lufe and gudenes, & ilkain auance oþir wid onur and gude dede; þe sekenes of youre bodi, þan it cumis, take it i*n* gude entente and i*n* pacience. Obedience, buxumnes, sal ilkain at oþ*ir* †lere hastiuelike, charite & gudenes ilkain lere oþi*r*, and chastite w*ith* luue. Ye sal

learn the good one!

[† leaf 42]

16. *to*, MS. *io*.

dute god and yure abbesse w*ith* luue and charite. And þat sal lede yow til þe ioy w*ith*-outen ende. god giue it vs.

LXXIII.

IN þis sentence mustirs sain B*enet* mikil mekenes þat in hym was. For pure mekenes mustirs he here *in* þe last ende of his reule. He sais þat he ne hauis noħt writyn alle þingis þ*at* fallis to rihtuisnes. Bott wha sam haldis wel þise cumaundemen*tis*, heȝ god, þat es fadir of alle, sal ȝelde þaim þair mede. We haue writin þis reule for to mustir til þa þ*at* ere suuerainis of hali kirke haue clene luue til god and to þaire prome, And ilke sistir til oþir. Bot wha sua wil cume til þe heȝnes and til þe sikirnes of religiun, Loke þat tay do eftir þe kening of þe haly fadir þat wnis in manhed in þe heȝnes þat lastis ay. Of what boke sam ye here, of anikin kening of þalde lai ouþir of þe neu testament, Ouþir what sum it es, þan es it þe riħt reule of þis life here. Of na boke ne make ȝe force, bot ȝe †may ga þe righ̄t gate to god alle-mihti. þe life of þe haly armitis and þaire cumandemens, And þe reule of sain basili, alle suilke þingis salle ȝe filiȝ. Til hali men, þat gude lif haldes & luuis obedience and gude vertus, þat may halde þis lif. Bot we, sais sain benet, þat er febil and for-getil and of febil lif, þis gude lif schamis vs, And confundis. Bot ye þat wille cume hastelike to þe heȝe ioy þat lastis ay, Haldes first þurȝ þe helpe of iesu crist þis litil beginning of þe reule þat I haue writin yu, And salle ye cume til þe heȝnes of mare v*er*tu þurȝ þe kenning þat I haue musterd. Þa þat it vnderstandis and haldis, Til þaim sal be oppind þe ȝatis of heuin. Laue*r*d, bigining and ending of alle gude dedis, giue vs sua þis reule of sain benet for to ȝeme, þat te rengne of heuin be oppind til vs. Godde gif it vs for his misericorde. AmeN. Qui v*iuis* & R*egnas*, D*eus*, P*er* O*mnia* S*ecula* S*eculorum*. AMEN.

This rule does not hold all that belongs to such a life: it is only a beginning.

There are other and nobler patterns besides,

[† lf. 42, bk.]

preservatory to the strong,

confusing to the feeble.

Keep, however, this little beginning, and thou shalt rise higher,

and pass through the gates of heaven!

29. *vs* omitted and then added above the line.

II. THE NORTHERN METRICAL VERSION

OF

The Rule of St. Benet.

(*Cotton MS. Vespasian A.* 25, *British Museum.*)

[leaf 66]

Regula beati benedicti anglicis v*er*bis tr*a*nsl*ata*.

Aƚƚ þat wyħ lely lyue in land
Als sant Benet has ordand,
Or wyħ gyf þair deuocioun
Vn-to þe rowle of religioun,
In þis boke þay may see sett
þe suthfast rewle of sant Benett
Wit*h* sere pont*es* þ*at* partens þar-to,
Nyght & day how þay saƚƚ do.
Monkes & als aƚƚ leryd meñ
In latyn may it lyghtly ken,
And wytt þarby how þay saƚƚ wyrk
To sarue god and haly kyrk.
Bott tyƚƚ women to mak it coutħ,
þ*at* leris no latyn in þar ȝoutħ,
In ingles is it ordand here,
So þ*at* þay may it lygħtly lere.
For ilkon þ*at* þar-to er vuñ
Er haldyn it clerly for to kuñ
And to fulfyƚƚ it att þar mygħt
In word and dede botħ day & nygħt.
And ryght to gar þis reule up-ryse,
þe wytty man says on þis wyse:
Asculta, o filia, disciplina[m] mag*ist*re tue—
Dogħter, he says, tak tent & lere
þe techynges of þi maystres here,
And lat þine eris bowand be
To þe bydynges of þi moder fre,
Whylk moder es cald haly kyrk,

This is the rule of St. Benet,

translated for women into English.

Prologue.

Hear the voice of the church!

[leaf 66, bk.]

4, 5, 26, and often: MS. þ^{e}, þ^{is}, þ^{i}. 22 b. MS. *disciplina*.

Whas wyll vs aw alway to wyrk.
þarfor þou sall fande to fulfyll
All þat þi modir tels þe vntyll,
And be bowsum to þi souerayn;
þan sall þou turn to god o-gayn,
Fro wham þat þou depayrtyd es
Thurth þine awin vn-bowsumnes.
And doghter, to my tale tak tent:
For godes sak we sall assent
All fleschly wyll for to for-sak
And gostly armurs vntill vs tak,
Thurth obediens by day and nyght
O-gans þe fend, our fa, to fyght.
Doghter, when þou dose ony dede,
Pray specially god þe to spede,
And what werk so þou sall to wend,
Pray hym at bryng it tyll gude end,
So þat, sen he vowches saue
For hys doghters here vs to haue,
þat we neuer *with* oure wykkydnes
Wreth hym, þat oure fader es,
So for to mak hym turn hys mode
To hald fro vs hys gostly gode,
Or vs deseryd by þat skyll
Fro þe blys þat he boght vs tyll,
And put vs vn-to pyen for þi,
Als wykkyd saruandes er worthy,
þe whylk, yf þay dyde wele, myght wend
To blys þat es *with*-outyn end.
And þarfor suld we vs a-vyse
Out of our syn sone for to ryse
And our hertes vnto heuy*n* at rayse,
Als haly wrytt on þis wyse sayse:
"þe houre es now, if we tak kepe,
In whilk vs aw to ryse fro slepe."
þat is, we suld ryse out of syn,
And wyrk so þat we heuy*n* may wyn,
And opyn our eghen to cryst on hyght,
þat namyd es ailastand lyght,
And opyn our eris, hys vose to here,

Through obedience thou shouldst return to God, from whom thou hast departed through disobedience.

Let us invoke God's help,

[leaf 67]

rise from our sins,

listen to and follow the precepts of Holy Scripture.

Als bokes vs bydes on þis manere:
Hebr. iii. 7, 8. “**Hodie si vocem ei*us* audierit*is*,
Nolite obdurare corda u*es*tra**—
If þ*at* ȝe here hys vose þis day,
[leaf 67, bk.] Turn nogħt ȝoure hertes fro hym oway”—
Take heed to God's voice. Bott tyƚƚ hys voce ȝe tak gude hede,
And fandes to fulfill yd in dede,
Sen god hase geuen ȝow eris & wytt;
For on þis wyse says haly wrytt:
Mat. xi. 15. “**Qui h*ab*et aures audiendi audiat.**”
Crist vs kens on þis manere,
He that has ears, let him hear. And says: “he þ*at* hase eris suld here
þe law of god, and þan tak hede
To fulfyll yd in word and dede.”
For þus þe haly gost wyƚƚ ken
Thruth haly kyrk aƚƚ cristyn men:
Ps. xxxiv. 11. “**Venite, filii, audite me**—
Cums hider, suns, my wordes to here!
þe drede of god I saƚƚ ȝow lere.”
Haly kyrk, for our be-houe,
Leris how we oure lord saƚƚ lufe
Let us live so as to please God. And lede oure lyf to hys lykyng
And drede [hym] ouer aƚƚ oder thyng.
Ryn we suld, whyls we haue day,
þ*at* mirknes mare vs nogħt þe way.
þ*at* mens, we suld lyf wele ilkane,
Or we w*ith* dynt of dede be tayne.
For in oure lyf here may we chese,
Whyder we our-self wyƚƚ saue or lese.
[leaf 68] And oure lord sekes in world aƚƚ-wase
Who wyƚƚ be sauyd, and þusgayt sayse:
Ps. xxxiv. 12. “**Quis est homo qui v*u*lt vitam**—
Whilk man is he þ*at* lyf wyl haue
Who wants to save his soul? And se gude days, hys saule to saue?
Als-so say of hym am I fayne.”
And if þou þan answer o-gayne
And says þus: “lord, þ*at* man am I,”
þan to þe says god almygħty:

72, 78. MS. *fulfillyd, fulfyllyd.* 79. MS. þ^{us}; like wise 99. 86. MS. *drede ouer.*

"Man, if þou wyƚƚ haue lastand lyf
And won in weltħ *with*-outyn stryf,
On þis wyse be-houes þe do,
Als I saƚƚ teƚƚ þe vn-to:
Proibe lingua*m* tua*m* a malo—
In þe begining, still þi tung,
And spek no uyl of ald na ȝong,
And spayr þi lipes, & hald þam stiƚƚ,
So þ*at* þay opyn noghŧ *with* iƚƚ!
Turn fro euil, & seke to gude,
And seke to pese *with* mayn & mode!"
And þus if we wyƚƚ wirk alway,
þan wyƚƚ oure lord þus tyƚƚ vs say:
"Myne eghen on ȝow saƚƚ luk ful clere,
And min eris saƚƚ ȝour p*ra*yers here,
And when ȝe to me caƚƚ or cry,
þan saƚƚ I say þus: Here am I."
What mirtħ to man myghŧ mor acord
þan to here þis voce of oure lord?
Lo, how mekly & how euen
þ*at* he vs techħes þe way to heuen!
Now, sen our mighty lord Ie*sus*
Vnto hys kyngdom eu*er* cals vs,
Ordand we vs in word & dede
At wend to hym *with*-outen drede
And *with* our werk mak vs wortħy
In endles blis to beld hym by!
For of þ*at* blis may we not spede,
Bot if our werks be worthy mede,
And if he ask here in oure steuen:
"Whylk er þo men saƚƚ won in heuen?"
Als dauid in þe sawter boke
Askes of oure lord, who likes to loke:
"**D*omi*ne, quis ha*b*itabit in taberna*cu*lo tuo?**"
þus of our lord he askes & says:
"Lord, who saƚƚ won in þi palays
Or ryst a-pon þi haly hyƚƚ?"
And þus oure lord answers þer-till:
"**Qui ingreditur sine ma*cu*la.**"

To win everlasting life,

(Ps. xxxiv. 13, 14)

control thy tongue,

turn from evil, and seek good.

Ps. xxxiv. 15.

[leaf 68, bk.]

In order to get to Christ,

let us ask with David,

Ps. xv. 1,

'Who shall rest on Thy holy hill?'

Ps. xv. 2.

136. *lord* omitted and then added above the line.

[leaf 69] God answers,
He answers þus by p*ro*phet steuen,
Wysand vs þe way to heuen :
Ps. xv. 2 ff.,
"He þ*at* enters þis world within
'The pure,
Clensid cłen of aƚƚ hys syn̄,
And always wyrkes þ*at* ryghtwis es,
truthful,
And says no thyng bot suthfastnes ;
þ*at* in hert hase no wykkyd thoght,
Ne *with* hys tong no uil hase wroght ;
þ*at* to hys neghburs dose no noy
In stede ne stayƚƚ, þare staite to stroy ;
steadfast,
And þay þ*at* standes and dwels til end
Ogans þe fandyng of þe fend,
And wyƚƚ not doy efter hys rede,
Ne suffer hym in þam hafe no stede,
lovers of Christ,
Bot settes þair hert & þare powere
Aƚƚ vnto crist, þ*at* boght þam dere ;
And for godes sake who wiƚƚ assent
To be bowsum and obidient,
who for His sake lead holy lives.'
And for his luf lyfes halily,
And es not egh in hert for þi,
Bot knaws þ*at* þaire gude dedes ilkon
Er of þe grace of god aƚƚon."
We should ever give the glory to God,
For thurth oure mightes, mor no les,
May we begyn nonekyns gude.*
Euil dedes er of oure awn entent,
[leaf 69, bk.]
And aƚƚ gude dedes fro god er sent.
þerfor hym suld we lofe aƚƚ-ways
With þe p*ro*phett, þ*at* þusgayt says :
like the psalmist
"**Non nobis, d*omi*ne, s*ed* no*mi*ni tuo da gl*ori*am**—
Lord, vntil vs be no loueyng,
Bot to þi naym ou*er* alkins thyng !"
For of oure-self we haf bot sin,
And al gude bose in þe bygin,
Namly þ*at* helpes to hele of saule.
and St. Paul.
þare-for on þis wyse says sant paule :
"**Gr*ati*a dei sum id quod sum**—
Aƚƚ þ*at* in erth to me es ton̄,
Itt is of þe grace of god aƚƚon.
Mine awn̄ power es noght to p*ra*yse,

148. MS. *fendyng*. 159–160. See Notes.

Bot wirchep be to god always."
And who so makes myrtħ, mor or min,
In god be-houes his ioy begin;
For aƚƚ oure comforth in hym dwels,
Als hym-self in þe godspel tels.
He says: "who to my wordes takes hede
And fandes to fulfiƚƚ þam in dede,
I saƚƚ mak hym wele like to be
A ful wyse man in aƚƚ degre,
Whylk man, for his hous sal last,
A-pon a ston hase byggid itt fast.
When it saƚƚ windes or flodes feƚƚ,
Euer may itt stand stifli & wele,
And harm þair-to may þai do none,
Be-caus itt es biggid on a stone.
þis stone es crist, þ*at* we on caƚƚ.
He gifes vs force, þ*at* we not faƚƚ,
And ilka day til vs he techis
Thurtħ haly wordes, þ*at* his men p*re*chis,
And als thurgħ law of hali kyrk,
How we in world saƚƚ wisely wirk.
And al þe days of oure lifyng
Er lent vs allane for þis thyng:
For we suld here oure mis amend
Thurgħ hali kirk, os crist hase kend;
þair-for god lens vs oure lif-days,
Als þe appostil p*ro*ues & says.
He says: "kan ȝe not vnder-stand
þe sufferance of god alweldand?
Vnto penance it suld ȝow lede
To mak a-mendes for ȝoure misdede."
Of swilk sufferance god schewes til vs
In his godspel, whaire he says þus:
"**Nolo morte*m* peccatoris *sed* vt mag*is***—
I wil not þe dede of sinful man,
Bot þ*at* he turn hym & lif þan;
And if he of me ask mercy,
Ful gladly for-gyf hym wyl I."
þus if we þis question craue,
Whilk þai er þat heuy*n* sal haue

All our comfort is in God.

Who heeds His words is like the wise man that built his house upon a rock, [leaf 70]

the true foundation Christ.

Our life is granted us for the mending of our sins,

as is shown in Holy Scripture.

[leaf 70, bk.]

And won *with* god in blisses clere,
Answer haue we halili here.
And hardeli if we ful-fiƚƚ
þe offese þ*at* fals þaim vntiƚƚ
þat er ordand in blisses to be,
þan aires of þ*at* ilk blis er we.

Thus, again, let us begin to serve God,

þan is it gude þ*at* we here dresse
Our hartes *with* aƚƚ oure bisines
For to fulfiƚƚ, in þ*at* we may,
Godes bidinges boþ nigħt & day;
And þat we may nott be oure migħt,

invoking His help.

Pray hym to p*er*fourn it rigħt,
And for to g*ra*nt vs migħt & maine,
Thurgħ his g*ra*ce, þat most may gaine,
þ*at* we may fle fro paines of heƚƚ
And be worthi in blis to dweƚƚ.
Gude councel es to man & wife,
Whils we lend in þis dedely life,
Vn-to swilk warkes for to take hede
þ*at* vs to lastand life may lede,
And gif vs fully, aƚƚ folk in-fere,

[leaf 71]

Let us enter the schools of Jesus, and there, steadfast in all tribulations,

To iesu skoles his laus to lere,
þ*at* er þe laus of haly kirk,
Of whilk vs aw not to be irk.
Al if vs thynk it hard to take,
We saƚƚ it suffer for godes sake;
And if sere enmis vs assayle,
þaire-for we saƚƚ not fayntly faile,

look forward to the sweet reward.

Bot thynk, if it be heuy & hard,
What mede we sal haue afterward.
For who to wele-lifing saƚƚ win,
With greu*aun*s grete þaim bus bigin;
Bot sethin a swetnes haue þai saƚƚ
And at þe last swetest of aƚƚ.
For who so wil godes lesons lere
May saue þair saules, & hele þaim here,
And mak [þaim] thrugħ meknes heueyn
Comu*n*ers in þe kyngdom of heuyn.

244. *þaim;* the first letter looks like a *p.* 249. MS. *mak thrugh.*

I.

De iiii^or condicionib*us* relig*ionis*.

In þis ilk rewle of sant Benett
Er sere folk in sere plasses sett
(There are various classes of monks and nuns:)
To serue god in sere degre,
Men or wemen whider þai be,
þ*at* sum er gude & sum not so;
Four maners mai men fynd of þo.
þe first es men here or womeñ
(1. those who live under a [leaf 71, bk.] rule and a superior;)
þat þair awn kynde wyħ clerly keñ,
And wilfully alway wil wirke
Efter þe laus of haly kirke,
And euer-mor be bowsum & baine
Vn-to þe sawes of þeir sufferaine,
Als þai may leire in þis boke
Efter-ward, who likes to loke.
þe secund maner es ful p*er*fite
(2. hermits,)
Als to be anger or eremete,
A-gains þe fend thurgħ faitħ to fegħt
W*ith* dedes of penance day & nigħt,
Not ainly bi lereing on buke,
Bot bi þe order þ*at* þai tuke.
And penance þat þai put þaime to
Sal mak þam mygħty so to do.
Anely life alħ if þai lede,
(living in solitude;)
Of þe deuel haue þai no drede.
For god makes þam so mekħ of mayne
And stalworthħ to stand him a-gayne,
þat al his dartes may þam not dere,
Ne his faindinges may þam not fere.
þe thrid degre es not so gude:
(3. those who (living apart) have no superior,)
Men or wemen of wilful mode,
þat order of religion takes,
And al obseru*aunce* þ*at* syne for-sakes,
þat nowder will be obidient
([leaf 72])
Vntyl sufferayne ne til couent
For no thing þ*at* men telles þam til,
Bot lifes efter þair wordly wilħ
And serues more to worldly thyng
þan vnto god, of heuen kyng.

no monastic habit,

Syngne of religion haue þai non,
Ne takyn, bot tonsure aƚƚon.
Vnto no hird þai wil tak kepe,
Bot raykes forħ als raueand scħep.
And whar-to so þai turn þair mode,
þat think þaym law and reson gude.
And whar-to þai haue no likyng,
þat think þam es vn-lefful thyng.

and no rule;

Be no rewle wil þai be arrest,
Bot lifes als ane vnskilful best.

4. vagrants,

þe fortt degre ȝit es þair als
Of sum þat er in order fals,
þat ligħtli leues al heuy thing
And folous euer þair flessħ likyng.
þai raik o-bout in sere contresse,
For þai þair likyng wil not lese.
In non abbay wil þai dweƚƚ,

[leaf 72, bk.] who go about, telling lies,

Bot wendes a-bout fro cel to cel
And tels lesynges here & þair
To gar men mak þam mery fare.

fornicating, and getting drunk.

þai lede þair lif in lechori
And in dronkynnes & in clotony.
þair lifyng es ay war and were;
þair-for of þam I spek no fare,

Only the first class is considered here.

Bot to þe first I wend o-gayn
For to p*er*fourn our p*ro*cesse playn,
To tel what pont*es* falles þam vnto,
And als what dedes þam aw to do
þat for godes sake here sett
Vnder þe band of sant Benett.
Whare priores es principaƚƚ,
And what pontes þ*er*-to suld faƚƚ,
In þis begynnyng sal be kend.
God help þat it mygħt haue gude end!

II.

Vlteri*us* de priorissa et ei*us* condicionibus.

The prioress, being the chief,

A Priores aw for to be
Principaƚƚ in gude degre

319. MS. *priours.*

Botħ in þe abba & witħ-oute,
Whar so sche ganges or rides o-boute,
And to be honored euer hir aw ;
Bot in her-self sche sal be law,
Pryde in hert for to haue none,
Bot loue god euer of al his lone
And wirchip him werld al-wais,
Als þe apostel plainly sais
Vn-to aƚƚ folk, who so it be,
þat takes swilk staite of dignite :
"**Accepistis sp*iritu*m adepcionis.**"
He sais : "ȝe take þe gaste of mede,
þat lele folk vnto lif suld lede,
In þe whilk gaste we caƚƚ & cry
Vnto our lord god al-myghty,
And 'fader, abbot,' þus we say."
Bi ȝer wordes vnderstand we may
þat soueranse aw no thing to do
Bot anely als crist kens þam to,
Ne no thyng suld þai tecħ ne lere,
Ne no thyng bid by þaire power,
Bot þat myghtturn in feld & towne
þair sogetes to saluacioune.
Techyng sal be to þam it beres
Als gastly sede sawn in þair eres,
And to teching þai sal be bayne
Als gude soietes to þair souerane.
For wele wit sche, & so wit þai,
þat in dome, on þe dredful day,
Sal reknyng by, how sche þam leres,
And als who wele hir lessons heres,
And botħ þan sal þai haue þair mede
Efter þair lif þat þai here lede.
A priores may knaw wele þan,
Scħe beres þe charcħ of a hird-man.
And als a graue bihoues hir be,
þat cure hase tayn to kepe hir fe.
And hir awn sawle wele may sche saue,
Al if hir schepe vnryght wyl raue :
If scho gude techyng teƚƚ þam to

and honoured as such, should humbly
[leaf 73]
and devoutly
follow Christ alone; teach her convent,
for the salvation of their souls
[leaf 73, bk.]
and of her own, for she
bears the charge of a herdsman.

And chastes als hir aw to do,
Efter þe rewle þat crist hase kend,
If offenders will not amend, And þai wil not þair mys amend,
Bott reklisly hir rede refuse,
To crist þan may scho hir excuse
In dome, a-pon þe dredful day,
And with þe pro*phet* þusgate say:
(Ps. xl. 10) "**Iusticia*m* tua*m* [non] abscondi in corde meo,**
Veritate*m* tua*m* & salutare tuu*m* dixi."
they shall be damned. þus for hir werk scho may haue mede,
And þai dampned for þair mysdede.

[leaf 74] Also we se ȝit to þe same:
The prioress must, in deed and word, Of priores who takes þe name,
In dede and saw her bus assent
To fulfil it to dubte intent;
fulfil þat es, scho sal in wark fulfyll
Al þat scho sal tech oþer vntill,
So þat al hir doghters dere
þat godes law lightly wil lere,
Bi wordes allayn may haue knawyng,
How þai sal do in al thyng,
And oþer, þ*a*t of hertes er herd
And oute of mesure more fraward,
Mai be informed bi hir dede
And lere how þai þair lif suld lede.
her own commandments, þus aw hir-self in dede to do
Al þat scho sal tech oþer vnto.
And when scho hir sugetes rep*r*oues,
On al maners luk hir be-houes,
not doing the deeds which he forbids to others. So þat scho hafe not done þo dedes
Whilk scho vntil oder for-bedes.
For þan hir lare is not to prays,
And crist þan vnto hir þus sais:
Ps. l. 16. "**Quare tu enarras iusticiam tua*m***—
Whi teches þu in rightwisnes,
[leaf 74, bk.] And þu þi-self mor synful es?
þu hates my techyng & my lare,
Sen þou þi-self hase sined mare,
And my wordes putes þ*ou* þe be-hinde,

370b. MS. *tuam abscondi.*

The prioress must not see a mote in a sister's eye, and overlook the beam in her own.

For of my teching ert þou blind.
Ful wele þou may p*er*ceaue & se
A litil mote in þi sister ee,
Bott a grete balk in þin awn
Vnto þi sigħt may not be knawn."
þus nedes þam-self for to be clere,
þat oþer folk saƚƚ tecħ & lere.

She must love all alike

A Priores aw to be slike,
þat scho luf ilkon in-like
And nogħt til on for fauor spare
And mak a-noþer to trauel mare,
Bot serue ilkon in þair degre
Samen, als sisters aw to be.
For haly writ sais wele þair-bi:
"In crist we er aƚƚ o body."
And aƚƚ þat serues vnto a lord,
In anhede aw þam to a-corde.

without regard to riches.

And rigħt als god takes no rewarde,
For riches þat no man be sparde,
Ne non put doun for pouerte,

[leaf 75]

So suld it emang sisters be.
For crist on cristyn folk es heued
And we his lyms þat here er leuyde;
And godes seruandes in haly kirk,
þat er ordand his werk to wirk,
Aw to be lufid in ewyn degre
Of hir þat sal þair souerayn be.

De ead*em*.

She must chastise each one according to her disposition.

A Priores þ*at* wil wirchep win
Aw to chastes on maners th[r]in
þam þ*at* scho sese wil be schrews,
Als þe apostil playnly schews;
"**Argue, obsecra, & increpa!**"
þat es to mene on þis manere:
þai þat er herd & latħ to lere,
þam sal scho chasti *with* hardnes
Of werk & word, als wortħy es.

426b. This heading, like several of the following, is written in the right margin. 428. MS. *thin.*

Meek sisters

And þay þ*at* er meke & obedient
And to hir saws wil eue*r* assent,

are only to be chid.

þai sal be chastede, wħen þai sin,
W*ith* fair wordes þam forto wyñ.
And þai þ*at* wil hir lare despise

Rebellious ones

Or als rebels o-gans hir rise,

[leaf 75, bk.]

Witħ þam aw hir for to trete

she must punish severely and without delay,

W*ith* preson & w*ith* penance grete;
And sone when þat scho mai p*er*saiue
þair syn, lat nogħt þe tym oue*r* wayue,
Bot chaistese þam & tery nogħt
Efter þe wark þat þa[i ha]ue wrogħt

taking warning from the prophet Hely.

For parel þat mai faƚƚ þarby,
Als wos p*ro*ued of þe p*ro*phet hely
And oþer mo þat men may teƚƚ,
How grete drede es yn sin to dweƚƚ.

However, she shall first warn them.

Bot first hir-self, & rigħt non els,
Sal councel þam, als crist vs tels,
Bi wordes warli anes or twis.
And if þai wil not þair-for rise,
To chastese þam scho sal not spare
With penance hard, als I said aire.
For hali writ sais on þis wise:
"þe fole witħ word may non chastese."
For þai wil set bi no man saw,
þarfor þam bus haue harder aw.
And to þis sam, als clerks may kun,
þe wiseman sais: "chastise þi sun
And bete him w*ith* a wand, I rede,
þan liuers þou his saule fro drede."

[leaf 76]

De ead*em*.

She must ever remember her great responsibility

A Priores aw for to wite,
Als beres witnes in haly writ,
Who mekel takes in town or felde,
Of mekil be-houes þam rekni[n]g ȝelde.
And so hir aw to vnderstand

446. MS. *þaue*. 468. MS. *reknig*. The scribe seems first to have written *-in-*, then to have altered *-in-* into *-ni-*, forgetting, however, that there should be an *n* also after *i* (or a contraction mark above it).

What hard wark scho takes on hand
To gouerne þe saules of sere women *for so many different souls,*
And aƚƚ þair ertħly maners ken:
Sum gude, sum iƚƚ, sum eueyn bitweyn,
Als es in ilk a-semble sene.
And þair-for scho þat ȝeme þam saƚƚ
Bus haue hir euynly vntil aƚƚ
And fully knaw what falles þam to,
Als a gude hird aw for to do,
So þat al hir flok may p*ro*ue
And encrese vnto crist*es* bi-houe.
No gude hirdes sal set þair thogħt *seeking not earthly,*
On erthli gudes, þ*at* gase to nogħt,
Mor þan þe saules for to saue
Of wham þai sal here keping haue.
For mor we suld ȝern hele of saule
þan of bodi, os sais sant paule.
And also crist in his godspeƚƚ
Of þis same makes minde o-meƚƚ: [leaf 76, bk.]
"**Primu*m* querite regnu*m* dei**—
First sal ȝe seke þe blis of heuyn *but heavenly weal,*
And þe rightwisnes of it ful euyn,
And þan aƚƚ þat nedes ȝou vntiƚƚ
Sal ȝe haue at ȝour awne wyƚƚ."
And forþermare ȝit may men rede:
Oure lord here if we luf & drede,
þan sal no thing here fro vs fayle
þat to our saule hele may a-vayle.
And man or woman þ*at* here wil haue
Cure of saules fro syn to saue,
Vnto reknyng saƚƚ þai cum *and thinking of the Judg-ment-day.*
For þo saules on þe day of dom.
For al þe saules þai hase in welde
And for his awn saule saƚƚ he ȝelde
Reknyng to crist, þe domes-man.
It nedes þat þai a-vise þam þan
For to do þat in þam es;
For if ony of þair schep peris,
And þe faute be not in þam fun,

þair awn saule þen haue [þai] vn-bun.
The prioress shall win reward for the souls she saves.
And souerans ȝit sal haue *þer* mede
For saules þai wyn *with* word or dede,
With gude ensampil *þat* þai gife,
[leaf 77]
Or *with* gude lifyng *þat* þai lif,
Or els *with* riġħtwise chastisyng;
þam falles gret mede for al swilk thyng.

III.

De adhibendis ad consilium sororibus.

In matters of great importance the prioress should consult the whole convent.

IN aƚƚ tymes, when oġħt es to do
 þat any grete charge fals vnto,
þe priores sal to-geder caƚƚ
All þe conuent, grete & smaƚƚ,
þat orderd er, boþħ old & ȝing,
And ask þair counsel in *þat* thing.
When ilkon hase said þair a-vise,
þe priores þan, if scho be wise,
She should take the best advice,
Sal se who a-cordes reson vnto,
And efter þair rede sal scho do.
And god schewś his myġħt, be ȝe bald,
Als wele in ȝong folk als in ald;
And þairfor sal in swilk a thing
Samyn com boþħ olde & ȝyng,
And mekely ilkon sai þair saw
And nother let for luf ne aw.
And when þai al *þer* sawes hafe saide,
and all should be [leaf 77, bk.] contented,
Als scho assentes þai sal be paide,
Als gude discipels saƚƚ al-ways
Be paide, what so þair maistres sais.
And scho *with* gude descreciouñ
Sal rewle hir wordes bi riġħt reson,
And aƚƚ þai aw be day & niġħt
To saue þis rewle in aƚƚ *þer* myġħt,
following the rule in everything.
And in no ponte, for gude ne iƚƚ,
To wirk efter þair awn wiƚƚ,
Bot euer to be bowsum & bayn
Vnto þe sawes of þair sufferane.
And who so wil not for grete harte,

508. MS. *haue vn bun.*

With greu*auns* aw to be gart.
Bot luke þe priores for no thing
Pase þe rigħt rewle of chastising,
Bot soberly to wirk al-way
For drede of dome in þe last day.
When oder lese thynges er to do,
þan may þe priores cal hir to
iii or iiii wysest women,
And do als þair counsel wil ken,
So þat scho hase witnes al-ways,
Als þe wise man witnes & says:
"Fac cu*m* consilio, et post factu*m* non pe*n*itebis!—
Do al þi dedes be gude counseƚƚ,
þan saƚƚ þe nogħt rew þi trauayle."
þair-for a souerayn sal not do,
Bot if scho ask counsel þair-to
Owþer of sum or els of aƚƚ,
Efter þe thyng es grete or smaƚƚ.

The prioress is not to chastise sisters too severely.

In matters of less importance she needs only consult a few of the wisest.

[leaf 78]

But she shall always take some advice.

IV.

De vij^tem operib*us* m*isericord*ie.

Here er þe warkes on raw to rede
þ*at* sesis oure sins & makes mede.
First sal we luf god loud & stiƚƚ
Witħ al our hert & al our wiƚƚ,
And syen our negħburs sal we luf
Als our-self for our saul be-houe;
No man ne women slay *with* wrang
Noþer *with* word ne wapyn strang.
Of oþer mens we sal not steyl
Ne couet here no wordly wele.
Fals witnes we sal non bere,
Bot honor al þ*at* cristynd ere.
Godes naym we sal not tak in vayn,
Ne swer it bot for thyng sartayn.
And to non here sal we do
Bot als we wold war don vs to.
Oure awn self we sal deny,

Summary of a good life.

We should love God

and our neighbours.

We must not kill,

not steal,

not covet,

not bear false witness,

not take God's name in vain,

but do as we would be done to.

555. Originally *counsaile*, or the like. Cf. 1518. 570. *no*, MS. *ne*.

And folow oure lord god al-myghty,
We should do penance,
Pine oure flescħ *with* penance grete,
And couet non delici*us* mete,
[leaf 78, bk.]
Fast & do gude almus-dede,
clothe the naked,
And cletħ þe naked þat hase nede.
visit the sick,
Seke men suld we viset wele,
bury the dead,
And bring þe dede vn-to biriele,
help the hurt,
Help al þo þat harmes haues,
And counsaile þam þ*at* counsele craues,
And rek not of þis erthli gude,
Bot vnto [crist] turn al our mode.
forego revenge
In our hertes sal we hold non ire,
Ne vengeance saƚƚ we non desire.
Fals frenschep we sal non make,
Trew charite so for to sake.
and swearing,
We sal not swer on euy*n* ne morn
For fardnes for to be for-sworn.
Euyl for euyl we sal not ȝelde,
Bot mayntene right in town & felde;
suffer wrongs,
And if we wranges of oþer take,
We sal it suffer for godes sake.
love foes,
Our enmys aw vs for to lufe,
And noght ban þam þ*at* vs rep*ro*ue;
For mekely suld we, mor & les,
Suffer rep*ro*ue for rightwisnes.
be humble,
W*ith* pride in hert we sal not rise,
Ne be to slaw in god saruyse.
[leaf 79]
No vs aw lightly to lac,
Ne speke no harme be-hind þair bac.
set all our thought on God,
In god we sal set al our thoght
And think þat of our-self es noght
Bot sin & sorow & wrechidnes,
And ilka gude dede of god es.
Þe day of dome vs aw to drede,
An vn-to heƚƚ we suld take hede,
And were vs euer w*ith* al our mayn
keep from sin,
Fro filth of sin, þ*at* sarues payn,
and covet heaven.
And couaite heuy*n* eue*r* inwardly,
And thynk ilk day þ*at* we sal dy,

588. MS. *vnto turn.*

And rewle our warkes by reson rygħt,
And think þai er eu*er* in godes sigħt;
We should act as ever in God's sight,
If euyl thogħtes our hert*es* tak,
Kast þam oute for godes sake;
And kepe our motħ fro grete carpyng
speak no wickedness,
Of wikkidnes or of wordly thing.
Vn-to p*ra*yers we sal vs spede,
pray,
And hali lessones here & rede;
And for our mysdedes don be-forn
mourn for misdeeds,
Suld we mourn botħ euy*n* & morn.
In p*ra*ers to god we [sal] vs schriue
And mak a-mendes so in our life.
We sal hate to wirk our awn wiƚƚ
[leaf 79, bk.]
Or our fleschħ ȝernyng to fulfiƚƚ;
keep chaste,
And on al wise we sal be bayn
Vnto þe saws of our souerayn,
be obedient,
þat we aw our obidience to.
And also if we se hir do
Oþerwise or wer, als god for-bede,
þan scho teches vs to do in dede,
þan sal we ordand our wirkyng
Als crist vs teches, in al thyng:
"**Sec*und*u*m* ope*ra* eoru*m* nolite facere!**"
following good instruction, not evil deeds,
He sais þus: "workes efter þ*er* saw,
And to þair dedes luke ȝe not draw!"
þ*at* es to say, if þai wirk wrang,
And techħ ȝou gratħly for to gang.
We sal not couet in our mode
W*ith* folk for to be haldyn gude.
Godes bidynges we sal fulfiƚƚ
fulfil God's bidding,
Airly & laite and loud & stiƚƚ,
And luf clennes and chastite,
And frendly vnto al folk be.
be friendly to all folk,
Fast suld we fle al vayn louyng,
And mak no strif w*ith* old no ȝing.
To old folk suld we do honour,
And febil we sal sucoure.
and help the weak.
For our enmes sal we pray,
[leaf 80]
Til a recorde be redy ay,

627. MS. *And praers to god we vs.* See Notes.

And seker help ay sal we haue
Of godes mercy our saules to saue.
These 'points of perfect living' will bring the reward
þer er þe pontes of p*er*fite lifyng
þat nedful er to old & ȝing;
For if we wil þam gladli do,
Ful fair reward fals vs vnto,
in endless bliss,
þat es in endles blis to dweƚƚ,
Als crist sais þus in his godspel:
"**Oc*ul*us non vidit, nec aures aud***iuerunt*—
prepared for the followers of the Lord.
None eghen mai se, ne eris here,
Ne hertes thynk þe blisses clere
Whilk god ordand to þ*er* bi-houe
þat yn þair liues hym lely luf."
þarfor es gude þat we tak hede
Hym for to luf & als to drede
þat vn-to slik blis may vs bryng.
Vn-to þ*at* lord be euer loueyng!

V.

De obediencia ad deum.

Now wil I tel, who wil tak tent,
Obedience is due to God,
How we sal be obedient
To honowr god wit*h* ilka lym
And luf no thynk better þan hym.
[leaf 80, bk.] for three reasons
God suld we luf for thynges thre,
Namely al þ*at* hase dignite
And in haly kirk to sing & rede:
(1. for the church service, 2. for dread of hell, 3. for desire to gain heaven),
For he til vs merkes slik mede,
And for drede of þe payns of heƚƚ,
And for ȝernyng in blis to dweƚƚ.
For merit of þer thynges thre
Suld we euermor bowsu*m* be,
And hertli faunde for to fulfil
and to the prioress,
Aƚƚ þ*at* oure souerayn telles vs tiƚƚ.
þan wil god of our wark be paide,
And þan vntil vs salbe saide,
Als crist sais in þe sauter buke
Thurgħ þe p*ro*phet, who likes to luke:
"Als sone als euer he heres my wiƚƚ,
Bowes he baynly me vntiƚƚ."

þus may be saide be old & ȝyng
þat baynly bowes to godes bedyng.
And also ȝit our lord iesus
Vntil his techers tels þus:
"Who so heres ȝou, he heres me."
þan be þ*er* sawes wele may we se:
þai þat er to þ*er* souerayn bayne,
To god he dose þe same o-gayne.
And þarfore who so wil be bown
To lif bi rewle of religiown,
Fro tyme þai wit þ*er* souerayn wiłł,
In wark þai sal it fast fulfiłł;
þair souerayn wil & þ*er* wirkyng
Suld go to-geder euyn als a thing.
And al þat wil do þus in dede,
þe way to heuy*n* it wil þam lede.
And harder it es þan oþer ways,
Als god vntil vs sutħli sais:
"þe way of lif, who likes to layte,
þai sal find botħ hard & straite."
For whi al þ*at* wil com þ*er*-tiłł
Mai not wirk *with* þ*er* awin wiłł;
Bot hard or softe whid*er* it semys,
Ai bus þai do os oþer demys.
þan of þ*er* wark es crist wele paide,
þat þus til his discipils saide:
"**Non veni facere volu*n*tate*m* mea*m*** &c.—
I com not to wirk myne entent,
Bot aynly his þat hase me sent."
Ensampil þus he techis vs til
þat we sal wirk our souerains wil.
Obediens *þus*, if it be stabil,
To god & ma*n* es acceptabil,
Not to tary ne grucħ o-gayne,
Ne to answer *with* worde in vayn̄,
Ne to be heuy in hert or thogħt,
For swilk obedience p*ro*fites nogħt.
Bot if þe hert & wark acorde,
It es not likand til our lord;
For al if we fulfil þe dede,

God's representative.

[leaf 81]

Obedience should be prompt, to

whatever is commanded,

uncomplaining, and cheerful.

[leaf 81, bk.]

Otherwise

we shall receive no reward.

We gete þ*er*-for no g*race* to mede,
Bot titter payn, þ*at* ordand es
To þam þ*at* vses vnbousu*m*nes.
And if we answer oght o-gayn,
Ful mekil mor mu*n* be his payn.

VI.

Þ*er*for es alway gude to do
Als þe p*ro*phet telles vs to;
For in þe sauter þ*us* he sais:
" I said þat I sal ȝeme my wais
In ilka tyme, both old & ȝung,

Silence.

Þ*at* I trispast not in my tung;
To ȝeme my moth also I seke,
And on þis wises I am maide meke,
And gude warkes hafe I non don els."
Lo, how þe p*ro*phet playnly tels:

observed sometimes even where only kind words would have been uttered,

Wise men su*m* tyme letes to say
Wordes þ*at* menes bot wele alway,
Becaus þai wil no iangters be.

[leaf 82]

must be kept all the more where there is danger of sin.

Þan of mare force may we se
Þat euyl wordes suld non here speke,
Þe whilk w*it*h wo er worthi wreke.
And mykel spekyng who so vse,
If it oft gayn, sum tym it nuse.
For þe wisman witnes & sais:
"If þu vse many wordes always,
Fro syn on no wise may þow fle."
And in a-noþer stede sais he

For in the tongue lies life and death.

Þat in a manes tung es contende
Life & dede to fa & frende.
And namly þai þat soietes er,
Gret spekyng þai suld for-bere.
For til a maistres fals ij thynges:
To spek & tech hir vnderlynges.

Disciples have to listen.

And þe discipels suld be stil
And here what es tald þam vntil.
And if þai oght wil aske or haue,
W*it*h gret reuerence þai sal it craue,
And al spekyng þai sal for-bere,

739. *ȝung* corrected from *ȝing*. 755. *no*, MS. *on*.

And hering, þ*at* þe saule may dere,
And gif þam vnto god allayn,
Whas trauel þai haf vnder-tayne.

VII.

De xij gradib*us* humilitat*is*.

Of meknes may we merure take — [leaf 82, bk.]
Of crist, þ*at* sais þ*us* for our sake — Humility
In his gospel, als clerkes ken,
Confortand al cristin men:
"**Qui se humiliat exaltabit*ur***—
Who higħes him-self, he bese made law."
Proude men rep*ro*ues he in þis saw.
And þam to confort þ*at* er meke,
þus he says, who so wele seke:
"**Qui se exaltat humiliabit*ur***—
He þat laws hy*m*-self here,
He salbe higħ in heuy*n* clere." — brings exaltation,
þus schews he wele, & sutħ it es,
þat oute of pride comes al egħnes.
And for [þe] p*ro*phet wald it fle, — as the prophet David
In þe sauter þus sais he: — tells us.
"**D*om*ine, non est exaltatu*m* cor meu*m***—
Lord, my herte ne mi egħen sigħt
Haf I not rasit vp in higħt,
Ne in gret thinges haf I not gayn
To mak maruayls many ayn,
Bot my lif mekly haf I spende,
And highed my saule in-to þi hende.
þ*er*-for, lord, fra scham me schylde,
Als þe moder dose þe childe." — [leaf 83]
If we our dedes wil duly drese
To haue þe meret of mekenes — If we will be
And win vnto þe higħt of heuy*n*, — meek, and
To whilk mekenes may lede vs heuy*n*, — rise to
Hus bus be-gin wi*th* hert & wil — heaven,
To rase þe stegħ þat rechis þ*er*-til, — we must set
Bi whilk Iacob in visioun — up a ladder
Saw angels wend botħ vp & doun. — like Jacob's.

774b and 778b are misplaced. 783. MS. *for prophet.*

This ladder

And þis ilk stegħ, als clerkes tels,
To vnderstandyng es not els
Bot thurgħ hegħnes doun to descend
And thurgħ lawnes vpward to wend.
And als þe stegħ, *with*-outin strife,

resembles our earthly life.

Es likand til our erthli life,
þe whilk stegħ thurgħ our mekenes euy*n*
God rases vp rigħt to þe heuyn.

Its sides are our soul and body;

Two sides þ*er*-of may signifi
Botħ oure saules & our bodi,
In þe whilk sides, als men may se,

Its 12 rungs are the 12 steps of meekness, and lead to heaven.

Er xij steles ordand to be,
Whilk er xij degrese of mekenes,
And right way vnto heuy*n* þ*at* es.
And who so likes þ*at* way to lere,
þe xij degres þus may þai here.

Prim*us* gr*a*dus humilitat*is*.

[leaf 83, bk.]

1. *The first step of the ladder of humility* implies the fear of God,

The first degre of meknes rygħt
Es euer to set be-for our sigħt
þe drede of god in ilk degre,
So þ*at* it neuer for-getin be,
And thinke how þai þ*at* him for-sakes
þair mede in helł *with* m*ur*nyng takes;
And who so hym wil luf & drede,
In heuyn sal þai haf þair mede.
þarfor our lord ay suld we luf,
And drede him for our saule bi-houe,
And kepe fro sin & fro foly
Al þe limes of our body,
And do oway al fleschħ likinges,

who sees both deeds and thoughts,

Thynkand þ*at* god þ*at* sese al thinges
þat we in world here eu*er* wrogħt
Ouþer in wark, or word, or thogħt—

according to Scripture.

For, als þe p*r*ophet p*r*oues & sais,
God enserches & sese al-wais
þe hertes & þe ententes of men,
Als clerkes on þis maner may ken:

Ps. vii. 9.

"Scrutans corda & renes de*us*."

And also ȝit þe p*r*ophet sais:

801. *clerkes*, MS. *crakes*. See Notes.

"Lord, þou wate my wil alwais, Jer. xii. 3.
And thoħtes þat in my hert er hide,
Vnto þe er þai knawne & kide."
þarfor who wil life wele alway, [leaf 84]
In his hert sal he think & say : He who will live well
"Be-for godes siħt I salbe clene,
Yf I waste myne euil dedes be-dene."
It is for-bed þus for þis skiƚƚ must not follow his
Any to folow þ*er* fleschly wiƚƚ ; own fleshly will
Als haly write comaundes & sais :
"Turn þe fro flescħ likynges alwais." (1 Pet. ii. 11),
And pray we god w*ith* wil & thoħt but pray God to work in
þat his wil in vs euer be wroħt ! him His will.
Hali write schews certan skil,
Whi we sal not wirk our awn wil.
For sum warkes þat vs think pe*r*fite,
In godes siħt er dedely delite.
Sum þat þe bodi thynk gude & fine
Wil lede þe saule vntil hel pyne.
And for þi of slike rekles warkes
Sais haly writ, os kens þir clerkes :
"**Corrupti sunt et abho*m*inabil*es***— Ps. xiv. 1.
þai er corrumpid & maide ful vile
þ*at* uses w*ith* filtħ þair flescħ to file."
And when so we ȝern ony thing All our desire
þat may faƚƚ vnto flescħ likyng,
Thinke we god waites vs weterly !
Als þe p*ro*phet sais þus þerby :
"Al my desire botħ day & nyght, (Ps. xxxviii. 9)
Lord, es set be-for þi sight ; [leaf 84, bk.]
And al mi ȝarnyng may þou se, must be in God's sight,
Il or gude wheder it be."
þ*er*for euyl desire suld we fle,
For dede es eue*r* in þe entre,
Redey to fel vs in þ*at* fit ;
And þ*er*for þus sais hali writ :
"Wend þou not, for hard ne nescħ, and not after the yearnings
Efter þe ȝarnynges of þi flescħ— of the flesh.
Sec*und*u*m* desideria cordis non ambul*es*!"

848. MS. *flescħlikynges.* 867. *mi*, MS. *in*.

þen, sen we wote our lord ie*sus*
Es euer bihaldand vntil vs,
And sese who sekes to godes se*r*uyse
And wil not als wriches vnwise,

As our good angel will tell God all our works,

And als we wote oure gude angel
Al our warkes to god wil tel,
Al be it neuer so litil a schar—
þan es wisdom to be-war

let us do nothing to grieve Him.

No warkes to do our god to greue.
For al if he here lene vs leue
For to a-mend vs, whils we may,
Neuer-þe-lese on þe last day
Sal he reherce & sai vs til:

Ps. l. 21.

"þus did þou, & I held me stil."

Secundus gradus humilitatis.

[leaf 85]

2. *The second step of the ladder of humility* is the giving up of one's own wishes and desires;

Ane oþer degre our meknes p*r*oues:
þat es who hir awn wil not lufes,
Ne hase no likyng to fulfil
þat hir desire entisice hir til,
Bot of þir wordes makes hir myrour,
Whilk ie*sus* saide, our sauiour:

as Jesus came, not to do his own will, but his Father's,

"**Non veni facere voluntatem mea***m*—
I com not to do myn entent,
Bot his allaine þat hase me sent,
þat es my fader in heuy*n* on hiĥt;
His wil I do boĥ day & niĥt."
And hali writ wil p*r*oue ful playn
þat our awn wil es worthi payn,
And who so of þe*r* wil here misses
Serues þe croun of endles blisses.
þarfor for-sake we here our wil,
þat we may cum þat blis vntil.

iij grad*us*.

3. *The third step* is obedience to the superior,

The third degre es þis to take:
Who þat gladli for goddis sake
Wilbe obedient w*ith* þe*r* mayne
Vnto [þe] wil of þeir souerayne,
And þat w*ith* gude cher wil fulfil
What so þair souerayne tels þa*m* vntil;

889. In the right margin: *ij gradus*. 908. MS. *Vnto wil.*

Al[s] be þe apostil es pupplist,
þat sais þus of our lord crist: [leaf 85, bk.] after the example of Christ.
"He wos meke to his fad*er* rede
And obedient vnto þe dede."
[. . . . .]
To gif ensaumpil mor & lese,
þat þai suld so obedient be
To þeir souerayns in þ*er* degre,
And tent no thyng to þ*er* awn wil,
Bot þ*er* souerayns fast to fulfil
Wi*th* obedience in word & dede;
Than es þ*er* wark worth mikyl mede.

iiij **g*r*ad*us*.**

The fourt degre of mekenes clere
Es of al þai þat suffers here
And dose what so þ*er* souerayn sais
Al if þe wark be wrang alwais
Or greuus til þam for to do,
ȝet sal þai sone assent þ*er*-to,
And do it wele wi*th* al our mayn
Wi*th*-outyn ony grochin ogayne,
And irk not þan, or it be done;
Als hali writ wil tech ful son:

4. The fourth step of the ladder of humility is patience and perseverance as taught by Christ,

"**Qui perseue*r*auerit vsq*ue* in finem**—
He þat lastes vntil þe end,
Salbe safe & vnto blis wende."
And also haly writ sais þus [leaf 86]
Ane oþer claus [to] comford vs:
"þi hert," he sais, "sal comford take
To be souerand for godes sake."
In oþer places he p*ro*ues alway
How souerand men to god suld say:
"**Propt*er* te mortificam*ur* tota die**—
Lord, we suffer here wi*th* sere payn
Al þe day for þi sake for to be slayn."
þat mens: "we suffer payn mekely
Als lams þat er lede for to dy,

St. Paul,

911. MS. *Albe*. 915. A line is omitted. 923. The *h* in *The* was added subsequently. 936. MS. *claus comford*. 941. MS. *suffor*. 942. Partly on erasure. See Notes.

And we er not ouer*cumen* þer-in,
For mede we hope þerby to wyn;
Bot al we suffer it for ies*us*
And for his sake þat so lufyd vs,
þat with his awn wil & his rede
For our sake wold suffer dede
So to saue vs thurtħ his grace."

and David.

And also in ane oþer place
May meke men say on þis manere:

Ps. lxvi. 10, 11.

"Lord, þou hase asayde vs here
With angers a-gayns our desire,

[leaf 86, bk.]

Als siluer es asaide with fire,
þou hase vs * vnto þe snare
And made vs to haue angers þair."
For to assay vs in swilk thing,
If we be meke to his bidyng,

These show us that we should obey our superior,

And also for to schew þat we
Suld to a souerayn bowsu*m* be
And wirk efter þer wil alway,
Vnto our lord þus may he say:
"Lord, o-bouen set hase þou
Souerayns to wham vs bus bew."

and for God's sake suffer persecution.

þus for god sake we suld be bown
To suffer sere p*er*secucioun,
What so men wil vn-til vs do;
Als þe gospel techis vs to:
Who so betes vs on a scheke,
To bede oþer we suld be meke,

To those who wrong us, we should give more than they ask,

And wrang of vs who wil oghֹt haue,
To bede þam mor þan þai wold craue;
þan es our mekenes mykil at prase;
Als sant paule þe appostil sais:
It be-houes folk of religioun
Suffer tenes & tribulacioun,

and honour those who harm us.

And honor þam þat dose þam scatħ,
Whider þai be wele paide or wratħ.

[leaf 87]

And þer meret it may not eke,
Bot if þai in þer hertes be meke
To suffer wilfuly alwais

957. A participle (*don, led, put, set*?) is omitted.

What so men to þ*am* dose or sais,
And be not greuyd w*ith* word ne dede;
Swilk mekenes makes vs mykil mede.

v gr*a*dus.

The fift degre es to be swift
Eftir our sin to seke to schrift,
And trewly tel w*ith*-outyn trayne
Al our lif & nothing layne,

5. The fifth step of the ladder of humility is undelayed and unreserved confession.

Als hali writ on þis wise sais:
"Vnto god sal I schew my wais,
And al my sines w*ith* mayn & mode
Sal I schew to god so gude;
For his mercy may mend & pas
All wikkidnes þ*at* in world eu*er* was."

God's mercy exceeds all sin.

And þai þ*at* þus þ*er* sines wil bete,
þus may þai sai w*ith* þe p*ro*[p]hete:
"Lord, all þe sines þ*at* er myn awne,

Ps. xxxii. 5.

Vnto þe haue I made þ*am* knawn̄;
And all onright þ*at* eu*er* I dide,
Lord, vnto þe I haue not hide;
Bot I sal p*ro*nunce for sertane
All my mysdedes my-self ogayne.
þarfore, der lord, do þ*o*u to me

[leaf 87, bk.]

Efter þi grace so grete plente,
And lord, not efter my misdede,
Bot efter þi mercy gr*a*unte me mede."

vj*tus* gr*a*d*us*.

The sext degre of mekenes þan:
Who salbe meke, man or woman,
Bus hald þam-self vile & worthy
Al maners of charch to vnderly,

6. The sixth step is self-depreciation, and readiness to do menial work.

And think þai er worthi to do
Mor þan oni wil put þ*am* to,
And þ*at* þai er worthi to haue
Wor þan any on þ*am* vouches safe,
So litil be þam-self to set,
Say þan þus w*ith* þe p*ro*phet:
"**Consu*m*pt*us* su*m* et humiliatus**—
I am wastid wor þan I wend,

998. MS. *prohete.*

For myne awn kind not I kend.
Now als a best meke sal I be
Aneli, lord, for luf of þe."
God len vs so to be bowsum,
þat we may til his kingdom cu*m*.

7. The seventh step of the ladder of humility is thinking oneself the lowest of the low.

[leaf 88]

vij gr*a*dus.

The seuent degre þa*n* of þe twelue
Es þat vs aw to law our-selue,
And in hert hald vs vnworthi
To cum in any gude company,
And of our-self we sal say þen
Os þe p*ro*phet wil clerely ken:

Ps. xxii. 6.

"**Ego sum vermis & non homo**—
I am a worm & no woman."
And þusgaite folos þar-on þan:
"Mine awne condicions wil I ken,
Rep*ro*ue & oute-kast of al women.
My hyghnes in herth þen wil I knaw,
Bot, lord, þi law hase mayd me law.
Wele es me yn þis lif here
To be so meke þi laws to lere."
God len vs so his laws to lufe,
þat we bide in blis obufe.

viij gr*a*d*us*.

8. The eighth step is compliance with rule and good examples.

The aght degre of meke lifyng
Es þat non sal do no thing,
Ne no wark þat es for to wirk,
Bot efter þe rewle of þe*r* kirk
Or be ensampil to vnd*er*stand
Of þam we knaw er wele lifand.
For ensawmpil of oþer dede
Salbe merure vs for to lede
In our doing both nyght & day,
So þat we folow our rewle alway.

[leaf 88, bk.]

ix grad*us*.

9. The ninth step is refraining from much talk;

The neyntt degre to ald & ȝong
Es þat vs aw to ȝem our tong
And spek not bot we be requerde.
For hali writ þus hase vs lerde,
þat who so mykil speking vse,

Of sin þai may not þa*m* excuse;
And gret spekers er not worthy
For to cum in gude *com*pany.
þarfor es gude to take reward
W*ith* onest folk þ*at* spech̄ be spaird,
And ordan vs to spek no thyng
Bot honestly to godes loueyng.

for great talkers are not worthy to come in good company.

x g*r*adus.

The x degre es þ*us* to lere:
Not to lagh̄ w*ith* oue*r*-lygh̄t cher'
Ne w*ith* laghing our voce to raise.
For hali writ þus leres & sais:
"A fole," he sais, "bi day & nygh̄t
In laghyng rais his vose on high̄t."
þarfor es gude to man & childe
For to ler' at be laghter-myld
And of al cowntnanse myld & stil
W*ith*-outyn ony mater of il.

10. *The tenth step of the ladder of humility* is keeping from much laughter.

xj gradus.

The xj wisses þus alway:
Al if vs aw litil to say
And in lagh̄ing not rudely rise,
ȝit es gude þ*at* we vs avise,
When so we speke bi morn or noun̄,
To say our wil in wordes fou*n*e,
And þ*at* our wordes be wittely.
For þus þe wisman sais þ*er*bi:
"**Sapiens in pauc*is* verbis exped*it*—**
He þ*at* is wise in word & dede,
His wark w*ith* fone wordes wil he spede."
And naymly women nygh̄t & day
Aw to vse fune wordes alway.

11. *The eleventh step* is conciseness and prudence in speech.

[leaf 89]

xij g*r*adus.

The twelft degre wele for to seke
Es, of þam þ*at* salbe meke,
Not aynli to be meke in wil,
Bot in wark mekely to fulfil
Al þat es to þam cumand:
To gang, or ride, or sit, or stand,

12. *The twelfth step* is lowliness in carriage.

1089. MS. *cunand.*

In kirk, in closter, in town & feld,
In way, in ȝerd, in ȝouth̄ & eld.
W*ith* law lowting þai salbe bayn
W*ith*-outyn ony gruching o-gayn.

We must look on the ground like the publican,

Vnto erth̄ down sal þai luke
Sorowand for syn, os sais þe buke

[leaf 89, bk.]

Of þe pupplicane, þ*at* prayde

Luke xviii. 13,

Vnto god & þusgaite saide:
"**Miserere m*ih*i pe*cca*tori**—
Lord, al thinges wele knaw þ*o*u can;

as unworthy to lift up our eyes to heaven.

Haue mercy on me, sinful man!
I am vn-worthi, lord," said he,
"To lift myn egh̄en vp vnto þe
Or for to luke vp vnto heuyn."
And also sais þe þ*ro*phet hewyn:

Ps. xxxviii. 6.

"**Curuat*us* sum & humilia*tus* su*m* nimis**—
I am bowed to þe erth̄," he sais,
"And so I am meke mayd alwais."

These are the twelve degrees of humility, which,

Now haue I tald þir twelf degrese
þat er of meknes for to chese,
þe whilk may bring vs for to be
W*ith* god in pe*r*fite charite
And al our lif lely to lede

if we do them gladly,

W*ith*-outyn trauel or ony drede.
We sal do gladli of custu*m*
þat air til vs wos ful irksu*m*,
And not aynli payn to eschew,
Bot allayn for luf of iesu.
And þat lufe & swete delite

will bring us to endless bliss.

þat in vs salbe so parfite,
Oute of al wais it sal vs wise
And bryng vs vnto endles blis.

[leaf 90]

VIII.

De officiis in noctibus.

Nocturnal divine offices are held at different hours in winter

IN tyme of winter, in Descember,
Fro þe kalandes of Nouember
Vn-to þe pase, es risyng righ̄t
At þe agh̄t our of þe nygh̄t,
And after mydnygh̄t for to rest,

þat þar mete may bi wele degest.
þan sal þai rise to syng & rede;
And after þan who so hase nede
May haue þ*er* meditacioune*s*
In sawters, saulms, & orisowns.
And fro al tyme of pase bi al left
Vn-to þo same kalandes cu*m* eft,
þan es it ordand on þis wise,
þ*at* nunes sal vnto matens rise
When þe day be-gyns to daw,
þat þai litters bi light may knaw.

and in summer.

IX–XVIII.

Mor how þai sal serues do,
Nedes not her' to tel þam to;
þai knaw þer salmes & ilka verse.
þarfor þe rowle I wil reherce,
How þai sal do wirchep alway,
When þai to god sal sing or say.

More about services need not be given here.

XIX.

Vbiq*ue* credim*us* diuinam esse p*resen*ciam—

We trow & wele we vnderstand
þ*at* our lord god alweldand
In ilka place es redi bown
To here our p*ra*yer & orisown;
And euyl & gude, al heres he,
Rich & pouer in ilk degre.
And most we trow he be present
In haly kirk bi þis entent
þ*at* his seru*au*ndes most comy*n*li
Serues hi*m* þ*er*, als es worthy.
þan sen we wote þ*at* he es þer,
Oure mynd on hym suld be þe mayr
To serue hym dredfully always,
Als þe p*ro*phet vs teches & sais:
"Seruite do*mi*no cum timore!"
He sais þus: "serues ȝor god in drede,
Hopand of hym to haue ȝor mede."
And wisely, sais he, we suld sing

[leaf 90, bk.]
In all divine service the presence of God should be remembered.

We should serve Him with fear (Ps. ii. 11),

wisdom,

1153. þ*er*, originally þ*air*, or the like.

Lessons vn-to goddes loueyng.
In ayn oþer plase sais he
þat angel[s] sal our synging se:
(Ps. cxxxviii. 1)
"**In conspectu anglor*um* psallam t*ib*i.**"
On þis maner til vs he teles
And sais: "lord, in sight of angels
[leaf 91]
Sal we syng to þi wirchep."
þan aght vs for to tak gude kepe
þ*at* our p*ra*yer & orisoune
and devotion.
Be done w*ith* gude deuocioune,
So þ*at* our hert & moth acord;
þan es it likand til our lord
And vnto his angels also,
Sen we may se, al þ*at* we do
And þ*at* we say bi day or nyght,
Al es set befor þare sight.

XX.

As we would obey a lord here, who could benefit us,
Bi gude ensau*m*pil may we se,
How bayn & bowsum we wold be
Vn-to a lord, her' whar we lif,
þat ony gude myght til vs gif.
We wold hym loute, es not at layn,
And til his bidyng be ful bayn
W*ith* al wirchep þat we may weld.
þan of mor force in town & feld
much more should we worship God with reverence and humility.
Wirchep suld we til him bede
þat in heuy*n* sal merk vs our mede.
W*ith* sorow of syn we suld hi*m* seke
And wirchep w*ith* wordes meke.
For haly writ lely vs leres
þ*at* law hertes lightly he heres.
We should pray to Him [leaf 91, bk.] briefly and in purity.
Our prayers suld be ordand euy*n*
Schort & clen to god of heuyn,
Bot if deuociou*n* cu*m* emang
And likyng for to hald þam lang.
For haly writ þus leli leres:
Heuy*n* es thirld w*ith* schort p*ra*yers;
þat es to say, if þ*at* þai be

1162. MS. *angel*.

Mellid w*ith* no kyns vanite,
Bot vnto godes wirchep alway.
God gr*a*nt vs gr*a*ce so for to pray.

XXII.

Quomodo sanctimonialles dormiant.

All should sleep in one house,

Aƚƚ samyn o nygħtes lig þai saƚƚ,
If a hows wil herber þa*m* aƚƚ,

in separate beds, and with their clothes on (cf. l. 2015).

And ilkon serly in a bede,
And ilkon in a kirtil clede
And girdid o-bown on al wise,
þ*a*t þai may be redy to rise.

But when beds are too few,

And if þar be gret company,
þat al may not in a hows ly

novices may sleep with old nuns.

In sere bedes, als I said hare,
þan ald women & wise of lare
May haue ȝong nou*i*ces, þ*a*t þai lere,
To lig in a bed botħ infere.

Light should burn all night.

In þe hows whar [þai] lig o nygħt,
Candel or lau*m*pe sal euer be lygħt.

Knives should not be taken into bed.

And kniues to bed þai sal non bere,
For dred þ*a*t þai mygħt do þa*m* dere.

[leaf 92]

All should rise punctually.

When tyme es ordand, on al wise,
W*ith*-outyn tareyng luk þai rise
And hast þa*m* hertly for to cum
Vnto godes serues al & sum.
And þis es þe encheson why
þat þai sal al in a hows ly:
Be-caus no idilnes sal vse,
Ne fro godes serues þam excuse.

XXIII.

Punishment gradation:

And if þar ony vn-bowsu*m* bene,
Or prowd in hert, os su*m* er sene,
þat to þar rewle ne þ*er* souerayn
Wil not bow, bot grucħ o-gayn,

1. privy admonition, 2. open admonition and atonement,

Twise preuely þai salbe blamyd
And, bot þai sese, opynly schamyd.
And if ane wil not mend her so,

1203. MS. *alwise.* 1211. MS. *whar lig.*

Opyn reprofe falis hir vnto
Omang þe couent eu*er*-ilkane.
And if sche ȝit be ouer-tayn,
And sche ken þe p*er*ils of cursing,
3. excommunication,
Sche salbe cursid for þ*at* same þing.
And if sche wil not mend hir mynd,
4. beating.
þan bodely sche salbe pynd.
And in hert penance sal sche lende,
[leaf 92, bk.]
Vntiƚƚ sche wil hir mys amend.

XXIV.

Modus castigacionis.

Noman suld curs mor ne lese
Bot for thyng þ*at* ful greu*us* es.
The punishment should be measured by the fault: be lighter
And so sal penance mor & myn
Be gyfyn & getyn efter þe sin,
Als lig*h*t penance for litil thing,
or heavier,
And for gret greu*us* chastying.
Als if a non be nyg*h*t or day
Forget þ*at* sche suld sing or say
Or ony werk þ*at* sche suld wirk
In couent or yn hali kirk,
as suspension from meals only,
Sche salbe suspend fro þe mete
Al tyme þ*at* hir felows sal ete.
Allayn at mete syne sal sche sit,
þ*at* oþer may hir t*r*ispas wit.
Su*m* seruyse salbe fro her let
[. . . . .]
Mor þan for oþer on raw,
þ*at* sche may so hir trispase knaw.

XXV.

Mor greu*us* syns if on wil wirk,
or from church, meals, and all company,
Sche salbe suspend fro þe kirk,
Fro mete, & fro al company
þ*at* sche myg*h*t og*h*t be cu*m*fort bi.
[leaf 93]
Allone by hir-self sal sche do
What wark so sche es put vnto,
So for to punyc*h* hir body;

1254. Here, for the second time, a whole line is omitted.
1259. *fro al*, MS. *for al.* Cf. 2463.

Als þe appostil speks þerbi:
Swilk men, he sais, sal trauel tast
W*ith* grete fullyng þ*er* flescħ to wast,
So þat þ*er* saules may safly cum
Bi-for god on þe day of dom̄.

in accordance with the words of the apostle.

XXVI.

Vt no*n* co*mmun*icent cu*m* ex-co*mmun*icat*is*.

[If] None or nouese, mor or lese,
Comyn w*ith* þam þat cursed es,
Or cu*m* vntyl hir whar' sche dwels
To ete or speke or do ogħt els,
þe same payn sal þai vnderly
þ*at* sche suffers for hir foly,
Vntil þai haue þ*at* mys amend,
Bot if þar souerayn haf þa*m* send:
þan may þai baldly speke & do
Als far os þai haf leue vnto.

Whoever communes with one excommunicated incurs the same punishment, unless sent by the superior.

XXVII.

De pe*r*tinentib*us* ad custodem.

Ane Abbot or a priorese,
þ*at* so ouer oder kepers es,
Aw besily for to be-gyn
To hele þa*m* þ*at* er hurt w*ith* syn,
Thurgħ haly lernyng þa*m* to lecħ,
Als crist þus in þe gospel tecħ;
He sais: "to hel folk es no nede
Ficiciens her for to bede,
Bot þo men þ*at* er seke & sore
Nedes for to haue medcyns mor."
A souerayn aw þarfor to send
To þe synful, þair mys to mend,
Of þe eldest & þe most wise,
Bi þair resons to ger þa*m* rise,
And tecħ þam turmentes for to take
And suffer þa*m* for godes sake,
And so assay bi þ*er* soft saw
The synful to meknes at draw.

The superior should be eagerly concerned about the one sick in sin, [leaf 93, bk.] send sisters to her, show her she should suffer for God's sake,

1269. See Notes.

pray for her,

For ane sinful al suld þai pray
þat god wise hir to better way.

and act like the good shepherd to

Ilka hird aw to do þis,
So þat non of his schep p*er*ise.
And in case þ*at* on p*er*ist were,
Ensaumpil of crist may we ler
To comford þam at our power.
For he tels vs on þis maner
Bi ensaumpil how a hird-man

the straying sheep,

A febil schepe warest & wane:
He left al his flok os him list
And went to seke ane þat he myst;

[leaf 94]

And sune when he had fon þ*at* same,

who brought it home on his back

A-pon his bak he broght it ham̄;
And þ*er*of wos he so wele payd,
þ*at* to his neghburs þus he said:

(Luc. xv. 6).

"**Cong*ra*tulam*ini* m*ih*i q*uia* inueni ouem q*uam*** &c.—
Bes glad & makes mery w*ith* me!
My schep wos lorn, & fun es he."
So aw a souerayn for to seke
þam þ*at* dose wrang, w*ith* wordes meke,
And fathly faund w*ith* myght & mayne
To get þam til þe flok ogayne.

XXVIII.

If the said modes of correction,

And if it fall, als god for-bede,
þat ony haue don gret mysdede
And wil not mend her bi no way
For noght þat men may do or say,
For fair wordes ne for chaistying,
Ne for dred of þe gret cursyng,

as well as prayers,

þan sal þe souerayn nyght & day
Ger al hir sisters for hir pray.

prove inefficient, there remains only

And if sche non wise wil amend,
þan, als þe appostil hase vs kend,

5. expulsion,

Sche salbe catchid fro cu*m*pany,
þat oþer bi not hermyt hir by.

as one sheep with the rot may give it to many.

For thurgh a schep þ*at* rote hase hent
May many schep w*ith* rote be schent.

[leaf 94, bk.]

So may a synful man do scath

Vnto him-self & oþer bath.
Swilk foles es best forto for-sake,
Sen þ*at* þai wil no m*er*cy take.

XXIX.

One who has left the convent can be

And if ane so for wikkid dede
Leue hir abbay & hir wede,
And lif in world eft*er* þer wil,
And sine wold turn þe hows vntil,
þe penance to hir sche sal restore
Of þat dede þat sche went oute fore,
And profer hir-self to suffer payne
At þe ordenance of hir sofferayne,
So þat men may hir meknes knaw
Thurgh hir lifyng, if it be law.

re-admitted twice,

And if sche eft a-way wil go,
Eft sal sche be resauyd so.

but not oftener.

And þe third tyme if sche be gone,
A-gayn hir aw not to be tone,
Bot whar hir list þan lat hir pas,
Als sche þ*at* neuer of order was.

XXX.

Children should be punished differently from grown-up people.

Chastying aw mesured to be
To ald & ȝung in sere degre.
For þe trispas of childer ȝing
Aw men to vse soft schastisyng,

[leaf 95]

They should be beaten with a rod only.

Als fastyng & betyng wit*h* wande
And noþer strakes of staf ne hande.
And if þai wil of wordes haf drede,
To bete þam þan it es no nede.

LXV.

De p*re*pocita, i*d est* subpriorissa.

A subprioress should not be chosen except by the prioress' provision,

IN þis maner it ordand es,
þat a president subp*ri*ores
Sal non be chosin for no chanch
Bot by þe p*ri*ores puruyanch.
For [if] it wor done oþer-wise,

1365. MS. *For it.*

lest contentions

Strif & debate myght lighͭtly rise.
For if sche wor chosin be þo same
þat chays þe priores by nayme,
þan thurgh̄ eggyng of þe fende

and pride should arise, and she should think, 'If the prioress died, I should be chosen prioress.'

A high̄nes in hir hert mygh̄t lend,
Thinkand þus in hir awn rede :
"If *þat* þe priores wor dede,
þo same by wham sche chosin es,
Wold ches me vnto priores."
And so p*er*chanch̄ in swilk a case,
If contek in þe couent rase,
þe subpriores so w*ith* pride
A-gayns hir souerayn suld sone chide,
And gete oþer of hir assent
To maynteyn hir in swilk entent

| [leaf 95, bk.]

And for to supplant hir souerayn ;
And in swilk case mygh̄t su*m* be slayn
And perels fal̄l, als folk may fele.
And þarfor es it ordand wele,

The same holds good of the sacristan and other functionaries.

þat subpriores & segerstone
And oþer offecers ilkon
Sal non be chosin bi no way
Bot als þe priores wil puruay.
And who so oþer-wise hase chose,
þe p*r*iores aw þam to depose
And oþer in þar' stede to take
In gude luf & for godes sake.

The subprioress must be submissive;

Subpriores sal euer be bayne
Vnto þe saws of hir souerayne,
And no thing wirk a-gayns hir wil
Arely ne layte, ne loude ne stil.
For þe mor high̄ state *þat* þai haue,
þe mor þam aw þer rewle to saue.

otherwise

And if sche groch̄ ogh̄t for to do
Of thyng þat touches þe rewle vnto,
Or if sche maynteyn mor or lese
For to myspay hir priores,
Or els rebel a-gayns hir rise,

she is liable to correction

Be word sche salbe warnyd thrise,
And bi þe iiij tyme, bot if sche mende,

Be chasted als þe rewle hase kende.
And if sche wil not mend hir so,
Sche salbe pute hir office fro,
And ordand in hir stede to be
On þat es abil to þat degre.
And if sche wil not mend hir ȝit,
Oute of þair flok sche salbe flit.
Bot euer þe priores bus nede
Haue gude discreciun in hir dede.
Scho bus wirk be non enuy,
Bot for þe luf of god anely,
Be charite & concience clene,
And þe rewle right to maynteyn.
And if sche so ordand hir dede,
Of god þan getes sche mykil mede.

[leaf 96]
and deposal.
The prioress, however, should be discreet, and led by pure motives.

XXXI.

De eleccione celarar*ie*.

A Celerer sal schosin be
Bi counsel of þe comu*n*alte
And fully bi þe hale assent
Of þe priores & þe couent,
Wise & meke & of myld thews,
Not prowd ne lither, like to schrews,
Not slaw ne grochand in hir dede,
Bot swilk als wil god loue & drede.
Scho sal tak ȝeme to mor & les
Bi puruyance of þe Priores.
For al sal cu*m* into her hend
þat salbe in hir offece spend.
Hir offece sal sche gladly do,
And ȝeme wele þ*at* es takyn her to.
And who so askes hir skilwis thyng,
Sche sal not greue þ*am* w*ith* groching.
Bot if it a-cord not w*ith* wit,
Mekely sal scho warn þam it.
And if it aw forto be done,
Scho sal it gif gladly & soñe.
So vnto hir gret mede may rise,

The cellaress is to be chosen by the convent,
to be meek and gentle,
and care for all,
[leaf 96, bk.]
as she has so much in hand.
She shall grant all reasonable requests.
Great will be her reward

1418. *þe* omitted and then added above the line.

Als þe appostel sais on þis wise :
(1 Tim. iii. 13) "**Qui bene administrauerit,**
g*ra*dum bonu*m* sibi adquirit—
for duties fulfilled. Who serues wele, w*it*h hertes fre,
Wins to þam-self a gud degre."
A cellaress must be kind to children and the poor, A celerer aw to be myld & meke
For to serue þam þ*at* er seke,
And ȝong childer, & gestes pore,
And oþer þat askes at þe dore.
Vnto al swilk tent sal sche take
And serue þa*m* for godes sake,
as accountable on Doomsday. Witand of all swilk doing
[leaf 97] On domesday sal [sche] mak reknyng.
She shall look after all the abbey utensils, Al þe vessel of þe abbay
Aw hir to ȝeme in right aray,
So þ*at* non perise ne be lorn
Be hir defaute ne euy*n* ne morn.
Scho sal not saue hir-selu vntil,
Bot wirk al be [hir] souerayn wil.
be fair of answer Fair of answer sal sche be
To euer ilkon in þ*er* degre.
For meke answer es mykil at p*ra*ys,
Als hali writ witnes & says :
(Ecclesiasticus xviii. 17), "**Sermo bon*us* sup*er* datu*m* optimu*m***—
Fair wordes in ilka plase
Er oboun oþer giftes of g*ra*ce."
A celerer sal gladly fulfil
Al þ*at* fals hir offece vntil,
and gladly give when others crave. And gladly gif when oþer craue,
And mekely ask what so wil haue.
And if scho so rewle al hir dede,
þan may scho serue ful mykil mede.

XXXII.

De offic*io* sacriste.

The sacristan should ring the bells, The Priores, & oþer nane,
Aw for to ches a segerstane
To ring þe bels in right aray

1452. *sche* or *scho* is omitted after (or before) *sal.* 1458. MS. *albe souerayn.* 1468. *so,* see Notes.

Til al þer seruys nyght & day.
And wisely aw hir forto wirk
To kepe enourmentes of þe kirk,
Als chalese, boke, & vestmentes,
Relekes, waxe, & a*n*nual rentes.
Er aw to ordan al bedene,
Als vessel, close, & kep þa*m* clene.
Indentures suld þai *be ilkon,
And þe priores sal kepe þe tone,
So þ*at* when on sal out flit,
By þe*r* endenturs may þai wit,
What thynges efter on er left
To hir þ*at* sal resaf þam eft.
And who so wil reklesly wirk
Or files þe þinges of haly kirk,
þai salbe chasted greuusly
Efter þe*r* warkes es worthi.

[leaf 97, bk.]

have the charge of the belongings of the church, and its rent.

She and the prioress shall each have an inventory of the convent's property.

XXXV.

De septimariis co*q*uine.

IN þe kechin sal þai serue oboute,
Ilkon þe*r* wouke wit*h*-outyn doute,
And serues sal non refuse,
Bot if skilwis caus þa*m* excuse,
þat þai til oþer thinges takes tent
Mor profetabil to þe couent.
And euer þam aw to tak rewarde
At euer þe eldest most be sparde.
And when on hase endid hir wouke,
Besily hir aw to luke,
þat al be clene þat to hir fell,
Both howses, clothes, & wessell,
To liuer os clene os scho kan
Vnto hir þat sal serue þan,
So þ*at*, if oght wantand be,
In whom defaut es, may men se.
And who so þus salbe seruand
May tak a sop wele be-for-hand,

Weekly kitchen-service is obligatory,

with certain exceptions.

[leaf 98]

Those serving should keep everything clean,

and take a sop early,

1481. We had expected a transitive verb. 1501. MS. *albe.*

before the regular meal.

So þ*at* þ*er* penance bi not gret
Forto bide til þe latter mete,
And for þai sal wi*th* meri cher'
Serue ilkon on sides sere.

At the week-end, she shall kneel to the convent,

When on hase seruyd a wouk to end
And sal oute of þ*er* seruys wend,
Kneland bi-for þe couent
þ*us* sal scho say wi*th* gud entent:

(Ps. lxxxvi. 17)

"**Benedict*us* es, d*omi*ne, q*ui* adiuuisti me—**
Blissid be þou, lord, þ*at* neu*er* falled,
þat hase me helpid & counseld!"

and thank God thrice.

Thris on þis wise sal scho say,
And blisyng take, & wend hir way.

[leaf 98, bk.] Her successor

And scho þat enters in seruese,
Kneland sal say on þis wise:

(Ps. lxx. 1)

"**Deus, in adiutoriu*m* meu*m* intende—**

shall pray for God's help.

Lord, to my helping þou take hede,
And hast þe hertly me to spede!"
And wi*th* hir hed scho sal bow down
And mekely take hir benysoun;
And on þis wise when sche don has,
Vntil hir serues sal scho pas.

XLV.

De delinquentibus in eccl*es*ia.

For mistakes in divine service,

If þat on faile in ony thing,
In verses or saulms to rede or sing,
Or in lessons þam er kend,

atonement must be made;

Bot þai mekely þ*at* mys amend
þair in presens of company,
Grete payn sal þai vnderly.
And þe nouices, whils þai er ȝing,
Aw to be scorid for swilk a thing.

XLVI.

likewise for carelessness about work

And als who so wil fayntly faile
And not trewly do þer trauayle

in kitchen

In kechin, celer, or in cels,

bakehouse, etc.,

In bakkows, brewhows, or ourels,
Or els þat loises mor or les

1518. Originally *counsailed*, or the like.

Bi resoun of þer reklesnes, [leaf 99]
And comes not son to þer souerayne
For þat trispas to tak þer payne,
Bot layns it stil, os no man wist,
Til it *with* oþer be puplist,
þan sal mor payn to þa*m* be layde
þan if þam-self þe suth̄ had saide.
For if none wit þe*r*of bot þay,
Vnto þer souerayn suld þai sai
Or til þer confessure in hi,
þat may þa*m* mend al preuely.

particularly if not acknowledged at once.

XLVII.

De horis assignandis.

Subp*r*iores, als woman wise,
Sal kepe þe oures of god seruyse,
Or els a-noþer bi her assent
Vnto þa*t* office sal tak tent,
So þa*t* seruyse bi day & nyght̄
In ilk seson be rewlid right̄.
And scho sal assigne old & ȝing
Til all̄ þa*t* þai sal rede or sing,
And se þa*t* non sal syng ne rede
Bot þa*t* er abil vnto þa*t* dede.
And dredefully ilkon sal do
Al þa*t* þai er assigned vnto.

On the subprioress or her substitute falls the duty of maintaining and regulating the worship.

XXXIX.

De mensura cibor*um*.

Who to þe kechin sal tak tent [leaf 99, bk.]
Sal ordan wele for þe couent
Euer-ilk-a day ij maners of mete,
Bi-caus þa*t* who so may not ete
Of þe ton for nokins nede,
Of þe toþer þai may þa*m* fede.
So til a couent suffes may
ij maner of potege ilka day.
If þai hafe appils or oþer thing
Ordand of þeir awn growyng,

Regulations about food. Two kinds of meat shall be provided, and two kinds of soup; also fruit, if they have any.

1555. *Or*, MS. *Er*.

þen sal þai make seruys of slike
Vnto euer-ilkon in-like.

Every lady shall have 1 lb. of bread daily

To ilka lady suffise may
A pond of bred a-pon a day,
Wheder þai wil ete ons or twise.
If it be ordand on þis wise,

(keeping a third for her supper),

þat euer-ilkon wil of hir laue
þe third part til hir sopper saue,
And to þe celerer wil it seme
Swilk seruys for to saf & ȝeme.

but more during hard work,

And who so wendes gret trauel til
Salbe seruyd at þer souerans wil,

though always with moderation.

W*ith* mor or les þ*at* es to mene,
Bot euer þat non outrage be sene;

[leaf 100]

For no thyng es [als] gret enmy
Vnto godes folk als glotony.
And þarfor þus sais ie*sus* crist,
Als witnes wele þe eu*au*ngelest:

Luc. xxi. 34.

"**Videte ne grauent*ur* corda u*est*ra crapula et ebrietate**—
Greues not ȝour hartes for no nede
W*ith* glotony & dronkenhede."

Children shall have less.

And les mesur in ilka thing
Salbe vsid to childer ȝyng.

XL.

De mensura pot*us*.

Similarly in the case of drink,

THE mesure salbe of þ*er* drink
Set efter þ*er* souerayn think,
Efter þai trauel arely & late,
And after þe plais es cald or hate;
Bot at þai neuer assent vntil
þair flesch ȝernyng fully to fil.
Softly sal þai tast, & fair,

particularly strong wine or noble ale.

Drynk þ*at* may þ*er* hedes inpair,
Als myghty wyne or nobil aile.
For þe wisman tels slik a taile:
"Wyne þ*at* es myghty & strang
Mase witty men forto wirk wrang."

1589. MS. *es gret;* cf. p. 28, ll. 11–12. 1600. MS. *hete;* cf. 2004.

þarfor es wit, to lest & mast, All should be moderate
Wine or aile softly to tast.
And if þai in slik places be,
þat þai of noþer haf plente, [leaf 100, bk.]
Swilk os þai find þen sal þai fande, and grateful.
And loue god hertly of his sande.

XXXIII.

Vt nichil *pro*prium h*ab*eant.

IN relegion, als it es knawn,
Sal þai haf no thing of þ*er* awn, Individual property is not allowed
Ne no þing clame be p*ro*pirte,
Bot al þing sal in comu*n* be.
No giftes sal [þai] gif ne take
Bot anly for þeir souerayn sake,
Ne no þing sal þai clayme ne craue
Bot als þer souerayn wouches saue.
Tabels, boke, ne oþer gere either in tables or books, or anything else.
W*ith*-outyn hir wil sal þai none were,
Bot whatkyn þing so on haf saH, Everything should be had in common,
þat salbe comu*n* vnto þam aH.
Scho þ*at* wil not wirk on þis wise,
Scho salbe warned anes or twise;
And if scho so mend not hir hert,
W*ith* greter payn scho salbe gert.

XXXIV.

For haly writ witnes & sais
How þai þ*at* wons so in abbais
Aw to haue leuer' of al thing
þat leful es to þeir lifing.
And ilkon aw in-like to haue,
And efter mor aw non to craue. [leaf 101]
Bot euer-ilkon, als I air saide, and every-body be satisfied.
Of hir part sal hald hir paide.
And if ony be so vnbayne Grumblers
In word or werk to groch ogayn,
And scho þer-of þan be ascried,
With penance sal scho be chastid. shall be chastised.

1619. MS. *sal gif.*

XXXVI.

De sororibus infirmis.

Special care and kindness should be bestowed on the sick,

When ony of godes saynd[s] es seke,
Aƚƚ þe oþer sal *with* hertes meke
Confort hir & *with* hir dweƚƚ,
Als crist vs kens in his gospeƚƚ:
"Seke I wos," sutħly sais he,
"And kindly com ȝe vnto me.
For þat ȝe did oþer in my name,
Vnto my-self ȝe did þe same."

who, on their part, must be humble

þai þat er seke sal vnder-take
þat oþer þ*am* serues for gode sake
And forto fulfil charite,
And nothing for þ*er* awn degre.

and patient.

In seknes suld þai haf sufferans
And loue god euer of alkyn chancħ.
For þe mor þai er meke & stil,
þe mor mede es ordand þam til.
And so a souerayn sal eue*r* be meke

[leaf 101, bk.]

And bowsum to þam þat er seke,

All provisions should be made for their recovery and comfort,

And *with* gude [wil] alway to spend
On ony þing þat mygħt þ*am* mend,
And ordan seruandes þam vntil,
þat wil þam serue *with* gude wil,

as quiet rooms,

And honest place for to be in,
Whor þai may [s]it *with*-outyn dyn.

baths, balms,

Bathes & bawmes sal þai haue
Als oft-sithes os þai wil craue.
And gladli sal me*n* to þ*am* gete

and meat or fish to eat.

Flesch or fisch, what þai wil ete.
And when þai er fulli amend,
Lif furtħ als þe rewle hase kend.

XXXVII.

Also age should be considered;

A souerayn aw forto be-hald
Ȝapli vnto ȝong & ald,

1643. MS. *saynd.* 1661. MS. *gude alway.* 1666. MS. *it*, apparently a blunder for some verb, possibly *sit* or *li.* 1669. *men* omitted and then added above the line.

þat euer-ilkon in þ*er* degre
Be ordand als þa*m* aw to be,
So þ*at* þe ȝong may trauel tast,
And þe eldest be hordand mast.

the young should do more work.

XXXVIII.

De leccione ad prandium.

During meals one sister should read, conforming to certain rules.

THE couent, when þai set at mete,
For to rede sal þai not for-gete.
On þe sunnday sal on begin,
And al þ*at* wouke scho sal not blin.
Vnto hir felos sal scho say,
Besekand þ*at* þai for hir pray.
And sone when þ*at* scho enters in,
þis vers to say scho sal be-gin :
"**D*omi*ne, labia mea aparies**—
Lord, opin my lippes als gastly lecħ,
And my mothħ sal þi louyng tecħ."
Hir souerain sal blis hir gud spede,
And so scho sal be-gin to rede.
þan of al nose þai salbe stil
And grathly tak entent hir til.
If any of þam nede ogħt to haue,
Softly w*ith* signes þai sal it craue.
And scho þ*at* redes sal sithen ete
W*ith* þa*m* þ*at* serues at þe mete.
And in order þai sal not rede,
Bot who so best can do þ*at* dede,
And most likandly tels & leres
Vnto þa*m* þ*at* þe lesson heres.

[leaf 102]

Ps. li. 15.

Then the others should be silent,

making signs for what they want.

The best reader is to read.

XLI.

In q*ui*b*us* horis reficiant*ur*.

Regulations about meals.

Of time of mete now es to lere,
In times & sesons of þe ȝere.
Fro pas righ̄t vnto witsunñday
At þe sext our ete sal þai,
þe whilk es midday for to mene,
And sine sal þai soupe bedene.

After Easter: dine at the sixth hour, and sup.

1686, 1690. MS. *salbe gin.*

[leaf 102, bk.] In summer: feed at the ninth hour on Wednesday and Friday (save at haytime and harvest),

In somer, fro witsunday be past,
Wedinsday & friday sal þai fast,
Bot if þai oþer swink or swete
In hay or corn *with* trauel grete.
And if þai non slike trauel done,
On þos days sal þai fast to none.

at the sixth hour on other days.

And on oþer days, als I air saide,
At mydday sal þer mete be graide.
Bot al þis salbe purued playn
At þe ordinance of þer souerayn.
What seson so scho putes þa*m* to,
W*ith*-outin groching sal þai do.

In winter: feed at the ninth hour.

Fro time þ*at* december be-gin
Vntil clene lentyn cu*m* in,
At hi none sal þai ete;
þer lesons sal þai not for-gete.

During Lent: fast,

In lentyn sal non to mete gang,
Or efter þe our of euyn-sang;
And al seruys þan sal þai sai
Efter mete bi light of day,
So þ*at* al be rewlid right

and go to bed by daylight.

At wend to bede bi dais lyght.

XLII.

Vt non loq*ua*nt*ur* post complectoriu*m*.

After the last meal

IN times when þai sal soup infere,
þen sal þai set efter soppere

[leaf 103] follows collation with reading of the Bible or lives of saints—

Al in a stede, whor þai wil sit,
And rede lessons of hali writ
Or els of liues of hali men,
þat gastly co*m*fort may þa*m* ken.
Tales of trofils þai sal non tel,
Ne oþer maters þa*n* of mel,
þat may let haly orisoun
Or driue þam fro deuocioun.

on fasting-days it is after evensong—

On fastyngdais, in ilka place,
Efter euynsang a litil space
In a stede þai sal set down
And mak a schort colaciown.

1727. MS. *albe.*

And als son os þai haf doñe,
Al samen sal þai wend ful son
Vnto complin, mor & myñ.
And efter þe our of complin
In þ*er* hertes al sal þai hurd,
And non haue lef to spek a word,
Bot gestes or oþer þinges it gar—
Bot þai spek it mygħt be-war—
Or if þ*er* souerayn say þam to
Nedeful thinges þai er to do.
Vnto hir sal þai answer þan
Als curtesly als euer þai kan.
And preuely so sal þai say,
Þat non þam here bot scho & þay.
And oþer speking salbe none
Fro tyme þ*at* þai haue complyn done.

and then compline, whereafter all speaking is forbidden except to guests, or by the superior's orders.

[leaf 103, bk.]

XLIII.

Vt cito veni*a*nt ad missam & ad mensa*m*.

Als son als þai here þe beles
To mes, matyns, or ogħt els,
Þan sal þai hast þam on al wise
Sone to com to godes seruyse.
Wheder so euer þai sit or stand,
Al thyng sone sal þai lef of hand
And wigħtly to þe kirk at win;
Bot neuer-þe-les þai sal not ryn.
And who es not redy grayd,
When glo*r*ia efter þe first saulm es said,
In order þen þai sal not be,
Bot stand in þe lawest degre,
Þat þai be of þer souerayn sene
And of þair sisters al be-dene.
And so þai sal wi*th* repentans
Mak amendes for swilk a chanħ.
For in þam-self þai sal haue schame

All should be punctual about worship hours.

Those who come late to night-service shall stand in the lowest place.

1756. *þay* was subsequently altered into *day;* cf. Notes. 1772. MS. *albe dene.* 1775–1778 were written, by mistake, in this order: 1776, 1778, 1775, 1777. Then, by way of correction, the letters *b, d, a, c* were added in the margin.

þat þai er worthi to ber' slik blaym.
In þe quer' sal þai stand algate,
And al if on cu*m* neue*r* so late;
[leaf 104] For els sum wold take no kepe,
Bot oþer ianglyng or els slepe,
And als for þai þat standes in quere
Sal haue part of al þ*at* þai here.
Those late for day-service
And if on dwel so lang oway
At ony of þe houres of þe day,
shall receive the same punishment.
þe same þan salbe þeir mede,
And noþer sal þai sing ne rede.
In þe lawest stede sal þai stand,
Bot if þeir souerayn þa*m* co*m*mand.
Those not punctual about their meals
At þe mete so sal it fair
Of þam þ*at* er not redi þair
To say þe grace & take þe*r* sete;
shall wait till later
þai sal bide to þe latte*r* mete.
And who so wil not be chastid,
Til langer efter sal scho bide
And sine be hir allayn to sit,
and have less to eat or drink.
And su*m* seruice sal hir want ȝit
Of mete or drynk þ*at* myght hir glade,
Vntil scho haue amendes mayde.
þe same payn es to þa*m* puruayde
þat bides [not] til þe grace be sayde
Efter mete, als it es vsed,
Bot þai haue caus to be excused.

XLIV.

[leaf 104, bk.]

De mo*d*o satisfaccionis.

Atonement is to be made by such as are excommunicated.

Scho þ*at* es for cursed kend
And wilfully wil hir amend,
Scho sal wait þe tyme of þe day
When þe couent in þe schapite*r* pray,
They shall fall face down on the floor before the church-door;
And doun scho sal fall in þe flore
Opon hir face be-for þe dore,
And oblis hir vntil þe*r* fete
Murnand sore hir mys to bete.
And ilk day sal þis be hir mese,

1800. MS. *bides til.* 1811. MS. *ilkday.*

Vntil hir souerayn bid hir sese.
And if hir souerayn þedir hir caƚƚ, — *and then in the church they shall lie down,*
Vntil hir fete first sal scho faƚƚ,
And sine lig in hir aller way
Besekand þa*m* for hir to pray.
If hir souerayn, þ*at* hase powerʼ,
Gif hir leue to cum in querʼ,
On hir knes doun sal scho faƚƚ, — *and kneel,*
þat scho may be sene of þam aƚƚ. — *so as to be seen of all.*
þis penance ilk day sal scho do,
Vntil hir souerayn se þerto.
And when scho ful mendyng may trow,
Scho sal say: "sese! it suffes now."

XLVIII.

De ope*r*ibus cotidianis.

Aƚƚ þ*at* wons in religioun — *All should be active in worship,*
Aw to haue sum ocupacioun
Ouþer in kirk of hali bedes — [leaf 105]
Or stodying in oder stedes. — *study,*
For ydilnes, os sais sant paul,
Es grete enmy vnto þe saul.
And þerfor es ordand þ*at* þai
Sum gude warkes sal wirk alway,
And sum certane times of þe ȝerʼ
To wirk wi*th* hand, os men may herʼ. — *or manual labour.*
Fro pase, thurgħ al cristyndome, — *In summer:*
Til þe kalandes of october cum,
Vnto p*r*ime sone sal þai rise, — *rise at prime,*
And sine ilkon wirk on þer wise — *work till the third hour,*
What so es most nedeful labore
Vntil þe tyme of þe third oure.
And lessons sal þai rede þan next — *read till the sixth,*
Fro þe third our vnto þe sext.
And efterward thurgħ wirchep * — *go to worship,*
Fro oures & mes wend vnto mete. — *have a meal,*
And efter mete, þen sal þai slepe, — *and sleep;*
And silence al samen sal þai kepe,

1821. MS. *ilkday.* 1843. The rhyme-word is missing, possibly *kete,* 'glad,' 'gladdened,' 'strengthened.'

So þ*a*t none do oþer disese,
Bot ilkon paid oþer to plese.
Sone efterward, when þis es done
> after the ninth hour, work till

And þai haf said þe our of none,
Vntil þeir werk þen sal þai gang
> [leaf 105, bk.]

Vnto þe tyme of euynsang,
> evensong in the field, &c.

To scher' or bind, if it be nede,
Or dike or els do oþer dede.
For vnto trauel wor we born,
And al our elders vs be-forn.
Bot trauel aw mesurd to be
Til ilkon efter þer degre,
To men or women, old or ȝing,
Ilkon to do diuers þing.
> In winter:

Fro october, os I are sayd,
Vnto lentyn es þus puruayd:
> pray and do lessons.

In orisons & in þer oures
And lessons salbe þer laboures.

De obseruanciis in xl^{esima}.

> In Lent:

IN lentyn tyme þen sal þai rise
Arly, & say þer seruyse
> pray till past the third hour,

And orisons til godes honoure,
Vntil it be past þe third oure.
> work till the tenth, and serve in church.

Þan to þe tent our sal þai wirk,
And sine til non serue in þe kirk.
And in lentyn aw þa*m* to luke
Þat ilkon haue ordand a buke,
> A book is to be read through.

Whilk salbe red right to þe end,
Als þe cours of þe rewl hase kend.
And who so groches oght here-o-gayn
> [leaf 106]

Salbe punest w*ith* greu*us* payne.
Who tentes to trofils & wil not rede
And þai ouertayn w*ith* þ*a*t dede,
W*ith* payn þai sal amendes make,
So þ*a*t oþer ensaumpil take.

XLIX.

> During Lent special

In lentyn aw þa*m* to be clere
Be-for all oþer times of þe ȝere,

1864b originally belongs to the following chapter.

In haly bedes þ*at* tyme to lif,
And vnto god haly þa*m* gif,
Abstenand þa*m* fro drynk & mete,
And gif þam vnto penance grete,
And fand to fle al flescħ likyng
And honor god ouer alkines þing.
W*ith* clene desire so sal þai bide
þe tyme of paise, þai sal þ*at* tide,
And kepe þ*at*, lord, so w*ith* clene life,
þ*at* medcyn es to man & wife.

purity, devotion, and abstinence are required.

L.

þai þ*at* sal walk bi way, or wirk,
And may not cum to haly kirk,
In what stede so þai be sett,
þeir seruyse sal þai not for-gete,
Bot kepe alƚ þe oures of þe day
W*ith* als grete honoure os þai may,
And say þ*er* seruyse in ilk seson
Witħ wil & gude deuocioun.

Sisters out far away from the church should observe the hours of worship as well as circumstances allow.

[leaf 106, bk.]

LI.

And if on sal on erand wend
Furthward vnto ony frend
A þinkes to com a-gayn þ*at* day,
Al if men vnto mete þam pray,
For to ete sal þai not assent,
Bot if þai asked leue, or þai went.
And who so trispas in þis þing,
þai ryn in peryl of cursyng.

Those out for the day must accept no food.

LII.

De orac*ione* in secret*is*.

IN chapit*er* or kirk who likes to lend,
When godes seruys is sayd til end,
To mak þeir meditaciouns
In haly p*ra*yers & orisouns,
So preuely þen sal þai pray,
þat non oþer here quat þai say.
And preualy furtħ sal þai wyn,

Private devotion should be quiet,

so as not to disturb any one else.

þat þai let none þ*at* lefes þerin.
þus euer ilkon sal hald silence,
When þai sal p*ray* in godes p*re*cens,
Noghħ w*ith* crying ne voce ful grete,
Bot wiħ murnyng on brest to bete.
Who so wil not do os I tel,
In p*ra*yng þai sal not dwel,
Bot furħ þai sal be had in hy,
[leaf 107] þat oþer be not harmyd þerby.

LIII.

De hospitib*us* suscipiend*is*.

Guests should be received charitably

A Priores aw to be prest
Forto resaue ilka gude gest
And at hir myghħ þam mere make
Soueraynly for godes sake,
Namely þam þ*at* er pilgrams knawn,
And pouer þ*at* hase not of þe*r* awn.
For god vntil [vs] þus sal say
In dome, a-pon þe dredful day :

(Matth. xxv. 35) for Christ's sake,

" **Hospes eram et colligist*is* me**—
I wos a gest in my degre,
And in ȝour hous ȝe herberd me."
þan aw vs gestes & gud pilgrims
For to releue in al þere lims
And for to refresħ in al righħ,
Als it es det be day & nyghħ,

be given the kiss of peace,

And oblis þam kissink of pese
Perfite luf forto encres.
And when þai cu*m*, bi day or nyghħ,
And also when þai wend to flighħ,

be bowed humbly to,

Loute vnto þam aw grete & smaƚƚ
Or els vnto þer fete at faƚƚ,
Witand wele in þat sesoune
þai honour crist in þer pe*r*soune.
For who so resaues þe pure man
[leaf 107, bk.] In crist name, resaues crist þan.
A souerayn sal ger gestes kepe

1931. MS. *vntil þus.*

Witħ honour & wit*h* gret wirchepe
and treated honourably.
Or rede to þa*m*, or ger be rede,
How hali men þe*r* liues lede,
So þ*a*t *he be to þam puplist,
How þai sal lif be þe law of crist.
A priores hir fast sal breke,
A prioress may eat with and talk to her guests,
And silence, when scho suld not speke,
To myrtħ hir gestes in þ*a*t scho may,
Bot if it be dere fasting day
except on special days.
And ymbrin-days or els vigil,
Whilk ilka man es bun vntil.
Bot al if scho brek, be ȝe bold,
þe couent sal þeir rigħt curs hald.
Scho sal gif water vnto þe*r* hend
She shall give them water, and wash their feet.
And wescħ þeir fete, als crist hase kend.
When þai so do, þai sal reherce,
Word bi word, & say þis verce:
" **Suscepim***us*, **de***us*, **mi***sericordi***am tua***m* **in med***io*—
Ps. xlviii. 9.
We haue resauyd, lord, þi mercy
In þe mydes of þe hows haly."
On þis maner crist wil vs ken
To resaue pilgrims & pouer men,
For when we þa*m* resaue wit*h* wil,
[leaf 108]
Crist resaue we vs vntil.
þe gestes kechin salbe set
They shall have a kitchen to themselves,
Allone, þ*a*t it no noþer let,
So þat þai be seruyd at ese,
And ilkman redy þa*m* to plese.
And luk þer bedes ordand bene
beds with litter and clean clothes,
Wit*h* litter larcħ & clotħes clene,
And swilk seruandes assigned þa*m* til
and servants to attend them.
þat wil þam serue wit*h* gude wil.
None aw þam do forto greue,
Ne speke wit*h* þam wit*h*-outyn leue,
Bot loutand hals þam wher þai go
And wit*h* blissing pase furtħ þam fro.

1953. *he* is a mistake, possibly for *þer* or *it*. 1961. Originally *bald*. 1963. MS. *hand*. 1968. Originally *þi hows*.

LIV.

Vt nichil accipiant sine lisencia.

Letters and gifts can be accepted and disposed of

If litters or bils be sent to rede,
Or oþer giftes of greter mede
Be send fro frendes in feld or toun
Til women of religioun,

only at the discretion of the prioress.

Scho sal resaue non hir vntil,
Bot scho first wit hir souerayn wil.
And if hir frendes fer or nere
Send hir gudes or giftes sere,
Or scho þam tak for ony nede,

[leaf 108, bk.]

To þe priores scho sal þa*m* bede.

If she gives them away,

And if þe priores at hir wil
Gif þo giftes a-noder vntil,

the sister must not be grieved.

Scho vnto wham þe giftes whor sent,
Sal not be greuyd in hir entent,
If hir presand be so puruayd,
Bot in hert sal scho hold hir payde.
For what þe*r* souerayn dose ilk dele
Aw þam to think worthi & wele.

LV.

De indumentis.

Regulations about clothes in different climates.

Thay sal be clede ful wele, we wate,
Efter þe*r* place es cald or hate.
For in cald stedes who so er sted,
þam nedes forto be better cled;
In who er in hate cuntre,
Sich clething to þa*m* may be.
And al it sal be puruayd playne
At þe ordinance of þeir souerayne.

Generally, a kirtle and coat are enough,

In comu*n* places for alkins note
Sufficis a kirtil & a cote;
And mantels sal þai haue certayne,
In winter dubil, in somer playne;

with another kirtle for night-use (cf. l. 1202).

And changing kirtils sal þai haue
In nyghtes þer oþer forto saue.
Schos þai sall haue, whor þai dwel,

[leaf 109]

Swilk os þai may find for to sel.
Of þe farest þai sal not by,

Bot þe vilist ful bowsumly.
And þeir souerayn aw forto se
þat þair gere euynly o[r]dand be,
Mete for þa*m* þat sal it fang,
And noþer to schort ne to lang.
When þai tak new, þe old sal þen
Be p*ar*tid til pouer women.
And when þai sal went in cuntre,
þair clething sal mor honest be;
And home a-gayn when þai cu*m* eft,
þen sal þai were slik os þai left.
Vntil þeir beddyng sal þai haue
At suffise þa*m* fro cauld to saue.
And oftsithes saƚƚ þer' bed be sene,
þat no tresure be þa*m* be-twene,
Ne no gude þ*at* to þa*m* may gayne;
Who so it hase, saƚƚ soffer payne.
For whi þ*er* souerayn sal þa*m* bede
Aƚƚ vnto þa*m* þat es nede.
Bot when scho gifes, scho sal be-hald
To þis þ*at* holi writ hase tald
And set to se for certayne
In þe dedes of þe appostil[s] playne:
"**Diuidebatur sing*u*lis, p*r*out cuiq*ue* op*us* erat.**"
He tels how crist depairtid hase
Intil ilkon, os myster was.
So suld a souerayn in hir daile
Tak reward to seke & haile,
To ȝing or old, wheder þai be,
And serue ilkon in þeir degre.

Old clothes shall be given to the poor.

When going out, nuns shall have better garments;

for beds, have only enough clothes to keep out the cold.

(Cf. ch. xxxiii, xxxiv.)

[leaf 109, bk.]

Acts iv. 35.

LVI.

De mensa priorisse.

A Priores bord aw forto be
Euer-mor vntil al gestes fre,
þ*at* es to mene vnto pouer men.
And when non cu*m*es, scho sal take þen
Of þe eldest & þe most nedy
Of hir sisters þat wons hir by,

The prioress' table should always be open to guests,

or else to some of the sisters.

2022. MS. *odand.* 2039. MS. *salbe hald.* 2042. MS. *appostil.*

In stede of pouer folk, þam to fede ;
So may scho wyn hir mykil mede.

LVII.

If any one can earn money at any work, it must be handed over to the superior

If ony woman can ogħt do
þat ony wining falles vnto,
Aħ þe p*ro*phet of þeir wyning
Vnto þeir souerayn sal þai bryng.
And if ony hafe pryde þ*er*-by,
It sal be tayn fro þ*am* in hy,
And neu*er* more sal þay negħ nere,
Bot þe priores gif þam power.

[leaf 110]

And þ*at* sal not faħ, bot scho se
þat þai be meke & obidient be,
And wil gif al þeir wyning fayn

and be disposed of by her.

To þe ordenance of þer souerayn,
And wil luf god in ilka place,
þat gifes to þam swilk giftes of grace.

LVIII.

De p*ro*bacione suscipiendor*um*.

If a woman of full age wants reception as a nun,

Aħ if a woman ful eld haue,
And religion wil to hir craue,
And hase non entisment þer-til
Bot oblis hir awn wil,

it should be granted only after long probation.

Fully resauyd sal scho not be,
Or tyme þai hir p*er*seuerans se
And prow hir botħ be nygħtes & days,
Als þe appostil playnly says.
Hir hert & wil er botħ to proue,
If þai be gifin til godes bi-houe,
And mak þam forto vnderstand
þe hardnes of religioun band.

She shall wait 4 or 5 days for leave to enter,

And if scho bide iiij days or fyue
And schews grete lawnes in hir liue,
Vnto hir salbe gr*au*nte entre ;
Bot als a gest ȝit sal scho be
And sine a place forto haue grayde,

and shall [leaf 110, bk.] then have a mistress

Als vnto nouysces es puruayd,
And a mastres her forto lere

2076. *þai*, MS. $þ^{t}$. See Notes.

Hir obseruandes & seruys sere,
to teach her.
And to schew hir botħ gude & ill
þat scho salbe obidient til.
And if scho be willy always
If she obeys her mistress 2 months,
To suffer what hir mastres sais,
Sithen efter ij monetħ space,
þan sal þai bring þis rewle in place
the rule shall be read to her;
And tel vntil hir opinly
þis law þ*at* hir aw to lif by.
When it es red on rigħt array,
þe priores sal til hir say:
"þis rewle if þou may ȝeme & saue,
We g*ra*nt þe entre here to haue;
And if þou may not þerwi*th* lend,
We g*ra*nt þe lefe frely to wend."
And if scho þan wil langer dwel,
and if she will obey it, she shall live as a novice
Scho sal bide in þe noues sel
At gud laser to lig & rise,
So þ*at* scho may hir wele awise
In hir hert, if scho be bald
þe rewle to tak þ*at* scho es tald.
When sex monetħs er fully goñ,
for 6 months. Then the [leaf 111] rule shall be read again to her;
þen saƚƚ þis rewel eft furtħ be toñ
And red to hir, os mykil os nedes,
How scho sal rewle botħ wordes & dedes.
And if scho ȝit wil lely last,
When xij moneths er playnly past,
and if after 4 more months
þis sal eft be to hir red,
So þat scho be not lyghtli led,
And þat scho wit be on & on
þe pontes wher-to scho hase hir tone.
And if scho so witħ a-visement
Hete to fulfil wi*th* gude entent
she keeps her resolve,
What so þai deme bi day or nygħt,
þen sal scho be resauyd right
Into þe kirk emang þam aƚƚ;
she shall be received in the church,
And þ*at* day þerin dwel scho saƚƚ.
In hir-self þen sal scho knaw
þ*at* scho sal neuer, for godes aw,
never to quit the rule again.
Fro þ*at* rewle reklisly gang,

Sen þ*at* scho es avised so lang.
Then in the chapter
To chapitur sine scho salbe tayn
In-mang þe couent euer-ilkayn,
she shall vow to God to fulfil her promise, [leaf 111, bk.]
And vnto god þer sal scho hete,
Falland doun be-for þer fete,
þat scho saƚƚ fathfuly fulfiƚƚ
Al þat þai haue told hir tiƚƚ.
and to Mary, and the saints.
Vnto mary, crist*es* moder dere,
And to al halows of heuy*n* clere
Sal scho hete þer þam emang.
þan may scho wit: if scho do wrang
Or maynten it not w*ith* hir mayine,
Al wil þai witnes hir ogayne.
þan sal scho make blitħly hir bown
She shall lay her petition
And puruay hir peticioun.
W*ith* hir awn hand it salbe wroght,
Or witħ a-noþer, if scho can noght;
Bot scho sal luke þ*at* it be lele,
And set þerto signet or sele.
on the altar,
On þe awter scho sal it lay,
And þer wordes þen sal scho say:
(Ps. cxix. 116)
"**Suscipe me, d*omi*ne, secu*n*dum eloq*u*ium tuu*m*, et viua*m*, & non confund*ar*.**"
And þir same [wordes] on þis wise
Sal þai ilkon reherce thrise
Witħ "**gl*or*ia p*at*ri**" put þerto
And "Sicut erat" sine also.
þe nouese þan be-for þam aƚƚ
fall flat on the earth,
Al flat vnto þe ertħ sal faƚƚ,
[leaf 112]
Besekand þam on ilka side
and ask all to pray for her.
For to pray for hir þat tide.
Then she shall be one of the convent,
Fro þat day sal scho rekynd be
On þe couent in hir degre.
and give all she has to the poor
And al þe þinges þ*at* scho hase þen,
Ouþer sal scho ȝif þa*m* to pouer men,
Besekand þam for hir to pray,
or to her abbey.
Or els vnto hir awn abbay.
Vnto hir-self scho sal haue noght
Of al þat scho hase þeder broght.

2141. MS. *hirmayine.* 2151. MS. *same on.*

Vntil oþer scho sal it take,
And hir awn wil scho sal for-sake.
Hir awn wedes scho sal lay doun
And take clotħs of religioun.
Hir cloths sal þan albedene
Be samyn layd & kepid clene,
Þat if case faƚƚ at þe ȝere end
Þ*at* scho in-to þe world wil wend,
Þe same wede þ*at* scho can for-sake,
Þat sal scho were & wi*th* hir take.
Bot hir bil of peticioun
Saƚƚ leue stil in religioun.

She shall put off her own clothes, and put on monastic ones.

But if, at a year's end, she returns to the world, she shall have her former dress.

LIX.

De nouicijs iuuenib*us* suscipiend*is*.

[leaf 112, bk.]

[M]ay fal þat ouþer man or wife
Wold haue þer' child * haly life,
And offer it vnto haly kirk;
On þis wise þam aw to wirk:
If þer child be so ȝung,
Þat it can not tel witħ tung
What es to leue ne what to take,
Þen sal þe frendes peticions make.
Tak þai sal þe childes hand
And bil & þer' awn offerand
Wi*th* reuerence, os þe rewle hase kend,
And law al on þe awter end.
And when þai mak peticioun,
A certayn soume þai sal lay doune,
Or els hete of þer gudes to gif
Whor-of þer child may lere to lif.
Til it-self sal þai gif no thing,
Gold ne siluer, brocħ ne ryng,
Bot opinly it gif sal þai
Vnto god & to þe abbay,
And childer þ*at* frenchep hase none,
For godes sake þai salbe tone.

If a young child is offered to the Church, its relatives shall lay their petition on the altar, and pay or promise money for its keep.

Poor children shall be taken for God's sake.

2179. Cf. p. 9, l. 22 ff. 2180. A prep. (*in*) or verb (*lede*, *lere*) seems to be omitted. 2183 and 2184 were written, by mistake, in the reverse order. Then the letters *b* and *a* were added in the margin. Cf. 1775 ff. The words *it* and *not* in 2184 were omitted and then added above the line.

LXIII.

Equals, in a sense, the [leaf 113] juniors and seniors should show each other

And fro time þai resauyd be,
Al salbe sarued in o degre,
Rich & pure, & ȝong & old,
In form os be-for es told.
Bot þe ȝong, whor so þai err,

reverence

Sal *ordan þam þat er elder,
And þe elder in alkins þing

and love.

Sal luf & lere þam þat er ȝing.

The youngest is 'Damsel,' the elder is 'Madam,' the prioress is 'Lady.'

"Damisel" þe ȝongest es,
þe elder "mad*au*m" & "mastres."
þe Priores als principall
Es "lady" & leder of þam all,
And not al for hir awn bi-houe,
Bot for hir staite & crist*es* luf.
And whor so euer þai gang o-boute,

The younger shall bow to the elder.

þe ȝonger sal þe elder loute
And do þam reuerence, als es right,
In word & dede, be day & nyght.

LXIV.

De elecc*ion*e priorisse.

The prioress should be elected by the whole convent,

A Priores aw to be chosen
þe best in lifyng leli losen,
Be ordinance & bi hali assent
And councel of al þe couent,

according to real merit.

Takand non for luf ne mede,
Ne leueand non for aw ne drede;
Bot for gude luf & for godes sake

[leaf 113, bk.]

A worthi souerayn sal þai take,
Whilk þai knaw perfite & stabil,
And als emang þai*m* most abill
Of wit & cunsel & of cunyng,
And vsand euynhed in al thing.

Otherwise

And if it fel, os god forbede,
þat ony wold for worldly mede
Samyn be þam-self assent,
Wit*h*-outyn consel of þe couent,
Forto chese swilk a souerayn

2206. *ordan*, corrupt for *honor* or the like? Cf. p. 9, l. 13.

Als to þer bedynges wold be bayn,
And þair doyng wor fundyn slike,
þen sal þe bisschop of þ*a*t rike
Swilk a p*r*iores sone depose,
And mak on bi þeir aller chose.

the election is void, the bishop shall depose her,

And foles þ*a*t in þer fatħ wil fayle,
þai salbe chastid fro cownsaile,
So þ*a*t in godes hows may be
A gude ȝemer of godes menȝe.
For wit þai wele þ*a*t þai sal cu*m*
To reknyng on þe day of dome
For þer myschesing þam omang,
Als sche sal for hir warkes wrang.

and the guilty will have to answer for it at the Day of doom.

And if þai chese wele & lely,
þa*n* falles a ful grete mede þerby,
So þat þai tak gude rewarde
þat noder on be spede ne oþerʼ sparde
For no ponte þ*a*t men may pruefe,
Bot anely for our lordes lufe.

[leaf 114]

When scho es chosin on þis manerʼ
And confermyd in hir playne powerʼ,
þen aw hir forto luke allayn
Vnto þ*a*t charcħ þ*a*t scho hase tayn
And vnto wham hir aw to ȝeld
Reknyng botħ in ȝoutħ in eld,
Iħ or wele wheþerʼ scho spend
þe charcħ þat scho hase tayn in hend.

The prioress has great responsibility.

Al if scho be highest in degre,
In hir-self lawest sal scho be.
Hir aw to be gude of forthoghħt
What thinges es to wirk & what noght,
Chaste & soberʼ, meke & myld,
Of bering bowsum os a child.
Sin & vices sal scho hate
And luf hir sisters ayrly & laite.

Though highest, she should be lowest, have forethought, be chaste and childlike, hate sin and love her sisters.

Scho salbe sober in al thyng
And naymly in hir chastying,
To lay on þam þ*a*t vnder hir erʼ
No euyer band þan þay may berʼ,

As ruler she must be considerate.

[leaf 114, bk.]

2257. MS. *alleyn*.

þat whils scho rubes a-way þe rust,
þe vessel fal not al to dust.
Hir maistri euer sal mesurd be,
The prioress must think of her own frailty, Thinkand on hir awn frelte
Lik to a rede in a forest,
þat bows *with* wind & wil not brest.
Scho sal so her' what ilkon sais,
be wise, And be wise in hir wordes alwais.

De condicionib*us* Priorisse.

A Priores hertly sal hast
zealous, Al vice & syns away to waist
And ordan for þam gastly bute,
Or tyme þ*at* þai haue takin rute,
And ordan alway hir entent
gain her sisters' love, For to be lufid of hir couent,
þ*at* þai hir honor in word & dede
For luf & not aynly for drede.
Scho sal not be *con*trarius
Ne ouer-lyghtly suspecius.
In al hir bidinges scho salbe
be reasonable, Resonabil & also avise,
Wheder it be for gastly thing
Or worldly þ*at* scho makes bidyng.
And when scho comaundes oght to do,
[leaf 115] Swilk rewling sal scho hafe þ*er*-to,
and moderate þat it be mesured on gude maners,
Als sant Ion þe apostil leres :
"**Si greges meos faciam &c.**—
If I ger my bestes," he sais,
" Trauel mor be nyghtes or dais
þan þer power p*er*fourn may,
þan wil þai fall down in þe way."
þus bi ensaumpil sal scho take
Materly al thinges to make,
in deed and speech. And þ*at* al thinges in dede & saw
Be mesured euermor os þa*m* aw,
And ilka thing in þer degre,
Bodely or gastly wheder it be.
If she fulfils her duty, And þis ilk rewle þus if scho rede

2276. MS. *alto.*

And fulfil it in word & dede,
þen may scho þer wordes vnderstand,
How crist says of a gud seruand :
“ **Sup*er* o*mn*ia bona sua constituet eum.**”
He þ*at* in life es funden lele
In word & wark alway to wele,
Hym wil þe lord w*ith*-outyn lete
Ouer al his gudes assingne & sett
And haly put in-til his hand
Botħ corn & katel, Hows & land,
And chancħ hym wil he for no new
Be reson þ*at* he findes him trew.
And efterward for his gude dede
þe lord wil larcħly gif him mede.
So sal al þo haue wele, we knaw,
þ*at* trewly dos euer os þam aw.

she will understand Christ's words in Matth. xxiv. 47, that a loyal servant will be set over goods, [leaf 115, bk.] house and land, and great will be his reward.

LXVIII.

Si inpossibilia iniungentur.

A Priores, als I sayd air,
Aw to be mesured euermair
To bind non bot als þai may bere,
And efter þer warkes worthi ere,
And bid non do by nygħt & day
Vn-mesurely mor þan þai may.
And if scho put any vntil
Mor wark þen þai may fulfil,
Til hir bedynges þai sal be bayn
And noþ*er* grucħ ne spek ogayn.
Bot forther, if þai se in sigħt
þ*at* þe trauel passes þ*er* mygħt,
Vn-to hir sal þai pray mekely
Forto relese þa*m* sum p*ar*ty,
Telland to hir al þ*er* encheson.
And if scho wil not her' þer reson,
ȝit saƚƚ þai not þam-self it slake,
Bot suffer it for godes sake,
Thinkand on þair mikil mede ;
þan sal god strengħ in þer dede.

A prioress, as is said before, should be moderate and just. But even if she sets a nun over-hard tasks, they should be received in humility [leaf 116] and patience, for God's sake.

2318. MS. *assingnes.* 2321. *he*, MS. *I.* 2329. MS. *als bot.*

LXIX.

Outward slander should be carefully avoided.

And on al wise þai sal take tent,
þat no þing be doñ in couent,
In word ne wark ne nokins wise,
Whar-of outward myght sclaunder rise.

LXX.

Vt nulla aliam cedat vel offendat.

Tham aw to tent vnto þis þing,
No nun shall beat another
þat non of þa*m* sal oþer dyng,
Ne none herdy oder to greue,
except by the prioress' leave.
Bot at þe Priores gifes leue
And power oþer to chasty
þat funden er in ony foly.
And þai þat opinly er blamyd,
Al opinly þai sal be shamyd,
So þat oþer may wernyd be
Fro al slik folis forto fle.
The novices should be under a mistress till the age of fifteen.
þe nouece þat þis rewle sal lere,
Vntil þai be past xv ȝere,
Sal be in keping of mastres
To chasty þam, when worthi es,
Als it falles þe trispas to.
[leaf 116, bk.]
And oþer-wise if þat scho do,
Scho sal be punyst for þat dede;
For it es writyn, os men may rede:
" Vntil a-noþer þou sal not do
Bot os þou wold wor don þe to."
On þe sam wise saƚƚ ilk souerayn
Do os þai wil take o-gayn.

LXVII.

De exeuntib*us* et redeuntibus.

When sisters set out on journeys,
A sister, when scho sal oute wende
To fadir or moder or oþer frend,
þan sal scho tak *with* gude entent
Hir leue of aƚƚ þe hale couent,
prayers should be offered;
Besekand þam for hir to pray
þat god hir wise in aƚƚ her way.

2351. The *h* in *Tham* was added subsequently.

And al þe couent, smaƚƚ & grete,
Aw no day forto for-gete,
Bot ilkay day to mak þer bone,
When seruys of þe day es done,
For þer sister þ*at* er not þair,
þ*at* god enforce þa*m* in þer fair.
And when on so hase bene to play,
When scho cu*m*mes ħome, al þe first day
Prayng sal þai put þa*m* to,
Besekand oder to pray also
þ*at* god for-gif wit*h* gude entent,
If þai oght wrethid hym, sen þai went,
In sigħt or in hering of eres,
In word or dede þ*at* þe sawle deres,
Or wantunly if þai haf wrogħt
Outher in word, or dede, or thogħt.
Of god þai sal ask for-gifnes
And make amendes for mor & lese.
To þer sisters þai sal not teƚƚ,
Whils þai wer furtħ how it befeƚƚ
Of thing þ*at* mygħt ogħt turn to tene;
For of slik hase harmes bene sene.
Ne outward sal þai no thing say
þ*at* es done wit*h*-in þeir abbay;
Ne oute of close sal þai not pas,
Bot þai leue of þ*er* souerayn ass;
Ne no charge and thing sal þai do,
Bot if þai haue hir lef þerto.
And who so dose ogħt here-ogayn
Efter þe rewle sal suffer' payn.

likewise during their absence

and on their return.

[leaf 117]

If they have displeased God in any way,

they must ask His forgiveness.

They must be silent about their experiences.

No one must go beyond bounds without permission.

LXVI.

De officio hostiarij.

An old man should be gate-keeper,

Ane old man sal þe ȝates ȝeme
þ*at* witti es & wele wil seme
For to welcu*m* wit*h* wordes fre
Euyr-ilk man in þer degre. [leaf 117, bk.]
His dwelling sal be dygħt algayte
In a cel be-side þe ȝate,

2405. MS. *chargeand.*

always ready

So *þat* he be redy ay
Til al *þat* cums be nyght or day.
And when so ony knok or caƚƚ,
Softli answer þam he saƚƚ.

and willing.

To herʼ þer wordes sal he be bayn
And bryng þam grath answer ogayn.
And baynly sal he bryng & take
Al *þat* men sendes for godes sake.
And euer him aw to ȝeme þe ȝate
For al auenturs arely & layte.

Well, offices, and gardens should be inside the enclosure.

In abbais aw to be al thing
Þat nedeful es to þeir lifing,
Als watter for to do al þer dedis,
Miln, kiln, & ouen, & al *þat* nedis,
Gardins, & al oþer gerʼ
With-in þa*m* wroght, *þat* þai sal werʼ,
So *þat* þai sal not outward gang
To say for dred, or wirk, oght wrang.

The rule should be frequently rehearsed.

Þus es þis rewle ordand to rede
[Als] Oft-sithes als it es nede,
So *þat* non sal þa*m* excuse,

[leaf 118]

To knaw þeir rewle & right it vse.

LXXI.

De obediencia ad inuicem.

The juniors should,

Ilk sister saƚƚ obedient be
Vnto oþerʼ in þair degre,
Witand *þat* es þe sekirʼ way
Vnto þe lif þat lastes ay.

with due preference given to the prioress and the functionaries,

Bot þe Priores os prencipaƚƚ
Sal be honord ouer þam aƚƚ;
And oþer, efter þai haue power,
Salbe honord *with* seruis serʼ.

honour and obey their seniors.

And sithen sal ilkon bainly bow
To honourʼ oder & wil þ*er* prow.

If any one disobeys or displeases the prioress,

And who so euer vnbowsu*m* es
Or rebel to þerʼ priores,
Or greues hir in ony degre,
Al if þe trispas litil be,

2434. MS. *Oft sithes als;* cf. 1668, 2113.

Be-for her fete down sal þai faƚƚ,
And so lang þ*er* lig þai saƚƚ.
And who so gruches herˀ-ogayn,
þai sal be gert w*it*h greu*us* payn.
And if þai wil not mend þerby,
þai sal be chaistid fro company.

she shall humbly ask her forgiveness.

LXXII.

For riħt os euel luf mor or les,
þat es fulfilid of bitternes,
Twins fro god, os clerkes teƚƚ,
And ledes a man to pyne of heƚƚ,
Riħt so gude luf in al degre,
þ*at* es fulfillid of charite,
Twins a man fro syn & strif
And ledes him vnto lastand lif.
And þ*at* ilk luf suld sisters haue
Emang þam-self þer saule to saue,
And ilkon honor oþerˀ alwais,
Als þe appostil playnly sais:
“**Honore inuecem preuenientes.**”
Sekenes sal þai gladly bere,
Bodily or gastly wheder þai ere.
þeir awn winyng þai sal not wayt,
þ*at* oþer win þai sal couayt.
God sal þai hertly drede & luf
And þ*er* souerayn for his be-houe,
So þ*at* þai set non erthly þing
Be-for þe luf of crist, heuyn kyng,
For his lofers ledes he euyn
Vntil his kyngdom heħ on heuyn.
Vnto þ*at* kingdom he vs lede,
þ*at* sufferd dede for our mysdede.

Out of the two kinds of love—one evil, [leaf 118, bk.] one good— the latter should pervade the convent (Rom. xii. 10), manifesting itself in patience, unselfishness, and devotion.

LXXIII.

Conclucio toci*us* reg*u*le.

This rewle es ordand þ*us* to rede
To mend our mys & merk vs mede,

This rule,

2463. *fro*, MS. *for*. 2481. The *h* in *This* was added subsequently.

[leaf 119]

And grath teching til vs at gif,
In cristes law [how] we sal lif,
And to draw fro alkin strife
Onto p*er*feccion of gude life.
For it teches to les & more
Of haly faders þat war before.
And if we þ*er*-in haue delite,
It ledes vs to lif p*er*fite.

like Holy Scripture itself,

For al lessons, als men may luke,
þ*at* wretyn er in haly buke,
Wheþer þai be of moises law
Or of cristes, whilk we suld knaw,

the lives of the saints,

And liues of marters & confessours,
And teching of godes dere doctours,
And þ*at* haly virgins lede,

and other rules,

And rewles, þ*at* [er] vntil vs rede,
Of basil, Bede, & oþer mo—

is instructive to the virtuous,

Al er þai teching vs vnto
And ensaumpil how we sal vse
Gude vertuse, & vices refuse.
To þam þ*at* lifes wele, old or ȝing,
Er swilk lessons ful grete likyng.

and confusing to the sinful.

And to þam þ*at* lifes synfully
And refuses to be rewlid þerby,

[leaf 119, bk.]

þan es it gret *con*fucioun
And hertly schame in ilk sesoun.
For if þeir lifyng be vnlele,
þam think dedeyn *with* it to dele.
þerfor al þ*at* þarto hase hight,
Saue þis rewle & ȝeme it ryght,

Pray to God for grace to keep it, and endless bliss shall be thy reward!

And p*ray* god hertly *with* gude wil
To gif þam myght & g*race* þertil.
þen endles lif sal be þair mede.
Vnto þ*at* lif our lord vs lede! //amen.//
A M E N.

//**Explicit.**//

2484. MS. *law we;* cf. 1954. 2497. Possibly: *And liues þat;* cf. 1952. 2498. MS. *þat vntil;* cf. 1951, 2117.

III. THE CAXTON ABSTRACT

OF

The Rule of St. Benet.

(*Cambridge University Library*, *AB.* 4. 64.)

[leaf *aa* 1]
Introduction.

¶ Here felowyth a compendious abstracte translate into englysshe out of the holy rule of saynte Benet for men and wym*m*en, of the habyte therof, the whiche vnderstonde lytyll laten or none / to þe ente*n*t þ*at* they maye often rede / execute the hole rewll and the better kepe it than it is / accordyng to the abyte & their streyte professyon / so that the welle of their sowlys and better emsa*m*ple of that holy relygyon maye be the sooner had and knowen.

(LXIV)
The superiors, duly elected,

HE or she *þ*at* is to be made hede or souereyn in a monestary / in whom all the hole congregac*i*on in one acorde after god consentyth / or els that the more parte therof and sadder wyth god cou*n*seyll chesith.

II.

WHan soo euer ony takyth by true eleccyon the name and dygnytee of an hede or souereyn in relygyon / they owne to shewe in their dedys to their disciples two doctrynes / that is to sey, that all suche good dedys and holy that they teche / þ*at* they first shewe hem by their owne dedys rather than by theyr wordys / And al thynges that they teche their †children and disciples to be contrari to god & their rule / lete her dedes shew openly suche thinges not to be done, soo þ*at* theimselfe be not fou*n*de gylty & reprouable in their doctryne & ensa*m*ple / & redy to see a lytill mote in their disciples eyen / but a grete blocke or beme in their owne they can not espie / but lete it lye styll. The souereyns also shulde not dissymyle in punyshme*n*t and chastysyng of theyr subgettes whan they offende / but assone as the

should live as they teach, and

[† leaf *aa* j, back]

chastise their inferiors.

4. Caxton regularly prints þ[e]. 10. Through þ*at* there arises an anocoluthon. 22. Caxton: *so o* þ[t].

synnes begyn to sprynge / forthwyth cut hem vp by the rote by correccyon accordyng to the rule wythoute accept-ynge of ony persone / Remembryng þ*a*t foles wyƚƚ neuer be corrected with wordis, but rather by chastisment /

III.

The superiors must consult their monks on important matters,

As ofte as ony grete maters arn to be doon in the monestary / aƚƚ þe congregac*i*on is to be caƚƚyd & to be enformed of hem by the souereyns / þe whiche owe to here the myndys of echone syngulerly / for oft tymes oure lorde shewyth to the symplest of the relygyon a thynge that is best therfore. how be it, what som euer shalbe seide of the subgettes / see that it be doon wyth al mekenes and submyssyon of spirite & body / And therevpon the souereyn ouħt to kepe weƚƚ in mynde [† leaf *aa* ij] †the resons or seyenges of euery of theim / and to doo therafter as can be fou*n*de best and proffitable /

and attend to their reasons.

For it is a token of an vnwytty mynde and of a prowde hert of theym that take their owne way oonly & cou*n*seyƚƚ. Also as it is accord-ynge to a disciple for to obey his mayster, soo it is requyred to the souereyn visely & warely and aƚƚ thynges of the place to dispose.

On less important things, the older monks only need be consulted,

To other thynges of lesse charge the souereyn owe to take counseyle of the senyours of the relygion & sadder / Soo þ*a*t euery thyng is to be doone at ony tyme wyth cou*n*seyle accordynge to scripture þ*a*t seyth: "Doo aƚƚ thynges wyth counseyle / & thou shaƚƚ not repente after."

everybody strictly following the rule.

Also bere in thy mynde this synguler note that the hede or the souereyn wyth aƚƚ the congre-gac*i*on streytly be bounde to folowe the rule in euery poynte / & that none of theim be soo bolde to declyne or departe therfro; So that none folowe the wyƚƚ of theyr owne mynde oonly / but euer be redy to be reformyd.

No strife must be raised against the superiors.

The subgettes also owe to be ryght ware þ*a*t they make no strife wythyn or wythout wyth theyr souereyns / yf that they doo, anone lete hem haue the streyt reguler punysshment wyth þe fere of god and in [† leaf *aa* ij, back] †kepynge the rule / remembrynge that the hede withoute ony dowte shaƚƚ yeue a fuƚƚ streyte accompte oo day of aƚƚ their Iugementes & byhauour to god atte ferefuƚƚ daye of rekenynge.

(LXIII)

¶ Also be they ware that they trowble not

13, 34. Caxton prints *a ij* instead of *aa ij*. 28. Caxton: *de-clyue*. 36. Caxton: *afull*.

their flocke that be*n* co*m*mytted vnto theim, and that they dyspose noo thynge of the place vnryȝtwysly, as though they wolde vse theim as their owne / the whyche is ayens god vterly & þe reule. Therfore it is good that they at aƚƚ tymes so behaue theim in vertue, that aƚƚ people may saye / "loo, suche one is worthy to occupye thys place and to haue thys dignytee." Wherfore suche owe not to be chosen therto by their age / but for their wertuo*us* lyuyng and wysdom, chastyte and sobre dealyng, and also for their pyte and mercy the whyche thei muste vse in aƚƚ their dedys / that they the rather maye haue the same of god whan someuer they trespasse / See then*n*e that they loue weƚƚ their chyldren / and hate their syn*n*es / & in amending of their maners and correccyon of their syn*n*es wysely to behaue theim / For to moche in ony thyng is nought, leeste þ*at* thei breke the †veseƚƚ / of the whiche wythoute discrecion and pyte they wolde haue taken of the rust / Also they must see that they prouffyte in theyr werkys more than for to loke for worship / and euer to studye to haue loue rather of the subgettes than drede / dooynge aƚƚ thynges wyth discrecion / whiche is moder of aƚƚ wertues / co*n*sideryng theyr owne freylte, where-thorough of theyr subgettes the better they may haue co*m*passion whan someuer they trespase. Also thei may not be yrefuƚƚ, vnrestfuƚƚ, or obstynate / or to be Ielouse / or moche suspeccyouse ouer theyr subgettes / for then*n*e they shaƚƚ neuer haue rest to-gyder in the relygyon / and euer kepe the rule. Also the souereyn & the subgettes owe euer to flee Idylnesse, þe norisshe of al syn*n*es, & to be ocupyed euer in vertu, louyng god wyth aƚƚ their herte of aƚƚ theyr soule and of aƚƚ their strength and theyr neyghbour as theyr selfe / doyng euer vnto theym as they wolde be done vnto / dyspisyng theyrselfe and folow crist by the crosse of penau*n*ce. Also they must chastyse theyr body and flee the pleasur therof / and to vse fastynge & refresshe the poore peple wyth dedes of mercy †goostly and bodely / and medle lytyƚƚ wyth worldly actes, no thyng preferryng aboue the loue of god / wrath or deceyte neuer to kepe in herte or to promyse ony false peas / kepynge euer charytee / And

The superiors are to be kind, and just,

LXIV.

virtuous, wise,

and loving

[† leaf *aa* iij]

in all their dealings,

and not angry or fidgety.

IV.

All must be industrious, love God

and their neighbours,

flee bodily pleasure, be charitable,

[† leaf *aa* iij, back]

devoted,

honest,

and kind.

They must forbear swearing, vse neuer to swere / leeste that by custome ye faƚƚ in periurie / and sey euer the trouth in herte & mouth / neuer yeldyng euyƚƚ for euyƚƚ / but rather good for euyƚƚ / *be patient,* doyng no wronge to ony, but for to suffre pacie*n*tly wha*n* it is done to you / loue your enmyes / & curse hem not / & be redy to take persecuc*i*on for a riȝtwys mater / *humble, sober, and contented,* neuer be prowde or dronklew nor moche etyng or slouthfuƚƚ / not grutchynge or bakbytynge / euer puttynge your trust in our lord god. Whan þ*at* ye see ony goodnes in your-selfe / anone put it to oure lorde & not to your-selfe. aƚƚ thinge that is euyƚƚ ascryue to your-selfe. Fere euer the daye of Iugement & the du*n*geon of heƚƚ / desyrynge wyth aƚƚ your mynde & herte þe euerlastyng lyfe / & haue euere deth suspecte afore your eyen / & gyde euer your dedes wysely in euery hour / And be certeyn þ*at* *put away evil thoughts* god beholdith theim in eueri place / & euery euyl thought that co*m*myth to your mynde, anone put it awaye by [† leaf *aa* iiij] thynkyng of cristes passyon / & shewe †theym by confessyon to your goostly fader / & kepe euer your tongue from euyƚƚ and shrewde langage / & speke lytyƚƚ & weƚƚ / *and words,* & euer auoyde vayn wordes and dissolute laughter & Iapes, and be glad to here gode lectures and lyues of sayntes with preyer / dayly waylyng your synnes & the syn*n*es & Ignorau*n*ce of the peple wyth ame*n*des makyng / *be obedient,* The preceptes of your souereyn in aƚƚ thynges obey lefuƚƚ as to god & fulfyƚƚ theym / *chaste,* Loue euer chastyte / & flee *and peaceable,* euer enuy / hatrede & stryff / & worship your elders / & fauour the yong in aƚƚ loue and drede of god. Euer pray for your enmyes / & or the sone goo downe, be in perfyte *and never despair of God's mercy.* peas wyth theym dayly to your power / & neuer dyspeyr of the grete mercy of god / Loo, thyes ben the Instrume*n*tes of the spirituеƚƚ crafte & occupac*i*on, þe which exercisid and doon, oure lorde hath promysed to you and vs that eye neuer sawe / nor ere euer herde, nor cowde euer in-to ma*n*nys herte ascende, þe whiche to al his louyng serua*n*tes he hath ordened. amen.

V.
Obedience

OBedyence is a grete vertu done without grutchyng or taryenge. It is the fyrst steppe vnto mekenes /

1. Caxton: *neuer / to swere leeste.*

& it is right specyo*us* & nedefull to be had for all peple & †namely for relygyous persones. True obedie*n*cers, assone as thei be called or co*m*maundid of theyr souereyn / anone after þe worde seyde / they be redy wyth all gladnesse to doo the dede so co*m*mau*n*did / settyng asyde all other thynges vndone & their owne wyll in euery poynt / and þ*at* wyth all quyknesse of herte & body for drede of our lorde. Wherfore he callyth suche a lyfe / a streyt waye to heuen / and not a comyn waye where syn*n*ers take her owne wyll / & be not vndir the yocke of obedye*n*ce to an other / Wythouten doubte trew obedye*n*cers folow surely oure lorde & his wordes where he seyth / "I come not in-to thys world to doo myn owne wyll, but the wyll of my fader the whiche sent me" / Then*n*e this obedience is gretly acceptable to god and swete to al criste*n* peple, whan it is done quikly and wythoute grutchynge or frowarde cou*n*tenau*n*ce in worde or in herte / Our lorde loueth a thyng done vnto hym cherefully in soule / and such obedience done to the souereyn / is done to god & for god, as he seyth hymselfe. Yf one obey with grutchyng either in worde or in their herte, fulfyllyng the co*m*mau*n*dement of theyr so†uereyn / yet it is not acceptable to god / the whiche beholdyth the herte euer & the wyll of the doer therof / & he shal haue noo grace but rather payne ordeined for grutchers, without he amende him.

[† leaf *aa* iiij, back]

should be prompt

and cheerful.

[† leaf *aa* v]

VI.

Silence should be kept,

AS for silence, doo aftir the cheyf prophete of god, dauid, where he seyth in þe sauter / "I haue seyd that I shall not offende in my tongue / I haue put a kepyng to my mowth / & am dompe and therwith made meke & silent" / In moche speche, as it is writen, syn*n*e can*n* not be auoyded / also in þe power of the tongue is deth & lyfe / As it accordith to a mayster to speke & teche, so it behoueth the disciple to here & be silent / wordes of vnclennes / voyde, or meuynge to disolucyon or to laughter, ben dampned by the rule in ony place to be had / & it is co*m*mau*n*did streytly by the same / none to be so bolde to open their mowth in suche maner of

1. Caxton: *specyou⁹*. 14. Caxton: *myfader*. 28. Caxton: *seydthat*.

XLII. *particularly after compline* talkyng / Also silence is to be kept by the rule at aƚƚ tymes & spyritueƚƚy at nyght after complyn, and noo licence then*n*e is to be gyuen to ony for to speke but oonly to officers / or to theim that grete nede causith to speke
(XXXVIII) with sadnesse & honestee / & silence also is to be kept at [† leaf *aa* v, back] †aƚƚ refeccions and meles & in other places / & at other *and during meals.* tymes specyfyed by the rule / Yf theyr be fou*n*de ony gylty in theis premyses, thei ouȝt to be punysshid streytly and greuously.

VII. *The twelve degrees of meekness:*

HOly scrypture cryeth and seyth / "he that wyƚƚ high hymselfe shal be made lowe, and he that mekyth hym selfe shaƚƚ be made high" / In thys is shewid that exaltacyon is þe doughter and nygh of kyne to pryde, whiche is mortaƚƚ / Yf we wyƚƚ atteyne and come to the heyth of perfyte mekenes, the whiche wyƚƚ bringe vs to the honour of heuen in body and soule, lete vs lyft vp our herte & mynde vnto heuen by þe skale and lader of Iacob, descendyng wyth the angels from ony exaltacyon / and clymme vp to theym by mekenes & humyliac*io*n. The *first,* fyrste steppe of thys ladder ascendyng by mekenes to heuen / is to be euer aferde of god and of your souereyn / and not to be foryetful / beringe in your mynde surely aƚƚ thynges that god hath co*m*maundyd you to be done, and your rule, and how they þ*at* contempnyth god & hys preceptes or the rule shal goo to heƚƚ / and to theim that loue & drede god & kepith his co*m*mau*n*dementes is ordeyned [† leaf *aa* vj] Ioye euerlastyng. Oure †lorde in euery place beholdyth the dedes & thoughtes of euery creature / and þe angels ben redy to shewe to the trynitee dayly the gode dedes of *second,* eche good creature. ¶ The seconde steppe or degree of thys ladder of mekenesse is whan one hath no delyte to fulfyƚƚ theyr owne wyƚƚ or desire / but oonli to folow crist / þ*at* seith: "I come not in-to the worlde to doo myn owne *third,* wyƚƚ but the wyƚƚ of my fader that sent me." The iij. degree is whan one subdewyth & mekyth hymselfe for god lowly to their souereyn / folowynge crist / of whom the apostyƚƚ seyth / "Ihesus was made obedient vnto deth of *fourth,* the crosse." ¶ The iiij. degree is whan one can suffre wyth

30. *or*, Caxton: *of*. 32. Caxton: *butoonli*.

aƚƚ obedience & pacyence aƚƚ Iniuries, wronges / wordes of rebuke, & suche other done or sayd vnto theim / & to take hem gladly for goddis sake their lyfe enduring / For þe gospel seith / "he þat contynueth to the ende / shall be sauff." The v. steppe of this ladder of mekenes is þat fifth, whan al euyƚƚ thoughtes that come vnto their herte or to their mynde, & their synnes a-fore hid & not confessyd / þat they wyƚƚ thenne open mekely to theyr souereyn wyth repentaunce / For it is writen / "shewe †thy wayes of thy [† leaf *aa* vj, back] lyuyng to our lord & trust in hym & in his mercy. for he is al goodnesse & piteful / & redy is to foryeue thy trespace & synne, yf thou wyƚƚ knowleche it wyth repentaunce & amende." ¶ The vj. degre of mekenes is whan sixth, one is weƚƚ content wyth symple araye or habite / & is glad to be set lytiƚƚ by & to be take as a drudge or outcast of the religion / & to be euer redy to doo al thynges that is boden hym to doo, Iugyng him an Idyƚƚ seruaunt and vnworthy to god and man / ¶ The vij. degree is yf he seventh, shew in dede hymself, not oonly with tongue but also wyth aƚƚ the inwardes of his herte & by outwarde behauour, the lothliest & the vilest of aƚƚ other / seyeng wyth the prophete / "I am a worme & noo man, the repreef of peple & abieccion / lord, I thanke the that þou hast mekid me, so that I may the beter lerne thy commaundementes." ¶ The viij: degree is yf that he doo no thynge but as the eighth, commyn rule of the place and holy ensample of his senyours doo shewe vnto him in our lorde / ¶ The ix. degree ninth, is yf one kepe his tongue in al silence to the tyme he be commaundid to speke / or els that he be askid a questyon. †¶ The x. degree is yf one be not lyght and redy to [†leaf *aa* vij] tenth, laughter or to dissolucyon. It is writen: "a fole wyƚƚe exalte his voyce in laughter." ¶ The enleuenth is for to eleventh, speke euer softely wyth sadnes / & mekely & with fewe wordes groundid vpon reason and godly / It is wryten: "The wyse man is knowen by hys wordes." ¶ The xij. twelfth. degree is whan one, not oonly in his mowthe but asweƚƚ in his body, shewyth meknesse to aƚƚ that beholde hym / as in al his dedes / in chaptour / in chirche, in garden / in felde, sittynge, walkynge, or standynge, & his hede enclynynge / and his sight to the grounde, shewynge hym selfe euery houre gylty of hys syn*n*e, hauynge euer suspect for to be brought to the ferefuƚƚ Iugement of god, seyeng thus wyth the publycan: "Good lorde, I a synner am not worthy to lyfte vp myn eyen to heuen." who som euer hath ascendyd al thise degrees of mekenesse shaƚƚ anone haue the charyte of god perfitely, þe whyche the*n*ne puttyth awaye aƚƚ drede in suche thynges / the whyche he dyde afore with drede / and also dooth the*n*ne al his actes of accustome, as it were naturalle to [† lf. *aa* vij, back] hym, cherefuƚƚy / & wythoute labour, & that not for the drede of heƚƚ he dooth it, but for feruent loue þ*at* he hath to god by a custome & delyte of vertue / þe whyche grace is yeuen of þe holy gooste.

These lead to perfect love.

VIII–XVIII.

Service regulations.

HOw the seruyse of god is to be doone at his howres acordyng to the tyme / is shewid in the hole rule distynctly by chaptours, where it is noted in þe ende þ*at* euery weke, begyn*n*ynge on the sonday, shal be songe the hole sawter of dauid wyth anthemes & other appropryed therfore / & finaƚƚy it is so of vs to doo in regarde of holy faders afore tyme, þ*at* dide deuoutly rendre & say euery daye of the yer' þe seyde hole sawter, as we rede.

XIX.

The presence of God should be remembered.

SIth it is so that our bileue is, that god is presente in euery place & beholdyth at eche howre both the gode & the euyƚƚ / the*n*ne it is to truste wythoute ony dowte / þ*at* moche more wha*n* we be occupied i*n* his seruyce in þe chirche or ony other holy place / wherfore he is to be serued in drede by the cou*n*seyle of the prophete / & wysely reme*m*bring his presence with innumerable angels / the whyche ben theyr surely at [† lf. *aa* viij] dyuyne seruyce / and lete vs euer soo syng and saye that our mynde accorde to our voys and the sentence / of the dyttee. Amen.

XX.

Right praying.

YF we shulde make ony suggestion to a state temporaƚƚ / we wolde not presume to doo it but with mekenes & reuerence / the*n*ne how moche more owe we to oure lorde god wyth aƚƚ mekenes and clennesse

12. Caxton: *of* (end of line) *of vertue.*

deuoutly to make our prayer and supplicacion, & that not in haste and moche seyenge, but in clennesse of the herte & co*m*punccion wyth wepyng / þ*at* we may the rather be herde in our prayer & petyc*io*n.

XXI. **Functionaries, etc.**

OF the eleccyon of the deanes & offycers of the religyon and of theyr good lyfe / & of their charges / by the whyche the souereyn maye in partie be discharged, And how they owe to be chosen for theyr good lyfe / theyr lernynge and wysdom / And how they shal be correct and blamed / and also depryued, if thei ame*n*de not after theyr defawte / And how that other better disposyd shaƚƚ occupye their place, and soo other offices / and also in what maner they shaƚƚ slepe in their clothes gyrde; [XXII.] †And how offenses and sinnes, grete & lesse dyuersly, owen to be corrected / And how þe souereyn owe to be dilyge*n*t aboute suche as a goode leche or phisicien in all charite & prayer; [XXIII–XXVII.] And also how they that oft haue ben corrupt & correcte wyƚƚ not amende by noo punysshement reguler, that prayer to god & good exhortacyon is the*n*ne euer to be had vnto theim; [XXVIII. **Punishments and atonements.**] Yf they wyƚƚ not dispose theim so to be reconsiled & to take grace, how that the*n*ne they shaƚƚ departe from the congregacyon, leest that suche a moreyne shepe / empoysen and enfecte the residue of þe flocke; [**One rotten sheep will infect a flock.**] And also how those þ*at* ones by their owne foly goone out of the religyon ben receyued ayen; [XXIX.] And how childern nouyces arn to be chastised: [XXX.] al thys afore wryten ben ordeyned afore by saynte benet in þe complete rule in seueraƚƚ chapitours full heuenly.

[† lf. *aa* viij, back]

XXXI. **The cellarer, his qualities.**

THe ceƚƚerer of the place is to be chosen of the congregacyon, suche one that is wyse, quicke, well condycyoned, & sobre, not prowde, impacient, not trowbel*ous*, ferefuƚƚ, nor large / but euer dredynge god / beyng as a fader or a louyng moder to al þe congregac*io*n. †¶ They must haue grete laboure & thought for aƚƚ theim / doyng noo thyng wythout þe co*m*mau*n*dement of the souereyn / the whiche agreyng to god and the rule is euer to be kept / soo that they cause not ony of the couent to

[† leaf *bb* j]

The cellarer grutche or be heuy / Yf cace be that ony aske a thynge vnresonable / yet they owe not to dysdeyne suche one or dispyse, makyng theim heuy with theyr cou*n*tenaunce or answere / but reasonably wyth aƚƚ mekenes and cheyrfuƚƚ
must be kind and gentle, cou*n*tenau*n*ce in softnes of spiritte denie their petyc*i*on. This sayd charge is dredefuƚƚ and also meritori*ous*; for the apostle seyth: "He or she that mynystrith wel / shal haue grete rewarde & crowned in heuen." Morouer theyr
see to the sick and helpless, charge is to see diligently and weƚƚ to the seke / and to Infau*n*tes, to strangers and to power peple / Reme*m*bring that wythout doubte / þ*at* they shaƚƚ yeue a streyt rekenyng and accompte for aƚƚ theys / and for the leest thyng in theyr office myskepte or myspendid, atte ferefuƚƚ daye
keep the vessels, of dome / Aƚƚ the vesels of þe place they owe to kepe weƚƚ / in that asweƚƚ as though thei were the sacrate
[† leaf *bb* j, back] vesels of the awter / Noo thynge they shulde doo nec†lygently / or to be couetous or ouerlarge or prodigous / but
be discreet, moderate, aƚƚ thynges to doo mesurably wyth discrecyon & after the co*m*mau*n*dement of the souereyn / And speciaƚƚy in thys offyce thei must haue mekenesse / & whan they haue not the thyng that is askyd of theym / then*n*e at leest to yeue an esy & gentiƚƚ answer / For it is writen: a soft & esy answere is a-boue ony yeft. The refresshynge and fode
and willing. that is to be yeuen to the couent or congregacyon is to be done euer without grutchyng or taryeng, so that thei haue noo cause to compleyne for the minystracyon / Aƚƚ thynges is to be askyd in dew houres / soo that none be trowbled or made pensy in the housholde of our lorde.

XXXII.
Caretakers.

FOr the other stuff of the monestary, and vesture of the couent wyth other necessaryes / þe souereyn owe to prouide suche officers of whos lyf & good maners he and other may be sure, for the kepyng therof & gaderyng of the same / and for delyueryng of hem to theym
Inventories of goods. þat haue nede / Of the whiche stuff the souereyn shaƚƚ haue wrytynge / wherby he maye delyuer the percels to
[† leaf *bb* ij] the offycers as they chau*n*ge / so þat †it maye be weƚƚ knowen what is yeuen and what is receyued / Who so

26. Caxton: *compleynefor.*

euer neclygently or sluttisshly entretyth ony thyng of the place / anone be they rebukyd & punysshid /

XXXIII.

Individual property is not allowed;

THe grete vice & syn of properte in relygyon is namely to be cutte awaye by þe rote / Presume none in relygyon to yeue ony thyng, or to take, wythout the wyll & co*m*mau*n*dement of the souereyn / nor it is leefull ony to haue a thyng to theyrself propre / not as moche as their owne body / or to haue their own wyll in their power / All thynges to theim necessary is to be had of the souereyn accordynge to theyr nede, not acceptynge ony persone more than an other, but accordyng to nede & in-firmyte / And all thynges must be co*m*myn emo*n*ge theym accordyng to the lyfe of þe apostles / None presume to sey: suche a thynge is myne. Yf ony be founde gylty in this venemouse offence of properte / lete hem twyes or thries be correct / yf they doo not amende / see the*n*ne to their cha[s]tysment / Yf at ony tyme one nede a lytyll thyng / thanke he our lorde and say he euer: "Deo gracias," not beyng sory that an[†]other that nede hath / that pite is shewid vppon hym / And he that hath suche pite shewyd vpo*n* hym shal not therof be proude by co*n*tenau*n*ce or by worde / and thus shall all the co*n*gregacyon be in rest and charitee / and grutchynge layd a syde / the whiche is perilous to be had eyther by worde or sygne / Yf ony therin be fou*n*de culpable, anone put theim to streyt disciplyne.

everything should be had in common

XXXIV.

[† leaf *bb* ij, back]

in true love.

XXXV.

Kitchen service regulations.

ECHe one be besy to serue other, & none is to be exscusid fro*m* þe dressing bord of þe kechyn / wythout they be seke or other wyse occupyed for þe co*m*myn well. In suche meke & low seruice is goten grete mede / charite and rewarde / and whan they shall departe wekely from the kechyn by cours / they owe to make al thynges clene at theyr departyng / and þe clothes þ*at* the couent hath fyled with theyr handes or fete they shall delyuer clene also wyth all mekenes. And moreouer theyr owne fete they shall make clene in theyr departyng, and delyuer al the naprye and clene clothes to the celerer.

17. Caxton: *to* (end of line) *to their chatysment.*

Suche seruytoures by þe rule may take a lytyƚƚ refresshing of mete & drynke afore high dyner / for by-cause of their atte*n*dau*n*ce & seruyse at þe same.

XXXVI.

[leaf *bb* iij]

Regulations for the sick

GRete attendau*n*ce is to be had aboute seke persones aboue aƚƚ other thynges: as though it were to criste hymselfe / the whiche doutlesse is seruyd in theym that is seke / as he seyth hymselfe: "I was seke and ye visited me, and that ye dide vnto the leest of theym that were seke, ye dide it vnto me" / Wherfore those that ben seke shulde considre that suche seruyce is doon to theym for the loue & honour of god, and therfore they shulde be righte ware to cause ony heuynese to theyr seruytoures by ony sup*er*fluite or vncurtees demenour. Not for thy, for theyr sekenes they owe pacye*n*tly to be suffred / for of suche is goten grete rewarde herafter in heuen. The souereyn may not be neclygent to the ouersyght of suche seke persones, serchyng wel that thei lacke noo helpe or comforte / or ony thing that is necessary for theim, as is wasshing, bathynge, and medicynes, yeuyng as oft as nedeth / and to suche is grauntid by the rule for theyr sooner ame*n*dement for to ete flesshe; so þ*a*t after thei recouer thei absteyn in ony wyse therfro. Prouyde alwey þ*a*t fauour be had to Infa*n*tes / seke persones & aged.

(who are not to lack washing, baths, and medicine),

XXXVII.

old people, and children.

XXXVIII.

[leaf *bb* iij, back]

Regulations about meals.

AT aƚƚ refeccyons and meles / redyng & lecture must be had / And the reder after the masse on the sonday shaƚƚ entre / and humbly desire of aƚƚ the congregacyon to pray for hym, makynge a crosse in his forhede / for the euyƚƚ spirite of pryde and other / and after the blessyng yeuen begyn to rede / and aƚƚ the tyme of refeccyon or meles / none to be soo hardy to speke / but to kepe high silence as speche, noys, or other wyse, preuy or aperte / how be it, the souereyn maye a lytyƚƚ speke of the processe that is rad or of other for edefieng of his ghestes or of other that here hym / and not els / Also þe congregacion shal be seruyd of al thynges necessary to theym at that tyme / so that none haue nede to aske ony thynge /

Silence to be kept.

15. Caxton: *goton.* 35. Caxton: *cls.*

Signs only to be made.

'Mixtum' for readers.

Yf cace be þ*at* suche nede befaƚƚ / then*n*e signes must be vsid and no speche / The reder may afore his lecture take a lytyƚƚ refeccyon that is caƚƚyd mixtum / yf nede be for by-cause of his redyng atte mete / And suche owe to rede euer / the whiche by theyr redyng may best edyfye the herers / And the same is to be obseruyd in aƚƚ syngyng and redynge in the chirche or in prechyng / and that †to be done in mekenes / sadnesse and drede.

[† leaf *bb* iv]

XXXIX–XLI.

Variation in meals at different seasons.

IT folowyth in the rule of the mesures of mete and drynke / and what howres after the season and tyme of the yere / the congregacyon sħaƚƚ take theyr repast and meles / And also how the souereyn must soo tempre and dispose aƚƚ suche thynges wyth other, so that the soules of his subgettes may be saaf.

XLIII.

All should be punctual about service hours.

Punishments for late arrival,

TO the seruyce of god as sone as is herde ony beƚƚ or token / aƚƚ thynges set aside, the couent owe to come in aƚƚ godely haste and relygyously therto / For noo thynge owe to be preferryd before the seruyce of god. And they that come late therto / shal not goo to their owne place in þe quere / but to the place assigned for suche late commers / to theyr rebuke, penau*n*ce, and amendement. How they shaƚƚ be punysshid that come late to meles / and of theyr sequestracyon from the feliship / and of theyr etynge alone in penau*n*ce after other / the rule with his expositour dooth specifye /

XLV.

[leaf *bb* iv, back]

for mistakes in divine service,

THo that fayle in psalmody / respons / anthemes or lesso*n*s, yf they meke not theyr-selfe openly afore aƚƚ the congregac*i*on / as puttynge theyr hede downe to the grounde or other wyse by the rule for a satysfacyon / els they must haue afterwarde more largelier & greter penaunce for their offence / And children euer for theyr trespace must be bette.

XLVI.

and for carelessness during work.

WHo that euer in his laboures / as in the kechyn, in celary / in the gardyn, or in ony other occupacyon, offendyth or brekyth ony thyng / or els

25. *with*, Caxton: *whiche.*

lesith, and wyll not knowleche his offence to the hede and souereyn or to the congregacyon / they owe to haue grete penau*n*ce, yf it be openly knowen, the offence / yf it be not knowen but oonly to hym selfe / then*n*e lete hym shew it bi confessyon to the souereyn or to his goostly fader and take his penaunce.

XLVIII.

Idleness must be avoided.

IDilnesse is the enmye of þe soule / wherfore lyke as the couent ben occupyed certeyn howres aboute the seruyce of god / soo certeyn other howres ben thei occupyed in redyng and studye*n*g of heuenly thynges / [† leaf *bb* v] and in labou†res wyth theyr body in thynges that is good and necessary to theim or þe place / for then*n*e thei ben very religious, whan thei thus folowe holy faders and doon as the apostles dyden.

During Lent there must be special study,

IN the tyme of lent echon by theyr-selfe haue the bible / the whiche they owe to rede complete and hole besyde theyr seruyse / and the seyde bible is to be delyuerd vnto theym atte begynnynge of lent. And the serchers of the relygyon owe to see warely about þ*a*t they be occupyed in lecture therof sonday and other / & not aboute fables / Iapes or sluggisshenes. Yf ony suche be fou*n*de / see that they be spoken vnto sharply ones or twyes / & yf they amende not theyr-wyth / lete theym be correct / soo that all other maye beware by theym. If theyr be ony so slouthfull or neclygent, that they maye not or wyll not be occupied in redyng or holy medytacyon / then*n*e lete theym be assigned to other occupacyons to doo / so that they be neuer vnoccupied in vertu / If they be seke or feble for age / then*n*e such an occupacyon is to be put vnto theym þ*a*t they maye awaye wyth / & not to be ydyll, by þe discrecio*n* of the souereyn.

under due control.

Non-readers must be set to work.

XLIX.

[leaf *bb* v, back]

HOw be it that a relygious persone owe euery tyme to kepe lent / yet for by-cause that fewe haue thys vertu / therfore we aduise and counseyll, seyth saynt benet, all of the relygyon spirituall*y* theys xl. dayes of lent to kepe in all clennesse of lyfe / and to put vtterly

Lent requires special purity,

33. Caxton: *relygions.*

awaye all theyr neclygences and olde custome of synne / and then*n*e more spiritually to gyue theim to prayer waylyng and wepinge / redinge / and abstinence in mete and drynke / wythdrawynge somwhat of theyr takynge in mete and drynke other wyse than they dide afore, and that wyth good wyll, offerynge it in his mynde to god and to the poore peple; And to wythdrawe some what of slepe and speche and wanton behauour. And as for abstynence of mete and drynke, it owe to be doon wyth the consente euer of the souereyn and the helpe of prayer. For yf it be otherwyse doon / it is to be taken of presumpcyon and vayne glory / and then*n*e it hath noo mede.

devotion, and abstinence, with less sleep and less talk.

LII.

[leaf *bb* vj] Use of the oratory.

NOo thynge is to be spoken in the chirche but prayer / And after that ony seruyce is there doon / all they owe to departe wyth silence and lowe reuerence doon to god. Yf ony after woll praye of deuocyon / none shall let hym by theyr noyse or ony other vncurteys delynge / and then*n*e suche owe secretly to praye wyth deuocyon and not on high, but wepynge for his synnes and the Ignoraunce of the peple and theyr synnes wyth all meke intencyon of herte and soule. All other not soo there occupyed owe to avoyde.

LIII.

Guests should be received charitably,

AL strangers or ghestes arn to be receyued for god & as god. For here-after they shal here hym saye to theim / "I was a stra*n*ger & ye toke me In / and gaue me mete & drynke and lodgynge" / and soo of other dedes of mercy / Euery persone is to be honourid for the ymage of god / then*n*e moche more those that ben of cristen religion and that co*m*men for god / Whan euer it is shewyd that a stranger is come / anone the souereyn or his bredern shulde †quykly goo to hym wyth all charyte / and after theyr prayer togider made and knyt togider in goddis peas / kissyng togyder and salutyng other / with after refresshing theim with mete and drynk and other necessaryes to their power / redynge amonge the lawes of god to theyr edyfieng of soule / The souereyn may breke his

[† leaf *bb* vj back]

be kissed, and given food.

3. Caxton: *wepnige.*

mele for a stranger, wythout it be a spiritueƚƚ fastynge daye / and the*n*ne he owe not to breke it / The bredern may not breke ony faste for strangers. Also the souereyn wyth the co*n*gregacion shulde with aƚƚ mekenes folow oure lorde / and wasshe the fete of the stra*n*gers, sayenge certeyn prayers / for in theim and poore folke is to be had dilige*n*t watche and cure / for crist in theym is surely receyued / He þ*a*t is asygned for suche gestes or poore folke, to gyue vnto theim necessaries, shulde drede god gretly and haue mekenes and pacience / and doo aƚƚ thynges with wisdom / and silence, euer fulfiƚƚyng the souereyns co*m*mau*n*dement / & whan they ony other mete or see / they owe to enclyne mekely and salute theim departyng with silence.

Strangers' feet are to be washed.

LIV.

[leaf *bb* vij]

Letters and gifts are to be subject to the disposal of the Superior.

NOo wyse be it leefuƚƚ to ony broder to take or receyue of fader or moder ony letters, tokens, or yeftes / or els to se*n*de hymself or to yeue ony without the wyƚƚ and comau*n*dement of his hede and souereyn / the whiche had, he the*n*ne maye receiue theim / not forthy the souereyn after may yeue suche stuff to suche as it shaƚƚ please hym, and he that it was sent vnto shaƚƚ take it in worthe & cherefuƚƚy / in that an other hath it / leest that occasion of grutchinge inwarde or outwarde be yeuen to the by thy goostly enmye.

LV.

Clothing is to be plain and cheap.

CLothynge to the couent, and habyte, is to be yeuen accordyng to the hete of the yere or to the coldenes of the cou*n*tre that they dweƚƚ in, lasse or more as nede is / And the souereyn must haue co*n*siderac*i*on therof / and to bye suche cloth that is made in that cou*n*tre or prouynce, of the vilest and lyghtest pryce / And as oft as they shal take new / the*n*ne to rendre vp the olde for the vse of pore peple / Of other thynges necessary for theyr body daye & nyght in wynter and somer, and of theyr ceƚƚes and lodgyng, and of their behauour in theim with other / the hole rule certifieth. And how the souereyne shal dyligently serche that thei lacke no †thyng to theym necessary / soo that aƚƚ occas*i*on of grutchyng, or for ony

[† leaf *bb* vij, back]

22. *it* /, Caxton: / *it.*

thynge werkynge, or for ony thynge kepyng / haue no place in þe relygyon / euer remembryng the wordes wrytyn in the actes of the apostles, where it is seyde / that it was distribute & delyuerd to echone of theym as theyr nede required.

LVI. The Superior's table.

THe borde or table of the souereyn is to be garnysshid wyth pilgrymes or ghestes / And whan there ben few strangers / the soouereyn maye caƚƚ vnto hym some of the brederen / so that parte of the senyours be left wyth the couent for theyr awe and disciplyne.

LVIII. Reception as a monk or nun should be granted only after long waiting,

WHan ony co*m*myth from the worlde to entre in-to religion / a light or soden entree is not to be grau*n*tyd; but for to doo after the apostle, preuynge the spirites / yf they be of god. Yf cace be that suche one be abydynge in hys purpose / and fou*n*de pacyent for ony Iniuryes done vnto hym / or for delayeng of his entree, & suche other, the*n*ne after iiij or v. dayes may be grau*n*ted vnto hym entree / abidyng after by †certeyn [† lf. *bb* viij] space in the ghestys chambre / and after in the ceƚƚ for nouices / theyr to be for a tyme in prayer and medytacyon / and for to ete and drynke. And a senyoure of the relygyon is to be assigned vnto hym / the whyche is apt to gete sowles to god / the whyche shaƚƚ see vnto hym warely and vysely that he be vertuously occupyed / sekynge our lorde by prayer, and to folow hym by obedyence and suffryng of repreues / Aƚƚ the hardnesse and sharpnesse of the ordre is to be tolde hym playnly / by the whiche he must goo to heuen. And yf he promyse to contynwe and to be stable in his purpoos, the*n*ne after two monethes / the rule shaƚƚ be red hole by ordre vnto hym / and thus it shaƚƚ be seyde vnto hym: "Beholde here the lawe vndyr whyche thou must sore laboure and fyght / Yf thou thynkyst that thou maye kepe it, come in / and yf thou may not / goo free ayen where it plesith þe." Yf he yet contynewe by hys promyse, the*n*ne he shaƚƚ be brought ayen to the nouyces ceƚƚ to be preued ayen, and yet ayen

preparation,

overseeing by a senior,

hearing of the rule,

and staying in the novices' cell.

34. */ goo*, Caxton: *goo /*.

[† lf. *bb* viij, back]

after in all pacience; †& then*n*e after six monethes the rule ayen shall be red vnto hym / soo that he may well know wherfore he entryth in-to relygyon / and yf he co*n*-tynue styll iiij. mou*n*thes after / yet not for thy þe rule ayen shall be red vnto hym / And yf he promyse then*n*e vtterly to kepe all thynges that is so ofte red vnto hym and to be obedie*n*t, then*n*e atte firste shall he be taken in-to the congregacyon / knowlechyng then*n*e that he is bou*n*de to the law of the rule / and then*n*e after he may not departe fro*m* þe monestarye / nor exscuse him, but that he is vnder the yocke of þe seyd rule to his deth.

After twelve months' probation,

¶ Then*n*e whan he is admyttid and taken in-to the chirche to be professid afore all the peple / there he shall pro-mytte of his stabylnesse and amendyng of his maners / & there-vpon make his obedience afore god and his sayntes / the whiche is to be done with all his mynde and herte, leest that he mocke our lorde god to his dampnacyon / Of his promyse and profession he shall make a peticyon in writynge to god and to all sayntes / whos relykes ben in that chirche and to the soucreyn assygned therto / the whiche he shal wryte with †his owne hande / or els an other of hym required, yf that he can not write / & marke it with his owne sygne / the whiche he shall put vpon þe awter afterwarde wyth his hande; & seye certayn prayers ther-wyth / And after this he shal fall downe prostrate at fete of the couent / prayeng theym to praye for hym / and after thys he shall be nombrid for euer / and named for one of the congregacyon / Suche stuff that he hath not yeuen before to folke þ*at* ben poore or other wyse, openly shall he then*n*e yeue to the monestary / noo thyng reseru-yng vnto hym-selfe; for after that tyme he may haue noo propirte / not as moche as his owne body / And whan in þe chirche he shall doo of his seculer arraye and be cladde with the habite of the place / those that he puttyth of shall be kept in the vestuary / leest that the enmye the fende perswade and cause hym after / the whiche god defende, for to departe from the relig*io*n / and then*n*e he must haue his seculer clothes ayen / and put out for euer. But his petycyon in wrytinge, that he put on the awter in

the vow is made. *The petition* [† leaf *cc* j] *is written, signed, and laid on the altar.* *The new member's goods are given away,* *and he puts on the monastic clothing.*

10. *from*, Caxton: *fŏr*.

his firste entree / ought euer to remayn and to be kept in the monestary.

LIX. [leaf *cc* j, bk.]

Rules for admission of children,

YF a man of worship offre a yong childe, his sone, to god and to the religion, then*n*e shaƚƚ he or his frendes make the petic*io*n, as is wryten afore, for him with writyng / and their offryng wyth the hande of þe childe / the whiche shaƚƚ be roƚƚyd togider in the paƚƚ or in the toweƚƚ of the awter / How poore children and seculer prestes / & how mounkes stra*n*gers owe to be receyued / and of the ordynac*io*n of prestes & of dekens wythin þe selfe religion, is shewid folowyngly in the complete rule by large processe / the whiche I passe ouer for the grete change that is in that religion, and the length.

LX–LXII. of strange monks, etc.

LXIII. Juniors and seniors.

WHan euer the bredern mete togider / the yonger shaƚƚ meke hymselfe / desirynge the blessynge of hys senyour / And whan ony senyour commyth at ony tyme before hym / he shal arise and gyue place to sytte; and the sayd Ionger shaƚƚ stande tyƚƚ he be co*m*mande to sitte. Yonge children of the religion both in chirche and at table & elswhere shaƚƚ kepe theyr place after their age in relygion / and they shal haue ouerseers, techinge theym & gyuynge disciplyne / tyƚƚ they come to the age of vndersto*n*dyng.

LXVI. [leaf *cc* ij] Gate-keeper

TO the gate of the monestary an aged persone, wise and weƚƚ manerd, is to be assigned / the whiche can take an answere wittely or a message / Whose good disposicyon woƚƚ not suffre hym to wandre aboute or to be idle / The whiche broder owe to lodge nygh the gate / soo that strangers that come maye euer fynde hym redy / of whom they shaƚƚ take an answere. / And whan someuer ony knockyth at gate, or els that the poore peple crye, anone he shaƚƚ seye: "Deo gracias" cherefully, and gyue theym an awnswere co*m*fortably in aƚƚ mekenes and soft-nesse and drede of god / The whiche broder portar shaƚƚ haue helpe of an other yonger broder, yf grete nede requyre. Suche a monestary is to be sette in suche a place where aƚƚ

to live near the gate,

and be kind to all.

Junior porter.

Situation of the convent.

5. Caxton: *as it*, for *as is*, or *as it is*.

thynges necessary soone maye be had / so that the couent nede not to passe the boundes of the clausures therof / the whiche yf thei dide / shulde be peryƚƚe for theyr soules / Saynt benet woƚƚ that the rule be red effectueƚƚy oftymes in the yere afore the co*n*gregac*i*on / for by-cause none of hem shal pretende Ignorance or ony exscuse.

Reading of the rule.

LXVII.

[lf. *cc* ij, bk.] Prescripts regarding those who go on journeys.

WHan ony of the bredern must doo a Iourney without the clausure of the place, after licence had, he shaƚƚ co*m*mende hym to the prayer of his souereyn / and euer at last oryson in the seruyse of god / shal a prayer be sayd for hi*m* and aƚƚ þ*at* is absent / And the daye that they come home ayen / they shal lye prostrate aƚƚ the seruyse tyme / & desyre the couent to praye for theym for theyr excesses done in the iourney / as in syght, heryng of ony vanytees / or euyƚƚ thynges, or ony voyde wordes / And they shaƚƚ not teƚƚ ony thyng þ*at* they sawe or herd in theyr iourney, for it is a grete meane to þe destrucc*i*on of suche a place of relygion / And he that presumyth to doo the contrary or to goo oute of the clausure of the monestary to ony place / thought it be neuer so lytil, wythout co*m*mandement or lice*n*ce of the souereyn / owe to be streytly punysshyd.

On coming back, they shall ask for prayers for their faults.

LXVIII.

Impossible injunctions

IF ony greuouse or impossible thynges be put vnto a broder of his souereyn to doo / he shaƚƚ wyth aƚƚ mekenesse and obedie*n*ce take the co*m*mau*n*dement vpon hym: Yf cace be that it passe his power in ony wise to fulfiƚƚ it, then*n*e wyth aƚƚ lowlynesse he shal teƚƚ it to [†]his souereyn / and the cause of impossibilytee. And yf cace be the souereyn contynew in his sentence & wyƚƚ / then*n*e the broder owe to know that it is to hym right profitable yet to obeye, puttynge his trust in the helpe of god / whiche woƚƚ not forsake all theym that truste in him.

[† leaf *cc* iij]

are to be obeyed, with trust to God.

LXIX.

Undue intercession.

ECHe one shuld beware þ*at* he exscuse not or defende an other in ony cause, though al he were neuer soo nygh to hym of blode / For of it lightly wolde

24. Caxton: *abroder*.

growe grete occasion of sclau*n*dre to the relig*i*on / Who þ*at* is fou*n*de fawty in this trespace owe to be punysshid greuosly.

LXX.

Unauthorized correction.

IT is ordeyned also that it is not lefuƚƚ to ony of the couent to punisshe or to bete an other of the same / but suche one as the souereyn hath yeuen power vnto / Those that offende openly / must be repreuyd and punysshid openly / that other maye be the rather aferd to offende / Children to the xv. yere of age shaƚƚ stande euer vndir streyt awe and diligent discipline / & aƚƚ thynges er to be doon vnto theym mesurably with discrecyon and reason / & vndir the co*m*mandeme*n*t euer of the souereyn / And he that otherwise dooth / shaƚƚ be correct wyth †reguler disciplyne / for it his writen in the gospeƚƚ / Aƚƚ thynges that ye wolde þ*at* other shuld doo vnto you / doo ye it to theym / and that ye wolde not haue done to you / doo it not to theim.

Children till 15 to be under strict discipline.

[† leaf *cc* iij, back]

LXXI.

Obedience to superior and seniors.

OBedience is not oonly to be yeuen of al the couent to the souereyn / but also echon to other must obeye / knowyng that by þe way of obedie*n*ce thei shaƚƚ come vnto heuen. Whan the co*m*mau*n*dement of the souereyn is doon by the subgette / saynt Benet woƚƚ that besyde that / þ*at* euer the yonger in religion obeye theyr senyours in aƚƚ charite / dilygence, & mekenesse; who þ*at* woƚƚ not must be correct / Yf ony brother be blamed of his souereyn for ony cause / though it be right smaƚƚ / as soone as that he knowyth that his souereyn or his senyour is greued wyth hym or trowbled, though it be right lityƚƚ / anone he owe to faƚƚ downe prosstrate at his fete / so longe to the tyme he that is greued be satisfied & plesid for his humyliacyon. Yf ony disdeyn to doo thys / lete hym be punysshid on the nakyd body / and yf he be obstynate / put hym out of the monestary.

A brother, when censured, must fall at the superior's feet, or be beaten on his naked body.

LXXII.

[leaf *cc* iv]

There is a bad and a good zeal.

AS there is an euyƚƚ ȝele / loue, or affeccyon / the whiche departyth one from god and bringith hym to heƚƚ / soo there is a ȝele or affecc*i*on the whiche

22. Caxton: *soueuereyn.*

The good zeal should pervade the convent. All should be meek, and help others, preferring God's cause, and so reach heaven.

departyth one from synne and bryngith hym to god to euerlastyng lyfe, the whiche is to be had in religion in all feruent desire / for by it echone gladly woll reuerence other, and echone suffre other for ony infirmytee or condycions / and that wyth all pacience / and moreouer echone be glad who can best meke hymselfe and to be obedient / neuer folowyng that thyng the whiche he demeth to be profitable oonly to hymselfe / but moche more that thyng that is profitable for other. Echone shewe charitee to other as brethern in all clene & chaste loue / dredyng euer god / and louynge theyr souereyn in charyte vnfeyned, preferryng euer goddis cause and mater afore all other / the whiche woll brynge hem all to-gider to reygne in the lyfe / the whiche is eternalle. AMEN.

Explicit.

Translator's solicitation.

¶ Of your charite praye for the translatour of thys sayd treatyse.

IV. THE NORTHERN LANSDOWNE RITUAL

FOR THE

Ordination of Nuns.

(*Lansdowne MS.* 378, *British Museum.*)

This is þe furme how A Nouice saƚƚ be made & resaiuid to religiun. [leaf 43]

After an applicant has been admitted into the convent,

IN þe first begining, when sho hase made hir peticiun, And askid þe howse, & priores and þe Couent hase graunt hir it, þan saƚƚ sho cume to þe priores and knele downe be-fore hir on hir kneis. And þe p*r*iores schaƚƚ take hyr hende in hirs and kisse hir, and sho saƚƚ be resauid.

has been examined the first time

Efterwarde, when þai likis to bringe hir to þe chaypitur for to be examen*d*, þai saƚƚ aray hir i*n* þat wede þat sho saƚƚ vse þe first ȝere to sho be profest. And þan, when chaipitur is done, sho þat saƚƚ be hir maistres saƚƚ say to þe p*r*iores: "þare is a Nouice for to be examend."

as to her desire to be a nun,

And þan [þe] priores saƚƚ byd bring hir in. And hir maistres saƚƚ bring hir in. And when sho comes whare þe cuuent takis þare venyse, þan saƚƚ sho p*ro*strate downe. And þan þe p*r*iores saƚƚ aske hir: "dere doughtir, what is þi asking?" And ligand stiƚƚ, sho saƚƚ say: "þe m*er*cy of god and ȝoures." And þe p*r*iores saƚƚ garre hir rise, and say tyƚƚ hir on þis wyse: "What is þat m*er*cy þat þu askes?" and sho saƚƚ say: "for to dwelle i*n* þis †place i*n* þe abet of religiun to serue godde, & for to punysce my sinnis, & for amen*d*men*t* of my life, & finally for saluacion of my saule." And þan þe priores saƚƚ say a-gayn: "Dere doght*ir*, þis thing þat þu askis is a harde thing & a strate. Neu*ir*-þeles, to þam þat [god] i*n*spires & [† lf. 43, bk.]

6. MS. þe. 15. MS. *þan priores.* 21. MS. þu; similarly p. 142, l. 12. 24. MS. *finally of saluacion.* 27. MS. *þat inspires.*

giffis grace, wiłł, and power to fulfil it, & standis stabiłł i*n*-to þe purpose þat þa be-gane, it is bott ligħt, meritory, & medefułł, & spedand to þe lif þat eu*ir* sałł last. Bott

and been told how she shall have to live in obedience,

at þe begining of þis spiritual life, thre thy*n*gis þar ar þat þe behuvis: to forsake þine awne p*ro*pir wiłł, & liffe vndir obedience, & be obediant p*r*incipally to þi p*r*iores & to þi elders i*n* þe ordir In ałł lefułł þingis & honeste. The

poverty,

secu*n*de is, þat þe behouis liue i*n* wilfułł power[te], na thing awand w*ith*-owtyn wittyng of þi p*r*iores, na nathi*n*g take of nane of þi frendis, golde ne silu*ir*, no na other gifte, bot at þi p*r*iores se it, And þ*at* it fully be disposid at hir wiłł, þat þu be nogħt p*ro*pirtarij and falle i*n* owre-hegħ daunger ene*n*ce þi religiun. For wha sa eu*ir* hase ani thing, golde,

[† leaf 44]

silu*ir*, iuel, or ony p*ro*pirte, w*ith*-outen †þe witting & sufferan*s* of hir p*r*iores, sho standis curste. The thirde is,

and chastity,

þat þe behouis to liue chaiste, and take god to þi spouse, and forsake ałł þi lust, & þi liking of þi flesche; þe be-

abstinence,

houis to giue þe to abstinens & faste, whe*n* oþ*ir* me*n* etis; þe behouis to rise to þe se*r*uise of godde, when oþ*ir* me*n*

and devotion;

slepis; þe be-houis gife þe to praier & deuocion for to purches grace, and stifly sta*n*de i*n* þe purpose þat þu takis þe to. And doht*ir*, giue þu seis þ*at* þu mai fulfiłł w*ith* þe grace of god ałł þeis poyntes þ*at* I haue reherced, Sais now her be-fore þe cuuent: what is þi wille?" And þan þe nouyce, if sho wiłł abide i*n* hir purpose, sałł say on þis wise: "The gude purpose þat I haue tane, I sałł fulfiłł it to my liuis ende thrugħ þe grace of god and ȝure gude i*n*formaciun." And þan þe p*r*iores sal say tyl hir: "Dere dogħt*ir*, godd of his grete grace, he giue þe gude pe*r*seue-

after she, subsequently, has received more instruction,

rans. Ga w*ith* þi maistres in þe name of crist." And hir mastres sall haue hir to þe Nouycery, & infurme as religiun wiłł. And whe*n* twa monethes er passid, hir maistres

[† lf. 44, bk.]

salle †expone hir þe rewle and ałł þe poyntis and stratenes of religiun, na thing lanande fra hir. And when hir

and been examined

maistres hase exponed hir þe rewle, sho sałł be examned

8. MS. *power.* 14, 15. MS. *siluir or ony iuel with outen þe witting & sufferans of hir priores propirte sho standis curste.* In a prior copy of the ritual, the word *propirte* was probably written in the margin. The scribe entered it in the wrong place, also putting *or ony* before *iuel* (jewel). 16. MS. þ^{i}. 21. MS. *stifly and stande.*

a-gain i*n* þe chaipitur on þe same wise os es be-fore saide. And giffe sho standis i*n* hir purpose eftir þe space of sex monethes, þe rewle eftir sone saƚƚ be exponed til hir of hir maistres. And þa*n* saƚƚ sho be examend i*n* þe chaipitur i*n* þe mane*r* be-fore saide. And giffe sho ȝitte abide fully i*n* hir purpose to hir ȝere ende, þan on þe day þat sho saƚƚ be p*ro*fest, sho saƚƚ be brogħt i*n*-to þe chaipitur, & þe fourte tyme be examend, as be-fore es rehercede. And þa*n* if sho fully agre hir to þe beheste þat sho made before, Efter þe gospeƚƚ on þe day þat sho saƚƚ be p*ro*feste, hir maistres saƚƚ cum til hir & lede hir til þe gree. And þare sho saƚƚ rede hir p*ro*fessiun, The preste þat singis þe messe sta*n*dand at þe rigħt corner of þe auter. And when sho hase redde hir p*ro*fession, hir maistres saƚƚ gyffe hir a penne w*ith* ynke, & þe nouyce sal make a crosse on þe buke of hir p*ro*fession, and sa wende vp to þe †hee auter, and hir maistres w*ith* hir, & lay it on þe right ende of þe auter, and kys þe auter, and encline deuotelie, and gange againe to þe gree, & singe þare thrise: "Suscipe me, d*omi*ne" &c. þe couent, aƚƚ-way standant i*n* þare stallis, saƚƚ reherce þe same again thrise, and "Gl*or*ia p*at*ri." þan þe nouice saƚƚ prostrate downe be-fore þe gree, when "Kirieleison, Chr*ist*eleison, Kiriel*eison*." And þa*n* þe preste saƚƚ say or sing: "Et ne nos." "S*ed* libera nos," saƚƚ þe qwere answer. And þa*n* þe chantur saƚƚ be-gine þis salme: "Miserere mei, de*us*," þe ta side a verse, & þe toþ*ir* a-noder, And "gl*or*ia patri," "Sic*ut*." And when þis salme es endit, þa*n* þe preste saƚƚ cume fra þe hee awter to þe gree, and on hir: "Salua*m* fac ancilla*m* tua*m*." And þe qwere saƚƚ answer: "Deus me*us*, sperantem i*n* te." And efter sune þe preste saƚƚ singe: "Mitte ei, do*mi*ne, auxiliu*m* de *sancto*." The qwere saƚƚ answer: "Et de sion tuere ea*m*." þe preste: "Esto ei, d*omi*ne, turris fortitudinis." þe qwere: "A facie i*n*imici." And þan þe preste: "Nichil †proficiet i*n*imicus i*n* ea." And þan þe quere: "Et fili*us* iniquitatis no*n* apponet nocere ei." þe preste: "D*omi*ne, deus vi*r*tutum, co[n]ue*r*te nos." þe quere: "Et ostende facie*m*." þe preste: "D*omi*n*us*

the second, third, and fourth time, she may be ordained. She shall then read out her vow, sign it, [† leaf 45] and place it on the High altar. After and under alternate songs and prayers, she shall prostrate herself before the altar steps, to which the priest also comes down from the altar, [† lf. 45, bk.]

29. MS. *Saluum;* cf. p. 144, l. 20, and p. 148, l. 2. 37. MS. *couerte.*

rise again, whilst the veil is being hallowed, receive the veil, repeat her obedience vow to the abbess [† leaf 46] and seniors, prostrate herself once more, take her stall, and then receive the Eucharist.

vobiscum." þe quere: "Et cu*m*." þe preste: "Orem*us*." And þa*n* he saƚƚ say fore colett*is* oure hir, The nouice ligand prostrate be þe gree, And þe p*r*iores and þe coue*n*t standand i*n* þe*r* stallis, and þar facis turned to þe autir. And whe*n* þe collett*is* are aƚƚ endid, þa*n* þe nouice saƚƚ sta*n*d qwil þe vaile es i*n* halowyng. And when þe preste hase halowid it, thre or fowre of hir sistirs w*ith* hir mastres saƚƚ cum oute of þe qwere & stand a-bowte hir, qwil hir vales ar i*n* doyng on,. Aƚƚ þe oþ*ir* remana*n*t of þe coue*n*t sta*n*dand i*n* þare stall*is*. þan, whe*n* sho is arayid vp i*n* hir valis, þe chantir saƚƚ be-ginne sole*m*ply þis hym: "Veni, creator," þe quere a verse, þe toþ*ir* a-noþ*ir*. And i*n* þe mene time saƚƚ þe Nouice make hir p*ro*fession to þe p*r*iores, kneland on hir kneis, saiand on þis mane*r*: "Promitto t*ib*i obedienciam *secun*d*um* regula*m* s*anc*t*i* benedicti." †And þe p*r*iores sais þan: "Det tibi Deus uita*m* eterna*m*." And on þe same wise saƚƚ sho ga downe þe p*r*iores side, and syne þe toþ*ir* syde. And when sho saƚƚ cume again, þare [saƚƚ] sho p*ro*strate and ligge hir downe. And þan þe preste at makis hir sal sai or sing: "Salua*m* fac," "Nichil p*ro*ficiet," As be-fore es saide, and þir colett*is*: "Deus, qui caritatis," "Acciones n*ost*ras," "Fidelium deus." Qwen þir thre colett*is* ar said, þe p*r*iores saƚƚ cume & lede hir til þe staƚƚ, whare sho sal stande, and þe preste saƚƚ ga to þe awter and be-gynne þe crede. And at þis [ah] hir to be howslid.

2. After *hir* nearly half a line is left blank. 19. MS. *þare sho.* 20. MS. *Saluum.* 26. MS. *þis hir.*

V. THE VESPASIAN RITUAL

FOR THE

Ordination of Nuns.

(*Cotton MS. Vespasian A.* 25, *British Museum.*)

The Method of makeing a Nunn. [leaf 120]

After a special mass, and epistle and gospel as usual,

Here bygyns þe manere forto make a nun. At þe first be-gynnyng þe mese salbe of our lady. þe offece of þe mese saƚ be "Salue, s*ancta* parens." þe Epistil & þe godspel & aƚ þe tother salbe als þe tyme of þe ȝer’ askes. Att þe bygynnyng of þe mese þe madyn þ*at* salbe mayde nun sal sit in þe quere a-pon a stole be-for þe priores stayle w*ith* hir prouese in hir hand. And at þe offerand tyme þe Priores sal lede þe madyn til þe toumbe in-mydes þe quer’, & þer’ sal scho betecħ hir vntil hir next frendes. And þai sal lede hir vp vnto þe hegħ auter. And þe Priores & þe conuent sal folow vp vnto þe auter’. And þen hir frendes sal offer’ hir vp tyl þe auter’, & þan byken hir’ to þe p*r*iores ogayn. And þe same tyme al þ*at* wil may offir’. And þen þai al sal sit down & here þe p*r*eching, And scho w*ith* hir p*r*ofesse-boke in hir hand. And when þe preching es done, þe Priores sal hafe hir be-for þe auter’ & vnclethħ hir of hir seculer’ clething. And in þe same tyme þe prelet saƚ halow hir habete w*ith*-outyn note, þer’ sayand: "Do*minus* vob[*iscum*]!

the novice's next of kin shall offer her to the High altar.

After the sermon,

her secular clothing shall be taken off, and the priest shall hallow her habit [leaf 120, bk.]

DEus, qui vestimentu*m* salutare et indumentu*m* eterne iocunditatis tuis fidelib*us* p*r*omisisti, clemencia*m* tuam suppliciter exoram*us*, vt hec indumenta, humilitate*m* cordis et contemptu*m* mu*n*di significancia, quib*us* famula (-e) tua (-e) N. s*an*cto visibilit*er* est (sunt) informanda (-e)

1. The heading is in a later hand. The English text (with some short Latin expressions) is underlined in red ink. 25 ff. The letters and words here placed within parentheses are, in the MS., written above (the endings of) the corresponding words.

propocito, propicius benedicas, et beate castitatis habitum, quem te inspirante susceperit (-perint), te protegente custodiat (-ant). Per christum dominum nostrum.

DEus, bonarum virtutum dator et omnium benediccionum largus infusor, exaudi preces nostras, et hanc (-as) vestem (-es), quam (-as) famula (-e) tua (-e) N. pro conseruande castitatis signo se ad-operiendam (-das) exposcit (-cunt), benedicere et sanctificare digneris. Per christum.

and her veil.

þe blissing our þe vayle: "Dominus vobiscum!

CAput omnium fidelium, deus, et tocius corporis saluator, hoc (-ec) operimentum (-ta) velaminis (-num), quod (que) famula (-e) tua (-e) propter tuam tueque genitricis beatissime sancte semper virginis marie amorem suo capiti est (sunt) impositura (-re), tua dextera et hoc, quod per illud (-a) mistice datur intelligi, tua semper custodia corpore pariter et animo incontaminato custodiat (-ant), vt quum ad perpetuam sanctorum remuneracionem uenerit (-int), cum prudentibus virginibus et ipsa (-e) preparata (-e) te perducente ad †perpetue felicitatis nupcias intrare meriatur (-an-). Per dominum."

[† leaf 121]

She shall receive habit

Efter þeir orisons kast haly watter o-pon þe clethyng, and þan þe prelete sal gyf þe madyn hir clethyng: first hir cote, sayand with-outen note:

"Accipe uestem! indue sanctitatis decorem! ornare habitu sancte religionis cum timore & reuerencia, quem interueniente beata dei genitrice Maria cum bonorum obseruancia operum ignita castitatis lampade suffulta immaculatum [ante] tribunal christi perferas. Qui viuit et regnat cum deo patre."

and mantle,

And sythen sal þe prelete gif hir þe mantiƚƚ, sayand: "Accipe uestem," vt supra.

and, after her hair has been cut off,

Efter þis, þen sal þe prelete with a payr of schers be-gyn forto kut hir hair befor at þe toppyng, sayand: "In nomine patris"—"et filii," behind—& "spiritus sancti"—"Amen," on aþer side. And þen sal þe priores kut o-way þe remnaunt of þe hair. And þen sal þe prelete gif hir hir wimpil, sayand:

wimple,

29. MS. *maculatum tribunal;* cf. p. 147, l. 2.—MS. *perfer/ras;* cf. p. 2, ll. 3, 7, footnotes. 33. MS. þe.

"Accipe peplum sacru*m*, puella, q*u*od pe*r*feras sine macu*la* ante t*r*ibunal do*mini* no*str*i ie*s*u chr*isti*, cui flectit*ur* om*ne* genu celestiu*m*, terrestriu*m*, & infernor*um*, in secula seculor*um*."

And þan þe prelete †sal lay þe vayle apon hir hede, sayand:

[† lf. 121, bk.] veil,

"Accipe velum sacru*m*, puella, quod pe*r*feras sine macu*la*," vt sup*ra*.

And þan sal he gif hir þe girdyl, sayand: "Accipe ȝonam," &c. þis orison "Accipe" salbe sayd at iij thynges, þ*at* es to wit: at þe gyfyng of þe wimpil, & of þe vayle, & of þe girdyl, als it es sayd be-for.

and girdle.

Efter þis sal þ*at* nun nouece stand stil befor þe auter & rede hir prouesse wit*h* note, sayand:

Then she shall sing her vow,

"Ego soror N., deo data, p*r*omitto stabilitate*m* meam et conuersionem mor*um* meor*um* et obidienciam sec*und*um regulam s*anct*i Benedicti cora*m* deo & om*nib*us s*anct*is eius in hoc monasterio, quod *con*structu*m* est in honorem s*anct*i N., in presencia domne N. priorisse."— þe p*ro*fession on english: "I sister N., giffyn to god, I hete my stabilnes & turnyng of my maners & buxsu*m*nes efter þe rewle of sant Benett, befor god & alł his halows in þis mynster, þ*at* es set in þe wirchep of sant N., in þe presence of daym N. priores."

When scho hase red †hir professe, scho sal wend vp to þe auter, And lay hir p*ro*fession-boke a-pon þe auter, & þe ryng wit*h*-al. And þan þe priores sal wind or lap þe maydyn handes in þe halowd towel of þe auter, & þan sal þ*at* nun nouece gay down be-nethen þe grece of þe auter, turnand hir vp vnto þe auter, standand, & sayand þis vers wit*h* note: "Suscipe me, d*omi*ne, sec*und*um eloquiu*m* tuu*m*, et viua*m*." And in þas wordes sayng, sal scho fałł down to þe erth, And þan rise vp & turn hir to þe pepil, sayand: "Et non confundas me ab exspectacione mea;" And lowte; & þis vers sal scho say iij tymes on þis maner. And þis same vers al þe congregacion, þ*at* es to wit, al þe conuent, sal answer thris, sayand wit*h*-outyn note: "Suscipe me, do*mi*ne" &c. wit*h* "Gloria p*at*ri;" And þan "kyriel*eison*, chr*iste*l*eison*, kyriel*eison*," "Pater no*ste*r." And þan sal þe nun be layd down grofelyng on lenghe be-

[† leaf 122] place it, with the ring, on the altar, have her hands wrapped in the altar cloth, return down, and sing 'Suscipe me,' etc.

The congregation shall answer;

she shall fall down

before the altar; and priest

[† lf. 122, bk.]

for þe ryght end of þe auter. And þan þe prelet sal say oue[r] hir with note: "Et ne nos," "Saluam (-as) [fac] ancillam (-as) tuam (-as)! Mitte ei (-is), domine, auxilium de sancto. Nichil †perficiat inimicus in ea (-is). Esto ei (-is), domine, turris fortitudinis. Domine, exaudi oracionem meam. Presta, quesumus, domine, huic (-iis) ancille (-is) tue (-is) renuncianti (-bus) secularibus pompis gracie tue ianuas aperire, que despectis mundi illecebris confugit (-unt) sub titulo christi, uenientem (-es) ad te sereno vultu suscipere, ne de ea (-is) valeat inimicus triumphare; tribue ei (-is), quesumus, infatigabile brachium auxilii tui; mentem eius (-arum) fidei lorica circumda, vt felici muro uallata (-e) mundum se gaudeat (-ant) euasisse. Per eundem dominum nostrum" &c.—And þen sal þe prelete, kneland be-for þe auter, begyn with note þe yme: "Veni, creator spiritus." And þe quere sal syng þe same vers to end. And þe prelete sal be-gyn ilka vers of þe yme kneland, & when he hase sayd al þat vers til end, he sal stand vp to þe tyme he begyn a-noþer vers; & on þis maner sal he do til þe yme all be endydde, & þe quer. sal syng þe remnant.

and congregation, alternately,

"VEni, creator spiritus, mentes tuorum visita, imple superna gracia que tu creasti pectora, Qui paraclitus diceris, donum dei."

[leaf 123] shall sing over her

when "veni, creator" es endyd, þe prelete sal say ouer hir with note þer orysons:

"Sancte spiritus, qui te deum ac dominum reuelare mortalibus dignatus es, immensam tue bonitatis graciam postulamus, vt sicut ubi-uis spiras, sic & huic ancille tue affectum deuocionis indulgeas, & que tua sapiencia est condita, tua quoque prouidencia gubernetur, quam iuxta consuetam graciam unccio tua de omnibus doceat, et per intercessionem beatissime dei genitricis Marie eam a vanitate seculi ueraciter conuerte, & sicut es omnium peccatorum remissio, deprimentes impietatis obligaciones in ea dissolue ad obseruanciam sancte castitatis vel virginitatis; fac eam certatim feruere in tribulacionibus & angustiis; tua difficiente consolacione valeat respirare, vt sobrie, iuste,

2. MS. *oue;* cf. Notes.—MS. *Saluam (-as) ancillam;* cf. p. 143, l. 29. 17. MS. *salbe gyn.* 20. MS. *þe tyme.*

& pie, per veram humilitatem atque deuocionem in christi caritate fundata, quod te donantę desiderat felici perseuerancia compleat in te; cui est honor et gloria cum patre & filio per omnia secula seculorum. amen.

Respice, domine propicius, super hanc famulam tuam N., vt virginitatis sancte propocitum, quod te inspirante suscepit, te gubernante custodiat. Per christum dominum. several

Da, quæsumus, Omnipotens deus, vt hec famula tua, que pro spe retribucionis eterne tibi domino desiderat consecrari, plena fide animoque in †sancto propocito permaneat; tu eam, omnipotens pater, sanctificare et benedicere et imperpetuum conseruare digneris; tribue ei humilitatem, castitatem, obedienciam, caritatem, & omnium bonorum quantitatem. Da ei, domine, pro operibus gloriam, pro pudore reuerenciam, pro pudicicia sanctitatem, vt ad meritum possit glorie peruenire; per christum. successive [† lf. 123, bk.

BEnedicat te conditor celi et terre, deus, pater omnipotens, qui te elegere dignatur ad sancte marie matris domini nostri iesu christi consorcium, vt integram et inmaculatam virginitatem, quam professa es coram domino et angelis eius, conserues, propocitum teneas, castitatem diligas, pacienciam serues, & coronam virginitatis accipere meriaris; per eundem christum. orisons.

BEnedicat te deus pater & filius & spiritus sanctus in omni benediccione spirituali, vt maneas sine macula sub vestimento marie, matris domini nostri iesu christi. Per dominum.

BEnedicat te & custodiat semper diuina maiestas patris et filii & spiritus sancti. Amen."

And þan cast hali water a-pon hir & encens hir'. And þe priores & þe couent sal þen go down into þe qwer' in-to þer stalles, & þan sal þe sub-priores lede þe ȝong nun to þe priores, & scho sal hald vp †botħ hir handes, & þe priores sal tak hir' handes be-twene hir handes & kis hir, & swa sal scho mak hir obedience, & swa fortħ til al þe couent, & þan saƚƚ scho be set in þe vttermest stale in þe quer', vnto þe "Agnus dei" of þe mese be down, & þen sal þe subpriores lede hir vp to þe auter'; & qwen þe prelete hase vsede & rineside, þan sal scho be howseld of hym, & þan

Holy water and incense having been used, [† leaf 124] she shall repeat her obedience vow to all, take her stall, receive the Eucharist, *remain in prayers till meal-time, observing silence for three days.*

At night her bed shall be hallowed

sal þe quer' sing þe comune of þe mese, & þe*n* sal þe sub-priores lede hir be-for þe lady auter', & þair sal scho sit in hir pr*a*yers vnto þe mete-tym. & þes iij days sal scho not spek vnto þe iiij day, þ*at* scho hafe leue of þe priores. And at euyn, when scho es in hir bede, þe p*r*iores & þe couent sal cu*m* vp in-to þe dortour, & þe prest & þe clerk wi*th* torcħ-lygħt forto halow hir bed; & he sal say wi*th*outyn note: "Ecce, non dor*m*itabit neq*ue* dor*m*itet D*omin*us vobiscu*m*.

BEnedic, do*mine*, hoc famularu*m* tuar*um* dormitoriu*m*, q*ui* non dormis neq*ue* dormitas, qui custodis isr*ae*l; famulam tua*m* in hac domo q*u*iescente*m* post labore*m* custodi ab illusionib*us*, fantasmat*is* sathane, vt vigilans in p*r*ecept*is* tuis meditetur, dormiens te p*er* sapore*m* senciat, & hic & vbiq*ue* defen†sionis tue auxilio muniat*ur*, P*er* d*omi*n*um* n*ostrum*."

[† lf. 124, bk.]

three times.

And efter þis orison sal he say "In principio"; & whe*n* þ*at* es sayd, þen sal he kest haly water, & encence hir & þe bede, & þe ij nygħtes efter þe conuent sal do þe same. //Amen.//

[*Here follows, in a later hand, a Latin prayer,* Benediccio Annule.]

NOTES.

NORTHERN PROSE VERSION.

1/14–16. THE negations, being double, have got out of gear. Lat. *ut non solum ut iratus pater suos non aliquando filios exheredet, sed nec ut metuendus dominus . . tradat.*

2/13. *þaim*, probably referring to *lippis*: "that thy life may follow thy lips." Cf. *sey euer the trouth in herte & mouth*, 122/2. But the Lat. has: *inquire pacem et sequere eam*; the Common Version: *sec sibbe and hyre ȝefolȝa.*

3/31–4/1. The passage is poetical (Introd. § 3) and deviates from the original text. Perhaps *þare may help þe here to* is a corruption of *þat þare may help þe, here do!* = Lat. *agendum est modo quod in perpetuum nobis expediat.*

4/4. *stresce*; thus I read the MS. It is well known that *ſt* and *ſc* are easily confused (as *storid* for *scorid*, p. 153, l. 10). Is not Halliwell's *streste* due to a mistake?

4/24. "So must be said of them as of the gold that thou mayst see, which . ."

4/29. "who neither want to be resident—but to go from place to place do they want—nor stay long (at each temporary abode)."

6/1. "For need's sake he may place one before another as to reverence (due to them), if he does not wish to have (or keep) each one in his order, as he takes it."

7/3. *of litil oresun*, "unable to pray much (and eloquently)." But the Lat. has: *ne causetur de minori forte substantia.*

7/8. *Nichil de-esse*; the Lat. text: *Nihil deest timentibus eum.*

7/23. "let her keep to the one which is best."

7/30. Lat. *omnes magistram sequantur regulam.*

7/32. *Yef any sal take discipline, gruching sal sho make nane.* But the Lat. has: *quod si presumpserit quisquam, disciplinae regulari subjaceat.*

10/26. An addition like "yea, it beseems you" would be quite in the style of the rule; see Introd. § 138. Another possibility: *for þi sal tu quite þe wid scrift, ye[f] it bi-timis yu*; cf. 17/6.

13/13–15. Lat. *Probasti nos, inquit, deus, igne nos examinasti, sicut examinatur argentum; induxisti nos in laqueum, posuisti tribulationes in dorso nostro.* Thus *laqueum* is the Lat. word apparently corresponding to *lay*, and the latter may be a corruption of *las*, "snare." Cf. Introd. § 45.

13/21. *weris taim*, "wears them" (*i. e.* the mantles). The whole passage is quite different from the original text: *auferenti tunicam dimittunt et pallium*, etc. (cf. Luke vi. 29).

14/32. *and helpis noht*, "and is no use."

15/29 ff. The Lat. rule speaks of vigils (2 a.m.), a short interval, matins (at day-break). Here: night-service, a short interval, work at day-break.

16/30. "in that same above-mentioned order."

17/10. *feste-dais . . sexe salmis.* But the Lat. has: *dominico die . . sexagesimus sextus psalmus.*

18/6. *And* (MS. *At*) *o niht ryse*, Lat. *et nocte surgamus.* Seven *at*'s before in those two lines!

18/10 ff. Thus: 1. the verse "Deus," 2. the hymn, 3. three psalms, 4. a lesson, etc.—For *te salme* the Lat. has: *psalmi* (pl.).

18/30–33. Not in the original. Cf. Luther's "Winkelmesse."

19/31. Where the Lat. rule makes an exception for *affectu inspirationis*, this version puts *mis-trouz.*

24/31. "and for utensils and other things she shall provide such of whose life and deed she is sure." Cf. 128/29 ff.

25/27. "To the needy shall she (*i. e.* the sound sister who gives) humble herself in their illness, and she (*i. e.* the sick sister) shall not . ."

30/9. *þe gloria patri of þe Venite*, the "Glory be to the Father," etc., which is sung after the 94th psalm.

35/6. *Alle . . And*; Lat. *omnibus congruus honor exibeatur, maxime domesticis fidei et peregrinis.* Cf. p. 102, l. 1929.

35/13. *alure* is a suspicious form. Murray, under the verb *allure*, quotes: *God's love alure* (1616), *alluring the mercy of God* (1622). Thus, certainly, it does not seem altogether impossible that the idea of worship, expressed by *anure* (Lat. *honorare*) and *aure* (Lat. *adorare*) was, at an early period, associated with the verb *alure.* But the expression *ouþir wid þe heuidis ouþir wid al þe bodi* would go better with an *alute*, "bow down in deference or worship"; the Lat. has: *inclinato capite vel prostrato toto corpore in terram*; and, as is well known, the letters *t* and *r* were easily confused (cf. 2/27). A third possibility is the assumption of a simple blunder for *anure* or *aure.*

36/20. *In caald cuntre es nede of warmer hend* makes the impression of being a proverbial saying. The Lat. has: *in frigidis regionibus amplius indigetur.*

38/39. *þat sho*, etc. The Lat. conveys quite a different thought: *ut si aliquando suadente diabolo consenserit, ut egrediatur de monasterio, quod absit, tunc exuta rebus monasterii proitiatur.*

39/18. *Sain Benet hauis te sperance of þoþir* means essentially the same as the Lat. *quod absit.*

39/21. *þat we*, etc., *i. e.* that we may act up to our high calling, our relatives having offered us to God.

39/34. *Yef þar*, etc. Here our version, or its pattern, deals rather freely with the original text.

40/6. *hym-selfe, He*, erroneous masculine forms (Introd. § 6).

40/18. Possibly an original *swilk* was misread as *hvilk* and changed into *whilk.*

42/16. "that she may refer, for testimony, both to the New and to the Old Testament."

42/25. *beli pipe* answers to the Lat. *calamum quassatum* (Common Version: *tocwysede hreod*), but it is hard to account for the form. A participle like *berid*, beaten, bruised, would seem acceptable. Or has *beli-pipe*, "bag-pipe" (not in N.E.D.), been introduced through some misunderstanding?

43/6. *þat yafe*, etc., Lat. *qui erogavit triticum conservis suis in tempore suo.*

43/18. Lat. *materia ei datur superbiendi.*

47/19. "For holy men, who lead a good life . . , such things may support (be a help to keep) this life."

NORTHERN METRICAL VERSION.

(B. = Böddeker; H. = Holthausen; K. = Kölbing; cf. Introd. § 1, *F.*)

I commence by giving a list of erroneous readings left uncorrected by K.: sely 1, here 116 ('123'), hafs 150 ('159,' in the note), amendes 204 ('215'), Commers in þe kingdom 250 ('262'), lighth 301 ('314'), folc 406 ('424'), þe 509 ('529'), ne 569 ('591'), honour 673 ('698'), bocksum 682 ('707'), te 883 ('918'), asaide 954 ('991'), haly 991 ('1028'), deuocion 1191 ('1235'), nunces 1209 ('1253'), chastyng 1244 ('1289'), That 1262 ('1306'), fast 1265 ('1309'), chastisyng 1356 ('1401'), omission of: *id est* 1360b ('1406'), celararii 1420b ('1467'), storid 1536 ('1589'), witsununday 1703 ('1764'), seruise 1896 ('1959'), wer 1997 ('2063'), hir mayne 2141 ('2210'), chaisted 2456 ('2533').

Some of these errors, and others not mentioned here, are of a more or less harmless nature. But sense and construction, and statements in grammars, essays, and dictionaries, are concerned when a text offers *sely* for *lely*, *commers* for *comuners*, *lighth* for *lightli*, *ne* for *not*, *bocksum* (!) for *bowsum*, *nunces* for *nouices*, *That* for *what*, *fast* for *tast*, *storid* for *scorid*, *wer* for *whor*, etc.

Fresh errors introduced by the collator: Thurch 34 ('35'; B. is right; the 't' is distinct enough both here, in l. 39, and other places), fulfillyd 78 ('82'), gudenes 160 ('169'; see below), Ne 570 ('592'), awm 712 ('737'; for B.'s 'awn'; both are wrong), it ho 890 ('925'; certainly 'who,' as B. prints it, although not unlike 'it ho'), fon*n*e 1078 ('1117'; for B.'s fone; both are wrong), *mihi* 1098b, 1312b ('1138b, 1357b'), Subpriores 1553 ('1607'), III 1576 ('1631'; see below), & ȝapli 1674 ('1733'; it is B.'s '& apli,' not his 'apli,' that is to be corrected into 'ȝapli'), loqu*antur* 1728b ('1790'; see below), þ*am* 1736 ('1798'; B. is right), m*od*o 1802b ('1865b'), Sicut (the first letter is n o t totally red; it is black with a perpendicular red stroke through it), 2154 ('2224').

Part of the inaccuracies and errors mentioned in these lists are due to inadvertency. Others — the majority — were deliberately accepted or advanced.

I may add that K. corrects B.'s þerfourn into p*ar*fourn 224 ('236'), but parfection into pe*r*feccion 2486 ('2564').

30 ('31'). 'þ*i*, ms. þ*ⁱ* (= þ*ai*).' B. Of course þ*ⁱ* means þ*i*, and nothing else; cf. p. 48, footnote.

55 ('56'). B. punctuates: Þe *whylk yf* þ*ay dyde, wele myght wend*, and adds the explanation: '*dyde*, i. e. be worthy.' Similar specimens of B.'s punctuation are to be found in 267 ('280'), 373 ('390'), 422–424 ('440–442'), 452 ('471') 1159 ('1202'), 1531 ('1584') ff., 1586 ('1641') ff., etc. Some others have been corrected by H.

97 ('103'). '*Als so say*, der sage es.' B. I render the line: "I am desirous, also, to speak of him."

129 ('136'). B. substitutes *we* for *he*. In either case the pron. must refer to the man who wishes to be saved.

145–146 ('154–155'). B. puts the comma after *noy*.

159–160. The lines may, as also H. suggests, have run something like this: *For thúrth oure míghtes mór no mýn Máy we nónekyns gúde begýn.* K. declares that the MS. has *gudenes* and that H.'s emendation thus 'sich erledigt.' But there is not even the slightest trace of another syllable after *gude*; and as B. saw the MS. in 1872, K. in 1896, the whole thing appears somewhat mysterious. Nor could I accept K.'s reading even as an emendation; it is not supported by the evidence of the text itself. For *gudenes* is not used anywhere else in the whole version, whereas *gude* occurs substantively twice on the same leaf (of my print): ll. 109 and 168, the latter passage answering very closely to the line in question. And the words *alkin(e)s, alkin (-kyn), nokins, whatkyn,* in all the nine instances in which they occur, are accentuated — ◡, followed as they are by a monosyllabic word (usually a rhyme-word).

The collocations *mor no min, mor or les,* etc., gradually wore down into mere expletives, or nearly so. Partly on this account, it is sometimes hard to decide whether the words should be looked on as pure adjectives, as adjectives used substantively, or as adverbs.

275 ('288'). '*mekli . .*, lies *mekil.*' H. See Glossary.

331 ('345'). [*in*] *werld.* B. But see Glossary.

334b. Properly *spiritum adopcionis* (Rom. viii. 15); but to judge from *gaste of mede,* the corruption must have been already in the copy used by the author.

340 ('355'). 'lies *þer . .* st. *ȝer.*' H. But see Introd. § 58, 1 (§ 59, 1).

372 ('389'). 'das verbum *be* fehlt vor oder hinter *dampned.*' H. True in a sense. But see Introd. § 128.

459 ('478'). B. substitutes *let* for *set.* But see Glossary.

588 ('610'). Lat. *nihil amori Christi preponere*; Common Version: *nan þing beforan Cristes lufe settan.* B. supplies: [god].

592. *for to sake,* possibly for original *to forsake.*

627. *praers* can hardly be explained as the direct object of *schriue,* the pronoun *vs* in such a case being the indirect object: "and prayers to God we should prescribe for ourselves as penance." Such a construction of the verb is not recorded elsewhere (as far as my knowledge goes). In all probability the original had *In.* As *in* was also a worn-down form of the conj. *and* (2007, 2260), and the whole passage (607 ff.) is full of *and's,* the substitution of *And* for *In* seems easily accounted for. Thus properly: "In prayers to God we should confess (and take penance)." B. makes the same emendation.

677 ('702'). 'Der text ist wahrscheinlich zum theil corrumpirt.' B. 'Die verderbniss des textes ist leicht zu beseitigen, wenn wir . . *And* streichen.' H. *And,* however, can be satisfactorily explained (whether used by the poet, or added by a scribe). In Northern languages, the corresponding *och* (*å'*, etc.) is freely used after an adj. or a quality-noun to introduce the expression for that in which the quality consists, or what it concerns: *han hade den vänligheten å' komma* (he had the kindness to come); *jag var färdig å' gråta* (I was on the point of crying). And in our texts, p. 44, ll. 20–21, we actually find: *þat þai . . alle timis finde hir redi and speke with þaim.* This sentence might, with a different word-order, easily have turned into: *redi and with þaim (for) to speke.* Thus, in 677, *And . . to* is practically the same as "to," and from our point of view we may term it pleonastic. But that, I believe, is all.

699. I am not certain of this *bown.* Cf. however 317–318.

796. *mekenes* is the subject (misunderstood by B. in Engl. Stud. ii, p. 364).

801. Even if *crakes* might have been tolerably understood as "talks," "tales" (?), there is not the smallest doubt but it is a corruption of *clerkes. Als clerkes tels* is, like *who likes to loke,* etc., one of those favourite phrases which, with various modifications (cf. 2459, 773, 461, 858, 836), were used in mediæval poetry both to give a stamp of authority to the exposition and to supply a convenient rhyme. The latter object is served by phrases like *in feld and town, arely and late, be day and night, loud and still,* which also meet us so often here and elsewhere. Cf. J. Ullmann's treatise on Richard Rolle de Hampole in Engl. Stud. vii, pp. 415 ff. (specially pp. 428-454).

867. *in ȝarning* (MS.) would certainly give some sense: even before it has become a thought or deed. Yet the alteration, made also by B., is probably right.

897. I might have mentioned that the two words *þat hase* in 896 were thoughtlessly repeated after *fader*, but immediately crossed out again.

915. To supply the missing line is out of the question. It may have conveyed a thought like: *For þi he shewed swilk bowsumnes.*

924 ('959'). 'wir haben ohne zweifel für *þai* einzuführen *þam.*' B. (Eng. Stud. ii, p. 360). But see Introd. §§ 37, 114.

929 ('964'). On account of the preceding *þai, þer, þam*, 'ist auch hier *þer* statt *our* einzusetzen.' H. But see Introd. § 138.

938, 940 ('974, 976'). 'lies *sofferand* st. *souerand.*' H. But cf. Introd. §§ 55, 89, 90, and *vnsouerable*, Wallace, ed. Jamieson, l. 267, etc.

942. The line has fared badly: *r þi sake for* is written on an erasure, *r sa e fo* being much blurred; *to* is squeezed in afterwards between *for* and *be*; traces of the old letters are left. In its present shape, it is cumbrously long. *Al (þe) dáy for þí sake tó be sláyn* would run smoothly.

965 ('1002'). '*o bouen* [*vs*].' B.

972 ('1008'). 'Vor *oþer* fehlt offenbar *þat* oder *þet.*' H. But cf. Glossary.

1045 ('1084'). 'nach dem beispiele, das zu ersehen ist an denjenigen.' B. Misconstruction. See Introd. § 135.

1070 ('1109'). B., misunderstanding the function of *laghter*, transposes *at* and *be*.

1126 ('1167'). 'lies *be* st. *bi.*' H. But cf. Glossary.

1131 ('1172'). 'lies *þe* statt des ersten *al.*' H.

1172 ff. The lines give fairly good sense without an alteration: "since we may see (from Scripture), that everything we do," etc. Nevertheless it is not unlikely that the first *we*, as H. suggests, stands in the place of an original *þai*: "since they can see all that we do."

1221 ('1265'). 'ergänze *þai* vor *vse.*' H. This does not improve the metre (cf. 1829). Yet it may be right. In both the lines (605 and 1221) where I wish to explain *no* as "none" (like *a*="an"), something may be omitted.

1198b ('1242b'). What I expand as *Quomodo sanctimonialles*, K. explains as *Quod singillatim.*

1253–54. The omitted line may as well have been the first in the pair, *for* being wrong for *fro*, like in 1259, etc.

1266 ('1310'). '*fullyng* zu mlat. *fullare*, neuengl. *to full.*' B. But see Glossary, and Introd. § 99.

1269 ff. Although *comyn* might be, and might have been, taken for an adj. ("familiar," "communicating") and *cum* for a participle, I believe, like B., that *If* is omitted: "If a nun . . communes . . or comes." Lat. *Si qua soror presumpserit*; Winteney Version: *Gyf hwilc swuster . . ȝedyrstlæcð.* In a prior copy, a blank had probably been left for the word; cf. 2179 and the footnotes on 923, 2151, 2481.

1306 ('1351'). 'lies *arest* (=*arested*) st. *warest.*' H. But see Glossary.

1317 ('1362'). K. corrects B.'s *found*, but puts a (!) after *faund*, thus appearing to misunderstand the word.

1403. *Or els* regularly means "or else;" thus: "or else rebellious rise against her." But it is tempting to compare the line with 440: "or as a rebel rise against her." Then *els* would be a corruption, or possibly a weakened form, of *als*; cf. *es* (8/3) = *as*.

1434 ('1481'). The end of the line, where all the letters stand rather far apart, may be transcribed *her to*, as I have done, or *herto*, as B. did. But the sense is "to her," not "hereto."

1457 ('1506'). B. substitutes *serue* for *saue*. Uncalled for.—B. prints *selu*, K. says the MS. has *seln*. It is quite true that the last character looks like an *n*. However, if K. had compared it *e.g.* with the fourth letter in *wayue* 444, he would have found that the last-mentioned letter has the same claims on being rendered by an *n*. But the word being a rhyme-word, K. silently put *u*.

1468. In M.V. *what so* means "whatever;" in P.V. the same words would have meant "what she." The latter signification suits the context much better and probably belonged to the original metrical text.

1476 ('1526'). 'lies *þe enournmentes*.' H.

1490 ('1540'). 'lies *er* st. *es*.' H. But see Glossaries.

1517 ('1568'). For B.'s erroneous *falted* H. substitutes *failed*. K. states that the MS. has *falled* and accepts H.'s emendation. Cf. however Introd. §§ 78, 99.

1576 ('1631'). B. correctly prints *in like*. K. declares the MS. has *III like*, and refers to the Lat. *addatur et tercium*! Cf. ll. 408, 1635.

1633 ('1691'). B. expands *leuerty*, which is impossible. The omission of a syllable (cf. 142/8) need not be supposed either. The meaning is, that they should not possess anything, but rather receive what is necessary to each one.

1728b ('1790'). B.'s reading, loquatur, is wrong, K.'s is impossible. But I wavered between loq*uantur* and loq*uantur*.

1756 ('1818'). K. thinks *day* was altered into *þay*. I admit that this would appear more natural. But the *d*-part of the hybrid character is written with specially black, bold strokes, as if intended to predominate.

1780 ('1843'). 'ergänze *be* vor *ianglyng*.' H. See my note on 372.

1868–70. The Lat. text mentions no other hour than *terciam* and *decimam*. Line 1780 seems as weak as *in Descember* 1121.

1878 ('1941'). 'ergänze *be* vor *writ*.' H. I would rather insert it before the participle. Cf. Introd. § 128, end.

1890 ('1953'). '*þai s* ist wol zu streichen.' H. This would be a metrical disimprovement. And cf. passages mentioned in Introd. § 138.

1929. "who are known to be pilgrims."

1968. The line corresponds to *in medio templi tui* 1966b, *I-middis ti tempil* 35/24.

2008 ('2074'). 'lies *Less* st. *Sich*, vgl. das original: *in calidis uero minus*.' H. Cf. Glossary.

2027 ('2093'). 'lies *wend*.' H. Cf. Introd. § 60, 2.

2076. ('2145') 'ergänze *men*, man, vor *hir*.' H. I have substituted *þai* for *þat*. My supposition is that the original had the shorter conjunctional phrase *Or tyme*, followed by the pron. *þai*. Equivalent to *or tyme*, and just as common, was the fuller *or tyme þat* (2286), analogously to *fro time* (2201) and *fro time þat* (1719), *do wilis* (2/7) and *to whilis þat* (40/29, 33). Thus the slip was easily made.

2190 ('2262'). 'lies *lay* st. *law*.' H. Cf. Introd. § 41, and Glossary.

2354 ('2430'). B. incorrectly substitutes *as* for *at*.

2346 ('2421'). 'B. ändert *strengh in* zu *strengthen*, was aber gar keinen sinn giebt. Es is einfach *þam* vor *in* einzuschieben.' H. *þam* is very acceptable, but does not seem quite necessary: "then God shall grant strength in their deed."

2385 ('2462'). '*to play* giebt in diesem zusammenhange keinen rechten sinn. Ich vermute, dass *to play* für ursprüngliches *o-way* geschrieben ist.' H. But cf. the opening lines of the chapter, and the statement in

W. Dugdale's Monasticon Anglicanum, vol. ii, p. 474a (London 1846), that a lady superior was allowed 'to go out of the monastery to one of her manors, to take the air and divert herself.'

2432. Cf. Introd. § 136.

CAXTON ABSTRACT.

119/4. "in order that they may often read and execute the whole rule, and keep it so much better than it is kept."

120/19. "to make arrangements wisely and carefully, and about all things in the place." Possibly *and* is due to an inadvertency.

125/5. "is this, when (*when* . . *þat*) they will confess to their superior, meekly and with repentance, all evil thoughts," etc.

128/14. "to keep well, so well as though . ."

129/7. "that anyone should have," "for anyone to have."

133/33. "and after their prayer (has been) made together and joined together in God's peace, (there shall be) kissing together and saluting of each other, with subsequent refreshing of themselves."

134/37. "occasion to grumble, or to work anything, or to keep anything."

LANSDOWNE RITUAL.

148/2. *one*[*r*]. Thus I read the MS., referring to 144/2, 146/10, 148/26. Possibly: *one*, "on"; cf. 143/29. The spelling *one* for *on*, however, occurs in no other instance in all the five texts.

GLOSSARY

TO THE NORTHERN TEXTS.

THE order is, on the whole, alphabetical (þ = th, v = u, ȝ = z), cross-references upholding due connections. The small displacements only involve that a word not found in its strictly alphabetical place, must be sought two steps above. An asterisk means: not so in the MS., not so in the Caxton Print. When used alone, *vb.* practically means: verb in the infinitive or subjunctive mood (or in an ambiguous form); *sg.*, *pl.* after a verb means: present indicative singular, pres. ind. (sometimes possibly subjunctive) plural. For other abbreviations see p. xix.

The occasional short etymological notes must only be regarded as expediential hints, in special cases, to lead the reader's thoughts in the right direction.

This Glossary, as well as the following, may from different points of view be considered to give both too much and too little. At all events they contain a good many words, forms, and significations not yet to be found in the New English or any other dictionary, or not yet recorded from the 15th century.

a, *indef. art.* 1/14, 15, 4/4, 182, 184, etc. an, 4/17. *num.* one, 6/4, 20/19, 23/10, 143/26, 144/12; 704, 971, 1200, 1206, etc. Cf. **an, ay, o, ta.**

a (unintentionally?) = **and,** 1903.

abba, *sb.* abbey, convent, 325. **abbais,** *pl.* 1632, 2425. **abbay,** 305, 1338, 1453, 2164, etc.

abbas, *sb.* abbess, 43/16, 22, 24. **abbes,** 12/37, 13/25, 37/15, 41/6, etc. *gen.* 37/5. **abbesse,** 42/2, 43/16, 20, 47/1, etc. **abes,** 7/32, 9/9, 31, 16/31, etc. Cf. **tabes, þabbasse.**

abbot, *sb.* 339, 1279. **-is** *pl.* 42/7. Cf. **abot.**

abet, *sb.* habit, 141/23. Cf. **abit, habete.**

abide, *vb.* 41/2, 142/25, 143/5. Cf. **obide.**

abil, *adj.* able, 1410, 1562. **abill,** 2228.

abit = **abet,** 4/27.

abot, *sb.* abbot, 5/5, 9, 14, etc. **-is,** *pl.* 5/25. Cf. **abbot, þabot.**

about, *adv.* 306. **abowte,** *prep.* 144/8. Cf. **abute, obout.**

abstenand, *ppr.* abstaining, 1885.

abstinens, *sb.* 28/27, 33/35, 142/18.

abute, *prep.* about, 24/22. Cf. **about.**

acceptabil, *adj.* acceptable, 722.

achesun, *sb.* occasion, 30/16, 36/14, 17, 45/26, etc. **for a-n,** for some reason, 41/22. **for nane a-n,** on any account, 45/22. Cf. **enchesun.**

achesunnir, *sb.* annoyer, harasser, disturber, 45/27. [O.F. *achesoner,* accuse, disquiet, harass, vex.]

acline, *vb.* bow down, 46/16. Cf. **enclind.**

acord, *vb.* accord, agree, 117, 1169, 1437. **-e,** 19/19, 416, 727. **-es,** *sg.* 523.

acumbird, *pp.* encumbered, 25/35, 26/6, 33/18.

after, *adv.* 1128. *prep.* 1125. *conj.* according as, 1600. Cf. **efter.**

afterward, *adv.* 242. Cf. **efterward.**

again, *adv.* again; back, 23/19, 143/21, 144/19. *prep.* against, 4/21, 19/3, 24/2, etc. **againe,** *adv.* 143/18. **agayn,** 141/26, 1350,

1903, 2029. **agayne,** 1/4, 31/7. *prep.* (postpos.) 276. Cf. **aigain, igain, ogain.**

againis, *prep.* against, 35/9. **agains,** 267. **agayns,** 955, 1378, 1395, 1403. Cf. **igainis, oganis.**

aght, *num.* eighth, 1041, 1124. Cf. **ahtend.**

aght, *vb. pt.-pr. sg.* ought; behoves, beseems, befits, 1166. Cf. **ahte, aȝht,** and **ah.**

agrè, *vb.* refl., agree, 143/9.

ah, *vb. sg.* ought, should; behoves, 5/5, 11, 12, 20/5, 24/11, etc. *pl.* 8/12, 14, 15, 9/33, 12/4, 21/26, 28, etc. owe, 34/21. **ahat** = **ah at,** 18/31, 32, 22/11. Cf. **aw, az, aȝh,** and **aght.**

ahe, *sb.* awe, 19/14. Cf. **aw, aze.**

ahen, *adj.* own, 7/31, 8/18, 10/4, 11, 12/9, etc. Cf. **awn.**

ahte, *vb. pt.-pr. pl.* ought, 19/26. Cf. **aght.**

ahtend, *num.* eighth, 14/16. Cf. **aztend** and **aght.**

ai, *adv.* ever, always, 714. Cf. **ay.**

aier, *vb. pl.* are, 34/18. Cf. **are.**

aigain, *prep.* against, 20/33. Cf. **again.**

ailastand, *adj.* everlasting, 66.

aile, *sb.* ale, 1605, 1610.

ainly, *adv.* only, 269. Cf. **anly.**

aioingne, *vb.* enjoin penance, 21/11.

aiont, *adv.* together, 16/1.

air, *adv.* ere, before, 1114, 1637, 1713, 2327. **aire,** 456. Cf. **are.**

aires, *sb. pl.* heirs, 218. Cf. **ayris.**

airly, *adv.* early, 646. Cf. **arely, ayrly.**

al, *adj., pron.* all, every, 1/13, 3/7, 8/2, 13, 145/14, etc. *adv.* all, quite, altogether, 39/12, 1552, 2156, 2358. as an expletive, 2213. **al be it,** albeit, 881. **al if,** even if, even though, 237, 362, 729, 884, etc. Cf. **all.**

alane, *adj.* alone, 21/30. *adv.* only, 46/10.

alanly, *adv.* alone, only, 1/15.

albedene = **al bedene,** 2171.

ald, *adj.* (*sb.*) old, 106, 526, 1051, 1208, etc. **alde,** 6/3, 7/25, 30, 8/4, etc. Cf. **old, þalde,** and **elder.**

algate, *adv.* always, 1777. **algayte,** 2413.

alkin, all kind of, 2485. **alkyn,** 1656. Cf. **allekin.**

alkines, do., 1888. **alkins,** 166, 2011, 2207. Cf. **kyns.**

all, *adj., pron.* 7/27, 8/2, 12/15, 1, 9, 30, 2376, etc. *adv.* all, quite, wholly, 2/35, 152. **alle,** 1/10, 2/33, 6/4, 7/24, etc. *adv.* 40/21. **all if,** *conj.* even if, even though, 273, 2071. Cf. **al.**

allaine, *adv.* alone, only, 896. **allane,** 196. **allayn,** *adj.* alone, 1251. *adv.* 381, 769, 1116, *2257, etc. Cf. **allon.**

allekin = **alkin,** 35/11.

alleluia, Halleluiah, 16/12, 32, 17/12, 21, etc.

allemihti, *adj.* almighty, 47/17. **-mihtye,** 38/6. Cf. **almihti.**

aller, *gen.* of all, 1815, 2240.

allon, *adv.* alone, only, 158, 172, 290, etc. **allone,** *adj.* 1261. Cf. **allaine.**

allwase, *adv.* always, 93. **allways,** 163. Cf. **alwais.**

allway, do., 143/20. Cf. **alway.**

almihten, *adj.* almighty, 14/4.

almihti, do., 2/17, 19/18, 46/30. **almyghty,** 100, 338, 578. Cf. **allemihti.**

almus, *sb.* alms, 39/12. **almus-dede,** *sb.* alms-deed, 581.

als, *adv.* so; as, 4/24, 7/11, 29, 16/18, 1668, 1743, etc. also, 9, 193, 299, 316, etc. *conj.* as, like, 1/21, 2/1, 3, 4/24, 2, 576, 689, *911, 976, 1243, 1357, 1590, 2329, 2434, etc. *rel.* 30/26, 1428, 2236. Cf. 10/21, 17/19, 40/27. **als . . þoz,** as though, 10/7. Cf. **also, as.**

also, *adv.* 1/15, 373, 487, etc. even, 634. **als-so,** 97. **als-sua,** 3/29, 19/5, 30/18, 33/14, etc. **alswa,** 43/26. Cf. **als.**

als-suilke, *pron.* the same, 30/27.

alure, *vb.* 35/13. See Notes.

alwais, *adv.* always, 331, 834, 838, etc. **always,** 141, 174, 533, etc. Cf. **allwase.**

alway, do., 28, 111, 547, 735, etc. Cf. **allway.**

alweldand, *adj.* almighty, 202, 1144.

am, *vb.* 1 *sg.* 97, 99, 116, 742.
ambrosine, *adj.* Ambrosian, 17/15.
amen, 2/18, 3/3, 26, 4/13, etc.
amend, *vb.* 197, 366, 1238, 1532. intr. 1327. refl. 20/8, 885, 1804. *pp.* 1275, 1671. **-e**, 21/2, 27/26, 30/17. intr. 20/9, 21/1, 2. refl. 9/8, 20/35, 30/17, etc. **-id**, *pp.* 20/31, 21/13, 16, 25/31, etc.
amendement, *sb.* amendment, 22/8, 23/15, 31/1, 46/22, etc. **amendment**, 46/21, 141/24.—**amendes**, *sb. pl.* amends, 204, 628, 1774, etc. **amendis**, 17/9, 33/16.
amise, *adv.* amiss, 13/20.
amonesce, *vb.* admonish, 6/19.
amoneste, do., 20/35. Cf. **moneste**.
an, *indef. art.* 22/7. a, 46/21. *num.* one, 16/19, 21/22, 25/15, etc. *pron.* 6/2, 25/14, etc. Cf. **a, ane, ay(n), on**.
an = **and**, 2/29, 612.
ancewer, *sb.* answer, 2/30. *vb.* 7/12, 44/23. Cf. **anscewer**.
and, *conj.* 1/3, 21, *3/7, *6/12, *18/6, etc. "to," 44/21. Cf. 677. "then," 1583. **&**, 1/2, 3, etc. Cf. **a, an, in**.
ane, *indef. art.* an, 298, 1279, 2409. a, 22/22. *num.* one, 20/8, 22/23, 1297, 1308, etc. *pron.* one; somebody, 38/28, 41/30, 42/6, 1229, 1337, etc. **þam ane**, alone, 4/22. **bi þam ane**, 4/19; similarly 18/10, 20/17, 26/35, 30/26, 35/28, etc. Cf. **an, tane**, also **alane, oþer**.
aneli, *adv.* only, 1022. **anely**, 342, 1416, 2254. *adj.* solitary, 273. Cf. **anly**.
anes, *adv.* once, 453, 1628. Cf. **anis, ons**.
angel, *sb.* 12/1, 21, 879. **-s**, *pl.* 11/16, 27, 19/17, 800, *1162, 1164, etc.
anger, *sb.* anchorite, 266.
angers, *sb. pl.* afflictions, 955, 958.
angri, *adj.* angry, 42/28.
anhede, *sb.* unity, 416.
ani, *adj.* any, 3/6, 6/15, 8/33, 17/8, etc. *pron.* any, anybody, 8/27, 24/36, 30/33. Cf. **any**.
anikin, any kind of, 47/14.
anis, *adv.* once, 28/26. Cf. **anes**.
anly, *adv.* only, 1620. Cf. **ainly, aneli, aynli**.
annual, *adj.* 1478.
a-noder, *adj.*, *pron.* another, 143/26, 1996. **a-noþer**, *6/2, 148/19, 410, 756, 1555, etc. **a-noþir**, *7/26, 10/5, 20/8, 10, 20, etc. Cf. **oþer**.
anoy, *vb.* annoy, trouble, injure, 32/6. Cf. **noid**.
anscewer, *vb.* answer, 24/15. **ansewere**, 38/33. **answer**, 143/25, 30, 32, 98, 724, 733, 1753, etc. *sb.* 44/18, 214, 1459, 1461, 2420. **answers**, *vb. sg.* 136, 137. Cf. **ancewer**.
antefen, *sb.* antiphon, 16/2, 17/16. **-fens**, *pl.* 16/4, 28, 17/11, 18, etc. **-fin**, 21/13, 31/15.
antente, *sb.* = **entent**, 12/14, 19/27, 27/5.
anure, *vb.* worship, 35/10. [O.F. *honourer*, Lat. *honorare.*]
any, *adj.* 19/24, 21/33, 39/4, 516, 1028. *pron.* any, anybody, 7/32, 19/31, 20/7, 31, 846, 1016, 1693, 2333, etc. Cf. **ani, ony**.
apendis, *vb. sg.* belongs 35/30. [O.F. *apendre.*]
apocalips, *sb.* Apocalypse, Revelation, 17/14.
apon, *prep.* upon, 42/33, 43/13, 135, 184, 369, etc. Cf. **opon**.
apostel, *sb.* apostle, 332. **apostil**, 23/8, 430, 911, 2300. **apostils**, *pl.* 36/33, 37/19, 20. **appostel**, 1442. **appostil**, 200, 976, 1264, 1328, etc. **appostils**, *pl.* *2042. Cf. **postil, ta-postil, þa-postil**.
appils, *sb. pl.* apples, 1573.
apreuid, *pp.* reproved *25/2.
aquaintance, *sb.* acquaintance, 45/23.
ar, *vb. pl.* are, 12/12, 17/12, 142/4, 144/9, etc. Cf. **are**.
ar, *prep.* ere, before, 27/12. *conj.* 36/9, 40/8. Cf. **are**.
aray, *sb.* array, order, 1454, 1473. *vb.* array, clothe, 141/10. **arayid**, *pp.* 144/10. Cf. **array**.
are, *vb. pl.* 144/5. Cf. **aier, ar, er, err**, and **is**.
are, *adv.* ere, before, 1861. *conj.* 9/15, 18/12, 30/20, 44/36, etc. Cf. **air, ar, hare, or**.
arely, *adv.* early, 1396, 1599, 2424. **arliker**, *comp.* 16/23. **arly**, 1866. Cf. **airly**.

armitis, *sb. pl.* hermits, 47/18. Cf. **eremete.**
armur, *sb.* armour, 1/8. **-s,** *pl.* 38.
array, *sb.* 2099. Cf. **aray.**
arrest, *pp.* stopped, checked, 297.
as, *conj.* 1/14, 44/21, 142/31, 143/8. Cf. **als, es, os.**
asaide, *pp.* tried, 956. **asayde,** 954. Cf. **assay.**
asaumpil, *sb.* example, 5/8, 26, 10/10. Cf. **ensampil, saumpyl.**
ascried, *pp.* decried, cried down, 1641.
ascuse, *vb.* excuse, 44/30. Cf. **excuse.**
asembil, *vb.* assemble, 29/25. **-d,** *pp.* 30/22.
asemblè, *sb.* assembly, 474.
ask, *vb.* ask, demand, require, 129, 209, 520, 558, etc. **aske,** 1/9, 19/24, 30/30, etc. *pl.* 2/27, 3/23, 19/25, etc. *imp.* 15/1. **asked,** *pt.* 1906. **askes,** *sg.* 141/22, 145/6, 132, 133, 1435. *pl.* beg, 1448. **askid,** *pt.* 37/21. *pp.* 2/30, 141/4. **askis,** *sg.* 24/2, 41/6, 43/34, 141/26. **askys,** 12/20.
asking, *sb.* asking, demand, 24/4, 38/2, 39/25, 41/2, etc.
asoile, *vb.* absolve, 31/23. **asoiles,** *sg.* 31/11. **asoilid,** *pp.* 31/9.
ass, *vb. pl.* have, 2404. Cf. **has.**
assay, *vb.* try, 959, 1295. Cf. **asaide.**
assayle, *vb.* assail, attack, 239.
assent, *sb.* 1423, 1555, 2221. *vb.* 36, 153, 375, 436, 1601, etc. **-es,** *sg.* 532. **of her assent,** who hold with her, 1379.
assigne, *vb.* assign, appoint, 1559. **assigned,** *pp.* 1564, 1979. **assingne,** *inf.* *2318.
at, *prep.* 1/13, 3/1, 29/32, 33/25, 246, 1124, 1303, 1696, etc. from, 5/11, 10/7, 19/24, 25/10, etc. before an inf. 2/31, 3/17, 26, 4/19, *24, etc. *conj.* that, 4/22, 1498. *rel.* that, who, 27/7, 144/20. **att,** *prep.* 19, 145/6. **atte** = **at te,** at the, 33/10. Cf. **bot at.**
atempir, *vb.* temperate, moderate, arrange, 29/11.
attendis, *vb. sg.* attends, 33/12.
aþer, *adj.* either, 146/36. Cf. **ayþar.**
auance, *vb.* advance, 40/12, 15, 42/15, 46/31, etc.
auantis, *vb. pl.* refl. vaunt, boast, command themselves, 37/12.
auayle, *vb.* avail, 496.
auen, *adj.* own, 4/30. Cf. **awn.**
auenturs, *sb. pl.* chances, occurrences, 2424. **par auenture,** peradventure, 24/1.
auis, *sb.* advice, opinion, 7/23. **avise,** 521. *vb.* refl. (wisely) make up their (our) minds, arrive at a conclusion, resolve, 504, 1076. Cf. 2294. **avised,** *pp.* advised, 2130. Cf. **avyse, awise.**
avisè, *adj.* well-adviced, prudent, 2294. [O.F. *avisé.*]
avisement, *sb.* consideration, 2121.
aune, *adj.* own, 1/14. Cf. **awn.**
aure, *vb.* do worship, honour, 34/30, 35/14. **aurid,** *pp.* 35/15. [O.F. *aourer*, Lat. *adorare.*]
auter, *sb.* altar, 31/22, 143/13, 16, 17, etc. **autir,** 30/10, 144/4. Cf. **awter, þauter.**
autors, *sb. pl.* authors, 43/29.
avyse, *vb.* = **avise,** 57.
aw, *sb.* fear, 530, 2128, 2224. punishment, 460. Cf. **ahe.**
aw, *vb. sg.* ought, should; behoves, beseems, befits, 10/36, 28, 62, 236, 323, 364, etc. *pl.* 341, 537, etc. owe, 633. **awand,** *ppr.* possessing, 142/9. Cf. **ah.**
away, *adv.* 8/19, 23/8, 10, 1347, etc. Cf. **oway.**
awin, *adj.* own, 34, 712. Cf. **awn.**
awise, *vb.* = **avise,** 2108.
awn, *adj.* own, 161, 173, 258, 361, 403, 540, 629, 2074, etc. **awne,** 1/7, 38/27, 38, 43/19, 492, 999, 1033, etc. Cf. **ahen, auen, aune, awin, azen.**
awter, *sb.* altar, 143/28, 144/25, 2149. *gen.* 2190.
ay, *adv.* ever, always, 3/32, 6/26, 31/18, 35/25, 311, 654, 655, 825, etc. Cf. **ai.**
ay, *indef. art.* a, 27/27, 28/33, 45/6. **ayn,** *pron.* one, 788. Cf. **a, an,** also **oþer.**
aynli, *adv.* only, 1087, 1115. **aynly,** 718, 2290. Cf. **anly.**

ayris, *sb. pl.* heirs, 3/25. Cf. **aires.**
ayrly, *adv.* early, 2270. Cf. **airly.**
ayþar, *pron.* either, 11/22. Cf. **aþer.**
az, aȝ, *vb. sg., pl.* ought, should; behoves, 5/*4, 13, 17, 29, 35, 6/6, 11, 26, 28, 7/1, 9, 11, 13, 19/11, 45/21. Cf. **ah.**
aze, *sb.* awe, fear, 35/27. Cf. **ahe.**
azen, aȝen, *adj.* own, 5/21, 35, 7/12, 25/14, 42/24, etc. Cf. **awn.**
aȝh, *vb. sg.* ought, should, 44/5. **aȝht,** 42/16, 18. Cf. **ah, aght.**
aztend, *num,* eighth, 15/24. Cf. **ahtend.**

bac, *sb.* back, 606. Cf. **bak.**
bad, *vb. pt.* bade, 5/20, 9/10. Cf. **bid.**
baine, *adj.* ready, willing, obedient, 261. Cf. **bayn.**
bainly, *adv.* readily, etc. 2445. Cf. **baynly.**
bak, *sb.* back, 13/15, 14/3, 1310. Cf. **bac.**
bakbytyngis, *sb. pl.* backbitings, 43/23.
bakehuse, *sb.* bakehouse, 44/26. **bakkows,** 1540.
bald, *adj.* bold, confident, 525. **be bald,** dare, 2109. Cf. **bold.**
baldly, *adv.* boldly, etc., 1277.
balk, *sb.* beam, 403. **balke,** 5/35.
ban, *vb.* ban, curse, 600. **banne,** 8/29.
band, *sb.* 318, 2082, 2274.
bar, *vb. pt.* bore, 22/28. Cf. **bere.**
barne, *sb.* child, 11/11. **barnis,** *pl.* 23/22, 24/7, 21, 27/9, etc.
basse, *vb.* kiss, 35/11. [O.F. < Lat. *basiare.*]
bath, *conj.* both; postpos. 1334. **baþe,** 5/27, 28, 6/3, etc. postpos. 4/28. *pron.* 37/23. Cf. **both.**
bathes, *sb. pl.* baths, 1667.
bawmes, *sb. pl.* balms, 1667.
bayly, *sb.* stewardship, 20/10.
bayn, *adj.* = **baine,** 541, 631, 1093, etc. **bayne,** 349, 697, 1393.
baynly, *adv.* = **bainly,** 690, 692, 2421.
be, *vb.* 1/6, 10, 12, 25, 2008, etc. Cf. 1481. *pl.* 2201. *imp.* 7/4. *imp. pl.* 525. Cf. **bi, by; bene, bes.**
be, *prep.* by, 1/12, 43/9, 19, 144/3, 223, 297, etc. of, 691. by way of, as, for, 1617. "for the," 2322. Cf. **bi, by.**
becaus, *conj.* because, 188, 747, 1221. **because,** 43/21. Cf. **bicaus.**
bed, *sb.* 20/23, 150/7, 1210, etc. **bedde,** 20/17, 32/29. **beddis,** *pl.* 20/26, 35/34, 36/28. **bede,** 150/5, 19, 1201, 1728. Cf. **bedes.**
beddyng, *sb.* bedding, 2031.
bede, *vb.* offer, 972, 974, 1183, 1994, 2037. call, summon, 1286.
bedene, *adv.* at once, (al)together, 844, 1706. **al bedene,** 1479, 1772. Cf. **albedene.**
bedes, *sb. pl.* beds, 1207, 1977. Cf. **bed.**
bedes, *sb. pl.* prayers, 1827, 1883.
bedyng, *sb.* bidding, command, 692. **-es,** *pl.* 2335. requests, demands, 2236. Cf. **bidinges.**
befell, *vb. pt.* 2398.
befor, *adv.* before; in front, 146/34, 147/12. *prep.* 9/18, 145/7, 1808, etc. **before,** *adv.* 43/16, 22, 143/1, 5, etc. *prep.* 12/19, 141/6, 142/24, etc. *conj.* 27/27. Cf. **bifor, byfor.**
beforhand, *adv.* beforehand, 1508.
beforn, *adv.* before, 625. *prep.* (postpos.) 1856.
begane, *vb. pt.* began, 142/2. **begin,** *inf.* 176, 797, 1681, 1686, etc. **begine,** 143/25. **beginne,** 18/12, 21/13, 27/16, 144/11. **begyn,** 146/33, 148/15, 17, 19, 160, 1281, etc. **begynne,** 144/25. **begyns,** *sg.* 1/10, 1135. Cf. **bigin, bygin.**
begining, *sb.* beginning, 15/31, 23/15, 25/20, 30/8, 105, etc. **beginning,** 29/15, 47/25. **begynnyng,** 43/18, 145/3, 321. Cf. **bigining, bygynnyng.**
behald, *vb.* look, see, 1673, 2039. Cf. **bihaldand.**
beheste, *sb.* promise, 143/9.
behind, *adv.* 146/35. *prep.* 606. **behinde,** (postpos.) 399. Cf. **byhinde.**
behoue, *sb.* behoof, sake, 83, 566, 2474. Cf. **bihoue.**
behoues, *vb. sg.* behoves, 103, 176,

390, 468, etc. **behouis,** 142/8, 16, 17, 19, 20. **behuvis,** *pl.* 142/5. Cf. **bihoues, bus, byhouid.**

bel, *sb.* bell, 20/24. **beles,** *pl.* 1759. Cf. **belle.**

beld, *vb.* dwell, 126.

beli? 42/25. See Notes.

belle, *sb.* bell, 29/31, 30/5, 31/4. **bels,** *pl.* 1473. Cf. **bel.**

belt, *vb.* girdle, 2/21. **belte,** 2/22. **beltyd,** *pp.* 20/22.

ben, *pp.* been, 18/30. **bene,** 2385, 2400. *sbj. pl.* 1223, 1977. Cf. **be.**

benecun, *sb.* blessing, 16/5, 31/24. Cf. **benichun.**

benediccion, *sb.* benediction, 27/19.

benethen, *prep.* beneath, 147/29.

benichun, *sb.* blessing, 26/17, 19, 22. **benichune,** 17/13. **benicun,** 16/32, 17/3, 18/26, 31/25, etc. **benysoun,** 1526. Cf. **benecun.**

bere, *vb.* bear, 11/23, 43/3, 571, 1213, etc. refl. 7/31, 25/28. **beres,** *sg.* 358, 466. *pl.* 347. Cf. **bar, beris, born.**

berid, *pp.* beaten, 21/4, 23/4.

beriing, *sb.* beating, 23/25, 25/31.

bering, *sb.* bearing, demeanour, 2268.

beris, *vb. sg.* bears, 5/6, 14/2, 28/15. Cf. **bere.**

bes, *vb. imp. pl.* be, 1313. **bese,** *ind. sg.* shall be, 775. Cf. **be.**

besekand, *ppr.* beseeching, 1684, 1816, 2157, 2163, etc.

beside, *prep.* 2414. Cf. **byside.**

besily, *adv.* busily, 1281, 1500.

best, *adj.* 4/22, 7/22, 24, 2220. *sb.* 23/5. *adv.* 20/4, 1335, 1698.

best, *sb.* beast, 298, 1021. **beste,** 28/15. **bestes,** *pl.* 2301.

besy, *adj.* busy, 1/10, 42/27.

betake, *vb.* 1/16.

betakins, *vb. sg.* signifies, 11/21. *pl.* 11/24. Cf. **bitakins, bytakins.**

bete, *vb.* amend, 997, 1810.

bete, *vb.* beat, 1360, 1920. *imp.* 463. **betes,** *sg.* 971.

betech, *vb.* commit, entrust, 145/10. Cf. **bitaht.**

betime, *vb.* happen, 17/6. Cf. **bitimis.**

beting, *sb.* beating, 22/34. Cf. **betyng.**

better, *adj.* 4/31, 24/16, 1298. *adv.* 674, 2006. **bettir,** 12/13, 24/22, 37/27. *adv.* 6/5.

betwene, *prep.* between, 149/35. (postpos.) 2034. Cf. **bitweyn.**

betyng = **beting,** 1357.

bew (by mistake?) = **bow,** 966.

bewar (be war), beware, avoid, 882, 1750.

bi, *vb.* be, 1126, 1131, 1330, 1509. Cf. **be.**

bi, *prep.* by, 4/19, 41/31, 269, 270, 381, 385, 453, etc. Cf. **be, by.**

bicaus þat, because, 1568. Cf. **becaus.**

bicimis, *vb. sg.* meant for **bisemis,** beseems? or for **bitimis,** happens? 10/26. See Notes.

bid, *vb.* bid, command, 344, 1812, 2331. **bidde,** 31/9. **biddis,** *sg.* 14/22, 36. **bide,** 9/4. **bides,** *sg.* 11/6. Cf. **bad, bidis, byd.**

bide, *vb.* wait, 1510, 1792, 1794, 2083, 2106. tr. abide, 1889. bide, dwell, live, 1040. **bides,** *pl.* 1800.

bidinges, *sb. pl.* biddings, commands, 222, 2293. **bidyng,** *sg.* 960, 1180, 2296. **bidynges,** *pl.* 645. Cf. **bedyng, bydynges.**

bidis, 3 *sg.* bids, commands, 1/20, 21, 2/8, 3/28, etc. Cf. **bid.**

bie, *vb.* buy, 36/24. Cf. **by.**

bifor, *prep.* before, 8/3, 20, 1268, 1515. **bifore,** 4/26, 6/2, 9/3, etc. *adv.* 16/17. Cf. **befor.**

biggid, *pp.* built, 188. Cf. **byggid.**

bigin, *vb.* begin, 244. **biginne,** 17/3, 32/16. Cf. **begane.**

bigining, *sb.* beginning, 33/8, 47/28. Cf. **begining.**

bihaldand, *ppr.* beholding, looking, 876. Cf. **behald.**

bihoue, *sb.* behoof, sake, 480, 665, 826, 2080, etc. Cf. **behoue.**

bihoues, *vb. sg.* behoves, 359. **bihouis,** 9/27, 10/21, 42/14. **bihus,** 4/20. Cf. **behoues.**

bil, *sb.* bill, note, document, 2177, 2188. **bils,** *pl.* 1985.

bileue, *vb.* remain, 39/16.

bind, *vb.* 1853, 2329. Cf. **bown, bun.**

birde, *vb. pt.-pr. sg.* behoves, 37/23. **birs,** *sg.* 27/12.

biriele, *sb.* burial, 584.
bisines, *sb.* business, 220.
bisschop, *sb.* bishop, 2238. **-e,** 40/19.
bitaht, *pp.* committed, entrusted, 6/29, 7/2, 24/25, 25/1, etc. **bi-teche,** *inf.* 35/33. Cf. **betech.**
bitakins, *vb.sg.* signifies, 5/9, 11/18. *pl.* 11/21, 23. Cf. **betakins.**
betide, *vb.* happen, 19/30.
bitimis, *vb. sg.* happens, 39/31. Cf. **betime.**
bitternes, *sb.* bitterness, 2458.
bitweyn, *adv.* between, 473. Cf. **betwene.**
blame, *sb.* 45/23. *vb. imp.* 6/12. **blamid,** *pp.* 5/16. **blamyd,** *pp.* 1227, 2357. **blaym,** *sb.* 1776.
blin, *vb.* cease, desist, 1682. **blinne,** 4/33, 12/10.
blind, *adj.* 400.
blis, *sb.* bliss, 1/18, 127, 218, 228, etc. **blisses,** *pl.* 213, 217, 664, 902. Cf. **blys.**
blis, *vb.* bless, 1689. **blisce,** 8/29. **blisced,** *pp.* 13/21. **blisse,** *inf.* 21/31. **blissed,** *pp.* 38/34. **blis-sid,** 1517.
blissing, *sb.* blessing, 146/10, 1984. **blisyng,** 1520.
bliþelike, *adv.* blithely, 9/6, 13/12. **blithly,** 2143.
blys, *sb.* = **blis,** 52.
bodely, *adj.* bodily, 2310. *adv.* 1236. **bodily,** 2470.
bodi, *sb.* body, 28/18, 35/14, 486, 810, etc. **bodis,** *pl.* 3/29. **body,** 11/22, 25/9, 27/8, 38/38, etc.
boght, *vb. pt.* bought, 52, 152. Cf. **by.**
boke, *sb.* book, Scripture, 7/4, 8/28, 13/5, 15/2, 5, 131, etc. **bokes,** *pl.* 68. **bokis,** 33/9. Cf. **buke.**
bold, *adj.* 1961. Cf. **bald.**
bone, *sb.* prayer, 2381.
bord, *sb.* board, table, 37/5, 2049. **borde,** 27/20, 30/4, 22.
born, *pp.* 1855. Cf. **bere.**
bose, *vb. sg.* should, 168. Cf. **bus.**
bot, *conj.* but, 1/15, 2/33, 39/11, 25, etc. unless, except if, 3/10, 41/31, 1228, 1532, 1749, 1750, 1802, etc. *prep.* (*or quasi-prep.*, followed by a nominative), except, 21/22, 41/21, 290, 342, 576, 1756, 2329, etc. more than, 6/1. *adv.* only, 167.
bott, *conj.* but, 40/18, 41/2, 13, 71, 367, 403, etc. *adv.* only, 142/2. **bot at,** unless, 142/10, 2354. only that, 1601. **bot if,** unless, 6/5, 17/5, 29/14, 128, 558, 727, 982, etc. **bot þat,** except that, only that, 17/18, 37/7. if only, as long as, 20/6 (the second; the first means: except such as). **bot yef,** unless, 19/30, 21/21, 25/34, 29/8, etc. without (there being), 14/24.
both, *adj.* 43/27, 149/34. *pron.* 355, 1210. *conj.* 43/25, 222, 325, 519, etc. Cf. **bath.**
bow, *vb.* bow, incline, 1226, 1525, 2445. **bowand,** *ppr.* 25. **bowed,** *pp.* 1105. **bowes,** *sg.* 690, 692. Cf. **bew, bows.**
bown, *adj.* ready, 967, 2143. **redi bown,** ready, willing, 1145. [O.I. *búinn*, Swed. *redobogen*, ready, willing.]
bown, *pp.* bound, 699 (cf. Notes). **bownyd,** bound, possessed, 43/11 (Lat. *inflati*). Cf. **bind.**
bows, *vb. sg.* 2280. Cf. **bow.**
bowsum, *adj.* compliant, yielding, willing, obedient, 31, 154, 261, 1660, etc. Cf. **buxum.**
bowsumly, *adv.* willingly, meekly, 2020.
bred, *sb.* bread, 26/14, 1578. **-e,** 28/6.
bref, *sb.* letter, 39/1.
brek, *vb.* break, 1961. **breke,** 35/18, 20, 1955. **brekis,** *sg.* 31/36, 38/25. Cf. **brokin.**
brenne, *vb.* burn, 44/15. Cf. **brind.**
brest, *sb.* breast, 1920.
brest, *vb.* break, 2280.
breue, *adj.* brief, 19/30, 32.
breuelike, *adv.* briefly, 27/26.
breuhuse, *sb.* brewhouse, 44/27. **brewhows,** 1540.
briht, *adj.* bright, 2/29.
brihtnes, *sb.* brightness, *1/23.
brind, *pp.* burned, 13/14. **brin-nande,** *ppr.* 20/22. Cf. **brenne.**
bring, *vb.* 141/15, 584, 1109, 2096, etc. **bringe,** 8/21, 21/6, 141/9. Cf. **bryng** and **broght.**
broch, *sb.* brooch, 2196.
broght, *vb. pt.* brought, 1310. *pp.* 33/8, 26, 143/7, 2166. **broht,** *pt.*

22/24. *pp.* 2/27, 3/9, 4/25, 14/5, etc. **broth,** *pt.* 38/38. *pp.* carried (out, or through), 42/8. Cf. **bring.**
brokin, *pp.* broken, 29/34, 42/25. Cf. **brek.**
broþir, *sb.* brother, 6/1, 21/34. *gen.* 5/34.
bryng, *vb.* bring, 44, 669, 1120, 2060, 2420, etc. Cf. **bring.**
buke, *sb.* book, Scripture, 143/15, 269, 687, 1096, etc. Cf. **boke.**
bun, *pp.* bound (in duty), 1960. Cf. **bind, vnbun.**
bus, *vb. sg.* behoves; should, 244, 375, 460, 476, 797, 966, 1413, 1415. *pl.* 43/25, 714, 1011. Cf. **behoues, bose.**
bute, *sb.* remedy, 2285.
butter, *sb.* 26/15.
buxsumnes, *sb.* compliance, obedience, 147/21. **buxumnes,** 38/24, 43/31, 44/23, 46/34, etc.
buxum, *adj.* compliant, yielding, obedient, 6/1, *15, 10/6, 13/26, 20/32, 24/14, etc. Cf. **bowsum.**
by, *vb.* buy, 2019. Cf. **bie, boght.**
by, *vb.* be, 353. Cf. **be.**
by, *prep.* 1/5, 18/10, 39, 51, 137, etc. (postpos.) 12/2, 126, 1330, 2054, 2098. Cf. **be, bi.**
bycom, *vb. pt.* became, 22/28.
byd, *vb.* bid, command, 20/8, 141/15. **bydes,** *pl.* 68. Cf. **bid.**
bydynges, *sb. pl.* biddings, commands, 26. Cf. **bidinges.**
byfor, *prep.* before, 26/18. **byfore,** 12/16, 23, 19/12, etc. *adv.* 16/20, 25, 29, etc. Cf. **befor.**
byggid, *pp.* built, 184. Cf. **biggid.**
bygin, *vb.* begin, 168. **byginne,** 16/36, 17/2, 31/15. **bygynne,** 16/34. **bygyns,** *sg.* 145/2. Cf. **begane.**
bygynnyng, *sb.* beginning, 145/6. Cf. **begining.**
byhinde, *adv.* behind, 38/37. *prep.* 15/13. Cf. **behind.**
byhouid, *vb. pt.-pr. sg.* behoves, is necessary, 28/27. **byhouis,** *vb. sg.* 4/21. Cf. **behoues.**
byken, *vb.* commit, entrust, 145/14. **bykenne,** 20/3.
byside, *prep.* = **beside,** 44/19.
bytakins, *vb. sg.* signifies, 13/20. Cf. **betakins.**
bytuix, *prep.* between, 20/26. **bytuixe,** 16/6. *adv.* 11/22. **bytwixe,** *prep.* 31/12.

caald, *adj.* cold, 36/20. Cf. **cald.**
cal, *vb.* call, 550. Cf. **cald.**
calanged, *pp.* accused, 6/32.
cald, *adj.* cold, 1600, 2004, 2005. Cf. **caald,** also **cauld.**
cald, *pp.* called, 7/25, 34/29, 27. **calde,** reckoned, 38/35. **call,** *inf.* 517, 1813. *pl.* 115, 189, 337, 2417. **calle,** 2/15, 7/21, 8/4, 25/13, 41/26, etc. **callid,** *pp.* 28/25, 41/28. **cals,** *sg.* 122. Cf. **cal, kald.**
calgard, *sb.* kailyard, vegetable garden, 31/35, 44/27.
can, *vb. sg.* can, knows (how to), is able for, 7/26, 27/29, 37/10, 1698. 2 *sg.* 4/9, 1099. *pl.* 10/19. 11/20, 20/4. **canne,** *sg.* 38/27. Cf. **kan** and **cune.**
candel, *sb.* candle, 1212. **candil,** 29/16.
cantikils, *sb. pl.* canticles, 16/31, 17/25. **cantikyl,** *sg.* 18/22.
carpyng, *sb.* talking, 621.
case, *sb.* 1301, 1375, 1382. **if case fall,** if it should happen, 2173.
cast, *vb. imp.* 149/31. **caste,** *inf.* 38/21. *pl.* 13/19. Cf. **kast.**
catchid, *pp.* taken, 1329.
cauld, *sb.* cold, 2032.
caus, *sb.* cause, 1494, 1802.
cel, *sb.* cell, 306, 2414. Cf. **celle, sel.**
celer, *sb.* cellar, 1539.
celerer, *sb.* cellaress, 1421, 1445, 1465, 1583.
celeres, do., 28/7. **celeresse,** 23/28, 24/24, 26/5, 12, 27/6, etc.
celle, *sb.* cell, 38/4. **cels,** *pl.* 1539. Cf. **cel.**
certan, *adj.* certain, sure, 851. **certane,** 1833. **certayn,** 2192. **certayne,** 2013, 2041. Cf. **sertane.**
chaipitur, *sb.* chapter (meeting), 141/12, 143/1, 4, 7. Cf. **chapiter, chaypitur.**
chaiste, *adj.* chaste, 142/16. Cf. **chaste.**
chaistid, *pp.* driven (by way of punishment), 2456. Cf. **chasti.**

chaistese, *vb.* chastise, 445. Cf. **chastes.**
chaistying, *sb.* chastisement, 1323. Cf. **chastying.**
chalese, *sb.* chalice, 1477.
chanch, *sb.* chance, accident, 1774. **for no c-h**, on any account, 1363. **of alkyn c-h**, whatever may befall, 1656.
chanch, *vb.* change, 2321.
changing, *sb.* 2015.
chantir, *sb.* chanter, 144/11. **chantur**, 143/25.
chapiter, *sb.* chapter-house, 1909. **chapitir**, 29/26, 31/10, 32/2. **chapitur**, 33/8, 2131. Cf. **chaipitur, schapiter.**
charch, *sb.* charge; weight, importance; responsibility, 358, 1012, 2258, 2262. **charge**, 4/7, 42/13, 45/14, 516, 2405.
chargid, *pp.* charged, 42/26.
charitè, *sb.* charity, love, 4/5, 5/10, 592, 1110, etc.
chartir, *sb.* charter, 39/14.
chaste, *adj.* 42/17, 2267. Cf. **chaiste.**
chaste, *vb.* chastise, 42/22. **chasted**, *pp.* 1406, 1489. **chastede**, 437. **chastes**, *sg.* 364. (Some of these and the following forms are ambiguous.)
chastes, *vb.* chastise, 428. **chastese**, 455, 458. Cf. **chaistese, chastise.**
chasti, *vb.* chastise, 5/18, 6/21, 12/17, 433. *imp.* 6/13. **chastid**, *pt.* 6/18. *pp.* 6/20, 21/26, 1642, 1793, etc. driven (by way of punishment), 2242. Cf. **chaistid, chasty.**
chastiing, *sb.* = **chastying**, 41/35.
chastiment, do., 2/21, 6/31.
chastise, *vb. imp.* 462. Cf. **chastes.**
chastising, *sb.* 546. **chastisyng**, 513. Cf. **schastisyng.**
chastitè, *sb.* chastity, 8/19, 9/11, 46/35, 647.
chasty, *vb.* chastise, 6/19, 31/31, 2355, 2364. **chastyd**, *pp.* 22/34. Cf. **chasti.**
chastying, *sb.* chastisement, 1244, 1353, 2272. Cf. **chaistying, chastiing.**
chaumber, *sb.* chamber, 44/20.
chaypitur, *sb.* chapter, 141/10. Cf. **chaipitur.**
chays, *vb. pt.* chose, 1368. Cf. **ches.**
chefly, *adv.* chiefly, 43/28.
chepe, *sb.* purchase. **of liht chepe**, cheap, 36/25. **bettir chepe**, cheaper, 37/27.
cher, *sb.* cheer, 909, 1064, 1511.
ches, *vb.* choose, 1374, 1472. **chese**, 42/1, 43/30, 91, 1108, 2235, 2249. **chesis**, *sg.* 42/5, 6. Cf. **chays, chose, schosin.**
chesyng, *sb.* choosing, 43/29.
chide, *vb.* 1378.
child, *sb.* 39/16, 2180, 2183, etc. **-e**, 39/6, 792, 1069, etc. **-es**, *gen.* 2187. **-er**, *pl.* 1355, 1447, 1596, 2199. **-ir**, 6/18, 39/20.
chose, *sb.* choice, 2240.
chose, *pp.* chosen, 1389. **chosen**, 2219. **chosin**, 23/29, 42/5, 1363, 1367, etc. **chossin**, 20/3. Cf. **ches.**
clad, *sb.* cloth, 36/22. Cf. **claþis.**
clad, *pp.* 20/22. Cf. **claþe.**
clame, *vb.* claim, 1617. Cf. **clayme.**
claþe, *vb.* clothe, 8/20. Cf. **clad, cleth.**
claþing, *sb.* clothing, 36/18. Cf. **clazing, clething.**
claþis, *sb. pl.* clothes, garments, 36/26. **clathis**, 38/38. Cf. **clad, close.**
claus, *sb.* clause, 936.
clayme, *vb.* claim, 1621. Cf. **clame.**
clazing, *sb.* clothing, 36/19. Cf. **claþing.**
cled, *pp.* clad, 2006. **clede**, 1202, 2003. Cf. **cleth.**
clen, *adj.* clean, pure, 140, 1190. **clene**, 4/11, 9/6, 19/30, 843, 1417, 1720, etc.
clennes, *sb.* cleanness, 647.
clensid, *pp.* cleansed, 140.
clere, *adj.* clear, bright; pure, 213, 405, 664, 780, etc. (*quasi*)*adv.* clear(ly), 113.
clerely, *adv.* clearly, 1030. **clerly**, 258.
clerk, *sb.* 150/6. **-e**, 40/1. **-s**, *pl.* 461. **-es**, 773, *801, 836, 858, etc.
cleth, *vb.* clothe, 582. Cf. **claþe, cled, vncleth.**
clething, *sb.* clothing, 145/18, 2008,

2028. **clethyng,** 146/22, 23. Cf. **claþing.**
cloister, *sb.* 9/22, 45/8. **cloistir,** 29/25. Cf. **closter.**
close, *sb.* enclosure, 2403.
close, *sb. pl.* clothes, 1480. **clothes,** 1502, 1978. **cloths,** 2170, 2171. Cf. **claþis.**
closter, *sb.* cloister, convent, 1091. Cf. **cloister.**
clotony, *sb.* gluttony, 310. Cf. **glotony.**
colaciown, *sb.* collation, conference, 1742. **colaciun,** 29/25, 31, 32.
colettis, *sb. pl.* collects, 144/2, 22, 23. **collettis,** 144/5.
com, *vb.* come, 528, 1762, 1903. *pt.* 6/17, 11/18, 22/26, 717, 895, 1648. **come,** 9/18. *pt.* 10/16, 40/13. **comes,** *sg.* 141/16, 782. *pl.* 1543. Cf. **cume.**
comaundes, *vb. sg.* commands, 847, 2297. **command,** *sbj.* 1788. Cf. **cumand.**
comford, *sb.* comfort, 937. *vb.* 936, 1303. **comfort,** 26/3, 1734. *vb.* 35/17. **comforth,** 177. *vb.* 22/7, 29/27. Cf. **confort, cumfort.**
commandementis, *sb. pl.* commandments, 1/2. **-dm-,** 42/31. Cf. **cumandemens.**
company, *sb.* 1028, 1058, 1205, 1259, etc. Cf. **cumpany.**
complin, *sb.* compline (the last service, about 6 p.m.), 1745, 1746. **complyn,** 1758. Cf. **cumplin.**
comun, *adj.* common, 25/12, 1626, 2011. *vb.* commune, 21/22, 34. **-e,** *adj., sb.* 150/1. **in comun,** 37/22, 41/16, 18, 1618. **til comun,** for all, 43/34. Cf. **comyn.**
comunaltè, *sb.* community, 1422.
comuners, *sb. pl.* participants, 250.
comunlike, *adv.* alike, 35/7.
comyn, *vb.* commune, 1270. See Notes. Cf. **comun.**
comynli, *adv.* commonly, 1151.
concience, *sb.* conscience, 1417.
condicions, *sb. pl.* conditions, 1033.
confermyd, *pp.* confirmed, 2256.
confessours, *sb. pl.* confessors, 2495. **confessure,** *sg.* 1551.
confort, *vb.* comfort, 777, 1645. **-and,** *ppr.* 774. Cf. **comford.**
confucioun, *sb.* confusion, 2507.
confundid, *pp.* confounded, 38/32. **confundis,** *sg.* 47/23.
congregacion, *sb.* congregation, 147/36.
consel, *sb.* counsel, 2234. Cf. **councel.**
consent, *vb.* 7/29, 42/6. **-is,** *sg.* 28/33, 40/14, 42/3, etc. *pl.* 7/27.
conseyue, *vb.* conceive, 43/17.
contek, *sb.* contention, 1376.
contende, *pp.* contained, held, 757. Cf. **cuntaine.**
contrarius, *adj.* contrarious, 2291.
contrary, *adj.* 43/24.
contresse, *sb. pl.* countries, 303. Cf. **cuntre.**
conuent, *sb.* convent, 145/12, 147/37, 150/19, 518. **-e,** 43/14.
corn, *sb.* 32/32, 1710, 2320. **corne,** 43/6.
corner, *sb.* 143/13.
correccion, *sb.* correction, 29/34, 31/30, 32/4, 45/7, etc.
corrumpid, *pp.* corrupted, 859.
cors, *sb.* body, 37/25.
costiue, *adj.* costive, 28/10.
cote, *sb.* coat, 146/24, 2012.
couaite, *vb.* covet, 615. **couayt,** 2472. **couet,** 570, 580, 643.
couent, *sb.* convent, 141/4, 143/20, 144/3, 10, 284, 1231, 1248, etc. Cf. **cuuent.**
couir, *vb.* heal, 27/4.
councel, *sb.* counsel, 229, 2222. *vb.* 452. **counsaile,** *vb.* 586. **counsel,** *sb.* 520, 552, 558, 1422. **counseld,** *pp.* 1518. **counsele,** *sb.* 586. **counsell,** 555. Cf. **consel, cownsaile, cunsaile.**
cours, *sb.* course, 1874. Cf. **curs.**
couth, *adj.* known, 13.
cownsaile, *sb.* counsel, 2242. Cf. **councel.**
cownte, *vb.* count, reckon, 1/11.
cowntnanse, *sb.* countenance, deportment, 1071.
(**crakes,** corrupt for **clerkes,** 801.)
craue, *vb.* 211, 766, 1467, 1621, etc. **craues,** *pl.* 586.
crede, *sb.* creed, 144/25.
crie, *vb.* 31/11, 46/19. *pl.* 44/22. *imp.* 15/1. Cf. **cry.**
cristen, *adj.* Christian, 28/12. **cristin,** 774. **cristyn,** 80, 421.

cristiante, *sb.* Christianity, 25/20.
cristynd, *pp.* christened, 572.
cristyndome, *sb.* Christendom, 1835.
croice, *sb.* cross, 38/29.
crosse, do., 143/15.
croun, *sb.* crown, 902. Cf. **curun.**
cry, *vb. pl.* 115, 337. Cf. **crie.**
crying, *sb.* 1919.
culur, *sb.* colour, 36/22.
cum, *vb.* come, 2/9, 3/32, 9/24, 30, 499, 1132, etc. *pl.* 44/20, 1941, etc. *imp.* 38/13. Cf. **cume.**
cumand, *pp.* commanded, *1089. **cumande**, *inf.* 5/11, 24/33, 46/12, etc. refl. commend herself, 44/36. *sbj.* 10/5, 21/22, etc. **cumandes**, *sg.* 9/31. **cumandid**, *pp.* 10/19, 34/3. **cumandis**, *sg.* 5/29, 8/28, 9/9, 32, etc. **cumaunde**, *inf.* 34/16. **cumaundis**, *sg.* 37/12. Cf. **comaundes, cummandis.**
cumandemens, *sb. pl.* commandments, 9/23, 10/3, 14/14, 46/8, etc. **-ment**, *sg.* 3/24, 4/9, 7/28, etc. **-mentis**, 3/17. **cumantemens**, 11/32. **cumaundement**, *sg.* 44/4. **-mentis**, 47/7. Cf. **commandementis.**
cume, *vb.* come, 2/25, 6/8, etc. *pl.* 9/4, 19/10, 30/13, etc. *pt.* 12/29. **cumen**, *pp.* 31/5, 39/29. **cumes**, *sg.* 31/7, 2052. Cf. **com, cum, cumis, cums.**
cumfort, *sb.* comfort, 6/15, 13/7. *pp.* comforted, 1260. **cumforth**, *sb.* 26/2. Cf. **comford.**
cuming, *sb.* coming, 23/19.
cumis, *vb. sg.* comes, 8/24, 19/27, 26/16, etc. *pl.* 26/10, 30/3, 8, etc. *imp. pl.* 2/5. **cummes**, *sg.* 2386. **cummis**, *pl.* 37/32, 40/25. Cf. **cume.**
cummandis, *vb. sg.* commands, 46/6. Cf. **cumand.**
cumpany, *sb.* company, 1329. Cf. **company.**
cumplin, *sb.* compline, 18/1, 6, 24, 29/21, etc. Cf. **complin.**
cums, *vb. sg.* comes, 2416. *imp. pl.* 81. Cf. **cume.**
cune, *vb.* know, 18/32. Cf. **kun** and **can, cuþe.**
cunsaile, *sb.* counsel, 5/13, 7/25, 44/1. **cunsal**, 8/7. **cunsale**, 7/21, 29, 8/4, 6, etc. **cunsel**, 2229. Cf. **councel.**
cuntaine, *vb.* contain, restrain, 35/1. Cf. **contende.**
cuntrè, *sb.* country, 36/20, 21, 23, 42/8, etc. Cf. **contresse.**
cunyng, *sb.* skill, 2229.
cure, *sb.* cure, charge, care, 360, 498.
curs, *sb.* course, 1962. Cf. **cours.**
curs, *vb.* curse; excommunicate, 1239. **curse**, 45/29. **cursed**, *pp.* 1270, 1803. **cursid**, 22/33, 23/4, 34/26, 1234. **curste**, 142/15. **cursyd**, 21/3.
cursing, *sb.* 21/4, 23/24, 31/2, etc. **cursyng**, 1324, 1908.
curtesly, *adv.* courteously, 1754.
curun, *sb.* tonsure, 5/6. **curune**, crown, 12/32. Cf. **croun.**
custum, *sb.* custom, 1113. **-e**, 40/27.
cuþe, *vb. pt.* knew, 18/30. Cf. **cune.**
cuuaitise, *sb.* covetousness, 37/26.
cuuatus, *adj.* covetous, 8/16.
cuuenant, *sb.* covenant, 38/25.
cuuent, *sb.* convent, 4/16, 5/14, 17, 6/11, etc. *gen.* 19/32. Cf. **couent.**

dai, *sb.* day, 29/6. **dais**, *gen.* 1728. *pl.* 2/9, 17/17, 29/7, 10, etc. Cf. **day.**
daile, *sb.* part, 2045.
dame, *sb.* 41/28. Cf. **daym.**
damisel, *sb.* damsel, 2209.
damne, *vb.* damn, 38/26. **dampned**, *pp.* 372.
dar, *vb. sg.* dare, 28/35.
dartes, *sb. pl.* darts, 277.
daunger, *sb.* danger, 142/12.
daw, *vb.* dawn, 1135.
day, *pron.* they, 1756, footnote. Cf. **þa.**
day, *sb.* 7/16, 9/2, 18, etc. **days**, *pl.* 150/3, 96, 195, 1712, etc. **o day**, to-day, 2/2. Cf. **dai.**
daym, *sb.* dame, lady, 147/24. Cf. **dame.**
debate, *sb.* 1366.
december, *sb.* 1719. Cf. **Descember.**
decipill, *sb.* disciple, 7/28. **decipils**, *pl.* 10/21, 37. **deciplis**, 9/11. Cf. **discipels.**

ded, *sb.* death, 2/7, 9/2, 10/35, etc. **dede,** 3/22, 90, 207, etc. *adj.* dead, 8/21, 37/23, 584, 1372.
ded, *sb.* deed, 24/32. **dede,** 2/22, 32, 5/28, etc. **dedes,** *pl.* 157, 161, 162, 268, etc. Acts, 2042. **in dede,** in deeds; indeed, 3/12, 7/13, 72, 180, etc. Cf. **dedis.**
dedely, *adj.* deadly, mortal, 230, 854. Cf. **dedly.**
dedeyn, *sb.* disdain; something below their dignity, 2510.
dedis, *sb. pl.* deeds, 1/13, 2/26, 5/7, 17, etc. Acts, 36/33. **dedys,** 1/16. Cf. **ded.**
dedly, *adj.* deadly, 10/32. Cf. **dedely.**
defaut, *sb.* default; want, 1506. **defaute,** 26/35, 27/5, 22, 1456.
defend, *vb.* defend; protect, preserve; prevent, hinder; forbid, 23/20. **-e,** 5/23, 23/1, 42/8, etc. *imp.* 25/17. **-id,** *pp.* forbidden, prohibited, 45/28. **-is,** *sg.* 24/18.
degest, *pp.* digested, 1126.
degrè, *sb.* degree; position; manner, way, 182, 253, 279, 299, 324, 2202, etc. **degrece,** 13/36, 14/7, 21. **degres,** *pl.* 816. **degrese,** *pl.* 813, 1107. [O.F. *degre, degrez.*]
dekin, *sb.* deacon, 40/5.
dele, *sb.* deal. **ilk dele,** (in) everything, 2001.
dele, *vb.* deal, 2510.
delite, *sb.* crime, 854. [Lat. *delictum.*]
delite, *sb.* delight, 1117, 2489.
delitis, *vb. pl.* refl. take delight, 25/14.
deliuer, *vb. imp.* deliver, free, 6/24. **deliuir,** 6/23. *inf.* 12/24. **deliuirs,** *sg.* hands over, 25/12.
deliuir, *adj.* free, 38/14, 41/15. [O.F. *delivre,* freed.]
demande, *sb.* demand, 27/24.
deme, *vb. pl.* deem, judge (over); decree, 2123. **demid,** *pt.* 41/20. **demys,** *pl.* 714.
demenance, *sb.* management, dealing, 43/1.
deny, *vb.* 577.
depairtid, *pp.* divided, distributed, 2043. **depart,** *sbj.* 36/33. **departid,** *pt.* 25/21. **departis,** *sg.* separates, 46/28, 29. **depayrtyd,** *pp.* 33.
depose, *vb.* 1390, 2239.
deppest, *adj.* deapest; used substantively, 24/23.
der, *adj.* dear, 1005. **dere,** 141/18, 26, 379, 2137, etc. high, special, 1958. *adv.* dearly, 152.
dere, *sb.* harm, injury, 1214. *vb.* harm, injure, hurt, 277, 768. **deres,** *sg.* (*or pl.*) 2392.
desaiue, *vb. pl.* deceive, 4/28.
Descember, *sb.* December, 1121. Cf. **december.**
descend, *vb.* 803.
descrecioun, *sb.* discretion, 535. Cf. **discrecion.**
dese, *sb.* daïs (a raised floor at the upper end of the refectory), 30/30.
deseryd, *vb.* disinherit, 51. Cf. **diseret.**
desire, *sb.* 12/28, 865, 869, 892, etc. *vb.* 43/2, 590. **desiris,** *sg.* 40/1.
despise, *vb.* 439.
despit, *sb.* contempt, 5/21, 20/34, 24/3. **-e,** 46/21. Cf. **dispite.**
destruciun, *sb.* destruction, 45/10.
desturbid, *pp.* disturbed, 35/2. Cf. **sturbe.**
det, *adj.* due, 1938.
deuel, *sb.* devil, 274. **deuil,** 4/21, 21/26, 29, 30/16, etc.
deuisid, *pp.* arranged, set forth, 18/8.
deuocion, *sb.* devotion, 16/13, 17/14, 19/29, 142/20. **-ioun,** 3, 1191, 1738, 1900. **-ioune,** 1168. **-iun,** 19/26. **-yon,** 19/12.
deuotelie, *adv.* devoutly, 143/18.
dicipils, *sb. pl.* disciples, 10/36. Cf. **discipels.**
dicipline, *sb.* discipline, etc. 4/17, 5/33. Cf. **discipline.**
did, *vb. pt.* 5/21, 8/17, 13/14, 25/20, 888, etc. **dide,** 1001. Cf. **do.**
die, *vb.* 42/35. Cf. **dy.**
digne, *adj.* worthy, 15/14. Cf. **dingne.**
dignitè, *sb.* dignity, 334, 676.
dike, *vb.* make ditches, 1854.
dingne, *adj.* worthy, 20/11, 40/7, 41/30, 42/10, etc. Cf. **digne, vndinge.**
directe, *pp.* directed, 1/7.

discerne, *vb.* discern, 42/32.
discipels, *sb. pl.* disciples, 533, 763. **discipilis,** 5/27. **discipils,** 716. **diciplis,** 29/12. Cf. **decipill, dicipils.**
discipline, *sb.* discipline; correction, punishment, 7/32, 10/7, 11/25, 36/15, etc. *vb.* punish, 45/30. **-ines,** *sb. pl.* regulations, 39/26. Cf. **dicipline.**
discrecion, *sb.* discretion, 42/33, 37. **-iun,** 29/19, 1414. Cf. **descrecioun.**
discrete, *adj.* 42/30.
diseret, *vb.* disinherit, 1/15. Cf. **deseryd.**
disese, *sb.* discomfort, 1847.
dispite, *sb.* contempt, 44/7. Cf. **despit.**
dispone, *vb.* dispose, 42/37.
disposid, *pp.* disposed of, 142/11.
dissensione, *sb.* dissension, 43/26. **-iones,** *pl.* 43/14, 23.
diuers, *adj.* diverse, 1860.
do, *def. art.* in the conjunctional phrase **do wilis,** whilst, 2/7. Cf. **to.**
do, *vb.* do, perform, execute, 2/6, 4/19, 31, 6/5, 8, 187, etc. "do so," 34/35. go through, suffer, 12/32. place, put, 6/2, 7, 20/10, 44/17. take, bring, 12/22. make, cause (to), 12/10, 40/20, 1981. *pl.* do, etc. 2/13. *imp.* 2/12, 26, 555, 1005, etc. make, cause, 6/12. **doe,** put, 12/16. do, execute, 14/2. Cf. **doy** and **did, don, dos, down, dyde.**
doctours, *sb. pl.* teachers, 2496.
doghter (-ir), 141/26, 142/29, 23, 35, 41. **doghters,** *pl.* 46, 379. **dohtir,** *sg.* 142/22. Cf. **doughtir, doȝtir.**
doghty, *adj.* doughty, powerful, 1/8.
doing, *sb.* 1049, 1451. Cf. **doyng.**
dom, *adj.* dumb, stupid, idle, 33/21.
dom, *sb.* judgment, 500. **dome,** 7/16, 9/19, 352, 369, etc.
domesday, *sb.* doomsday, 24/9, 44/14, 1452. **domisday,** 9/1, 26/28.
domesman, *sb.* judge, 503.
domnum, *sb.* lord, master, 4/6 (cf. footnote and 147/19).
don, *pp.* done; placed, put; taken; shown; finished, 3/21, 13/17, 576, 1320, etc. **done,** 11/11, 13/18, 23/7, 145/17, 391, 1743, etc. *pl.* (*sbj.*?) 1711. Cf. **do.**
dore, *sb.* door, 15/13, 31/4, 6, 8, etc.
dortour, *sb.* dormitory, 150/6.
dos, *vb. sg.* does, acts, makes, lets, etc., 2/34, 35, 3/13, 12/1, etc. 2 *sg.* 5/33, 10/23. *pl.* 3/24, 21/25, 2326. **dose,** *sg.* 28/34, 37/13, 38/8, 145, etc. 2 *sg.* 41. *pl.* 37/24, 27, 925, 979, etc. Cf. **do.**
doughtir, *sb.* daughter, 141/18. Cf. **doghter.**
doun, *adv.* down, 419, 800, 803, 1807, etc. **doune,** 2192. Cf. **down.**
doute, *sb.* doubt, fear, 28/22, 1492. Cf. **dowte, dut(and)e.**
down, *pp.* done, 149/38. Cf. **do.**
down, *adv.* 1095, 1741, 2304, 2451, etc. **downe,** 33/4, 37/23, 141/6, 17, etc. Cf. **doun, dun.**
dowte, *sb.* fear, 19/14, 32/20, 37/23. **dowtis,** *vb. sg.* 35/33. Cf. **doute.**
doy, *vb.* do, 149. Cf. **do.**
doyng, *sb.* doing; putting, 144/9, 2237. Cf. **doing.**
doȝtir, *sb.* daughter, 39/5. Cf. **doghter.**
drahe, *vb.* draw, 40/31. **draw,** 1296, 2485. intr. draw, go, have recourse, appeal, refer, 640. **draze,** refl. 34/4. **draȝe,** intr. 42/16.
dred, *sb.* dread, fear, 1214, 1324, 2432. **dredde,** *pp.* dreaded, 42/28. **drede,** *sb.* 82, 124, 274, etc. dreadful or dangerous position, risk, danger, 450, 464. *vb.* 86, 494, 611, 668, etc.
dredefully, *adv.* with fear, 1563. **dredfully,** 1155.
dredful, *adj.* dreadful, 1/15, 352, 369, 1932.
drese, *vb.* direct, prepare, 793. **dresse,** 219.
dreze, *vb.* endure, suffer, 21/28.
drinc, *vb.* drink, 8/31. **drink,** *sb.* 28/20, 1597. *vb.* 30/31. **drinke,** *sb.* 28/14, 30, 34, 29/2, etc. *vb.* 28/33, 35. Cf. **drynk** (and **drunkin**).
driue, *vb.* drive, 1738. **driuin,** *pp.* 13/11.

dronkenhede, *sb.* drunkenness, 1594.
dronkynnes, do., 310.
drunkin, *adj.* drunk, 28/30, 31.
drynk, *sb.* drink, 1604, 1797, 1885. Cf. **drinc.**
dubil, *adj.* double, 2014. **duble**, 376.
duelle, *vb.* stay, remain, 39/3, 41/2. **duellis**, *sg.* persists, 39/25. *pl.* delay, tarry, loiter, 30/15. Cf. **dwel.**
duelling, *sb.* delay, tarrying, 9/27, 24/19. Cf. **dwelling.**
duly, *adv.* 793.
dun, *adv.* down, 31/7. **dune**, 10/6, 11/16, 19. Cf. **down.**
dust, *sb.* 2276.
dutande, *ppr.* fearing, 23/31. **dute**, *sb.* fear, 2/6, 6/34, 8/1, 10/8, 11/31, etc. *vb.* 5/16, 8/34, 26/36, 47/1. **dutes (-is)**, *pl.* 3/6, 44/1. Cf. **dowte.**
dwel, *vb.* dwell, stay, remain, 1783, 1922, 2105, 2126. *pl.* 2017. **dwell**, 228, 305, 450, 661, etc. **dwelle**, 34/31, 35, 40/29, 41/3, etc. **dwels**, *sg.* 177, 1271. *pl.* 147. Cf. **duelle.**
dwelling, *sb.* 2413. remaining, 40/4. **dwellyng**, delay, 46/18. Cf. **duelling.**
dy, *vb.* die, 616, 944. Cf. **die.**
dyde, *vb. pt.* did, 55. Cf. **do.**
dyght, *pp.* prepared, 2413. [O.E. *dihtan.*]
dyn, *sb.* din, noise, 1666.
dyng, *vb.* strike, beat, 2352.
dynt, *sb.* dint, force, 90.

edefied, *pp.* edified, 32/18.
ee, *sb.* eye, 402. Cf. **eye.**
eere, *sb.* ear, 1/3. Cf. **eres.**
eft, *adv.* back; again; afterwards, 1132, 1347, 1348, 1486, etc.
efter, *adv.* after, 16/1, 3, 150/19, 1794, etc. *prep.* 16/34, 18/11, 20, 149, 260, 286, 356, 1485, etc. *conj.* according as, 21/10, 26/4, 560, 1490, etc. **eftir**, *adv.* 16/11, 12, 27, etc. *prep.* 6/32, 8/6, 15/26, 16/6, etc. **eftir an**, alike, 6/5. **eftir sone**, eftsoons, 143/3. **eftir sune**, 143/31. **eftir þat**, according as, 41/14. Cf. **after.**
efterward, *adv.* afterwards, 264, 1843, 1849, 2323. **efterwarde**, 141/9. Cf. **afterward.**
eggyng, *sb.* egging, 1369.
egh, *adj.* high, 156. Cf. **hez.**
eghen, *sb. pl.* eyes, 65, 113, 663, 1102. *gen.* 785. Cf. **eye.**
eghnes, *sb.* highness, loftiness, 782. Cf. **heghnes.**
ehe, *sb.* eye, 5/34. **ehin**, *pl.* 1/22. Cf. **eye.**
eke, *vb.* increase, 981.
eld, *sb.* age; old age, 1092, 2071, 2260. **elde**, 14/28, 23/21, 27/10, etc.
elder, *adj. comp.* (*sb.*) older, 2206, 2207, 2210, 2216. **eldest**, *superl.* 20/21, 1291, 1498, 1678, 2053. Cf. **þelder** and **ald.**
elders, *sb. pl.* 142/7, 1856.
ellofte, *num.* eleventh, 14/35.
els, *adv.* else; otherwise, 451, 513, 559, 802, 1272, 1555, etc. Cf. 1403 (see Notes).
emang, *adv.* among, 1191. *prep.* 420, 2125, 2139, 2228, etc. Cf. **imang.**
eminan, *sb.* a certain measure (Lat. *emina*), 28/25.
enbreuid, *pp.* entered into a book, made a list of, 24/34.
encens, *vb. imp.* incense, 149/31. **encence**, *inf.* 150/18.
encheson, *sb.* occasion, reason, 1219, 2341. Cf. **achesun.**
enclind, *pp.* inclined, bent, *15/10. **encline**, *inf.* bow down, 143/18. Cf. **acline.**
encres, *vb.* increase, 1940. **-e**, 480.
end, *sb.* 148/1, 16, 44, 56, etc. **ende**, 2/10, 23/17, 38/17, 26, etc.
endeles, *adj.* endless, 126. Cf. **endles.**
endenturs, *sb. pl.* indentures, 1484. Cf. **indentures.**
endid, *pp.* ended, 1/11, 17/7, 144/5, 1499, etc. **endit**, 143/28. Cf. **endyd.**
ending, *sb.* 8/24, 47/29. Cf. **endyng**, **þending.**
endles, *adj.* endless, 126, 661, 902, 1120, 2515. Cf. **endeles.**
endyd = **endid**, 148/25. **endydde**, 148/20.
endyng, *sb.* = **ending**, 13/16.

enemis, *sb. pl.* enemies, 8/28. Cf. **enmes.**
enence, *prep.* as to, 142/13. [*on* + *efen* + *t* + *es.*]
enforce, *vb.* strengthen, 2384.
english, *sb.* English, 147/20. Cf. **ingles.**
engreuid, *pp.* aggrieved, burdened, 27/28. [O.F. *engrever.*]
enmes, *sb. pl.* enemies, 653. **enmis,** 9/13, 239. **enmy,** *sg.* 1589, 1830. **enmys,** *pl.* 599. Cf. **enemis.**
enourmentes, *sb. pl.* ornaments, 1476.
ensampil, *sb.* example, 39/33, 511, 719, 1045. **ensaumpil,** 916, 1175, 1302, 1305, etc. **ensawmpil,** 1047. Cf. **asaumpil, examples.**
enserches, *vb. sg.* searches, 834.
entende, *vb.* give attention to, mind, 33/7.
entendement, *sb.* understanding. See **þentendement.**
entent, *sb.* intention, will; mind; attention, heed, 38/31, 161, 717, 895, 1998. **-e,** 33/34, 38/8, 46/33. **-es,** *pl.* 835. **bi þis e-t,** for this reason, 1150. **with gude e-t,** graciously, 2389. Cf. **antente, intent.**
ententiuelike, *adv.* attentively, 32/14, 46/2.
enters, *vb. sg.* 139, 1521, 1685. **entird,** *pp.* 39/35. Cf. **entre.**
enticement, *sb.* 38/40. Cf. **entisment, þenticement.**
entirmete, *vb.* refl. occupy herself, 22/12, 19. [Fr. *s'entremettre.*]
entirual, *sb.* interval, 15/30, 17/22, 29/31.
entisice, *vb. sg.* entices, 892.
entisment, *sb.* enticement, 2073. Cf. **enticement.**
entrè, *sb.* entry, admission, 37/33, 2085, 2102. **in þe entre,** approaching, near, 870.
entre, *vb.* enter, 2/31. Cf. **enters.**
envie, *sb.* envy, 44/15, 16. **enuy,** 1415.
enuius, *adj.* envious. See **þenuius.**
epistil, *sb.* epistle, 145/5.
er, *pron.* her, 1479. Cf. **her.**
er, *vb. pl.* are, 4/16, 23, 17, 18, 54, 130, 2273, etc. **ere,** 1/14, 2/31, 4/18, 5/17, 572, 2330, 2470, etc. Cf. **are, err.**
erand, *sb.* errand; message, 15/1, 22/1, 34/23, 36/6, etc. **-e,** 19/25.
eremete, *sb.* hermit, 266. **ermitis,** *pl.* 4/18, 19. Cf. **armitis.**
eres, *sb. pl.* ears, 348, 2391. **erin,** 2/4, 9/20. **eris,** 25, 67, 73, 76, etc. Cf. **eere.**
err, *vb. pl.* are, 2205. **ert,** *sg.* art, 400. Cf. **er.**
erth, *sb.* earth, 147/33, 171, 1095, 1105, 2156. **erþe,** 10/16, 12/20, 22/26, 31/28, etc. **ertht,** 19/25. **eryd,** 8/21. Cf. **þerþe.**
erþelike, *adj.* earthly, 7/1. **erthli,** 482, 587, 806. **erthly,** 472, 2475.
es, *vb. sg.* is, 1/21, 2/16, 10/18, 27, 48, 56, etc. art, 8/23, 39/29, 33. am, 2/15, 14/1, 9. are, 4/15, 16, 7/2, 13/2, 31/2, 34/3, 31, 1490, 2266. **es for to,** "you should," 16/23. **þat in þam es,** what they should do, 505. Cf. **is.**
es, *rel.* as. See **þar.**
eschew, *vb.* 1115.
ese, *sb.* ease; good health, 26/4, 33/21, 1975.
ete, *vb.* eat, 8/31, 21/15, 16, 30, etc. *pl.* (*sbj.*) 21/14, 15, 28/2, 29/18, etc. **etes,** *pl.* 27/21. **etin,** *pp.* 21/14, 32/28. **etis,** *pl.* 29/23? 142/18.
ethy, *adj.* easy, 43/17.
euaungelest, *sb.* evangelist, 1592.
euel, *adj.* evil, 2457. Cf. **euil.**
euen, *adv.* evenly, 119. Cf. **eueyn, euyn,** also **ewyn.**
euensang, *sb.* even-song (about 5 p.m.), 17/33, 18/6, 19, 29/15, etc. Cf. **euinsang, euynsang.**
euer, *adv.* ever, 5/15, 122, 186, 302, etc. Cf. **euir.**
euer-ilk-a, *adj.* every, 1567. **euer-ilkane,** *pron.* everybody, 1231. **-ilkayn,** 2132. **-ilkon,** 1576, 1581, 1637, 1675.
euermair, *adv.* evermore, 2328. **euermor,** 261, 682, 2050, 2308. Cf. **euirmare.**
eueyn, *adv.* even, 473. Cf. **euen.**
euil, *adj.* 161, 844. *sb.* 2/34, 5/30, 109. **evil,** *adj.* 11/32. Cf. **euel, euyl, iuel.**

euin, *sb.* evening, 21/16. Cf. **euyn.**
euinlike, *adv.* equally, alike, 6/6, 17/4.
euinsang = **euensang**, 18/30, 19/5.
euir, *adv.* ever, 2/25, 4/10, 11/34, 38/10, etc. Cf. **euer.**
euirmare, evermore, 38/25. Cf. **euermair.**
euyer, *adj. comp.* heavier, 2274. Cf. **heuy.**
euyl, *adj.* 1/13, 16, 619, 749. *sb.* 595. Cf. **euil.**
euyn, *sb.* evening, 28/6, 150/5, 593, 626, 1456. Cf. **euin.**
euyn, *adv.* even (sometimes as an expletive), 490, 704, 807, 1189, 2477. Cf. **euen, heuyn.**
euynhed, *sb.* equity, 2230.
euynly, *adv.* evenly, alike, 476, 2022.
euynsang = **euensang**, 1724, 1740, 1852.
euyr-ilk, *adj.* every, 2412.
ewyn, *adj.* even, like, 425.
examend, *pp.* examined, 141/10, 14, 143/4, 8, etc. **examned**, 142/35.
examples, *sb. pl.* 42/36. Cf. **ensampil.**
excuse, *vb.* 1222, 1494. refl. 368, 1056, 2435. **excused**, *pp.* 1802. Cf. **ascuse.**
expone, *vb.* expound, 142/33. **exponed**, *pp.* 142/35, 143/3.
exposiciuns, *sb. pl.* expositions, 16/10.
eye, *sb.* 9/20. **eyen**, *pl.* 11/9, 36. **ezin**, 2/13, 15/15, 17. Cf. **ee, eghen, ehe.**

fa, *sb.* foe, 40, 758.
fa, *adj.* few, 14/37, 15/3, 18/19. **faa**, 33/29.
face, *sb.* 1808. **facis**, *pl.* 144/4.
fader, *sb.* father, 1/14, 48, 339, 897. *gen.* 913. **faders**, *pl.* 2488. **fadir**, *sg.* 1/4, 5/9, 6/13, 47/7. **fadirs**, *gen.* 10/16, 12/30.
fagnis, *vb. pl.* fawn on, try to please, seek the favour of, *43/27.
faile, *vb.* fail; be missing or wanting, 7/8, 27/14, 240, 1529, 1537. *pl.* 31/26. **failed**, *pt.* 3/15. Cf. **fayle** and **falled.**
fain, *adj.* glad, 22/23. Cf. **fayne.**
faindinges, *sb. pl.* temptations, 278. Cf. **fandyng.**
fair, *sb.* journey, 2384. *vb.* fare, 1789. Cf. **fare.**
fair, *adj.* 438, 660, 1323, 1459, etc. *adv.* gently, 1603. **-e**, *adj.* 9/31, 23/3. *adv.* gently, kindly, 6/30, 15/1, 20/27, 24/15, etc. Cf. **farest.**
faith, *sb.* 267. Cf. **fath.**
fal, *vb.* fall; happen; arise; belong, 2179, 2276. **falis**, *sg.* 1230. **fall**, 447, 862, 1319, 1383, etc. *pl.* 190. **falland**, *ppr.* 2134. **falle**, 9/16, 19/31, 31/12, 42/22, etc. **fallen**, *pp.* 21/19. **falles**, *sg.* 477, 514, 2058, etc. *pl.* 315. **fallis**, *sg.* 8/27, 17/7, 8, etc. *pl.* 3/24, 13/3, etc. **fals**, *sg.* 216, 516, 660, 4166. *pl.* 761. Cf. **fel, fell.**
falled, *vb. pt.* failed, 1517. See Notes. Cf. **faile.**
fals, *adj.* false, 8/16, 13/19, 300, etc.
falslike, *adv.* falsely, 4/26.
fand, *vb.* try; endeavour, 1887. **-e**, 29, 1613. **-es**, *sg.* 180. *imp. pl.* 72. Cf. **faund.**
fandyng, *sb.* temptation, *148. Cf. **faindinges.**
fang, *vb.* get, receive, have, 2023.
fardnes, *sb.* fear, 594.
fare, *sb.* 308. Cf. **fair.**
fare, *adv.* further, 312.
farest, *adj.* fairest, 2019. Cf. **fair.**
fast, *adv.* fast; firmly; energetically; closely, 2/6, 184, 649, 702, 920.
fast, *sb.* 1955. *vb.* 29/14, 581, 1708, 1712. **-e**, *sb.* 142/18. *vb.* 29/7. *pl.* 29/17.
fasting, *sb.* 8/19, 23/24, 29/10, etc. **fastyng**, 29/19, 1357.
fastyngdais, *sb. pl.* fasting days, 1739. Cf. 29/30, 1958.
fat, *adj.* 22/17.
fath, *sb.* faith, 2241. Cf. **faith.**
fathfuly, *adv.* faithfully, 2135.
fathly, do., 1317.
faund, *vb.* try; endeavour, 1317. **-e**, 683. Cf. **fand.**
fauor, *sb.* favour, 409.
faute, *sb.* fault, 6/15, 17/9, 21/2, 507, etc. **fautes**, *pl.* 9/14, 12/23, 25, 19/2, etc. **fautis**, *pl.* 31/25. **fawte**, 46/15.
fayle, *vb.* be wanting, 495. Cf. **faile.**

fayn, *adv.* gladly, 2067. **-e,** *adj.* glad, desirous, 97. Cf. **fain.**
fayntly, *adv.* faintly, 240, 1537.
fe, *sb.* property, 360.
febil, *adj.* feeble, 26/2, 27/3, 28/16, 29/29, etc. **febyl,** 22/18, 20.
febilnes, *sb.* feebleness, 28/23.
fede, *vb.* feed, 2055. refl. eat, 1570.
feeste, *sb.* feast, 33/1. Cf. **feste.**
feeste-day, *sb.* feast-day, 29/9. Cf. **feste-dais.**
feet, *sb. pl.* 35/22. Cf. **fete.**
feght, *vb.* fight, 267. Cf. **fezte, fyght.**
fel, *vb.* fell, 871. Cf. **fell.**
fel, *vb. pt.* happened, 2231. Cf. **fal.**
felahe, *sb.* fellow, 14/38. **felaze,** 24/24. Cf. **felos.**
felahscap, *sb.* fellowship, 23/7. **felascap,** 22/26. **felazscap, felaȝscap,** *4/10, 11/26, 19/21, 22/28, 31, 40/2. common property or provision, 28/5. *vb.* associate, 40/34.
feld, *sb.* field, 345, 1091, 1182, 1987. **-e,** 15/9, 467, 596.
fele, *vb.* feel, 36/15, 39/33, 44/9, 46/5, etc. *pl.* 1383.
fell, *vb.* (try or threaten to) overthrow, 185. **-e,** 8/25. Cf. **fel.**
fell, *vb. pt.* 1501. **-e,** 37/23. Cf. **fal.**
fellike, *adv.* cruelly, 42/22.
felos, *sb. pl.* fellows, 1683. **felows,** 1250. Cf. **felahe.**
felun, *adj.* deceitful, false, wicked, 37/17, 42/8.
feluni, *sb.* deceit, etc., 8/24.
fend, *sb.* fiend, devil, 40, 148, 267. **-e,** 1369.
fer, *adv.* far, 34/15, 1991. *adj.* far, remote, 40/25.
ferde, *num.* fourth, 4/29. Cf. **ferþe.**
fere, *sb.* See **in-fere.**
fere, *vb.* frighten, terrify, 278.
feris, *vb. sg.* is becoming, is proper, 28/31. [O.F. *aferir*, pertain, behove.]
ferme, *sb.* rent, 39/14.
fermerier, *sb.* superintendent of the infirmary, 27/6.
ferþe, *num.* fourth, 13/1, 16/34. Cf. **ferde, fourt.**
feste, *sb.* feast, 29/14, 35/20. Cf. **feeste.**
feste-dais, *sb. pl.* feast-days, 17/10, 33/19. Cf. **feeste-day.**
fete, *sb. pl.* feet, 2/23, 11/36, 26/9, 10, etc. Cf. **feet.**
fezte, *vb.* fight, 4/20, 22. Cf. **feght.**
ficiciens, *sb. pl.* physicians, 1286.
fift, *num.* fifth, 987. **-e,** 13/24, 38/3.
fiftene, *num.* fifteen, 46/2.
fil, *vb.* fill, satisfy, 1602.
file, *vb.* defile, soil, 860. **files,** *sg.* (*pl.*) 1488.
filiȝ, *vb.* follow, 47/19. Cf. **folih.**
filth, *sb.* 614, 860.
finally, *adv.* 141/24.
find, *vb.* 710, 2018. *pl.* 1613. **-e,** 8/33, 26/2, 30/16, 35/31, etc. **-es,** *sg.* 40/27, 2322. **-is,** 3/6, 36/29, 40/28. Cf. **fynd,** and **fon, fun.**
fine, *adj.* 855.
finise, *vb.* finish, 16/14, 18/17, 32/13. **finist,** *pp.* 16/20, 35, 18/14, 32/12, etc.
fir, *sb.* fire, 9/1, 30. **fire,** 956.
firmitè, *sb.* infirmity, 45/17.
first, *num.* 1/20, 4/16, 15/32, etc. *adv.* 1/9, 7/5, 8/12, etc. **-e,** *num.* 9/26. *adv.* 11/30.
fisch, *sb.* fish, 1670.
fit, *sb.* attack, 871.
flat, *adj.*, *adv.* 2156.
fle, *vb.* flee, 3/32, 9/30, 11/12, 32, etc.
fleis, *sb.* flesh, 11/38, 13/9, 27/4. **fles,** 9/8. **flesch,** 579, 860, 874, etc. *gen.* 630, 829, 848, 862, etc. **flesche,** 142/17. **flessh,** *gen.* 302.
fleschly, *adj.* fleshly, 37, 846.
flight, *sb.* **wend to flight,** go away, 1942.
flit, *vb.* move, 1483. *pp.* removed, 1412.
flod, *sb.* flood, 3/15. **-es,** *pl.* 185.
flok, *sb.* flock, 23/11, 479, 1307, 1318, 1412.
flore, *sb.* floor, 1807.
fole, *sb.* fool, 21/3, 458, 1067. **foles,** *pl.* 1335, 2241. Cf. **fool.**
folie, *sb.* folly, 28/35. **folis,** *pl.* 2360. Cf. **foly.**
folih, *vb. pl.* follow, 13/12, 17/32. **folihe,** *inf.*, *sbj.* 2/12, 7/30. **folihis,** *pl.* 18/10. **foliz,** *inf.*, *sbj.* 8/18, 10/14, 17, 35/21. **folize,** *inf.* 22/21. **folos,** *sg.* 1032. **folous,** *pl.* 302. **folow,** *inf.*, *sbj.*, 1/17, 4/6, 578,

846, 1050, etc. **folu,** *inf., sbj.* 3/17, 7/31. Cf. **filiȝ** and **folyzed.**
folk, *sb.* 233, 252, 333, 336, 1590, etc. **-e,** 42/7.
foly, *sb.* folly, 30/7, 827, 1274, 2356. Cf. **folie.**
folyzed, *vb. pt.* followed, 12/13. Cf. **folih.**
fon, *pp.* found, 1309. Cf. **find.**
fone, *adj.* few, 1082. Cf. **foune.**
fool, *sb.* 14/32. Cf. **fole.**
for, *prep.* 1/13, 14, 36, 46, 83, 155, etc. instead of, 16/19. *conj.* 3/16, 4/33, 17, 74, 79, etc. because, *6/18, 41/27, 459, 678, 738. in order that, that, 183, 197, 1511, 1781. **for to** (before an inf.), 4/4, 16, 20, 32, 5/*5, 8, etc. Cf. **fore, forto,** also **na-for-þi, þi.**
forbed, *pp.* forbidden, 845. **-bede,** *sbj.* 635, 1319, 2231. **-bedes,** *sg.* 392.
forbere, *vb.* forbear, 28/23, 32, 760, 767.
force, *sb.* strength, 3/30, 45/15, 190. **make f-e of,** etc., pay heed to, care for, mind, 21/4, 47/16. **of mare f-e,** etc., more forcibly, 748, 1182.
forde, *adv.* forth, 18/19, 23, 26. Cf. **forth.**
fore, *num.* four, 144/2. Cf. **four.**
fore, *prep.* (postpos.) for, 1342. Cf. **for.**
forefadirs, *sb. pl.* forefathers, 16/10.
forest, *sb.* 2279.
forgat, *vb. pt.* forgotst, 5/34. **-get,** *sbj.* 1246. **-gete,** *inf., sbj.* 7/1, 40/10, 1680, 1722, etc. **-getin,** *pp.* 2/14, 820.
forgetil, *adj.* forgetful, 11/31, 24/11, 47/22. **forgetilnes,** *sb.* forgetfulness, 17/8, 27/6.
forgif, *vb.* forgive, 2389. **-giue,** 9/14, 19/1, 4, 5, etc. *pl.* 19/2. **-giuin,** *pp.* 19/7. **-gyf,** 210. **-gyvin,** *pp.* 13/34.
forgifnes, *sb.* forgiveness, 46/19, 2395.
forht, *adv.* forth, 4/25. Cf. **forth.**
forlokid, *pp.* provided, arranged, 28/23, 30/28, 36/21, 43/30, etc. **-lokis,** *sg.* 29/10. **-lokyd,** *pp.* 15/23.
forloking, *sb.* provision, 28/28.
form, *sb.* 2204. Cf. **furme.**
forsak, *vb.* forsake, 37. **-e,** 142/5, 17, 1335, etc. *imp. pl.* 903. **-es,** *pl.* 282, 821. **-is,** *sg.* 1/7.
forsworn, *adj.* 594.
forth, *adv.* 34/31, 42/8, 149/36, 292. Cf. **forde, forht, forz, furth.**
forþe, *vb.* bring about, effect, "manage," 44/25. Cf. **furde.**
forther, *adv.* further, 2337. Cf. 33/30.
forþermare, do., 493.
forthoght, *sb.* forethought, provident care, 2265.
forto = **for to,** 1981, 2049, 145/2, 146/34, etc.
fortt, *num.* fourth, 299. Cf. **fourt.**
forward, *adv.* 30/18, 38/20, 34, etc.
forz, *adv.* forth, 9/4, 21, 17/16, 31/7, etc. **forȝe,** "on," 45/18. Cf. **forth.**
foune, *adj.* few, 1078. Cf. **fone, fune.**
four, *num.* 256. **foure,** 4/15, 16/26, 29, 33, etc. **fowre,** 144/7. Cf. **fore.**
fourt, *num.* fourth, 923. **-e,** 143/7. Cf. **ferþe, fortt.**
fra, *prep.* from, 1/5, 2/11, 6/13, etc. (postpos.) 3/30. absent from, 30/28. safe or protected from, 3/15. Cf. **fro.**
fraitur, *sb.* refectory, 21/21, 31/3, 19, 37/8, etc.
fraward, *adj.* froward, 6/14, 384.
fre, *adj.* free; open; liberal; generous, noble, 26, 1443, 2050, 2411.
freendis, *sb. pl.* friends, 9/20. Cf. **frend.**
frelty, *sb.* frailty, 2278.
frely, *adv.* freely, 2104.
frenchep, *sb.* friends, 2199. Cf. **frenschep.**
frend, *sb.* friend; relation, 1902, 2374. **-e,** 18/3, 36/9, 39/17, 29, etc. **-es,** *pl.* 1987, 1991, 2186, 145/11, 13. **-is,** 2/25, 36/7, 39/7, 22, etc. Cf. **freendis.**
frendly, *adj.* friendly, 648.
frenschep, *sb.* friendship, 591. Cf. **frenchep.**
friday, *sb.* 1708. Cf. **fryday.**
fro, *prep.* from, 10/32, 33, 50, 52, etc. (postpos.) 1984. *conj.* from the time that, 1131, 1707. Cf. **fra.**
frute, *sb.* fruit, 28/5.

fryday, *sb.* Friday, 29/8. Cf. **friday.**
ful, *adj.* full, 8/33, 21/3, 28/34, 2071. *adv.* fully, quite, very, 1/17, 11/29, 19/25, 21/4, 113, 182, 401, etc. Cf. **full.**
ful, *adj.* foul, wrong, 24/4.
fulfil, *vb.* 12/27, 142/1, 376, 683, 729, 891, etc. *imp.* 1/3. **-fild,** *pp.* 15/18, 17/31. **-filid,** *pp.* filled, 2458. **-fill,** 142/22, 26, 72, 180, etc. *pl.* 215. **-fille,** 12/28, 13/18. **-fillid,** *pp.* filled, 2462. **-fyll,** 19, 29, 78, 377. **fullfille,** *pl.* 3/33.
full, *adv.* fully, quite, very, 7/13. Cf. **ful.**
fulli, *adv.* fully, 1671. **fully,** 142/11, 143/5, 233, 477, etc.
fullyng, *sb.* fouling, 1266.
fun, *pp.* found, 507, 1314. **funden,** 22/23, 25/31, 33/13, 2315, 2356, etc. **fundyn,** 2237. Cf. **find.**
fundes, *vb. sg.* founds, 3/14.
fune, *adj.* few, 1084. Cf. **foune.**
furde, *vb.* bring about, effect, afford, 28/25. Cf. **forþe.**
furme, *sb.* form, 141/1. Cf. **form.**
furth, *adv.* forth, 1672, 1915, 1923, 1984, etc. **-e,** 2398. Cf. **forth.**
furthward, *adv.* forth, out, 1902.
fyftyd, *num.* fiftieth, 17/11.
fyght, *vb.* fight, 40. Cf. **feght.**
fynd, *vb.* find, 256. Cf. **find.**
fyue, *num.* five, 2083.

ga, *vb.* go, 2/24, 4/13, 23, 5/23, etc. *pl.* 8/20, 26/9. *imp.* 38/13, 142/30. Cf. **gay, go,** and **gane, gas.**
gabbingis, *sb. pl.* jesting, prating, 34/5.
gadir, *vb.* gather, 32/32. **-d,** *pp.* 4/16.
gafe, *vb. pt.* gave, 43/6. Cf. **giue.**
gaine, *vb.* avail, profit, be useful, 226. Cf. **gayn.**
gainsaie, *vb.* gainsay, 7/27.
gainsaȝe, *sb.* gainsaying, 45/16.
gane, *pp.* gone, 1/5, 3/30. Cf. **ga.**
gang, *vb.* go, 11/18, 41/18, 642, 1090, 1723, 1851, 2215, etc. **-e,** 4/29, 30/12, 34/34, 35/9, etc. **-es,** *sg.* 326.
gar, *vb.* make, cause (to), 21, 308, 1749. Cf. **garre, ger.**
gard, *sb.* yard; garden, 31/35, 44/28. **-e,** 15/8.
gardins, *sb. pl.* gardens, 2429.
garre, *vb.* make, cause (to), 141/20. **gart,** *pp.* 544. Cf. **gar.**
gas, *vb. sg.* goes, 23/17, 26/16, 17. *pl.* 12/12. **gase,** *sg.* 45/8. *pl.* 482. Cf. **ga.**
gaste, *sb.* Ghost, 335, 337. Cf. **gost.**
gastly, *adj.* spiritual, 348, 1687, 1734, 2285, etc. Cf. **gostly.**
gate, *sb.* way; path; manner, 2/17, 5/14, 10/9, 35/20, etc. **gates,** *pl.* 12/12. **gatis,** 10/10. Cf. **algate.**
gay, *vb.* go, 147/29. **gayn,** *pp.* 787. Cf. **ga.**
gayn, *vb.* profit, be useful, do good, 752. **-e,** 2035. Cf. **gaine.**
gede, *vb.* guide, 22/14. Cf. **gyde.**
ger, *sb.* gear, apparel, 2429. **gere,** 1623, 2022.
ger, *vb.* make, cause (to), 1292, 1326, 1949, 1951. 1 *sg.* 2301. **gert,** *pp.* 1630. Cf. **gar.**
gerne, *adv.* eagerly, fervently, 19/31. Cf. **ȝerne.**
gest, *sb.* guest, 1926, 1933, 2086. **-e,** 35/6, 40/26, 34. **-es,** *pl.* 1447, 1749, 1935, etc. *pl. gen.* 1973. **-is,** *pl.* 29/35, 35/3, 8, etc. *pl. gen.* 35/19. **-ys,** *pl.* 24/7.
get, *vb.* get, receive, obtain, procure, 1318. **gete,** 1379, 1669. *pl.* 730. **getes,** *sg.* 1420. Cf. **getyn.**
gete, *vb.* watch, guard, hold, keep; observe, 5/20, 6/29, 30, 9/5, 11/35, etc. *imp.* 2/11, 27/7, etc. *imp. pl.* 12/8. *pp.* 39/2. **getes,** *imp. pl.* 12/22.
geting, *sb.* watching, care, 41/35.
getyn, *pp.* got, received, 43/33, 1242. Cf. **get.**
geuen, *pp.* given, 73. **geuin,** 43/18. **geuyn,** 43/19. **gif,** *inf., sbj., imp.* 3/26, 5/2, 10/27, 916, 1818, etc. refl. 233, 769. **gife,** 142/20. *pl.* 511. **gifes,** *sg.* 190, 2039, 2070, 2354. **giffis,** *sg.* 142/1. **giffyn,** *pp.* 147/20. **gifin,** 2080. Cf. **giue.**
giffe, *conj.* if, 143/2, 5. Cf. **giue.**
gifte, *sb.* gift, 24/17, 25/26, 28/20,

142/10. **giftes,** *pl.* 1464, 1619, 1986, 1992, etc. **giftis,** 36/7.
girdid, *pp.* girt, 1203.
girdyl, *sb.* girdle, 147/9, 12.
giue, *conj.* if, 142/22. Cf. **giffe, gyf, if, yef.**
giue, *vb.* give, 3/7, 5/8, 26, 9/19, etc. *pl.* 21/26. *imp.* 7/15, 22/30, 25/3, etc. **giuin,** *pp.* 6/33, 25/26, 41/15. **giuis,** *sg.* 3/18, 9/19, 24/35, 36/11, etc. Cf. **geuen, gyf,** and **gafe.**
glad, *adj.* 3/11, 1313.
glade, *vb.* gladden, 1797.
gladli, *adv.* gladly, 659, 906, 1113, 1669. **gladly,** 210, 1433, 1440, 1465, etc.
gloria, *sb.* (Lat.) 1768.
glotony, *sb.* gluttony, 1590, 1594. **glutunie,** 4/31. Cf. **clotony.**
gluterie, do., 28/12, 13.
go, *vb.* 149/32, 704, 1347. *pl.* 1983. Cf. **ga** and **gone.**
god, *sb.* God, 2/2, 6, etc. *gen.* 8/26, 604, 967, 1554. **godd,** 142/29. **godde,** 42/31, 43/8, 47/31, etc. **goddes,** *gen.* 1160. **goddis,** *gen.* 11/24, 42/16, 45/19, 906. **gode,** 11/16, 19/5, 26/36, 40/31, etc. *gen.* 1652. Cf. **godes.**
god, *adj.* good, 14/13. *sb.* 3/6. **gode,** *adj.* 2/22, 4/25, 5/7, etc. *sb.* 2/12, 5/30, 50. Cf. **gud.**
godenes, *sb.* goodness, 40/15. Cf. **gudenes.**
godes, *sb. gen.* God's, 3/19, 36, 153, 222, etc. **godis,** 1/23, 2/9, 27, etc. **godys,** 20/25. Cf. **god.**
godspel, *sb.* Gospel, 145/5, 178, 206, 662. **-spell,** 487. Cf. **gospel.**
gold, *sb.* 4/24, 2196. **-e,** 142/10, 13.
gon, *pp.* 2111. **gone,** 1349. Cf. **go.**
gospel, *sb.* 2/24, 3/13, 15/13, 16/36, etc. **gospell,** 143/10, 1646. Cf. **godspel.**
gost, *sb.* Ghost, 79. Cf. **gaste.**
gostly, *adj.* spiritual, 38, 50. Cf. **gastly.**
gouerne, *vb.* govern, rule, 471. Cf. **guuerne.**
grace, *sb.* 3/26, 13/34, 21/6, 31, etc. thanks, 3/7, 8/34. prayer, 1791. *vb.* thank, 28/36, 44/22.
graid, *pp., adj.* procured, prepared; ready, 9/21, 15/19. **graide,** 1714. **graiþe,** *inf.* procure, 24/18. **grath,** *adj.* ready, direct, 2420, 2483. Cf. **grayde.**
grant, *vb.* 225, 1198. *pl.* 2102, 2104. **-e,** *sbj.* 4/12. Cf. **graunt.**
grathly, *adv.* straight, 642, 1692.
graue, *sb.* steward, 359.
graunt, *vb.* grant, 39/25. *imp.* 15/20. *pp.* 141/5. **-e,** *imp.* 1008. *pp.* 2085. **-id,** *pp.* 39/30. Cf. **grant.**
grayde, *pp., adj.* prepared, ready, 2087. **redy grayd,** do., 1767. Cf. **graid.**
grece, *sb.* step(s), 30/10, 13, 17, 147/29, etc. **gree,** step, 143/11, 19, 22, 29, etc.
gret, *adj.* great, large, big, 20/23, 514, 760, 766, etc. **-e,** 24/17, 26/1, 244, 2379, etc. **-er,** *comp.* 1630, 1986.
greting, *sb.* weeping, lamentation, 21/23.
greuching, *sb.* grudging, grumbling, 20/32, *24/19. Cf. **gruching.**
greuauns, *sb.* hardship, 244, 544.
greue, *adj.* burden, grieve, 41/14, 42/26, 883, 1436, 2353. feel annoyed or distressed, 1981. Cf. **greues.**
greue, *adj.* heavy, oppressive, grievous; grave, serious, 4/3, 31/3, 36/30, 45/12, etc. **greuer,** *comp.* 21/20, 31/30, 32/4.
greuelike, *adv.* grievously, 45/25.
greues, *vb. sg.* grieves, 2449. *imp. pl.* burden, "overcharge," 1593. **greuid,** *pp.* 33/23. **greuyd,** 1/12, 985, 1998. Cf. **greue.**
greueus, *adj.* grievous, hard, 6/28. **greuus,** 43/10, 927, 1240, 1244, etc. **greuusly,** *adv.* 1489.
groch, *vb.* grudge, grumble, 1399, 1640. **-and,** *ppr.* 1427. **-es,** *sg.* 1875. Cf. **gruch.**
grochin, *sb.* grudging, grumbling, 930. **groching,** 1436, 1718. Cf. **gruching.**
grofelyng, *ppr.* 147/40.
growyng, *sb.* growing, 1574.
gruch, *vb.* grudge, grumble, 723, 1226, 2336. **-ande,** *ppr.* 8/32,

10/26, 29/1. **-e,** *inf.*, *sbj.* 10/22, 28/36, 32/33. **-es,** *sg.* 10/23, (*pl.*?) 2453. Cf. **groch.**

gruching, *sb.* grudging, grumbling, 7/33, 10/18, 26/15, 1094, etc. Cf. **greuching, grochin.**

gud, *adj.* good, 1444, 1516, 1689, 1935, etc. **gude,** 1/10, 11/23, 44, 71, etc. *sb.* 3/8, 12/18, 109, 160, etc. **gudes,** *pl.* goods, 482, 1992, 2193, 2318. **gudis,** bounties, 1/14. Cf. **god.**

gudenes, *sb.* goodness, 40/17, 46/31, 35. Cf. **godenes.**

guuerne, *vb.* govern, 42/9. Cf. **gouerne.**

gyde, *vb.* guide, manage, 39/21. Cf. **gede.**

gyf, *conj.* if, 37/12. Cf. **giue.**

gyf, *vb.* give, 12/5, 146/23, 3. **gyffe,** 143/14. **gyfyn,** *pp.* 1242. Cf. **giue.**

gyfyng, *sb.* giving, 147/11.

habete, *sb.* habit, 145/19. Cf. **abet.**

had, *vb. pt.* 1/5, 1309, 1548. *pp.* 1923. **haf,** *inf.*, *sbj.* 824, 1276, 1616,' etc. 1 *sg.* 786, 787, 789. *pl.* 167, 770, 1278, etc. **hafe,** *inf.*, *sbj.* 150, 391, 1573, 2061, etc. 1 *sg.* 743. *pl.* 531. *imp.* 1100. Cf. **haue.**

haile, *adj.* sound, 2046. Cf. **hale.**

hair, *sb.* 146/34, 37.

haite, *vb.* promise, 23/15, 38/24. *pl.* (*sbj.*?) 40/3. **haitis,** *sg.* 38/2, 10, 18. Cf. **hete** and **hight, hizte.**

hald, *vb.* hold, keep ; consider ; observe, 149/34, 50, 1011, 1027, etc. *imp.* 107. **-e,** 6/4, 7/24, 8/18, 38/36, etc. **-en,** *pp.* 14/33, 16/17. **-es,** *pl.* 47/20. *imp. pl.* 47/24. **-in,** *pp.* 10/23, 17/4, 20, 18/28, etc. **-is,** *sg.* (*pl.*) 47/7. intr. (holds on), remains, 45/17. *pl.* 47/27. **-yn,** *pp.* 644. bound, 18. Cf. **hold** and **held.**

hale, *adj.* whole, entire ; sound, 22/4, 23/6, 1423, 2376, etc. **haler,** *comp.* 42/4. Cf. **haile.**

hali, *adj.* whole, full, 2221.

hali, *adj.* holy, 7/25, 8/28, 193, 198, etc. Cf. **haly, holi.**

halili, *adv.* wholly, 214.

halily, *adv.* holily, 155.

halized, *pp.* hallowed, 24/11. **halow,** *inf.* 145/19, 150/7. **halowd,** *pp.* 147/28. **halowid,** 144/7.

halizes, *sb. pl.* saints, 16/8. **halizes,** 38/25. **halizis,** 29/26. **halows,** 2138, 147/22.

halowyng, *sb.* hallowing, 144/6.

hals, *sb.* neck, 24/23.

hals, *vb.* greet, salute, 1983.

haly, *adv.* wholly, 1884, 2319.

haly, *adj.* holy, 2/3, 146/22, 12, 2180, etc. Cf. **hali.**

halynes, *sb.* holiness, 5/27.

ham, *adv.* home, 1310. **hame,** 45/2. Cf. **home.**

hand, *sb.* 470, 1764, 1834, 145/8, etc. **-e,** 38/27, 39/7, 1358. **-es,** *pl.* 147/28, 149/34, 35. Cf. **hend.**

happins, *vb. sg.* happens, 43/9.

hard, *adj.* (*sb.*) 2/2, 237, 241, 456, etc. **-e,** 3/16, 5/28, 38/9, 141/26. Cf. **herd** and **harder.**

harde, *vb. pt.* heard, 43/6. Cf. **here.**

hardeli, *adv.* bravely, 215.

harder, *adj. comp.* 460, 707. Cf. **hard.**

hardi, *adj.* hardy, bold, 21/34. **hardy,** 25/6, 29/33, 34/25, 36/6, etc. Cf. **herdy.**

hardnes, *sb.* hardness, 433, 2082.

hare, *adv.* ere, 1207. Cf. **are.**

harm, *sb.* 187. **-e,** 606. **-es,** *pl.* 585, 2400.

harmyd, *pp.* harmed, 1924. Cf. **hermyt.**

hart, *sb.* heart, 5/28, 11/8. **-e,** 8/24. **-es,** *pl.* 220, 1593. **grete harte,** pride, 543. Cf. **hert.**

has, *vb. sg.* 2, 1527. **hase,** 1/11, 26/19, 42/13, 43/4, etc. 2 *sg.* 954, 957, 965, 1518. *pl.* 501, 582, 676, 1930, etc. Cf. **ass, haue.**

hast, *vb.* hasten, 2283. refl. 1217, 1761. *imp.* refl. 1524.

hastelie, *adv.* hastily, quickly, 39/24, 44/23. **hastelike,** 30/6, 46/18, 47/23.

hastiuelike, do., 46/34.

hate, *adj.* hot, *1600, 2004, 2007.

hate, *vb.* 12/27, 42/20, 629, 2269. **hates,** *sg.* 397. **hatid,** *pt.* 5/33.

haterede, *sb.* hatred, 43/23. **hateredin,** 44/15, 16.

haue, *vb.* have, 2/10, 22, 46, 1633, etc. refl. behave herself, act, 476. 1 *sg.* 3/10, 47/25, 1107, etc. *pl.* 2/7, 30, 3/7, 87, etc. **haues,** *pl.* 585. **hauid,** *pt.* 5/20, 12/13, 22/23, 27, etc. **hauide,** 12/31. **hauis,** *sg.* 3/21, 6/27, 28, etc. 2 *sg.* 10/25, 13/17. *pl.* 2/4, 25, 4/23, 19/3, etc. Cf. **had, has, þaue.**
hay, *sb.* 1710.
he, *adj.* high, 11/14. Cf. **hez.**
he, *pron.* 1/11, 147/9, 23, 45, *2321, etc. Cf. **him, his.**
hed, *sb.* head, 1525. **hede,** 147/5. **hedes,** *pl.* 1604. Cf. **heued.**
hede, *sb.* heed, 71, 77, 179, 231, etc.
hee, *adj.* high, 143/16, 28. **hegh,** 145/11. *adv.* 2478. Cf. **hez.**
heghnes, *sb.* highness, pride, 803. Cf. **eghnes, heȝnes, highnes.**
hel, *sb. gen.* hell's, 856. Cf. **hell.**
hel, *adj.* healthy, sound, 1285.
held, *vb. pt.* 11/9. **helde,** kept, withheld, 37/19. Cf. **hald.**
hele, *sb.* health; salvation, 15/27, 169, 485, 496.
hele, *vb.* heal; save, 22/6, 32/8, 248, 1282. **helid,** *pp.* 23/25.
hell, *sb.* 12/12, 227, 612, etc. **-e,** 3/32, 9/1, 11/34, etc. Cf. **hel.**
help, *sb.* 3/31, 4/22, 44/24, 655. *vb.* 4/1, 8/20, 322, etc. **-e,** *sb.* 25/28, 26/2, 35/31, etc. *vb.* 11/22, 23/5, 24/24. **-es,** *sg.* 169. **-id,** *pp.* 1518. **-is,** *sg.* helps, avails, 14/32.
helping, *sb.* 1523.
hend, *sb. pl.* hands, 11/36, 26/9, 36/21, 1431, *1963, 2262. **-e,** 30/6, 32/34, 33/5, 790, etc. Cf. **hand.**
hent, *pp.* seized, 1331.
her, *pron.* 375, 1434. refl. 1229, 1321. *adj.* 46/18, 1555, 2378, 2451, etc. Cf. **er, hir, hyr.**
her, *adv.* here, 3/20, 142/24, 1286. Cf. **here.**
herber, *vb.* tr. or intr. harbour, hold, lodge, dwell, 36/3, 1200. **-berd,** *pt.* 1934. **-berz,** *inf.* 36/3.
herd, *adj.* hard, 383, 432. Cf. **hard, hert.**
herd, *vb. pt.* heard, 2/2. *pp.* 45/6. **-e,** 19/28, 27/20, 29/29, etc. Cf. **here.**
herde, *sb.* shepherd, 22/21. Cf. **hird.**
herdis, *sb. pl.* herds, flocks, 42/35.
herdy, *adj.* bold, 2353. Cf. **hardi.**
here, *sb.* Lord, 4/1. See Notes.
here, *vb.* hear, 1/23, 2/14, 67, 76, etc. *pl.* 3/24, 9/33, 10/20, 19/3, 1759, 1782, etc. *imp.* 7/4. Cf. **harde, herd, heres.**
here, *vb.* praise, 19/14.
here, *adv.* 2/15, 25, 4/11, 11/21, 15, 24, 46, etc. Cf. **her.**
here-ogayn, *adv.* against this, 2407. Cf. **her-ogayn.**
heres, *vb. sg.* hears, 354, 689, 695, etc. *pl.* 1700. **heris,** *sg.* 3/13, 10/1. *pl.* 10/20, 27/29, 29/27, 32, etc. *imp. pl.* 3/12. Cf. **here.**
hering, *sb.* hearing, 768, 2391.
herkins, *vb. imp. pl.* hark, listen, 2/4. **herkyn,** *imp.* 1/2.
hermyt, *pp.* harmed, 1330. Cf. **harmyd.**
her-ogayn, *adv.* against this, 2453. Cf. **here-ogayn.**
herself, *pron.* 328. Cf. **hirself.**
hert, *adj.* hard, 1237. Cf. **herd.**
hert, *sb.* heart, 2/33, 4/7, 143, 151, etc. **-e,** 1/3, 8/13, 30, 9/21, etc. **-es,** *pl.* 59, 70, 383, 589, etc. **herth,** 1035. **hertis,** *pl.* 2/2, 3/29, 13/8, 28/13, etc. **of grete herte,** proud, 20/31. Cf. **hart.**
hertli, *adv.* heartily, lustily, vigorously, 683. **hertly,** *adj.* thorough, 2520. *adv.* 1217, 1524, 2283, etc.
hete, *sb.* heat, 28/28, 29/9.
hete, *vb.* promise, 2122, 2133, 2139, 2193. 1 *sg.* 147/21. Cf. **haite.**
heued, *sb.* head, 421. Cf. **hed, heuidis.**
heuen, *sb.* heaven, 120, 130, 138, 288. Cf. **heuin.**
heueyn, *adv.* even, 249. Cf. **heuyn.**
heuidis, *sb. pl.* heads, 15/10, 35/14. Cf. **heued.**
heuin, *sb.* heaven, 11/15, 34, 12/5, 19, etc. Cf. **heuen, heuyn.**
heuin, *vb.* avenge; refl. 8/23.
heuin-rike, *sb.* the kingdom of Heaven, 9/30.
heuy, *adj.* heavy, 241, 301, 725. Cf. **euyer.**
heuyn, *sb.* heaven, 59, 64, 212, 250, etc. *gen.* 2476. Cf. **heuin.**

heuyn, *adv.* even, 796. **hewyn,** 1104. Cf. **euyn, heueyn.**
heyed, *pp.* heightened, elevated, exalted, raised, 11/5. **heyes,** *pl.* 11/4. **heyid,** *pt.* 11/10. *pp.* 11/8. **heȝe,** *inf.* 42/18. **hezed,** *pp.* 11/17, 20, 14/10. **hezid, heȝid,** 11/14, 44/4. **heȝis,** *sg.* 41/22. Cf. **highed.**
hez, *adj.* high, 35/20, 47/7. **heze, heȝe,** 5/36, 7/31, 47/23, etc. *adv.* 25/28. **heȝer,** *comp.* 41/5. **heze-like,** *adv.* aloud, 18/29. **hezlike,** 19/6. Cf. **egh, he, hee, high.**
heȝnes, *sb.* highness, 41/28, 47/11, 13, 26, etc. Cf. **heghnes.**
hi, *sb.* haste, 1551. Cf. **hy.**
hi, *adj.* high, 1721. Cf. **high.**
hid, *vb. pt.* 5/19, 13/32. *pp.* 46/13. **hide,** *pp.* 839, 1002. Cf. **hyd.**
hider, *adv.* hither, 81.
high, *adj.* 780, 1397. **highest,** *sup.* 2263. Cf. **hez, hi.**
highed, *pp.* lifted, 790. **highes,** *sg.* heightens, etc., 775. Cf. **heyed, hyes.**
highnes, *sb.* highness, pride, 1370. Cf. **heghnes, hyghnes.**
hight, *sb.* height, 795. **in hight,** on high, 786. **on hight,** 897, 1068. Cf. **hyght.**
hight, *pp.* promised, 2511. Cf. **haite.**
him, *pron.* 3/7, 12, 276, 331, etc. refl. 3/1. Cf. **hym.**
himself, *pron.* 5/31, 10/20, 775, 1334. **-e,** 12/29, 26/27. Cf. **hymself.**
hir, *pron.* her, *21/4, 32/8, 16, 327, 359, etc. refl. 368, 2056. *adj.* 7/21, 8/2, 354, 360, etc. Cf. **her.**
hir, *adj.* their, 21/2, 1815. Cf. **ire.**
hird, *sb.* shepherd, 291, 478, 1299. **-es,** *pl.* 481. **-is,** 22/16. Cf. **herde.**
hird-man, *sb.* herdsman, 358, 1305.
hir-fra, *adv.* from this, 42/23.
hirs, *pron.* hers, 141/7.
hirself, *pron.* herself, 387, 451, 1261, 1343, etc. **-selfe,** 32/13, 38/28. **-selu,** 1457. Cf. **herself.**
his, *adj.* 2/6, 8, 155, 176, etc. **hise,** 2/25, 6/18, 9/20, etc. *pron.* 12/20. Cf. **hys.**
hizte, *vb. pt.* promised, 9/20. Cf. **haite.**
hold, *vb.* 589, 2000. **holde,** keep, 40/3. Cf. **hald.**
holi, *adj.* holy, 2040. Cf. **hali.**
home, *adv.* 2029. Cf. **ham.**
honest, *adj.* honest, worthy; decent, fine, 1665, 2028. **hon-este,** 142/7. Cf. **onest.**
honestly, *adv.* 1062.
honor, *vb.* 572, 979, 1888, etc. **-d,** *pp.* 2442, 2444. **-ed,** *pp.* 327. **honour,** 2446. *pl.* 1946. *sb.* 651, 1950. **honoure,** *sb.* 1867, 1898. **honowr,** *vb.* 673. **honur,** *sb.* 16/36, 35/27. Cf. **onur.**
hope, *vb. pl.* 946. **hopand,** *ppr.* 1158.
hordand, *pp.* appointed, 1678. Cf. **ordain.**
houre, *sb.* hour, 61. **houres,** *pl.* 1784. Cf. **hure, our, ure.**
hous, *sb.* house, 183, 1934. Cf. **hows, hus.**
how, *adv.* 10/29, 19/23, 8, 11, etc. **how . . þat,** how, 119. Cf. **hu.**
hows, *sb.* house, 1200, 1206, 1220, 1340, etc. **-e,** 35/32, 35, 37/13, 38/4, etc. **-es,** *pl.* 1502. Cf. **hous.**
howseld, *pp.* administered the Eucharist, 149/40. **howslid,** 144/26.
hu, *adv.* how, 2/20, 7/20, 13/1, 16, etc. Cf. **how.**
hundred seuintende, *num.* 117th, 17/12.
hundrez, *num.* hundred, 22/22.
hurd, *vb.* treasure up, keep, 1747.
hure, *sb.* hour, 18/14. **huris,** *pl.* 30/18. Cf. **houre.**
hurt, *pp.* 1282.
hus, *pron.* us, 797. Cf. **us.**
hus, *sb.* house, 3/14, 20/19, 24/27, etc. **huse,** 20/20, 24/13. Cf. **hous.**
hy, *sb.* haste, 1923, 2062. Cf. **hi.**
hyd, *pp.* hid(den), 12/19. **hydes,** *sg.* 32/3. Cf. **hid.**
hyes, *vb. sg.* heightens, exalts, 11/6 Cf. **highed.**
hyghnes, *sb.* highness, pride, 1035. Cf. **highnes.**
hyght, *sb.* = **hight,** 65.
hyll, *sb.* hill, 135.
hym, *sb.* hymn, 144/11. Cf. **yme.**
hym, *pron.* him, 1/5, 9, 44, 48, etc. Cf. **him.**

hymself, *pron.* 178, 779. **-e,** 35/4, 40/6. Cf. **himself.**
hyr, *pron.* her, 20/8, 23/4, 6, etc. refl. 20/8. *adj.* 10/36, 141/7. Cf. **her.**
hys, *adj.* 1/12, 14, 15, 46, 49, 50, etc. Cf. **his.**

I, i, *pron.* 2/5, 4/2, 82, 97, etc. Cf. **ic.**
ianglers, *sb. pl.* chatterers, 747.
ianglyng, *ppr.* chattering, 1780.
ic, *pron.* = **I,** 15/17. Cf. 14/2, 9, 10.
id, *pron.* it, 17/17. Cf. **it.**
idilnes, *sb.* idleness, 1221. Cf. **ydilnes.**
if, *conj.* 142/25, 143/8, 61, 98, etc. **if þat,** if, 69, 1195, 1372, 1529, etc. Cf. **giue, yef, yf.**
igain, *adv.* again, back, 23/14. *prep.* against, 28/12. Cf. **again.**
igainis, *prep.* against, 13/2. Cf. **againis.**
il, *adj.* ill, bad, 32/23, 40/34. *sb.* 868, 1072. Cf. **ill.**
ilk, *adj.* same, 218, 251, 801, 2311. Cf. **ilke.**
ịlk, *adj.* each, 29/14, 474, 616, 819, etc. Cf. **ilke.**
ilka, *adj.* each, 191, 610, 673, 739, etc. *pron.* each one, everybody, 14/8. **ilkain,** *adj.* 6/1. *pron.* 6/3, 6, 31, 7/23, *36/32, etc. **ilkane,** 46/10. **ilkay,** *adj.* 2381. Cf. **ilkon,** also **euerilk-a.**
ilke, *adj.* same, 9/19, 10/24, 16/30, 33, etc. Cf. **ilk.**
ilke, *adj.* each, 9/2, 13/10, 17/23, 24, etc. Cf. **ilk.**
ilkman, each one, everybody, 1976.
ilkon, do., 17, 157, 408, 411, etc. Cf. **ilka.**
ill, *adj.* ill, bad, wicked, 473. *sb.* 108, 539, 2091. *adv.* badly, 2261. **ille,** *adj.* 5/17, 8/24, 33/33, 40/8, etc. *adv. or sb.* 24/36. Cf. **il.**
imang, *adv.* among, amongst it, 14/25. *prep.* among(st), 38/19, 35, 44/30. Cf. **emang, inmang, omang.**
imangis, *prep.* amongst, 25/30, 33/10.
imiddis, *prep.* amidst, in the midst of, 35/24. Cf. **inmydes.**
immonesis (careless or corrupt) for **immondesis,** *sb. pl.* impurities, 43/22. [O.F. *immondices.*]
in, *prep.* 1/12, 14, 1, 5, etc. (postpos.) 1665. *adv.* 26/10, 16, 40/16, 141/15, 1685, etc. **in . . in,** 42/20, 21. Cf. **yn.**
in, *conj.* and, 2007, 2260. Cf. **and.**
inconueniens, *sb.* inconvenience, 43/17.
indentures, *sb. pl.* 1481. Cf. **endenturs.**
in-fere, *adv.* together, 233, 1210, 1729.
informaciun, *sb.* information, instruction, 142/28.
informed, *pp.* 385. **infurme,** *inf.* 142/31.
ingles, *sb.* English, 15. Cf. **englísh.**
in-like, *adv.* alike, 408, 1576, 1635.
in-mang, *prep.* among, 2132. Cf. **imang.**
in-mydes, *prep.* in the midst of, 145/10. Cf. **imiddis.**
inne, *prep.* (postpos.) in, 34/30, 35/34. *adv.* 38/13. **in . . inne,** 37/26.
inobedience, *sb.* 1/6.
inoh, *adj.* enough, 27/33, 28/6.
inpair, *vb.* impair, enfeeble, injure, 1604.
inspires, *vb. sg.* 141/27.
intent, *sb.* meaning, 376. Cf. **entent.**
in-til, *prep.* unto, to, into, 10/16, 14/8, 2044, 2319, etc. **in-tyl,** 12/19.
into, *prep.* into, in, 19/10, 20/25, 43/27, 142/2, etc.
invinis (**v** is a vowel), *vb. sg.* enjoins, 42/33.
inwardly, *adv.* in one's heart, eagerly, 615.
iois, corrupt for **erin**? 45/4.
iolyose, *adj.* jealous, 42/29.
ioy, *sb.* joy, 2/10, 18, 3/19, etc. joyful praise, 3/9. **ioye,** 2/10, 3/25.
ire, *sb.* 6/17, 8/23, 589.
ire, *adj.* their, 25/28. Cf. **hir.**
irk, *adj.* tired, 236. *vb.* tire, become tired, 931.
irksum, *adj.* irksome, tiresome, 1114.
is, *vb. sg.* 15/25, 16/35, 18/15, etc.

am, 14/2, 15/14, 17. **it is to,** "we should," 1/13. Cf. **es, are.**
it, *pron.* 1/13, 22, 2/1, etc. **itt,** 172, 184, 186, 188. Cf. **id, yd, yt.**
itself, *pron.* 2195.
iuel (i is a consonant), *sb.* jewel, 142/14.
iuil (i is a vowel), *adj.* 4/5, 6/13, 8/19, etc. *sb.* 2/12, 8/25, 12/8, 18, 21/3. illness, 26/32. **ivil,** *adj.* 45/4. **iuils,** *sb. pl.* 25/32, 27/8. Cf. **euil.**
iugemens, *sb. pl.* judgments, 8/2. **-ment,** *sg.* 5/18, 8/3, 30, 37/2, etc. **-mentis,** *pl.* 44/14. **iugiment,** *sg.* 15/11, 18/4, 25/2.

kalandes, -is, *sb.* "the first" (Lat. *Calendæ*), 15/22, 29, 16/16, 1122, 1132, 1836.
kald, *pp.* called, 35/26. greeted, 35/4. Cf. **cald.**
kan, *vb. sg.* can, 32/7, 39/6, 1503. *pl.* 201, 1754. Cf. **can** and **kun.**
kast, *vb.* cast, 620. *imp.* 146/22. **-e,** *imp. pl.* 9/12. Cf. **cast, kest.**
katel, *sb.* cattle, 2320. chattel, property, 38/35.
kechin, *sb.* kitchen, 1491, 1539, 1565, 1973. Cf. **kichin.**
ken, *vb.* know ; teach, 10, 79, 258, 472, 552, etc. *pl.* 773. **kend,** *pt.* 1020. *pp.* 198, 321, 365, 1803, etc. **kende,** *pp.* 1406. Cf. **kenne.**
kene, *adj.* bold, 6/20.
kening, *sb.* teaching, instruction, 47/12, 14. **kenning,** 4/20, 23, 47/26.
kenne, *vb.* teach, 2/17. **kennis,** *sg.* 3/16. 5/30, 11/30, 20/16, etc. **kennys,** 19/23. **kens,** 75, 342, 1646. *pl.* 858. Cf. **ken.**
kep, *vb.* keep, 1480. **kepe,** 34/27, 43/3, 360, 621, etc. *imp. pl.* 10/31, 32. Cf. **kepid.**
kepe, *sb.* heed, 61, 291, 1166, 1779.
kepers, *sb. pl.* keepers, 1280.
kepid, *pp.* kept, 2172. Cf. **kep.**
keping, *sb.* keeping, care, 484, 2363.
kest, *vb.* cast, 150/18. **-e,** *pt.* 5/33. Cf. **kast.**
kichin, *sb.* kitchen, 25/34, 26/6, 14, 31/34, etc. Cf. **kechin, kychin.**
kide, *pp.* made known, told, 840.
kiln, *sb.* 2428.
kind, *sb.* race, children, 1020. **manes kinde,** mankind, 22/28. Cf. **kynde.**
kindly, *adv.* 1648.
kingdom, *sb.* 1024, 2479. Cf. **kyngdom.**
kingis, *sb. pl.* kings, 29/28. Cf. **kyng.**
kinreden, *sb.* kindred, 25/24.
kirk, *sb.* church, 198, 235, 423, 677, etc. **-e,** 4/6, 5/7, 9/17, 260, etc. Cf. **kyrk.**
kirtil, *sb.* kirtle, gown, 1202, 2012. **kirtils,** *pl.* 2015.
kis, *vb.* kiss, 35/10, 149/35. **kisse,** 141/7. Cf. **kys.**
kissink, *sb.* kissing, 1939.
knau, *vb.* know, 4/9. make known, confess, 9/7. **knaus,** *imp. pl.* confess, 13/30. **knaw,** 41/7, 357, 477, 1035, 1099, etc. confess, 32/3. *pl.* 1046, 1139, etc. **knaws,** *sg.* or *pl.* 157. **knawn,** *pp.* 404, 1000, 1615, 1929. **knawne,** 840.
knawyng, *sb.* knowledge, 381.
knees, *sb. pl.* 31/12. **kneis,** 141/6, 144/14. **knes,** 31/17, 1819.
kneland, *pp.* kneeling, 144/14, 148/14, 17, 1515, 1522. **knele,** *inf.* 141/5.
kniues, *sb. pl.* knives, 1213. Cf. **knyvys.**
knok, *vb.* knock, 2417.
knyvys, *sb. pl.* knives, 20/23. Cf. **knives.**
kun, *vb.* know, 18, 461. Cf. **cune** and **kan.**
kut, *vb.* cut, 146/34, 36.
kychin, *sb.* kitchen, 35/27. Cf. **kichin.**
kynde, *sb.* kind, nature, 258. Cf. **kind.**
kyng, *sb.* king, 1/9, 288, 2476. Cf. **kingis.**
kyngdom, *sb.* kingdom, 122, 250, 2478. Cf. **kingdom.**
kyns, *sb. gen.* **no kyns,** of no kind, no manner of, 1196. Cf. **nokins,** also **alkines** and **alkin, anikin, oþirkin, whatkyn.**
Kyrieleison, Kyrie eleison, 16/14. **Kyryeleison,** 18/14, 17, 26.
kyrk, *sb.* church, 12, 27, 80, 83, etc. **-e,** 19/10, 20/25, 40/28. Cf. **kirk.**

kys, *vb.* kiss, 143/18. Cf. **kis.**

labore, *sb.* labour, work, 1839. **laboures**, *pl.* 1864. **labur**, *sg.* 1/5, 10/5, 15/7, 31, etc. *vb.* 42/35. **laburs**, *sb. pl.* 15/30, 25/35, etc.
lac, *vb.* blame, 605.
lady, *sb.* 1577, 2212, 145/3. *gen.* Our Lady's, 150/2.
lafe, *sb.* loaf, 28/5, 8. Cf. **laue.**
lagh, *vb.* laugh, 1064.
laghing, *sb.* laughing, laughter, 1065, 1075. **laghyng**, 1068.
laghter-myld, *adj.* gentle or quiet in laughing, 1070. Cf. **lazter.**
lai, *sb.* law, 47/14. Cf. **lay.**
laid, *pp.* 21/24, 23/2. **laide**, *pt.* 15/12. **laie**, *inf.* 10/6, 28/8. **lais**, *sg.* 14/3. Cf. **lay.**
laiser, *sb.* leisure, liberty, 38/22. Cf. **laser.**
laite, *vb.* seek, 22/26. Cf. **layte.**
laite, *adv.* late, 646, 2270. Cf. **late.**
lams, *sb. pl.* lambs, 944.
lanande, *ppr.* concealing, 142/34. Cf. **layn.**
land, *sb.* 1, 2320. **-e**, 37/19, 39/13. **-is**, *pl.* 40/25.
lang, *adj.* long, 1192, 2024. *adv.* 1783, 2452. **-e**, eternal, 4/1. *adv.* 4/30. **-er**, *adv. comp.* 1794, 2105.
langes, *vb. sg.* belongs, 40/27.
langing, *sb.* longing, desire, 11/37, 12/15, 28, 34/6, etc. **-is**, *pl.* 8/19.
lap, *vb.* wrap, 147/27.
larch, *adj.* large, broad, 1978.
larchly, *adv.* largely, abundantly, 2324.
lare, *sb.* teaching, lore, 393, 397, 439, 1208. **lares**, *pl.* 4/5.
laser, *sb.* leisure, 2107. Cf. **laiser.**
last, *adj.* 17/24, 47/5, 548, 886. **laste**, 23/17. **at þe last**, 246. **at te laste**, 38/34.
last, *vb.* last, endure, 142/3, 183, 2115. **-and**, *ppr.* 101, 232, 2464. **-es**, *sg.* 9/2, 10/28, 933, 2440, etc. **-is**, 44/33, 47/13, 24.
lat, *vb.* let, 444. *imp.* 28/3, 25, 1351. Cf. **latte.**
late, *adv.* 30/3, 13, 1599, 1778. Cf. **laite, latte, layte,** also **neuir-þe-later.**
lath, *adj.* loth, unwilling, 432.
latte, *vb.* let, 40/35. Cf. **lat.**
latte, *adj.* slow, 23/31. **latter,** *comp.* later, 1510, 1792. *adv.* "not so readily," 27/3. Cf. **late.**
latyn, *sb.* Latin, 10, 14.
laue, *sb.* loaf, 1581. Cf. **lafe.**
lauerd, *sb.* Lord, 2/27, 30, 3/1, 10, etc. Cf. **lord.**
laumpe, *sb.* lamp, 1212.
laus, *sb. pl.* laws, 234, 235, 260. **law**, *sg.* 42/16, 17, 77, 193, etc. Cf. **laws.**
? **law**, *vb.* heap or pile up, 2190. [Cf. O.E. *hlāw*, pile.] See Notes.
law, *vb.* humble; refl. 779, 1026. Cf. **lazed.**
law, *adj.* low, humble, 328, 775, 1036 (the second), 1093, etc. **lawest**, 1770, 1787, 2264.
lawnes, *sb.* lowness, humility, 804, 2084.
laws, *sb. pl.* 1038, 1039. Cf. **laus.**
lay, *sb.* law, 16/9, 33, 35/17, 45/19, etc. [O.F. *lai*, Lat. *legem.*] Cf. **lai.**
? **lay**, *sb.* flame, 13/15. [O.I. *leygr.*] See Notes.
lay, *vb. pt.* 11/17. Cf. **lie.**
lay, *vb.* 33/4, 38/29, 143/17, 147/5, etc. *imp.* 1/2. **layd**, *pp.* 147/40, 2172. **layde**, 1547. Cf. **laid.**
layn, *vb.* hide, conceal, 1179. **-e**, 990. **-s**, *sg.* 1545. Cf. **lanande.**
layte, *vb.* seek, try, 709. Cf. **laite.**
layte, *adv.* late, 1396, 2424. Cf. **late.**
lazed, *pp.* lowered, humbled, 14/11. **laȝis**, *sg.* lowers, degrades, 41/22. Cf. **law.**
lazter, *sb.* laughter, 14/32, 37. Cf. **laghter-myld.**
lecciun, *sb.* election, 42/3, 8.
lech, *sb.* physician, 1687. *vb.* heal, cure, 1283.
lechori, *sb.* lechery, 309. Cf. **licherie.**
led, *pp.* 2118. **lede**, *inf.* 2/20, 12/3, 47/2, etc. *pl.* 273, 309, 356. *imp.* 6/14. *pt.* 1952, 2497. *pp.* 944. Cf. **ledes.**
lede, *sb.* lead (metal), 4/26.
leder, *sb.* leader, 2212.
ledes, *vb. sg.* leads, 2460, 2464, 2477, 2490. **ledis**, 46/28, 30. Cf. **led.**

leel, *adj.* loyal, 20/7. Cf. **lele.**

lef, *sb.* leave, permission. 1748, 2406. **lefe,** 2104.

lef, *sg.* leave, 1764. l CH. LIX- mains, 1916. **left,** *pt.* left, 1307, 2030. *pp.* 1485, gone, 1131. **lefte,** *pt.* 22/21, 25. Cf. **leue.**

leful, *adj.* allowable, permissible, 1634. **lefull,** 142/7. [*lef-ful.*]

leire, *vb.* learn, 263. Cf. **ler.**

lele, *adj.* lawful; loyal; living according to a rule, 336, 2147, 2315. Cf. **leel.**

leli, *adv.* lawfully, etc. 1193, 2220. **lely,** 1, 666, 1111, 1187, etc.

len, *vb.*=**lene,** 1023, 1039.

lend, *vb.* come; dwell, remain, 1370, 1909, 2103; *pl.* 230. **-e,** 1237.

lendis, *sb. pl.* loins, 2/23.

lene, *vb.* lend, grant, 884. **lens,** *sg.* 199. **lent,** *pp.* 25/29, 196. Cf. **len.**

lenghe, *sb.* **on lenghe,** her full length, 147/40.

lentin, *sb.* Lent, 17/25, 33/1, 6, 28, etc. **lentyn,** 17/23, 29/14, 15, 33/8, etc.

ler, *vb.* learn, 6/34. **lerde,** *pp.* taught, 1054. **lere,** *inf.* teach, learn, 2/6, 5/10, 14, *26, 9/7, etc. *pl.* 1209. *imp.* 23. **lered,** *pt.* 5/21. *pp.* 5/16. **leres,** *sg.* 353, 1066, 1187, 1193, etc. **leris,** 9/34, 20/30, 40/24, 84, etc. *pl.* 4/27, 14. Cf. **leire, leryd.**

lereing, *sb.* learning, 269.

lernyng, *sb.* teaching, 1283.

leryd, *pp., adj.* learned, 9. Cf. **ler.**

les, *adj.* (*sb.*), *adv.* smaller, less, 15/7, 159, 601, 1429, 1541, 1595, 2487, etc. Cf. **lese.**

les, *vb.* loosen, absolve, 6/7, 9/9.

leschun, *sb.* lesson; reading, 17/14. **lescun,** 9/6, 16/13, 27/13, etc. **-is,** *pl.* 16/18. **-s,** 15/27, 16/5, 6, 11, etc. Cf. **lesons.**

lese, *vb.* lose, 92, 304. Cf. **lorn.**

lese, *adj.* (*sb.*), *adv.* smaller, less, 549, 916, 1239, 1269, etc. **lesse,** 14/8, 16/21, 17/6, 31/20, etc. **lest,** *adj.* least, 13/38. *sb.* 1609. Cf. **les.**

lesons, *sb. pl.* lessons, readings, 247, 1722. **lesson,** *sg.* 10/37, 1700. **-es,** *pl.* 624. **-s,** 354, 1160, 1531, 1732, etc. Cf. **leschun.**

lesynges, *sb. pl.* falsehoods, 307.

let, *vb.* let, allow, 22/18. leave alone, forsake, omit, 530. *pp.* "kept," 1253. Cf. **lete.**

let, *vb.* hinder, 1737, 1916, 1974.

letanie, *sb.* litany, 16/14, 17/16, 18/22.

lete, *sb.* delay, 2317.

lete, *pt.* let, allowed, 6/18. **letes,** *pl.* leave alone, forsake, 745. Cf. **let.**

letter, *sb.* Scripture, 13/16. **lettirs,** *pl.* letters, 36/6, 41/8. Cf. **litters.**

lettrun, *sb.* lectern, 16/6.

leue, *sb.* leave, permission, 25/7, 30/12, 30, 32, etc. Cf. **lef.**

leue, *vb.* leave; abandon; cease, 8/18, 9/8, 1338, 2185, etc. remain, 2178. *pl.* neglect, do not, 42/12. **leueand,** *ppr.* 2224. **leues,** *pl.* 301. **leuid,** *pt.* 11/10. **leuyde,** *pp.* 422. **leue of,** leave off, 31/19. Cf. **lef.**

leuer, *adv.* rather, 1633.

lezis, *vb. sg.* tells lies, 2/33.

licherie, *sb.* lechery, 8/15. Cf. **lechori.**

lie, *vb.* 20/18, 20, 22, 27, etc. Cf. **lig, ly,** and **lay.**

lif, *sb.* life, 2/9, 12, 309, 336, etc. **life,** 38/21, 40/15, 41/5, 42/5, etc. **lif-days,** *sb. pl.* days of life, 199. Cf. **liue, lyf.**

lif, *vb.* live, 208, 700, 1339, 1672, etc. *pl.* 512, 1177. **lifand,** *ppr.* 1046. **life,** *inf.* 38/12, 841. **lifes,** *pl.* 286, 298, 2503, 2505. **liffe,** *inf.* 142/5. Cf. **liue.**

lifing, *sb.* life, 1634, 2426. Cf. **lifyng, lyfing, lyuyng.**

liflade, *sb.* mode of life, 28/22, 33/29.

lift, *vb.* 1102. **lifte,** 15/14.

lifyng, *sb.* life, 311, 512, 657, 1041, etc. Cf. **lifing.**

lig, *vb.* lie, 1199, 1210, 1815, 2107, etc. *pl.* 1211. **ligand,** *ppr.* 141/19, 144/3. **ligge,** *inf.* 31/22, 46/19. **ligge hir downe,** lie down, 144/19. Cf. **lie.**

light, *sb.* 1136, 1726. **liht,** 2/7, 20/22. Cf. **lyght, lyth.**

light, *adj.* light, easy, 142/2,

1243. **liht,** 4/7, 36/24 (see chepe).—**lightli,** *adv.* lightly, easily, 301. **lightlike,** *37/32. **lightly,** 380, 1188, 1366. thoughtlessly, 605. Cf. **lyghtli.**

lik, *adj.* like, 2279. **like,** 14/2, 181, 1426. Cf. **in-like.**

likand, *ppr., adj.* pleasing, acceptable, 1170. resembling, 806. **likes,** *vb. sg.* likes, 132, 264, 688, 709, etc. **likis,** *pl.* 141/9. **likandly,** *adv.* pleasingly, acceptably, 1699. Cf. **lykand.**

liking, *sb.* liking, pleasure, desire, 142/17. **-es,** *pl.* 829. **likyng,** 295, 302, 304, 862, etc. **-es,** *pl.* 848. Cf. **lykyng.**

limes, *sb. pl.* limbs, 828. **lims,** 1936. Cf. **lym.**

lipes, *sb. pl.* lips, 107. **lippes,** 1687. **lippis,** 2/11, 10/31.

list, *vb. sg.* pleases, 1351. *pt.* 1307.

litel, *adj.* little, small, 45/9, 46/15. **litil,** 7/3, 21/10, 47/25, 402, etc. *sb.* 1017, 1074. *adv.* a little, 15/25. **ay litil,** a little, 27/27, 28/33. Cf. **lytil.**

lither, *adj.* bad, false, 1426.

litter, *sb.* straw-bed, 1978.

litters, *sb. pl.* writing, 1136. letters, 1985. Cf. **letter.**

liue, *sb.* life; manners, 4/1, 2084. Cf. **lif, liues.**

liue, *vb.* live, 3/22, 4/17, 5/8, 6/12, etc. *pl.* 32/33, 34. Cf. **lif, liues, lyf, lyue.**

liuer, *vb.* deliver, 1503. **-s,** *sg.* 464.

liues, *sb. pl.* lives, 666, 1733, 1952, 2495. **liuis,** *gen.* 142/27. Cf. **liue.**

liues, *vb. pl.* 4/26. **liuis,** 4/11, 20, 5/1. *sg. or pl.* 7/7. Cf. **liue.**

lo, *interj.* 119, 744.

lofe, *vb.* praise, 163. Cf. **loue.**

lofers, *sb. pl.* lovers, 2477.

loises, *vb. pl.* lose, 1541.

loke, *vb.* look, see, behold, look at, look after, see to, consider; observe; guard, protect; provide; appoint, 7/10, 22, 23/17, 25/30, 32/29, 33/10, 42/2, 132, 264, etc. *imp. sg. or pl.* 3/33, 4/6, 9/12, 10/35, 18/9, etc. **lokes,** *sg.* 12/20. *imp. pl.* 11/14. **lokis,** *sg.* 4/6, 12/19. *imp. pl.* 19/19. **lokys,** *sg.* 20/18. *imp. pl.* 12/21. Cf. **luk.**

lone, *sb.* loan, 330.

lord, *sb.* 3/8, 25, 11/5, 28/12, etc. **-e,** 1/8, 43/5. **-es,** *gen.* 2254. Cf. **lauerd.**

lorn, *pp.* lost, 1314, 1455. Cf. **lese.**

losen, strong *pp.* of the otherwise weak *vb.* **lose,** praise? 2220.

loud, *adv.* aloud, 563, 646. **-e,** 1396.

loue, *sb.* love, sake, 19/4. Cf. **luf, luue.**

loue, *vb.* love, 5/36, 1428. Cf. **louid, luf, luue.**

loue, *vb.* praise, 3/12, 18/7, 19/17, 330, 1614, 1656. Cf. **lofe.**

loueyng = louing, 165, 670, 1062, 1160.

louid, *pp.* loved, 6/4, 6. Cf. **loue.**

louing, *sb.* praise, glory, 3/7, 8/34, 17/30, 18/2, etc. **louyng,** 649, 1688. Cf. **loueyng.**

loutand, *ppr.* bowing (down), 1983. **loute,** *inf.* 1179, 1943, 2216. Cf. **lowte.**

lowe, *sb.* flame, 44/15.

lowsid, *pp.* released, 43/20.

lowte, *vb.* bow down, 147/35. Cf. **loute.**

lowting, *sb.* bowing, 1093.

luf, *sb.* love; sake, 155, 530, 1022, 1116, etc. **lufe,** 46/31, 1117. Cf. **loue.**

luf, *vb.* love, 408, 563, 565, 647, etc. *pl.* 493. **lufe,** *inf.* 43/2, 599, 1039. **lufes,** *sg.* 890. **lufid,** *pp.* 425, 2288. **lufyd,** *pt.* 948. Cf. **loue.**

luk, *vb.* look, etc. 113, 390. *imp.* 545, 1216, 1977. **luke,** *inf.* 688, 1095, 1103, 1500, etc. *imp. pl.* 640. Cf. **loke.**

lust, *sb.* 142/17. **-is,** *pl.* 1/7.

luue, *sb.* love; sake, 9/28, 10/9, 18, 13/9, etc. Cf. **loue.**

luue, *vb.* love, 7/9, 8/13, 19, 22, 28, etc. *pl.* 4/31. **luues,** *pl.* 9/22. *imp. pl.* 9/11, 22. **luuid,** *pp.* 42/27. **luuis,** *pl.* 3/5, 47/20. Cf. **loue.**

ly, *vb.* lie, 1206, 1220. Cf. **lie.**

lyf, *sb.* life, 12/11, 85, 91, 95, 101. Cf. **lif.**

lyf, *vb.* live, 89. **lyfes,** *sg.* 155. Cf. **liue.**

lyfing, *sb.* life, 195. Cf. **lifing.**

lyght, *sb.* light, 66, 1728; cf. 150/7. *pp.* lit, 1212. Cf. **light.**
lyghtli, *adv.* lightly, thoughtlessly, 2118. **lyghtly,** easily, 10, 16. Cf. **lightli.**
lykand, *ppr., adj.* pleasing, acceptable, 728. Cf. **likand.**
lykyng, *sb.* liking, pleasure, 85. Cf. **liking.**
lym, *sb.* limb, 673. **lyms,** *pl.* 422. Cf. **limes.**
lyth, *sb.* light, 15/31. Cf. **light.**
lytil, *adj.* little, 15/30. Cf. **litel.**
lyue, *vb.* live, 1. Cf. **liue.**
lyuyng, *sb.* life, 43/2. Cf. **lifing.**

ma, *adj.* more, 42/36. Cf. **mo,** also **mare.**
ma, *vb.* make, 2/3, 26/8. **made,** *pt.* 7/7, 37/22, 39/22, 43/21, etc. *pp.* 14/1, 43/16, 775, 958, etc. Cf. **mak, maide, mayd, mas.**
madaum, *sb.* Madam, 2210.
madyn, *sb.* maiden, 145/6, 9, 146/23. Cf. **maydyn.**
mai, *vb. sg.* may, 29/30, 30/11, 443, 447, etc. 2 *sg.* 1/4. *pl.* 11/26, 14/12, 256, 663, etc. Cf. **may.**
maide, *pp.* made, 742, 859. Cf. **ma.**
maine, *sb.* main, power, 225. Cf. **mayine.**
mainè, *sb.* household, 5/8. Cf. **menȝè.**
maister, *sb.* master, 7/30. *gen.* 7/28. Cf. **mastir.**
maistires, *sb.* mistress, 10/5, 36, 13/16. **maistiresse,** 9/34, 10/14. **maistres,** 14/18, 141/13, 142/30, 32, 534, 761, etc. Cf. **mastiresse, maystres.**
maistri, *sb.* mastery, authority, 42/15, 2277.
mak, *vb.* make, 13, 49, 125, 181, etc. **make,** 3/28, 4/4, 7/33, 591, 1575, 1927, etc. *imp.* 6/23. *imp. pl.* 9/15. **makes,** *sg.* 175, 275, 488, 893, etc. *pl.* 562. *imp. pl.* 1313. **makis,** *sg.* 37/16, 144/20. *pl.* 43/14. Cf. **ma.**
[**makeing,** *sb.* making, 145/1.]
man, *sb.* 2/34, 3/14, 5/4, 8/15, etc. *gen.* 39/19, 459. *pron.* one, 3/11, 6/21, 8/17, 9/27, etc. **manes,** *sb. gen.* 22/28, 757. Cf. **mannis, men.**
maner, *sb.* manner, way; kind, sort, 4/16, 18, 6/32, 265, etc. *pl.* 4/15, 5/26, 22/12, 1572, etc. **-e,** 68, 75, 431, 953, etc. **-s,** *pl.* 38/15, 256, 390, 472, etc.
manhed, *sb.* manhood; humanity, 35/18, 47/13.
mannis, *sb. gen.* of man, 15/19. Cf. **man.**
mantels, *sb. pl.* mantles, 2013. **mantil,** *sg.* 13/20. **mantill,** 146/31.
many, *adj.* 19/28, 38/14, 754, 788, 1332. Cf. **mony.**
mare, *adj.* (*sb.*), *adv.* greater; more, 5/36, 6/27, 7/14, 14/8, 34/1, etc. Cf. **mayr, mor,** also **ma.**
mare, *vb.* mar, spoil, 88.
marters, *sb. pl.* martyrs, 2495.
maruayls, *sb. pl.* marvels, 788.
mas, *vb. sg.* makes, 21/3. **mase,** 1608. Cf. **ma.**
mast, *adj.* (*sb.*) most, 1609, 1678. Cf. **most.**
mastir, *sb.* master, 1/2. Cf. **maister.**
mastiresse, *sb.* mistress, 10/8. **mastres,** 142/31, 144/8, 2089, 2094, etc. Cf. **maistires.**
matens, *sb.* matins, 1134. Cf. **matins.**
mater, *sb.* matter; cause, occasion, 43/18. **-s,** *pl.* 1736.
materly, *adv.* moderately, 2306. [Cf. O.F. *meitere,* a measure.]
matins, *sb.* divine office about 2 a.m., 15/26, 33, 16/15, 17/3, etc. **matyns,** 1760. Cf. **matens.**
maunde, *sb.* foot-washing, 26/8, 11. [Lat. *mandatum.*]
may, *vb. sg.* 4/1, 5/11, 186, 226, etc. 2 *sg.* 2/25, 3/20, 401, etc. *pl.* 2/6, 5/1, 5, 10, etc. Cf. **mai, myght.**
mayd, *pp.* made, 1036, 1106. **-e,** 1798, 145/7. Cf. **ma.**
maydyn, *gen.* maiden's, 147/28. Cf. **madyn.**
mayine, *sb.* main, power, 2141. **mayn,** 110, 613, 929, 993. **mayne,** 275, 907, 1317. Cf. **maine.**
maynten, *vb.* maintain, 2141. **-tene,** 596. **-teyn,** 1380, 1401, 1418.
mayr, *adv.* more, 1154. Cf. **mare.**

maystres, *sb.* mistress, 24. Cf. **maistires.**

me, *pron.* 2/5, 15, 115, 171, etc.

medcyn, *sb.* medicine, 1892. **-s,** *pl.* (possibly: physicians) 1288. Cf. **medicinis.**

mede, *sb.* reward, 4/27, 7/15, 9/19, 128, etc. value, 1986.

medefull, *adj.* bringing (or deserving of) reward, 142/3.

medicinis, *sb. pl.* medicines, 23/3. Cf. **medcyn.**

meditacioounes, *sb. pl.* meditations, 1129. **-iouns,** 1911.

meke, *adj.* meek, humble, 1/4, 6/15, 23, 9/27, etc.

meke, *vb.* humble, 15/6. refl. 13/2, 14/7, 25/27, etc. *imp. pl.* refl. 9/28. Cf. **mekes, mekyd.**

mekel, *sb.* much, 467. Cf. **mekil.**

mekelike, *adv.* meekly, 19/25, 24/3, 35/36. **mekely,** 13/39, 14/36, 529, 601, etc. Cf. **mekly.**

mekenes, *sb.* meekness, 3/29, 10/2, 12, 19, etc. *pl.* 15/18, 20. Cf. **meknes.**

mekes, *vb. pl.* humble; refl. 11/4. **mekid,** *pt.* refl. 9/28. *pp.* 11/4, 15/17. Cf. **meke.**

mekil, *adj.* much, 14/23, 23/30. *sb.* 468. *adv.* 19/26, 734. Cf. **mekel, mekyl, mikil.**

mekli, *adj.* great, 275. [O.I. *mikilligr.*] Or an error for **mekil**?

mekly, *adv.* = **mekelike,** 789.

meknes, *sb.* meekness, 249, 771, 817, 889, etc. Cf. **mekenes.**

mekyd, *vb. pt.* humbled, 14/13. Cf. **meke.**

mekyl, *adj.* great, 22/27. Cf. **mekil.**

mel, *vb.* speak, 1736. [O.E. *meþlan.*]

mellid, *pp.* mingled, 1196.

men, *sb. pl.* 8/17, 9/12, 12/12, 9, 130, 192, etc. *pron.* people, one, 811, 1506, 1834. Cf. **man, mens.**

mend, *vb.* 32/9, 995, 1235, 1290, etc. intr. 25/2. refl. amend, 1229. **-e,** 3/18, 15/11, 31/25, etc. "give more to," 28/9. intr. 1405. refl. 7/13. **-id,** *pp.* 6/16, 21/25. **-is,** *sg.* 7/14.

mendnis, *sb.* mending, amendment, 4/4.

mendyng, do., 1823.

mene, *adj.* middle, 40/2. **mene time,** meantime, 144/13.

mene, *vb.* mean; understand, "say," 431, 1587, 1705, 2051. **menes,** *pl.* 746. **mens,** *sg.* 89, 943.

mens, *sb. pl. gen.* men's, 10/4, 12, 28/22, 569. Cf. **men.**

menȝè, *sb.* household, 2244. Cf. **mainè.**

merci, *sb.* mercy, 22/30, 24/27, 25/3, etc. **mercy,** 3/25, 13/30, 41/35, etc.

mere, *sb.* mare, 14/2.

merè, *adj.* merry, 1927. **meri,** 1511. Cf. **mery.**

meret, *sb.* merit; sake, 794, 981. **merit,** 681.

meritory, *adj.* meritorious, 142/2.

merk, *vb.* mark, 1184, 2482. **-es,** *sg.* 678.

merure, *sb.* mirror, pattern, 771, 1048. Cf. **myrour.**

mery, *adj.* merry, 308, 1313. Cf. **merè.**

mes, *sb.* mass, 1760, 1844. **mese,** 1811, 145/3, 149/38, etc. Cf. **messe.**

mese, *sb. pl.* dishes, 28/3.

meself, *pron.* myself, 11/10. Cf. **myself.**

messe, *sb.* mass, 27/17, 39/31, 143/12. Cf. **mes.**

mester, *sb.* occupation, function, 24/10. Cf. **mister.**

mesur, *sb.* measure, 16/24, 23/22, 24/13, 27/32, etc. (concrete) 28/24, 25. **-d,** *pp.* measured, 36/25, 1857. *adj.* moderate, 2277. **-de,** 28/6. **-e,** *sb.* 384. **-ed,** *pp. adj.* 1353, 2299, 2308, 2328.

mesurlike, *adv.* moderately, 8/31, 28/17, 26, 32/35, etc.

mete, *sb.* food; meal, 21/31, 24/19, 1679, 1696, etc.

mete, *adj.* meet, suitable, 2023.

mete-tym, *sb.* meal-time, 150/3.

metis, *vb. sg.* meets, 35/36, 41/31.

[**method,** *sb.* 145/1.]

mi, *adj.* my, 4/2, 5/32, 10/16, 785. Cf. **min, my.**

midday, *sb.* 17/26, 33, 18/5, 14, etc. Cf. **mydday.**

midnyght, *sb.* midnight, 15/25. Cf. **mydnyght.**

might, *sb.* might, power, 223, 225. **-es,** *pl.* 159. Cf. **miht, myght.**

mighty, *adj.* 121. Cf. **myghty.**
Mihelmesse, *sb.* Michaelmas (29 Sept.), 32/25.
miht, *sb.* might, power, 3/31, 4/21, 24/8, 25/32, etc. "best," "utmost," 9/29, 26/36. Cf. **might.**
mikil, *adj.* great; much, 14/25, 2345, etc. *sb.* (*adv.*) 11/9, 14/24, etc. *adv.* 16/18, etc. **mikill,** 3/31, 4/8. **mikyl,** 922. *adv.* 11/12. Cf. **mekil, mykel.**
mikilnes, *sb.* coarseness, 36/22.
milke, *sb.* milk, 11/12.
miln, *sb.* mill, 2428. **-e,** 44/26.
milnestane, *sb.* mill-stone, 24/22.
min, *adj., adv.* less, 175. Cf. **myn.**
min, *adj.* my, 2/13, 11/9, 114. **mine,** 5/34, 15/15, 173, 1033, etc. Cf. **mi, myn.**
minde, *sb.* remembrance, mention, 488. Cf. **mynd.**
ministracion, *sb.* ministration, 43/5.
minning, *sb.* remembering, 31/27.
miri, *sb.* leech, physician, 22/5, 6, 23/2. [O.F. *mire*, Lat. *medicus.*]
mirkenes, *sb.* darkness, *2/7. **mirknes,** 88.
mirth, *sb.* joy, 117. Cf. **myrth.**
mis, *sb.* fault, 197. Cf. **mys.**
misancewer, *vb.* answer unkindly, 24/3.
misdede, *sb.* misdeed, 2/35, 31/32, 42/24, 204, 1007. **-dedis,** *pl.* 22/10. Cf. **mysdede.**
misdo, *vb.* 31/36. *pl.* 6/12, 9/14, 23/24, 27/7. **-don,** *pp.* 19/3, 45/3. **-dose,** *pl.* 22/4.
misericorde, *sb.* mercy, 11/25, 42/19, 47/31.
misga, *vb.* err, transgress, 5/17.
mishope, *vb.* despair, 9/16.
mislike, *vb.* displease, 8/6.
misses, *vb. pl.* (with **of**) are without, 901. Cf. **myst.**
mistrouz, *sb.* doubt, despair, 19/31.
miste, *vb.* have for a provisionary meal, 26/14, 27/27. [Lat. *accipere mistum.*]
mister, *sb.* need, 22/4, 5, 36/34, 44/24, etc. trade, art, 37/14. Cf. **mester, myster.**
mo, *adj.* more, 449, 2499. Cf. **ma,** also **mor.**
mode, *vb.* mind, 49, 110, 280, 293, etc.
moder, *sb.* mother, 42/37, 26, 27, 792, 2137, etc. **modir,** 30. *gen.* 11/12.
moneste, *vb.* admonish, 22/9. Cf. **amoneste.**
monesterys, *sb. pl.* monasteries, 43/10.
moneth, *sb. pl. gen.* 2095. **-es,** *pl.* 142/32, 143/3. **-s,** 2111, 2116.
monkes, *sb. pl.* monks, 9. Cf. **munkis.**
mony, *adj.* many, 6/29. Cf. **many.**
mor, *adj.* (*sb.*), *adv.* greater; more, 117, 159, 396, 734, 916, 1239, 1241, etc. **more,** 42/27, 287, 384, 2063, 2487. Cf. **mare,** also **mo.**
morn, *sb.* morning, 593, 626, 1077, 1456. **-e,** 26/17.
morning, *sb.* 15/31.
most, *adv.* 226, 1149, 1151, 1291, etc. Cf. **mast.**
mote, *sb.* 402.
moth, *sb.* mouth, 621, 741, 1169, 1688. Cf. **muþe.**
mourn, *vb.* 626. Cf. **murnand.**
multeplii, *vb.* intr. multiply, 7/6.
mun, *vb. sg.* will, 734. **munde,** *pt.* 2/2, 11/11.
munkis, *sb. pl.* monks, 4/15, 5/10, 15. Cf. **monkes.**
muntain, *sb.* mountain, 2/29.
munte, do., 22/22.
murnand, *ppr.* 1810. Cf. **mourn.**
murnyng, *sb.* mourning, 822, 1920.
muster, *vb.* show; tell; report, show up, 7/22, 13/34, 22/13, 40/19, etc. **-d,** *pp.* 12/23, 36/9, 45/17, 47/27, etc. **-s,** *sg.* refl. explains himself, 15/2. **mustir,** *inf.* 5/6, 34/7, 47/9. *imp.* 13/28. **-d,** *pt.* 13/32. *pp.* 32/5. **-s,** *sg.* 2/20, 5/4, 7/20, 8/11, etc.
muþe, *sb.* mouth, 11/7. **muþes,** *pl.* 9/5. **muz,** *sg.* 2/28, 5/33. Cf. **moth.**
my, *adj.* 1/6, 2/15, 35, etc. Cf. **mi.**
mydday, *sb.* midday, 1714. Cf. **midday.**
mydes, *sb.* midst, 1968.
mydnyght, *sb.* midnight, 1125. Cf. **midnyght.**
myght, *sb.* might, power, 19, 525, 538, 1317, etc. Cf. **might.**
myght, *vb. pt.* might, 55, 117, 322, 345, etc. Cf. **may.**

myghty, *adj.* mighty, powerful, 272, 1605, 1607. Cf. **mighty.**

mykel, *adj.* great, much, 751. **mykil,** 986, 1055, 1420, etc. *adv.* 975, 1461, 2113. Cf. **mikil.**

myld, *adj.* mild, gentle, quiet, 1071, 1425, 1445, etc.

myn, *adj.* (*sb.*) less, smaller, 1241, 1745. Cf. **min.**

myn, *adj.* my, 895, 999, 1102. **myne,** 13/32, 38/31, 113, 717, 844, 1020. *pron.* mine, 26/29. Cf. **min.**

mynd, *sb.* mind, 1154, 1235. **-e,** 43/19. Cf. **minde.**

mynster, *sb.* minster, 147/23.

myrour, *sb.* mirror, 893. Cf. **merure.**

myrth, *sb.* mirth, 175. *vb.* amuse, 1957. Cf. **mirth.**

mys, *sb.* fault, 366, 1238, 1275, 1290, etc. Cf. **mis.**

myschesing, *sb.* wrong choice, 2247.

mysdede, *sb.* misdeed, 372, 1320, 2480. **-dedes,** *pl.* 625, 1004. Cf. **misdede.**

myself, *pron.* 1004, 1650. Cf. **meself.**

myspay, *vb.* displease, 1402.

myst, *vb. pt.* missed, 1308. Cf. **misses.**

myster, *sb.* need, 2044. Cf. **mister.**

na, *adj.* no, 2/11, 16, 34, 4/23, etc. Cf. **nan, no.**

na, *conj.* nor, 4/3, 23, 8/15, 14/25, 106, etc. Cf. **no.**

na-for-þi, *adv.* nevertheless, 28/22.

naie, *adv.* no! 24/4.

naked, *adj.* 582. **nakid,** 8/20.

naman, nobody, 14/24, 25. Cf. 41/9 and **noman.**

name, *sb.* 3/9, 5/5, 8, 6/27, 374, 1649, etc. Cf. **naym.**

nameli, *adv.* especially, 43/14. **namely,** 676, 1929. **namli,** 43/3. **namly,** 169, 759. Cf. **naymly.**

namyd, *pp.* named, called, 66.

nan, *adj.* no 7/1. "nothing," 10/33, 29/28; cf. 5/30. *pron.* none, 2/34, 4/5, 7/27, 31, etc. **nane,** *adj.* 37/6. after its noun, 7/33, 20/23, 41/15 (rather so than *pron.* in dative). *pron.* 5/36, 20/26, 1471, etc. Cf. **na, non.**

nathing, nothing, 142/9. Cf. 7/8, 25/11, 142/8, etc., and **nothing.**

naym, *sb.* name, 166, 573. **by nayme** "so called," 1368. Cf. **name.**

naymly, *adv.* especially, 1083, 2272. Cf. **nameli.**

ne, *conj.* nor, 2/34, 8/16, 9/20, 144, 146, etc. **ne . . ne,** neither . . nor, 21/13, 1456. (pleonastic) before other negatives, 3/15, 4/33, 5/19, 8/25, etc.

neccligence, *sb.* negligence, 30/23.

ned, *sb.* need, 7/8, 24/33, 25/22, 25, etc. **nede,** 3/1, 5/13, 7/22, etc. *adv.* needs, 1413. **for nede,** for need's sake, 6/1. **for no nede,** on no (any) account, 1593; cf. 1569, 1993. Cf. **nedis.**

nede, *vb.* need, 1693. **nedes,** *sg.* is needed, is necessary, 405, 491, 504, 1138, etc. **nedis,** 2428.

nedeful, *adj.* needful, necessary, 1752, 1839, 2426. **nedful,** 658. needy, 25/27, 37/1.

nedis, *sb. pl.* needs, wants, 12/22. Cf. **ned.**

nedly, *adv.* needs, necessarily, 43/25.

nedy, *adj.* needy, 2053.

negh, *vb.* approach, 2063. **nehe,** 20/26.

neghburs, *sb. pl.* neighbours, 145, 565, 1312.

neis, *adj.* soft, 2/3. Cf. **nesch.**

nek, *sb.* neck, 38/21.

nere, *adv.* near, 1991, 2063.

nesch, *adj.* soft, 873. Cf. **neis.**

neu, *adj.* new, 47/15. Cf. **new.**

neuer, *adv.* never, 47, 820, 881, etc. **neuir,** 42/30, 45/9, 46/15. **neuir mare,** no more, 39/9.

neuer-þe-les, *adv.* nevertheless, 1766. **neuer-þe-lese,** 886. **neuir-þeles,** 141/27.

neuir-þe-later, do., 40/15.

new, *adj.* 16/33, 42/17, 2025, 2321. **newe,** 16/9, 36/25. Cf. **neu.**

next, *adj.* nearest, next, 145/10. *adv.* 1841.

neyntt, *num.* ninth, 1051. Cf. **nihend.**

night, *sb.* 18/2, 222, 268, 537, 898. Cf. **niht, nyght.**
nihend, *num.* **neyntt,** 14/21.
nihend-ferþe, *num.* 94th, 16/2. **nihende-ferþe,** 16/22.
niht, *sb.* night, 17/24, 18/3, 9, 32/13, etc. **-is,** *pl.* 16/18. **nith,** *sg.* 18/6. Cf. **night.**
no, *adj.* 10/25, 31, 14, 143, *755, etc. "nothing," 106. *pron.* none, 605, 1221 (cf. Notes). *adv.* 312. Cf. **na, non.**
no, *conj.* nor, 142/10, 159, 650. Cf. **na.**
nobil, *adj.* noble, strong, 1605.
nocturne, *sb.* nocturn, 17/24.
noder, *conj.* neither, 2252. Cf. **noþer.**
noght, *pron.* nought, nothing, 12/19, 482, 608, 2165, etc. *adv.* not, 11/31, 12/23, 70, 88, etc. **noht,** *pron.* 2/35, 3/10. *adv.* 2/2, 8, 14, 9/11, etc. Cf. **not.**
noid, *pp.* annoyed, 24/27. Cf. **anoy.**
noise, *sb.* 27/23, 25, 34/33. Cf. **nose.**
noius, *adj.* annoying, troublesome, 23/30.
nokins, of no kind, no manner of, no (any), 1569, 2349. Cf. **kyns, nonekyns.**
noman, nobody, 1239. Cf. 1545 and **naman.**
non, *sb.* "noon," 1870. Cf. **none.**
non, *sb.* nun, 1245. **none,** 1269. Cf. **nun.**
non, *adj.* no, 305, 451, 580, 1327, etc. after its noun: none, 289. *pron.* 419, 2052, 2331, 2352, etc. **none,** *adj.* 663, etc. after its noun, 187, 329. *pron.* 1549, 1981, 2353. Cf. **nan, no.**
none, *sb.* "noon," divine office about 3 p.m., 28/2, 6, 1712. 1850. **noon,** 17/26, 33, 18/6, 15, etc. **hi none,** 1721. Cf. **non, noun.**
nonekyns = **nokins,** 160.
nor, *conj.* 42/28, 29. Cf. **noure.**
nose, *sb.* noise, 1691. Cf. **noise.**
not, *pron.* nought, nothing, 557. *adv.* not, 1/12, 15, 17, 127, etc. Cf. **noght, nott.**
note, *sb.* note, music, 145/20, 146/24, 147/14, etc.
note, *sb.* business, work, 2011.
noþer, *pron.* neither, 1612. *conj.* 568, 1358, 1786, etc. **nother,** 530. Cf. **noder, nouþer, nowder.**
noþer; no noþer=non oþer, no one else, 1974. **na noþir,** 46/6. **an noþir,** another, 33/36. Cf. **oþer.**
nothing, 990, 1654. Cf. 142, 919, 1042, 2195, etc., and **nathing.**
nott, *adv.* not, 42/28, 223. Cf. **not.**
nouece, *sb. pl.* novices, 2361. **noues,** *pl. gen.* 2106. **nouese,** *sg.* 1269, 2155. **nouice,** 141/1, 13, 143/21, 144/2, 5, etc. *pl. gen.* 20/26. **nouices,** *pl.* 1209, 1535. **nouicis,** 38/4. Cf. **nouyce,** also **nun.**
Nouember, *sb.* November, 1122. **nouembir,** 15/23, 29, 16/16.
noun, *sb.* "noon," 1077. Cf. **none.**
noure, *conj.* nor, 4/30. Cf. **nor.**
nouþer, *conj.* neither, 4/29. **nouþir,** 20/23. Cf. **noþer.**
nouyce, *sb.* novice, 142/25, 143/15. **nouysces,** *pl.* 2088. Cf. **nouece.**
nouycery, *sb.* novices' house or cells, 142/31. [O.F. *novicerie,* time of probation, etc.; formed like *nunnery.*]
now, *adv.* 1/6, 4/32, 18/8, 9, etc.
nowder, *conj.* neither, 283. Cf. **noþer.**
noy, *sb.* annoyance, trouble, tribulation, suffering, 13/15, 26/16, 145. *vb.* annoy, trouble, disturb, injure, 24/1, 26/31, 32/30, 34/36, etc. **noyd,** *pp.* 28/13. **noye,** *sb.* 26/3.
numbir, *sb.* number, 7/11. **nummer,** 1/12.
nun, *sb.* 145/2, 7, 147/40, 149/33, etc. **nunes,** *pl.* 1134. **nunn,** 32/14, [145/1]. **nunne,** 13/26, 22/7, 33/10, 35/8, etc. **nunnis,** *pl.* 40/25. **nun nouece,** novice about to become a nun, 147/13, 29. Cf. **non.**
nurischis, *vb. pl.* nourish, 43/13.
nuse, *vb. sg.* hurts, 752.
nyght, *sb.* night, 15/24, 8, 39, 865, 1049, etc. **-es,** *pl.* 2016, 2077, 2302, etc. **nyht,** 16/21, 20/22. Cf. **night,** also **o,** *prep.*
nym, *vb.* take, 16/5.

o, *num.* one ; the same, 414, 2202. Cf. **a.**

o, *prep.* of, on, in, to, 2/7, 4/24, 9/33, 11/9, 26, 12/26, 26/14, etc. **o day,** to-day, 2/2. a day, each day, 28/6. **o night,** at night, in the night, 18/2. **o niht,** 18/3. **o nyght,** 1211. **o nyghtes,** 1199. Cf. **of, on.**

obac, *adv.* behind, 5/34.

obediant, *adj.* obedient, 142/6. **-ient,** 435, 672, 907, 914, etc. Cf. **obidient.**

obedience, *sb.* 1/5, 8, 7/28, 9/25, etc. obeisance, 149/36. **-iens,** 46/10, 11, 24, 39, 721. Cf. **obidience.**

obey, *vb.* 1/13.

obide, *vb.* abide, 34/13. Cf. **abide, obidis, obyde.**

obidience = obedience, 633.

obidient = obediant, 154, 283, 2066, 2092.

obidis, *vb. sg.* abides, persists, 38/4. **obied,** *inf.* stay, wait, 31/5. Cf. **obide.**

oblis, *vb.* "courteously (or kindly) give," 1939. serve, gratify, 2074. refl. "beseechingly throw herself," 1809.

obouen, *adv.* above, 965. **oboun,** *prep.* 1464. **obown,** *adv.* 1203. Cf. **obufe.**

obout, *adv.* about, 303. **-e,** 326, 1491, 2215. Cf. **about, obute.**

obseruandes, *sb. pl.* observances, 2090. **obseruaunce,** *sg.* 282.

obufe, *adv.* = **obouen,** 1040.

obute, *prep.* about, 24/11. Cf. **obout.**

obyde, *vb.* abide, 34/6. Cf. **obide.**

october, *sb.* October, 1836, 1861.

ocupacioun, *sb.* occupation, 1826.

oder, *adj.* other, 86, 549, 1828. *pron.* others, 392, 1280, 2388, 2446. **odir,** *adj.* another, 13/29. other, 25/35, 42/36. *pron.* others, 13/38. **odyr,** *adj.* another, 12/30. Cf. **oþer.**

of, *prep.* 1/2, 3, 4, 6, etc. (postpos.) 1736. with, 4/27, 35/18. by, 43/15, 149/40. as to, in, with regard to, 13/2, 45/3, 127. to, 24/4, 400. *adv.* off, 31/19. **offe** (postpos.), of, 20/6. Cf. **o.**

offece, *sb.* office, 1432, 1433, 1466, 145/4. Cf. **offese.**

offecers, *sb. pl.* officials, 1386.

offer, *vb.* 145/13. *pl.* 2181. Cf. **offir.**

offerand, *sb.* offering, 2188, 145/9. **-e,** 39/21. Cf. **offrand.**

offese, *sb.* office, 216. **office,** 19/9, 20/8, 13, 24/28, etc. **officis,** *pl.* 20/2, 3, 24/36. Cf. **offece, ofice.**

offir, *vb.* offer, 34/2, 7, 39/20, 145/15. *pl.* 39/7. **-d,** *pp.* 39/19. **-s,** *sg.* 30/33, 39/5. Cf. **offer.**

offrand, *sb.* offering, 38/36. Cf. **offerand.**

ofice, *sb.* office, 27/29. Cf. **offese.**

ofte, *adv.* often, 7/26, 22/32, 28/34, 36/28, etc.

ofte-timis, do., 43/9.

oft-sithes, do., 1668, 2033, 2434.

ogain, *prep.* against, 4/27, 5/22, 7/32, 8/29, etc. towards, before, 9/8. Cf. **again, ogayn.**

oganis, *prep.* against, 13/9. **ogans,** 40, 148, 440. Cf. **againis.**

ogayn, *adv.* again, 32, 313, 733, etc. **-e,** 98, 698, 723, etc. Cf. **ogain.**

oght, *pron.* aught, 515, 733, 765, 973, etc. **ohte,** 12/21, 24/2.

old, *adj.* (*sb.*) 519, 650, 651, 658, etc. **olde,** 528. Cf. **ald.**

omang, *prep.* among, 1231. (postpos.) 2247. Cf. **imang.**

omell, *adv.* in between, 488.

on, *num., pron.* one ; somebody, any one, 409, 1257, 1301, 1410, etc. **one,** 42/35. **be on & on,** one by one, 2119. Cf. **an, ton.**

on, *prep.* 2/13, 15/10, 17/8, 1016, etc. (postpos.) 189. in, 22, 60, 68, etc. Cf. **o.**

onest, *adj.* honest, 1060. Cf. **honest.**

onestelike, *adv.* honourably, 24/10. Cf. **honestly.**

oni, *pron.* anybody, 1014. Cf. **ony.**

onlong, *adj.* depending, owing, 17/8.

onright, *adj., sb.* wrong, 1001.

ons, *adv.* once, 1579. Cf. **anes.**

onto, *prep.* unto, 2486. Cf. **vnto.**

onur, *sb.* honour, 16/8, 26/29, 41/29, 30, etc. *vb.* 8/16, 9/13, 41/25, 32, etc. Cf. **honor.**

ony, *adj.* any, 1/12, 46/16, 41, 861,

etc. *pron.* any, one, anybody, 44/21, 506, 1223, 1320, 1639, 1643, etc. Cf. **any, oni.**
opo, *prep.* upon, 17/30, 18/1, 26/7, 27/16. Cf. **opon.**
opin, *adj.* open, 1/22. *vb. imp.* 1687. Cf. **oppind.**
opinlie, *adv.* openly, 40/21. **-like,** 39/12. **-ly,** 2097, 2197, 2357, 2358. Cf. **opynly.**
opon, *prep.* upon, 3/15, 16, 9/2, 15/1, etc. Cf. **apon, opo.**
oppind, *pp.* opened, 47/28, 30.
opyn, *inf.* 65, 67, 108. *adj.* 1230. Cf. **opin.**
opynion, *sb.* opinion, 43/25.
opynly, *adv.* openly, 1228. Cf. **opinlie.**
or, *conj.* 42/31, 3, 51, 92, *1555, etc. Cf. **ouþer.**
or, *conj.* ere, before, 90, 931, 1906, 1993. **or þat,** do., 2/14. Cf. **are** and **tym.**
ordain, *vb.* ordain, institute, appoint, provide, arrange, regulate, establish, dispose, decree, prescribe, 27/28, 29/11. **-d,** *pp.* 32/25, 35/35. **-de,** 16/25, 26, 40/6, 41/18, etc. **ordan,** *inf.* 1479, 1566, 1663, 2285, etc.; cf. 2206. refl. dispose ourselves, 1061. **-d,** *inf., sbj.* 637, 1419. *imp. pl.* refl. 123. *pt.* 665. *pp.* 2, 15, 217, 1574, etc. **-de,** *pp.* 43/15. **-id,** 43/21. Cf. **hordand.**
ordanè, *adj.* ordinate, regular, 22/7. Cf. **ordenè.**
ordanment, *sb.* ordination, appointment, *43/31.
ordenance, *sb.* ordinance, disposal, 1344, 2068. Cf. **ordinance.**
ordenè, *adj.* ordinate, regular (as a member), 37/8, 42/3. **ordenest,** *sup.* 20/6. Cf. **ordanè.**
order, *sb.* 41/13, 270, 281, 300, etc. Cf. **ordir.**
orderd, *pp.* ordained, entered into the order, 519.
ordinance, *sb.* appointment; provision, 43/9, 19, 1716, 2010, 2221. **ordinansis,** *pl.* 43/23. Cf. **ordenance.**
ordir, *sb.* order, 5/1, 6/3, 10/17, 28, etc. *vb.* enter the (Benedictine) order? 40/1. Cf. **order, þordir.**

orison, *sb.* 147/10, 150/17. **-ons,** *pl.* 146/22, 1863, 1867. **-oun,** 1737. **-oune,** 1167. **-ouns,** *pl.* 1912. **-own,** 1146. **-owns,** *pl.* 1130. **orysons,** 148/26. Cf. **uresun.**
ortorie, *sb.* oratory, 34/28.
os, *adv.* as, 2113. *conj.* 1/15, 43/12, 143/1, 198, etc. *rel.* 2030. Cf. **as.**
oþer, *conj.* either, 1709, 1780. Cf. **ouþer.**
oþer, *adj.* other, 10/12, 406, 569, etc. *pron.* others, 378, 383, 388, 449, etc. another, the other(s), 972, 2252, 2438, 2467. *gen.* of others, 1047, 2472. **other,** *adj.* 142/10. **oþir,** *adj.* 6/1, 10/4, 16/11, etc. another, 3/11, 10/34, 19/15, 23/9. *pron.* others, 4/28, 5/8, 29, 30, etc. another, the other(s), *5/36, 10/7, 11/22, 14/8, 20/19, etc. **ane oþer,** another, 889, 936, 952. **ayn oþer,** 1161. Cf. **a-noder, noþer, oder, þoþir, toþer.**
oþerwise, *adv.* otherwise, 635, 1365, 1389, 2366.
oþirgate, do., 40/17.
oþirkin, other kind of, 28/5.
ouen, *sb.* oven, 2428.
ouer, *prep.* over, 86, 1280, 1888, 2318, *148/2, etc. *adv.* by, 444. Cf. **ouir, our.**
ouercumen, *pp.* overcome, 945. Cf. **ouircumin.**
ouer-lyght, *adj.* too light, 1064.
ouer-lyghtly, *adv.* too easily, 2292.
ouertayn, *pp.* overtaken, caught, 1232, 1878. Cf. **ourtake.**
ouir, *prep.* over, above, 4/17, 8/23, 10/14, 13/17, etc. *adv.* 33/9. Cf. **ouer.**
ouir-arlike, *adv.* too early, 11/12.
ouircumin, *pp.* overcome, 14/11. Cf. **ouercumen.**
ouir-ful, *adj.* too full, 28/30.
ouirgase, *vb. sg.* is beyond, 45/14.
ouir-late, *adv.* too late, 17/5.
ouir-lazand, *adj.* laughing too much, 14/31.
ouir-mikil, *adj.* too great; too much, 26/3, 28/34, 29/2. *sb., adv.* 8/31, 24/12, 27/28. Cf. **our-mikil.**
ouir-obstinate, *adj.* too obstinate, 42/29.

ouir-suspiciose, *adj.* too suspicious, 42/29.
our, *sb.* hour, 1124, 1704, 1724, 1746, etc. Cf. **houre, oure, owre, ure.**
our, *adj.* 1/8, 13, 40, 58, etc. **oure,** 11/23, 15/16, 47, 48, etc. Cf. **owre, ure.**
our, *prep.* over, 146/10. **oure,** 144/2. Cf. **ouer.**
oure, *sb.* hour, 1840, 1868. **oures,** *pl.* 1554, 1844, 1863, 1897. Cf. **our.**
ourels, *sb. pl.* oriels, closets, 1540. [O.F. *oeurieul.*]
oureself, *pron.* ourselves, 167. **ourself,** 92, 566, 608, 1029. **ourselue,** 1026. Cf. **usself.**
our-mikil, *sb., adv.* too much, 8/31. Cf. **ouir-mikil.**
ourtake, *vb.* overtake, 2/7. Cf. **ouertayn.**
out, *adv.* 1483. **oute,** 620. **out of,** 26/7, 58, 63. **oute of,** 23/7, 144/8, 384, 782, etc. Cf. **owte, ut.**
outekast, *sb.* outcast, 1034.
ouþer, *conj.* either, 832, 1827, 2162, 2179. **outher,** 2394. **ouþir,** or, 15/8, 9, 16/2, etc. Cf. **or, oþer, ouȝir, owþer.**
outrage, *sb.* 1588. Cf. **owterage, vtrage.**
outward, *adv.* outside, 2350, 2401, 2431.
ouyr-litel, *adj.* too small, 20/19.
ouȝir, *conj.* or, 41/7. Cf. **ouþer.**
oway, *adv.* away, 9/4, 12, 11/37, 12/16, etc. Cf. **away.**
owre, *sb.* hour, 31/4, 41/23. Cf. **our.**
owre, *adj.* our, 37/4, 39/3, 22. Cf. **our.**
owre-hegh, *adj.* too high or great, 142/12.
owte, *adv.* out, 34/25. **owte of,** 31/2, 3, 7, etc. Cf. **out.**
owterage, *sb.* outrage, excess, 46/5. **owtrage,** 28/10. Cf. **outrage.**
owþer, *conj.* either, 559. Cf. **ouþer.**

pacience, *sb.* patience, 8/27, 13/4, 8, 26/33, etc.
pai, *vb.* please, satisfy, 27/29, 31. **paid,** *pp.* 10/24, 1848. **paide,** 532, 534, 685, etc. Cf. **payd.**
paine, *sb.* pain, 4/11, 5/23, 6/23, 24, etc. **paines,** *pl.* 227. **painis,** 3/32. Cf. **payn.**
paire, *sb. pl.* pair, 36/26. Cf. **payr.**
pais, *sb.* peace, 4/17, 12/9, 25/29. Cf. **pes.**
paise, *sb.* Easter, 1890. Cf. **pas.**
palays, *sb.* palace, 134.
par. See **auenturs.**
paradis, *sb.* Paradise, 22/29. **paradise,** 30/37.
parcaiuid, *pp.* aware, 37/21.
parel, *sb.* peril, 447. Cf. **perils.**
parfite, *adj.* perfect, 1118. Cf. **perfite.**
part, *sb.* 4/12, 30/26, 1582, 1638, 1782.
parte, *vb.* divide, distribute, 38/35. Cf. **partid.**
partens, *vb. pl.* pertain, 7.
parti, *sb.* part, 28/7. **partie,** 37/19, 20, 42/4. **partis,** *pl.* parties, 43/27. **party,** 2340.
partid, *pp.* distributed, 2026. Cf. **parte.**
pas, *sb.* Easter, 1703. **pase,** 1123, 1131, 1835. Cf. **paise.**
pas, *vb.* pass, go; surpass; go beyond, 995, 1351, 1528, 2403. **pase,** 546, 1984. **passe,** 36/1. **passes,** *sg.* 2338. **passid,** *pp.* 31/8, 142/32. **past,** 1707, 2116. *prep.* 1868, 2362.
paskis, *sb.* Easter, 15/28, 16/16, 17/21, 27, etc. **paskys,** 15/23.
pater noster (Lat.), 18/23, 29, 31, 32, etc.
pay, *sb.* satisfaction, 26/23.
payd, *pp.* (*adj.*) pleased, satisfied, 1311. **-e,** 37/28, 29, 2000. Cf. **pai.**
payn, *sb.* pain; penitence, 614, 731, 734, 1799, etc. **-e,** 1/17, 1343, 1544, etc. (take) pains, 29/22. **-s,** *pl.* 679. Cf. **paine.**
payr, *sb.* pair, 146/33. Cf. **paire.**
penance, *sb.* 21/24, 28, 203, 268, etc.
penne, *sb.* pen, 143/14.
pepil, *sb.* people, 147/33.
perchanch, *adv.* perchance, 1375.
perceaue, *vb.* perceive, 401. Cf. **persaiue.**
perel, *sb.* peril, 43/25, 27. **-s,** *pl.* 1383. Cf. **perils.**
perfeccion, *sb.* perfection, 2486.

perfite, *adj.* 15/19, 265, 657, 853, etc. Cf. **parfite.**
perfourn, *vb.* perform, 224, 314, 2303.
perfytely, *adv.* perfectly, 1/11.
perils, *sb. pl.* 1233. Cf. **parel, perel, peryl.**
peris, *vb.* perish, 506. **-e,** 1300, 1455. **-t,** *pp.* 1301.
perpetual, *adj.* 1/16.
persaiue, *vb.* perceive, 443. **-saue,** 40/33. Cf. **perceaue.**
persecucioun, *sb.* persecution, 968.
perseuerans, *sb.* perseverance, 142/29, 2076.
persones, *sb. pl.* persons, 43/21. **-soune,** *sg.* 1946.
peryl, *sb.* peril, 1908. Cf. **perils.**
pes, *sb.* peace, 8/25, 9/15, 13/29. **pese,** 43/31, 110, 1939. Cf. **pais.**
peticions, *sb. pl.* petitions, 2186. **-ioun,** *sg.* 2144, 2177, 2191. **-iun,** 39/6, 20, 141/3.
pilegrimis, *sb. pl.* 35/25, 37/6. **pilgrams,** 1929. **pilgrims,** 35/7, 1935, 1970.
pine, *vb.* torment, 579. **pines,** *sb. pl.* torments, 11/34. **pinis,** 46/28. Cf. **pyen.**
pipe, *sb.* reed, 42/25. Cf. Notes.
pitè, *sb.* pity, 23/26, 25/17, 27/12, 29/1, etc. Cf. **pytè.**
place, *sb.* 141/22, 952, 1145, 1665, etc. **places,** *pl.* 43/15, 939, 1611, 2011. **plais,** 1600. **in place,** "forth," 2096. Cf. **plase.**
plainly, *adv.* 332. Cf. **playnly.**
plaisters, *sb. pl.* plasters, 23/3.
plane, *adv.* = **playn,** 18/19.
plase, *sb.* place, 1161, 1463. **plasses,** *pl.* 252. Cf. **place.**
play, *vb.* amuse or divert herself, 2385.
playn, *adj., adv.* plain; plainly, 314, 899, 1715. **-e,** 2009, 2014, 2042. "full," 2256. Cf. **plane.**
playnly, *adv.* plainly, 430, 744, 2078, etc. "fully," 2116. Cf. **plainly.**
plentè, *sb.* plenty, 1006, 1612.
plese, *vb.* please, 1848, 1976.
pointe, *sb.* point; tip, 10/35. **ponte,** 539, 2253. **pontes,** *pl.* 320, 657, 2120. **pontis,** 7, 315. Cf. **poyntes.**
pond, *sb.* pound, 1578.
pore, *adj.* poor, 1447. Cf. **pouer.**
postil, *sb.* apostle, 3/19. Cf. **apostel.**
potage, *sb.* soup, 28/1. **potege,** 1572.
pouer, *adj.* (*sb.*) poor, 1148, 1930, 1970, 2026, etc. **pouir,** 8/20, 24/7, 35/25, 38/36, etc. Cf. **pore, pure.**
pouertè, *sb.* poverty, 419.
poustè, *sb.* power, 6/27, 7/1, 21/29, 25/10, etc.
power, do., 43/20, 142/1, 173, 344, etc. **-e,** 151.
powertè = **pouertè,** *142/8.
poyntes, *sb. pl.* points, 142/23. **poyntis,** 142/33. Cf. **pointe.**
praers, *sb. pl.* prayers, 627. **praier,** *sg.* 2/14, 142/20. Cf. **prayer.**
prai, *vb.* pray, 22/11. *pl.* 3/1, 11/25, 19/1, 33, etc. **praie,** 14/4. **prais,** *sg.* 27/10, 39/23, 40/5. **pray,** 9/13, 19/26, 224, 653, etc. ask, invite, 1904. *pl.* 3/30, 8/7, 12/33, etc. *imp.* 42, 44. *imp.* 1 *pl.* 849. **prayde,** *pt.* 1097. Cf. **prayis.**
praise, *vb.* 11/9. **prase,** 975. Cf. **prays.**
prayer, *sb.* 1/10, 19/23, 1146, 1167. **-s,** *pl.* 114, 623, 1189, 1194, etc. Cf. **praers.**
prayis, *vb. sg.* prays, 39/26. Cf. **prai.**
prayng, *sb.* praying, 1922, 2387.
prays, *vb.* praise, 393, 1461. **-e,** 14/25, 173. Cf. **praise.**
precens, *sb.* presence, 1918. Cf. **presence.**
preching, *sb.* preaching, 145/16, 17.
prechis, *vb. pl.* preach, 192.
prelet, *sb.* prelate, 145/19, 148/1. **-e,** 146/23, 31, 33, etc.
prencipall = **principall,** 2441.
presand, *sb.* present, 1999.
presence, *sb.* 147/24. **presens,** 1533. Cf. **precens.**
present, *adj.* 43/4, 1149.
president, *adj.* presiding, 1362.
preson, *sb.* prison, 442.
prest, *adj.* ready, quick, 1925.
prest, *sb.* priest, 6/17, 150/6. **-e,** 32/7, 39/23, 36, 40/5, etc.
preualy, *adv.* privily, 1915. **preuely,** 1227, 1552, 1755, 1913. Cf. **priuelike.**

price, *sb.* 37/17, 20.
pride, *sb.* 9/12, 11/5, 603, 782, etc. Cf. **pryde.**
prime, *sb.* divine office about 5 or 6 a.m., 17/26, 33, 18/5, 1837, etc.
principall, *sb.* principal, ruler, head, 319, 324, 2211. Cf. **prencipall.**
principally, *adv.* 142/6.
priores, *sb.* prioress (abbess), 141/4, 145/9, *319, 323, 357, etc. *gen.* 144/18, 145/8, 1364, 2049. **-rese,** 1279. **-resse,** (sub)prioress, 43/10, 15, 17, 21, etc. Cf. **priures.**
priuè, *adj.* privy, 8/3, 32/6, 34/1, 32, etc.
priuelike, *adv.* privily, 20/34, 22/6, 32/6. Cf. **preualy.**
priures, *sb.* (sub)prioress, 41/27. **-resse,** 20/12, 35/8, 43/35, 44/2, etc. Cf. **priores.**
processe, *sb.* proceeding, course, 314.
profer, *vb.* proffer, 1343.
professe, *sb.* vow, 38/23, 39/1, 147/25. [O.F. *professe.*] Cf. **prouese.**
professe-boke, *sb.* scroll or document containing the vow, 145/16. **profession-boke,** 147/26.
profession, *sb.* profession, vow, 143/14, 16, 144/13, 147/20. **-iun,** 143/12.
profest, *pp.* **be profest,** make (has made) the vow, 141/11, 143/7. **be profeste,** 143/10.
profetabil, *adj.* profitable, 1496.
profete, *sb.* prophet, 2/28. Cf. **prophet.**
profites, *vb. sg.* is profitable, 726.
prome, *sb.* neighbour, 8/14, 10/18, 47/10. [OF. *prome, prosme, proisme,* Lat. *proximum.*]
pronunce, *vb.* pronounce, 1003.
prophet, *sb.* profit, 2059.
prophet, *sb.* prophet, 370, 448, 688, etc. *gen.* 137. **-e,** 3/8, 5/19, 10/30, *998, etc. **-is,** *pl.* 16/31. **prophett,** *sg.* 164. Cf. **profete.**
propir, *adj.* proper, own, 10/4, 12/6, 27, 28/20, etc.
propirlie, *adv.* as property, 39/16.
propirtarij, *sb.* proprietor, 142/12.
propirtè, *sb.* property, 25/5, 8, 36/29, 31, 1617.
prostrate, *adj.* 144/3. *vb.* prostrate herself, 141/17, 143/22, 144/19.
proude, *adj.* proud, 776. Cf. **prowd.**
proue, *vb.* prove, test, try, 7/23, 899, 2079. thrive, 479. *imp.* prove, etc., 38/1. **proued,** *pp.* 448. **proues,** *sg.* 200, 833, 889, 939. **prouid,** *pp.* 38/14. **prouis,** *sg.* 13/14. **prow,** *inf.* 2077. Cf. **pruefe.**
prouese, *sb.* profession, vow, 145/8. **-uesse,** 147/14. Cf. **professe.**
prow, *sb.* profit, advantage, 2446. **prowe,** 45/18.
prowd, *adj.* proud, *43/18, 1224, 1426. **-e,** 40/22, 44/6. **prudde,** 20/12. **prude,** 6/20, 8/30, 20/7, 23/30, etc. Cf. **proude.**
pruefe, *vb.* = **proue,** 2253.
pryde, *sb.* pride, 329, 2061. Cf. **pride.**
punest, *pp.* punished, 1876. **punych,** *inf.* 1263. **punysce,** 141/23. **punyst,** *pp.* 2367.
puplicane, *sb.* publican, 15/12. **pupplicane,** 1097.
puplist, *pp.* made public or known, 1546, 1953. **pupplist,** 911.
purches, *vb.* purchase, 142/21.
pure, *adj.* poor, 36/26, 39/19, 1947, 2203. Cf. **pouer.**
pure, *adj.* pure, 47/4.
purpose, *sb.* 142/2, 21, 25, 26, etc.
puruaie, *vb.* provide, 24/32. **-uay,** 35/34, 1388, 2144. **-uayd,** *pp.* 1862, 1999, 2009, 2088. **-uayde,** 1799. **-ued,** 1715.
puruyance, *sb.* provision, 1430. **-anch,** 1364.
put, *vb.* 38/3, 53, 1014, 2319, etc. *pl.* 271. *pp.* 419, 1262, 2153. **pute,** *pp.* 1408. **putes,** *sg.* 399, 1717. **putt,** *pp.* 46/23.
pyen, *sb.* torment, 53. **pynd,** *pp.* tormented, 1236. **pyne,** *sb.* 856, 2460. Cf. **pine.**
pytè, *sb.* pity, 22/27. Cf. **pitè.**

quaintelike, *adv.* prudently, 40/30.
quantitè, *sb.* quantity, number, 16/17.
quat, *pron.* what, 1914. Cf. **what.**
quer, *sb.* choir, 31/18, 145/10, 148/20, 149/37, 150/1. **quere,** 143/36, 38, 144/1, 12, etc. Cf. **qwer.**
question, *sb.* 211.

quit, *adj*. free, 5/18, 25/34, 26/5.
quite, *vb*. acquit, free; refl. 9/5, 10/26, 18/31. **quites**, *sg*. refl. 3/1.
qwen, *conj*. when, 144/23, 149/39. Cf. **when**.
qwer, *sb*. choir, 149/32. **qwere**, 143/24, 30, 32, 34, etc. Cf. **quer**.
qwil, *conj*. while, 144/6, 9. Cf. **while**.

rad, *adj*. afraid, 15/11.
raik, *vb*. wander, 303. Cf. **raykes**.
rais, *vb*. *sg*. raises, 1068. **raise**, *inf*. 1065. **rase**, 798. **rases**, *sg*. 808. **rasit**, *pp*. raised, exalted, 786. Cf. **rayse**.
ras, *vb*. *pt*. rose, 18/3. **rase**, 1376. Cf. **rise**.
raue, *vb*. rove, 362. **raueand**, *ppr*. 292.
raw, *sb*. row, 561, 1255.
raykes, *vb*. *pl*. wander, 292. Cf. **raik**.
rayse, *vb*. raise, 59. **raysid**, *pp*. 43/22. Cf. **rais**.
rebel, *sb*., *adj*. rebel, rebellious, 40/18, 46/22, 1403, 2448. rebellion, 46/25. **-s**, *pl*. 440.
recaiue, *vb*. receive, 26/17, 29, 27/19, 31/24, etc. **-uid**, *pt*. 35/6. *pp*. 23/16, 18, 35/24, 38/3, etc. **-uis**, *sg*. 26/13. **recauis**, 24/35. **rechaiue**, *inf*. 26/22. **rechaiuid**, *pp*. 26/19, 35/15. Cf. **resaf**.
rechis, *vb*. *sg*. reaches, 798.
recles, *adj*. = **rekles**, 6/14.
reclusis, *sb*. *pl*. recluses, 4/18, 19.
recorde, *sb*. accord, agreement, 654.
recorde, *vb*. take to heart, remember, 11/32.
red, *pp*. read, 16/5, 9, 1873, 2099, etc. **redde**, 16/12, 44/30, 143/14. Cf. **rede**.
rede, *sb*. advice; decision, will; mind, 149, 367, 524, 913, etc. Cf. **reed**.
rede, *sb*. reed, 2279.
rede, *vb*. read, 5/7, 21/14, 493, 561, etc. 1 *sg*. advise, 463. *pl*. read, 28/30. *pp*. 1951 (the second), 2498. **redes**, *sg*. 1695. **redis**, 27/21. Cf. **red**.
redey, *adj*. ready, 871. **redi**, 44/21, 1145, 1790. **redy**, 3/29, 20/24, 654, 1204, etc.
reed, *sb*. advice, 2/8. Cf. **rede**.
refresch, *vb*. refresh, 1937.
refuse, *vb*. 30/33, 367, 1493, 2502. **-ses**, *pl*. 2506. **-sid**, *pp*. 40/32. **-sis**, *sg*. 5/31.
regne, *sb*. kingdom, 6/9. Cf. **rengne**.
reherce, *vb*. rehearse, go through (again), 143/20, 887, 1140, 1965, 2152. **-ced**, *pp*. 142/23. **-cede**, 143/8.
rehtuisnes, *sb*. justice, 5/19. Cf. **rightwisnes**.
rek, *vb*. care, 587.
rekles, *adj*. reckless, 857. Cf. **recles**.
reklesly, *adv*. recklessly, 1487. **reklisly**, 367, 2129.
reklesnes, *sb*. carelessness, 1542.
rekning, *sb*. reckoning, account, *468. **reknyng**, 353, 499, 503, 1452, etc.
rekynd, *pp*. reckoned, 2159.
relegion, *sb*. = **religion**, 1615.
relekes, *sb*. *pl*. relics, 1478.
reles, *sb*. relaxation, 39/27.
relese, *vb*. release, 2340. **relesses**, *sg*. remits, 29/9.
releue, *vb*. relieve, 1936.
religion, *sb*. religion; pious or monastic life; "the convent," 281, 289, 2072. **-ioun**, 4, 977, 1825, 2178, etc. *gen*. 2082. **-iown**, 700. **-iun**, 4/6, 15, 5/27, 6/5, etc. Cf. **relegion**.
religius, *adj*. religious, pious, 6/1.
remanant, *sb*. remainder, 144/9. **remnaunt**, 146/37.
remue, *vb*. remove, 24/36.
rengne, *sb*. kingdom, 2/24, 26, 7/6, 21/18, etc. Cf. **regne**.
renne, *vb*. run, 3/33, 4/9. **rennes**, *imp*. *pl*. 2/6. **rennis**, *pl*. 13/20. Cf. **rinne**.
rentes, *sb*. *pl*. rents, 1478.
repentans, *sb*. repentance, 1773.
repreue, *vb*. reprove, 40/18. **repreuid**, *pp*. 44/8.
reprofe, *sb*. reproof, reprehension, 1230. **reproue**, 602, 1034. *vb*. *pl*. reprove, 600. **reproues**, *sg*. 2/34, 389, 776.
requerde, *pp*. required, asked, 1053.
resaf, *vb*. receive, 1486. **resaiuid**,

pp. 141/1. **resaue,** 1926, 1970, 1989. *pl.* 1971, 1972. **resaues,** *sg.* 1947, 1948. **resauid,** *pp.* 141/8. **resauyd,** 1348, 1967, 2075, 2124, etc. Cf. **recaiue.**
reson, *sb.* reason, 294, 523, 536, 617, 2322, etc. **-ons,** *pl.* 1292. **-oun,** 1542. Cf. **resun.**
resonabil, *adj.* reasonable, 2294. **resonabillike,** *adv.* reasonably, 43/34. Cf. **resunnabil.**
respit, *sb.* respite, 3/18.
respun, *sb.* response, 16/7, 19, 34, 17/15, etc. **-s,** *pl.* 16/6, 11, 26, 30, etc.
rest, *sb.* 9/16. *vb.* 1125. **-e,** *sb.* 42/30. *vb.* 32/28. Cf. **ryst.**
restore, *vb.* 1341. store, 38/39.
resun, *sb.* reason; account; sense, meaning, 6/32, 7/3, 10, 8/2, etc. Cf. **reson.**
resunnabil, *adj.* reasonable, 13/39. Cf. **resonabil.**
reuerance, *sb.* reverence, 6/2. **-rence,** 16/28, 19/24, 766, etc.
reul, *sb.* rule, 4/17, 23, 6/4, 11/26, etc. **-e,** 7/30, 10/7, 27/11, 21, etc. Cf. **rewel.**
reuþe, *sb.* regret, repentance, 21/23, 28, 22/9, 33/35, etc.
rew, *vb.* cause regret, 556.
reward, *sb.* 660. regard, heed, care, 1059, 2046. **-e,** regard, etc. 417, 1497, 2251.
rewel, *sb.* rule, 2112. **rewl,** 1874. **rewle,** 142/33, 35, 143/3, 147/22, etc. *vb.* 536, 617, 1469, 2114. **rewles,** *sb. pl.* 2498. **rewlid,** *pp.* 1558, 1727, 2506. Cf. **reul, rowle.**
rewling, *sb.* ruling, 2298.
rich, *adj.* 1148, 2203. **-e,** 39/4. Cf. **rike, ryche.**
riches, *sb.* 418.
ride, *vb.* 1090. **rides,** *sg.* 326.
right, *sb.* 596, 1937. *adj.* 47/17, 536, 546, 814, etc. (on the right hand), 143/13, 17. *adv.* right, rightly, 32/13, 33, 224, 417, 808, etc. "at all," 451. **riht,** *sb.* 2/31. *adj.* 2/22, 23, 5/14, 7/4, etc. *adv.* 5/8, 6/12, 7/7, etc. **rihte,** *adj.* 2/17, 12/11, 38/12. **wid rihte,** by right, 33/29. Cf. **ryght.**
rightwise, *adj.* just, 513. **rihtuis,** 2/32, 5/12, 8/3, etc.—**rightwisnes,** *sb.* justice, 395, 490, 602. **rihtuisnes,** *5/32, 7/6, 47/6. **rihtvisnes,** 18/5.—Cf. **rehtuisnes, ryghtwis.**
rike, *sb.* country, 2238.
rike, *adj.* rich, 35/26. Cf. **rich.**
rineside, *pp.* rinsed, 149/40.
ring, *vb.* 1473. **-is,** *sg.* intr. 20/24, 29/25, 31, 31/4, etc. Cf. **rungen.**
rinne, *vb.* run, 30/6. Cf. **renne, ryn.**
ripe, *vb.* search, 36/28.
rise, *vb.* rise; arise, 1/21, 15/25, 27/25, 141/20, 1216, etc. ("raise our voices") 1075. *pl.* 17/5, 29/24. **rises,** *sg.* 9/15. Cf. **ras, ryse.**
risyng, *sb.* (time for) rising, 1123.
rodes, *sb. gen.* rood's, 29/13. **rodis,** 29/6. (The day was Sept. 14th.)
rote, *sb.* rot (in sheep), 1331, 1332.
rotyn, *adj.* rotten, 12/13.
rowle, *sb.* rule, 4, 1140. Cf. **rewle.**
rubes, *vb. sg.* rubs, 2275.
rudely, *adv.* 1075.
rungen, *pp.* rung, 32/31. Cf. **ring.**
rust, *sb.* 2275.
rute, *sb.* root, 2286.
ryche, *adj.* powerful, rich, 19/25. Cf. **rich.**
ryght, *adj.* right, 1/7, 617, 817. (on the right hand), 148/1. *adv.* right, rightly, 21, 2512. Cf. **right.**
ryghtwis, *adj.* just, 141. Cf. **rightwise.**
ryn, *vb.* run, 87, 1766. *pl.* 1908. Cf. **rinne.**
ryng, *sb.* ring, 2196, 147/27.
ryse, *vb.* rise, 15/24, 16/23, 58, 62, 63, etc. **rysis,** *pl.* 18/2, 43/10. Cf. **rise.**
ryst, *vb.* rest, 135. Cf. **rest.**

sa, *adv.* so, 22/23, 43/1. then, 1/13, 143/16. *rel.* see **wha.** Cf. **so, sua.**
saf, *vb.* save, 1584. Cf. **saue.**
safe, *adj.* 934. Cf. **sauf, vochyd.**
safly, *adv.* safely, 1267.
sahtil, *vb.* reconcile, 8/21.
sai, *vb.* say, 14/12, 34/20, 529, 887, etc. **saiand,** *ppr.* 144/14. **said,** *pt.* 456, 738, 1101, 1207, etc. *pp.* 7/23, 16/4, 521, 1768, etc. **saide,**

pt. 11/5, 7, 12/37, 716, etc. *pp.* 16/21, 17/17, 531, 686, etc. **saie,** *inf.* 2/15, 4/24, 5/18, 9/26, etc. 1 *sg.* 2/16, 17/30, etc. *pl.* 18/34. **sais,** *sg.* 2/5, 16, 332, 335, etc. "is said," 2/1, 9/34, etc. *pl.* 984. *imp.* 142/23. **sais . . owte,** discloses, tells on, 32/4. Cf. **say.**

sain, *adj.* Saint, 1/20, 2/17, 20, 3/5, etc. **sainte,** 42/34. Cf. **sant.**

sak, *sb.* sake, 36. **sake,** 35/19, 153, 238, 317, etc.

sake, *vb.* forsake, 592. Cf. Notes.

sal, *sb.* soul, 27/8. Cf. **saul.**

sal, *vb. sg.* shall (will), 2/5, *14, 183, 272, etc. shalt, 2369. *pl.* 2/13, 14, 212, 242, etc. **salbe = sal be,** 16/12, 321, 145/3, 5, 7, 147/10. Cf. **sale, schall, shal, suld.**

salde, *vb. pt.* sold, 37/18. *pp.* 37/16. Cf. **sel.**

sale, *sb.* 37/28.

sale, *vb. pl.* shall, 13/33. **sall,** *sg.* shall (will), 3/23, 32, 4/7, 82, 104, 243, etc. shalt, 29, 32, 43. *pl.* 3/25, 8, 11, 113, etc. **salle,** *sg.* 21/15, 25/22, 23, 27/23. shalt, 38/12. *pl.* 13/25, 17/21, 21/24, 130. Cf. **sal.**

salme, *sb.* psalm, 7/7, 16/2, 22, etc. **salmes,** *pl.* 16/25, 18/20, 31/27, 1139. **salmis,** 16/3, 12, 17, 21, etc. Cf. **saulm.**

saluacion, *sb.* salvation, 141/25. **-ioune,** 346.

sam, *rel.* See under **wha, what, whar, whilk, wilke.**

sam, *adj.* same, 2371. **same,** 43/15, 21, 143/1, 1234, etc. *pron.* 143/21, 488, 698, etc. **to þe same,** to the same effect, 373. **to þis sam,** 461.

samen, *adv.* together, 412, 1744, 1846. **samyn,** 528, 1199, etc.

sampil, *sb.* example, 41/4. Cf. **saumpil.**

sande, *sb.* thing or gift sent, 1614.

sant, *adj.* Saint, 2, 6, 170, 251, etc. Cf. **sain.**

sari, *adj.* sorry, 21/29, 25/26.

sartayn, *adj.* certain, 574. Cf. **sertane.**

saruandes, *sb. pl.* servants, 54. Cf. **seruand.**

sarue, *vb.* serve, 12. **sarued,** *pp.* 2202. **sarues,** *sg.* deserves, 614. Cf. **serue.**

saruyse, *sb.* service, 604. Cf. **serues.**

saue. See **vochyd.**

saue, *vb.* save; keep, observe, 92, 538, 1398, 2512, etc. Cf. **saf, sauyd.**

sauf, *adj.* safe; saved, 7/12, 13/6, 29/12, 20, etc. Cf. **safe.**

sauflike, *adv.* safely, 33/33.

sauiour, *sb.* Saviour, 894.

saul, *sb.* soul, 6/23, 7/12, 8/13, 1830, etc. *gen.* 566. **-e,** 21/27, 32/23, 96, 169, etc. *gen.* 826. **-es,** *pl.* 22/14, 43/25, 248, 471, etc. **-is,** 29/11. **-s,** 6/29, 7/2, 9, 37/24, etc. Cf. **sal, sawle.**

saulm, *sb.* psalm, 1768. **-s,** *pl.* 1130, 1530. Cf. **salme.**

saumpyl, *sb.* example, 22/21. Cf. **a-saumpil, sampil.**

sauter, *sb.* Psalter, 687, 737, 784. **-s,** *pl.* 15/27. Cf. **sawter.**

sauyd, *pp.* saved, 94. Cf. **saue.**

saw, *vb. pt.* 800. Cf. **saz** and **se.**

saw, *sb.* saying, utterance, word; command, 375, 459, 529, 639, etc. **sawes,** *pl.* 262, 531, 542, 696. Cf. **saws.**

sawle, *sb.* soul, 361, 2392. Cf. **saul.**

sawn, *pp.* sown, 348.

saws, *pl. of* **saw,** *sb.* 436, 632, 1394.

sawter, *sb.* Psalter, 131. **-s,** *pl.* 1130. Cf. **sauter.**

say, *vb.* say; read, 11/6, 15/28, 1142, 1683, etc. *pl.* 339, 1914. **sayand,** *ppr.* 145/20, 146/24, 31, etc. **sayd,** *pt.* 1861, 2327. *pp.* 1910, 147/10, 12, etc. **saye,** *inf.* 38/11. **sayng,** *ppr.* saying, 42/34. *ger.* 147/32. **says,** *sg.* 2/3, 22, 23, 99, etc. **sayse,** 60, 94. Cf. **sai.**

saynds, *sb. pl.* messengers, *1643.

saz, *vb. pt.* saw, 11/15, 15/11. Cf. **saw** and **se.**

scath, *sb.* harm, injury, 979, 1333. **scaþe,** 2/11, 10/31, 11/35.

scere, *vb.* cut, 11/37. Cf. **scher, scorn.**

schall, *vb. sg.* shall, 141/6. Cf. **sal, shal.**

scham, *sb.* shame, 791. **-e,** 1775. Cf. **shame.**

schamis, *vb. sg.* makes ashamed, 47/22. **schamyd,** *pp.* 1228. Cf. **shamyd.**
schapiter, *sb.* chapter-house, 1806. Cf. **chapiter.**
schar, *sb.* scar, mark, spot, blemish, 881. [O.F. *eschare.*]
schastisyng, *sb.* chastisement, 1356. Cf. **chastising.**
sche, *pron.* she, 326, 328, 351, 353, etc. Cf. **scho.**
scheke, *sb.* cheek, 971.
schent, *pp.* ruined, 1332.
schep, *sb.* sheep, 1314, 1331. *pl.* 506, 1300, 1332. **-e,** *sg.* 1306. *pl.* 362. Cf. **shep.**
scher, *vb.* cut, reap, 1853. Cf. **scere.**
schers, *sb. pl.* scissors, 146/33.
schew, *vb.* show, 961, 992, 994, 2091. **-s,** *sg.* 430, 525, 781, 851, etc. **-es,** 205.
schilde, *vb.* shield, protect, 21/5. Cf. **schylde, silde.**
scho, *pron.* she, 7/21, 10/6, 8, 363, 368, 371, etc. Cf. **sche, sho.**
schort, *adj.* short, 1190, 1194, 1742, 2024. Cf. **scort.**
schos, *sb. pl.* shoes, 2017.
schosin, *pp.* chosen, 1421. Cf. **ches.**
schrews, *sb. pl.* shrews, 429, 1426.
schrift, *sb.* shrift, confession, 988. Cf. **scrift.**
schriue, *vb.* refl. confess (and take penance), 32/7, 9, 627. Cf. **scriue.**
schuldirs, *sb. pl.* shoulders, 22/24.
schylde, *vb. imp.* shield, 791. Cf. **schilde.**
scifte, *vb.* shift, change, 36/27.
sclandir, *sb.* scandal, offence, slander, 18/30, 45/26. **sclandirs,** *vb. sg.* scandalizes, causes offence to, 24/21. **sclaunder,** *sb.* 2350. **-s,** *pl.* 43/13. **sclaundird,** *pp.* 24/20. Cf. **sklaunders.**
scole, *sb.* school, 4/2. Cf. **skoles.**
scorid, *pp.* scourged, beaten, 1536.
scorn, *pp.* cut (off), curtailed, 36/28, 31. Cf. **scere.**
scort, *adj.* short, 16/19, 19/28. **scorte,** 16/18. Cf. **schort.**
scrift, *sb.* shrift, confession, penance, 4/11, *6/6, 9/5, 10/26. **-e,** 14/11, 21/17. Cf. **schrift.**
scripture, *sb.* 11/3.
scriue, *vb.* = **schriue,** 13/25, 26.
se, *sb.* sea, 24/23.
se, *vb.* see, 2/9, 4/8, 9/3, 96, etc. *pl.* 15/17, 373. Cf. **see** and **ses, saw, saz, sene.**
seculer, *adj.* secular, 145/18.
secund, *num.* second, 265. **-e,** 41/22, 142/8. Cf. 17/13.
sede, *sb.* seed, 348.
see, *vb.* 5. **seis,** *sg.* 42/25, 142/22. Cf. **se.**
segerstane, *sb.* sacristan, 1472. **-stone,** 1385.
seke, *adj.* (*sb.*) sick, ill, 8/21, 22/5, 583, 1287, etc.
seke, *vb.* seek, 7/5, 22/22, 489, 988, etc. 1 *sg.* 741. *imp.* 109, 110. Cf. **sekes.**
sekenes, *sb.* sickness, illness, 15/28, 25/24, 28, 2469, etc. Cf. **seknes.**
seker, *adj.* sure, 655. Cf. **sekir.**
sekes, *vb. sg.* seeks, 93, 877. Cf. **seke.**
sekil, *sb.* world (as opposed to religion), 37/31, 39/4.
sekir, *adj.* sure, 2439. Cf. **seker, sikir.**
seknes, *sb.* sickness, illness, 1655. Cf. **sekenes.**
sel, *sb.* cell, 2106. Cf. **cel.**
sel, *vb.* sell. **for to sel,** for sale, 2018. Cf. **salde, selle.**
selden, *adv.* seldom, 10/32.
sele, *sb.* seal, 2148.
self, *sb.* 577.
selle, *vb.* sell, 37/26, 27, 29. Cf. **sel.**
semande, *ppr., adj.* seeming, seemly, 4/26. Cf. **seme.**
sembils, *vb. sg.* resembles, 3/14.
seme, *vb.* beseem, be suitable, suit, 1583, 2410. **semis,** *sg.* seems, 4/24. **semys,** 713. Cf. **semande.**
semtembir, *sb.* September, 29/6.
sen, *conj.* since, as, 45, 73, 121, 875, etc. (temporal) 2390. **sen þat,** do., 1336, 2130. Cf. **sine.**
send, *vb.* 1289, 1992. *imp.* 14/34. *pp.* 1276, 1987. **-e,** 3/10, 22/7, 39/10, 44/28. **-es,** *pl.* 2422. **-is,** *sg.* 7/26, 22/1, 44/35. **sent,** *pt.* 10/17, 12/30, 40/31, etc. *pp.* 3/19, 7/14, 162, 1985, etc. **sente,** *pp.* 36/8. **sent forz,** properly :

dismissed (said of the congregation at the end of the mass; cf. Lat. "ite, missa est!"); then: finished (said of the canonical hours), 17/16. **sent forde,** 18/23, 26.

sene, *pp.* seen, 45/5, 474, 1224, 1588, etc. Cf. **se.**

sentence, *sb.* sentence, paragraph, 1/20, 2/20, 36/33, etc. judgment, 21/9, 12, 22/1, 7, etc. sense, wisdom, 22/13.

sep, *sb.pl.* sheep, 22/13, 22. Cf. **shep.**

sere, *adj.* several, various, different, 7, 239, 252, 253, etc.

serly, *adv.* separately, by herself, 1201.

sertane, *adj.* certain, 1003. Cf. **sartayn, certan.**

seruand, *sb.* servant, 1507, 2314. **-e,** 43/6. **-es,** *pl.* 423, 1663, 1979. **-is,** 1/17, 43/7. **seruaundes,** 1151. Cf. **saruandes.**

serue, *vb.* serve, 3/2, 5/27, 253, 411, etc. deserve, 1470. *pl.* 26/11, 14, 27/21. **serued,** *pp.* 26/27. **serues,** *pl.* 287, 415, 902, 1152, 1443, etc. *imp. pl.* 1157. **seruis,** *sg.* 24/6. *pl.* 26/31. **seruyd,** *pp.* 1513, 1586, 1975. **seryf,** *inf.* 1/8. Cf. **sarue.**

serues, *sb.* service, 1137, 1218, 1222, 1493, etc. **seruese,** 1521. **seruice** (concrete), 1796. **seruis,** 2444. **seruise,** 4/2, 9/29, 11/24, 12/37, etc. **seruys,** 1474, 1514, 1575, etc. (concrete) 1584. **seruyse,** 877, 1554, 1557, 1762, etc. (concrete) 1253. Cf. **saruyse.**

ses, *vb. sg.* sees(t), 5/35, 10/24, 11/38, etc. **sese,** 43/35, 429, 830, etc. Cf. **se.**

sese, *vb.* cease, 1228, 1812. *imp.* 1824. **sesis,** *pl.* tr. stop, 562.

seson, *sb.* season; time, occasion, 1899. (diet or life according to season), 1717. **-ons,** *pl.* 1702. **-oun,** *sg.* 2508. **-oune,** 1945.

set, *vb.* set; arrange, regulate, fix; appoint; intr. settle or place oneself; sit down, 20/5, 32/14, 459, 481, 607, 1730, 1741, 2475. *pl.* 1679. *pp.* 8/2, 15/26, 866, 965, etc. **set litil be,** think little of, 1017. Cf. **sett.**

sete, *sb.* seat, 1791. sitting, 32/23.

sethin, *adv.* afterwards, 245. Cf. **sithen.**

setirday, *sb.* Saturday, 26/8.

sett, *vb.* = **set,** 43/8, 2318. *pl.* intr. 317. *pp.* 29/18, 5, 252, 1895. **-e,** *sbj.* 37/17. **-es,** *pl.* 151.

seuent, *num.* seventh, 1025. **seuind,** 14/6.

seuin, *num.* seven, 17/30, 31, 18/1.

seuintende. See **hundred.**

sex, *num.* six, 143/2, 2111. **sexe,** 16/3, 12, 24, 28, etc.

sext, *num.* sixth, 1009, 1704, 1842. **-e,** 13/36.

sextid þe secunde, *num.* the 62nd, 17/13.

shal, *vb. sg.* shall, 23/18, 30/16. Cf. **sal, schall.**

shame, *sb.* 30/14, 41/1, 2508. Cf. **scham.**

shamyd, *pp.* shamed, 2358. Cf. **schamis.**

shep, *sb.* sheep, 23/10. *pl.* 13/11. Cf. **schep, sep.**

sho, *pron.* she, 7/33, 8/2, 4, 21/2, etc. Cf. **scho, so.**

shod, *pp.* 2/23.

sibredin, *sb.* relationship, 45/23.

? **sich,** *adj.* such, corresponding, 2008. Cf. Notes and **suik.**

side, *sb.* 143/26, 144/18, 146/36, 2157. **sides,** *pl.* 809, 811, 1512. Cf. **syde.**

sience, *sb.* knowledge, 39/32.

sight, *sb.* 404, 618, 785, 866, etc. **in s-t,** evidently, 2337. Cf. **siht.**

signes, *sb. pl.* signs, 1694. Cf. **singne.**

signet, *sb.* 2148.

signifi, *vb.* signify, 809. Cf. **singnefiis.**

siht, *sb.* sight, 19/17, 42/24, 45/4. Cf. **sight.**

sikir, *adj.* sure, 20/6, 24/33. Cf. **sekir.**

sikirnes, *sb.* surety, 47/12.

silde, *vb.* shield, protect, 21/31. Cf. **schilde.**

silence, *sb.* 10/29, 14/26, 1846, etc.

siluer, *sb.* silver, 956, 2196. **siluir,** 13/14, 142/10, 14.

simpelie, *adv.* simply, 39/19. **-like,** 34/33, 40/28.

simpil, *adj.* artless, 33/10.

simplis, *sb. pl.* simple or artless persons, 5/28.
sin, *sb.* 167, 450, 609, etc. *vb. pl.* 437. **sines**, *sb. pl.* 993, 997, 999. Cf. **sinne, syn.**
sine, *adv.* afterwards, then, 1340, 1706, 1795, 1815, etc. Cf. **sen, sithen, syen.**
sinful, *adj.* (*sb.*) 207, 1100, 1297. **-full**, 3/22. Cf. **synful.**
sing, *vb.* 143/24, 144/20, 677, 1142, etc. 1 *sg.* 19/17. *pl.* 19/19, 20. **-e**, 5/7, 19/15, 27/30, 32/17, etc. **-is**, *sg.* 143/12. Cf. **syng** and **songen, sung.**
singne, *sb.* sign, 38/29. **sinis**, *pl.* 27/24. Cf. **signes, syngne.**
singnefiis, *vb. sg.* signifies, 5/6. Cf. **signifi.**
sinne, *vb.* sin, 12/10. *sb.* 1/21, 2/32, 35, 3/18, etc. **sinnes**, *pl.* 9/9, 13/34, 15/15, etc. **sinnis**, 6/7, 13/27, 19/2, etc. **sins**, 562. Cf. **sin.**
sister, *sb.* 44/17, 147/20, 2373, etc. *gen.* 402. *pl.* 2383. **-s**, *pl.* 43/1, 412, 420, 1326, etc. **sistir**, 13/26, 21/33, 35/9, etc. **-s**, *pl.* 2/15, 13/25, 37, 14/6, etc. **sisturs**, 30/33.
sit, *vb.* 1090, 1251, 1731, 1795, etc. *pl.* 1763. **sitande**, *ppr.* 16/25. befitting, suiting, 15/3. **site**, 16/5, 29/24, 31/13, 33/11. Cf. **sitte.**
siþe, *sb. pl.* times, 17/30, 44/8. Cf. **syþe.**
sithen, *adv.* afterwards, then, 1695, 2095, 2445. **siþin**, 3/18, 12/25, 14/10, 15/26, etc. Cf. **sethin, sine, sythen.**
sitte, *vb.* sit. 33/21, 22, 35/16, 41/31. Cf. **sit.**
sizing, *sb.* sighing, 9/7.
skil, *sb.* reason, 851. **skill**, 845. Cf. **skyll.**
skilwis, *adj.* reasonable, 1435, 1494.
sklaunders, *sb. pl.* scandals, 43/10. Cf. **sclandir.**
skoles, *sb. pl.* schools, 234. Cf. **scole.**
skyll, *sb.* reason, 51. Cf. **skil.**
sla, *vb.* slay, 8/15. Cf. **slay.**
slake, *vb.* make loose, relax, 2343.
slapande, *pp.* sleeping, 11/15. **slape**, *inf.* 20/17, 30/15, 38/5. Cf. **slepe.**
slau, *adj.* slow, 8/32. **slaw**, 604, 1427.
slay, *vb.* 567. **slayn**, *pp.* 942, 1382. Cf. **sla.**
slepe, *sb.* sleep, 34/5, 62. *vb.* 8/31, 1780, 1845. **slepis**, *pl.* 142/20. Cf. **slapande.**
slewth, *sb.* sloth, 1/6.
sleze, *adj.* skilful, 23/2.
slik, *adj.* such, 669, 678, 1606, 1611, etc. **-e**, 407, 857, 1710, etc. *pron.* 1575. Cf. **suik.**
smal, *adj.* (*sb.*) small, 20/24. **small**, 518, 560, 1943, 2379.
smerte, *adj.* smart, 22/34, 23/24, 25/31, 29/34, etc.
smite, *vb. imp.* beat, 6/22. **smitis**, *sg.* or *pl.* rap(s), knock(s), 44/22.
snare, *sb.* 957.
so, *pron.* she, 22/18, 23/10, 24/28, 33, 25/16, 26, 26/16, 19, 36. Cf. 1468 (see Notes) and **sho.**
so, *adv.* 49, 255, 272, 1280, 1632, 2281, 2452, etc. *rel.* see **whar,** etc. (p. 213). **so þat,** so that, that, 16, 45, 64, 108, 379, etc. Cf. **sa.**
sober, *adj.* 2267, 2271. **sobir,** 42/18. **sobur,** 23/29.
soberly, *adv.* 547.
soffer, *vb.* suffer, 2036. Cf. **souerand, suffer.**
sofferayne, *sb.* = **souerain,** 1344.
soft, *adj.* 1295, 1356. **softe,** 713.
softelie, *adv.* softly, 45/13. **softli,** 2418. **softly,** 1603, 1610, 1694.
sogetes, *sb. pl.* subjects, 346. **soietes,** 350, 759. Cf. **sugetes.**
solemply, *adv.* solemnly, 144/11.
somer, *sb.* summer, 1707, 2014. Cf. **sumir.**
son, *sb.* 1/2. Cf. **sons, sun.**
son, *adv.* soon; at once, 932, 1543, 1743, etc. **sone,** 6/16, 58, 689, 1378, 1764, etc. **sone when þat,** at once when, as soon as, 443, 1685. Cf. **sune.**
songen, *pp.* sung, 16/31. Cf. **sing.**
sons, *sb. pl.* 1/12, 15. Cf. **son.**
sop, *sb.* 1508.
sopper, *sb.* supper, 1582. **-e,** 1730. Cf. **super.**
sore, *adj.* wounded, 1287. *adv.* sorely, intensely, 1810.
sorow, *sb.* sorrow, 609, 1185. **-and,** *ppr.* grieving, 1096.

soth, *sb.* sooth. **for soth,** 1/13, 43/7. Cf. **suth.**

sothfastnes, *sb.* truthfulness, 2/33. Cf. **suthfastnes.**

sothly, *adv.* truly, 43/9. Cf. **suthli.**

souerain, *sb.* superior, prioress, 1689. **-ains,** *pl.* 720. **-ane,** 350. **-ans,** *gen.* 1586. *pl.* 509. **-anse,** *pl.* 341. **-ayn,** 31, 426, 557, 632, etc. *gen.* 701, 703, 1458, 1620, 1990. **-ayne,** 908, 910, 1394, 1543, etc. Cf. **sofferayne, souerayns, sufferaine.**

souerand, *ppr.* suffering, 938, 940. Cf. **soffer.**

soueraynly, *adv.* as behoves a superior, 1928.

souerayns, *sb. gen.* superior's, 920. *pl.* 918, 966. Cf. **souerain.**

soume, *sb.* sum, 2192.

soup, *vb.* sup, 1729. **-e,** 1706. Cf. **supe.**

spac, *vb. pt.* spoke, 11/7. Cf. **spek.**

space, *sb.* 15/26, 143/2, 1740, 2095.

spaird, *pp.* spared, 1060. **sparde,** 418, 1498, 2252. **spare,** *inf., sbj.* 409, 455. **spayr,** *imp.* 107.

speche, *sb.* speech, talk, 2/32, 5/13, 11/36, 14/25, 1060, etc.

specially, *adv.* 42.

spede, *sb.* speed, 1689. *vb.* tr. advance, help forward; despatch, manage, 42, 1082, 1524. intr. get on, succeed, 127. refl. hasten, be quick, 623. *pp.* 2252. **spedand,** *ppr.* helpful, 142/3.

spedily, *adv.* speedily, 1/3.

spek, *vb.* speak, 762. 1053, 1061, 1748, etc. 1 *sg.* 312. *imp.* 106. **-e,** 2/11, 4/32, 33, 606, etc. *pl.* 14/26, 37, 1077. Cf. **spac, spekis.**

spekers, *sb. pl.* talkers, 1057.

speking, *sb.* speaking, talk, 1055, 1757. **spekyng,** 751, 760, 767.

spekis, *vb. sg.* speaks, 5/25, 8/11, 9/25, etc. **speks,** 1264. **spekys,** 12/35, 13/1, 20/1, etc. Cf. **spek.**

spend, *vb.* intr. make expenditure, 1661. tr. manage, perform, 2261. *pp.* spent, 1432. **-e,** *pp.* 789.

sperance, *sb.* hope, 39/18.

spille, *vb.* spoil, ruin, 23/11.

spirit, *sb.* 34/12. **spirt,** 2/4, 8. **spirte,** 38/7. Cf. **sprete.**

spiritel, *adj.* spiritual, 34/6, 9. **spiritual,** 142/4.

spouse, *sb.* 142/16.

sprete, *sb.* spirit, 43/11. **sprite,** 34/4. Cf. **spirit.**

stabelike, *adv.* steadily, 32/19.

stabelis, *vb. sg.* establishes, fixes, arranges, 28/21. **stabilist,** *pp.* 27/14. Cf. **stablis.**

stabil, *adj.* stable, 14/38, 16/11, 721, 2227, etc. **stabill,** 142/1.

stabilnes, *sb.* stability, 38/10, 24, 40/16, 147/21. **make s-s,** settle down, 40/32.

stablis, *vb.* establish, fix, arrange, appoint, 4/2, 3. *sg.* 16/31, 41/13. **-t,** *pp.* 34/19, 41/16, 18, 44/25, etc. Cf. **stabelis.**

staf, *sb.* stick, 1358.

staite, *sb.* estate, condition, 146, 334, 2214. Cf. **state.**

stale, *sg.* stall, 149/37. **stall,** 144/24. **stalle,** 30/10, 12, 20. **stalles,** *pl.* 149/33. **stallis,** 143/20, 144/4, 10. Cf. **stayle.**

stalworth, *adj.* 276.

stan, *sb.* stone, rock, 3/15. **-e,** 3/16. Cf. **ston.**

stand, *vb.* 144/6, 8, 186, 276, etc. **-and,** *ppr.* 143/13, 144/4, 10, 147/30. **-ande,** 16/7. **-ant,** 143/20. **-e,** *inf.* 16/27, 17/1, etc. **-es,** *sg.* 31/17. *pl.* 147, 1781. **-is,** *sg.* 142/15, 143/2. *pl.* 142/1. Cf. **stode.**

state, *sb.* 1397. Cf. **staite.**

stayle, *sb.* stall; stand, 145/8, 146. Cf. **stale.**

sted, *pp.* placed, living, 2005.

stede, *sb.* stead, place, 3/11, 40/3 (rank), 41/28, 146, 150, etc. **stedes,** *pl.* 1828, 2005. **stedis,** 9/3, 19/11, 41/4, 34, etc.

stedfast, *adj.* steadfast, 19/32.

stegh, *sb.* ladder, 798, 801, 805, 807. Cf. **stize.**

steles, *sb. pl.* rounds, rungs, 812. **stelis,** 11/22.

steuen, *sb.* voice, 129, 137.

steyl, *vb.* steal, 569.

stifli, *adv.* stiffly, firmly, 186. **stifly,** 142/21.

stil, *adj., adv.* still; quiet, silent; quietly, silently, 763, 888, 1071, 1396, 1545, 1675, 2178, etc. **still,**

107, 563, 646. *vb. imp.* still, check, 105. **stille,** *adj.* 4/31.
stize, *sb.* ladder, 11/14, 18, 21. Cf. **stegh.**
stode, *vb. pt.* stood, 19/12, 18. Cf. **stand.**
stodying, *sb.* studying, 1828.
stole, *sb.* stool, 145/7.
ston, *sb.* stone, rock, 184. **-e,** 188, 189. Cf. **stan.**
stra, *sb.* straw, 5/35.
straite, *adj.* narrow; strict, 10/10, 710. **straiter,** *adv. comp.* more strictly, 6/14. Cf. **strate.**
strakes, *sb. pl.* strokes, 1358.
strang, *adj.* strong, 1/8, 22/19, 43/2, 568, 1607.
strate, *adj.* narrow; strict, 10/9, 141/27. Cf. **straite.**
strateness, *sb.* strictness, 142/33.
strengh, *vb.* strengthen, 2346.
stresce, *sb.* constraint, restraint, forcible control, 4/4. Cf. Notes.
strif, *sb.* strife, 650, 1366, 2463. **-e,** 2485. **-is,** *pl.* 43/22. **withoutin strife,** indisputably, 805. Cf. **stryf.**
striue, *vb.* strive, 7/32, 8/29, 22/15.
stroy, *vb.* destroy, spoil, 146.
stryf, *sb.* strife, 102. Cf. **strif.**
studie, *vb.* 33/2, 18, 20, 38/5, etc.
sturbe, *vb.* disturb, 34/33.
sua, *adv.* so, 2/16, 23, 3/2, 4/12, etc. *rel.* see **whar, whilk.** Cf. **sa, swa.**
subpriores, *sb.* subprioress, 1362, 1377, 149/33, 38, etc.
sucoure, *vb.* succour, help, 652.
suere, *vb.* swear, 39/9. Cf. **swer.**
suete, *adj.* sweet, 2/15, 4/10, 11/29. **sueter,** *comp.* 2/16. Cf. **swete.**
suetnes, *sb.* sweetness, bliss, 4/8. Cf. **swetnes.**
suffer, *vb.* 150, 238, 598, 950, 2408, etc. *pl.* 941, 943, 947. Cf. **soffer, sufferd.**
sufferaine, *sb.* superior, prioress, 262. **-ane,** 542. **-ayne,** 284. Cf. **souerain, suuerainis.**
sufferance, *sb.* long-suffering, patience, 202, 205. **-ans,** 3/20, 1655. permission, 142/15. Cf. **suffrance.**
sufferd, *vb. pt.* suffered, 2480. **suffers,** *sg.* 1274. *pl.* 924. **suffir,** *inf.* 8/30, 25/3, 37/25, 38/2, etc. bear with, 26/32. *pl.* 13/12. Cf. **suffer.**
suffes, *vb.* suffice, 1571. *sg.* 1824. **sufficis,** *sg. or pl.* 2012. **suffise,** *inf.* 1577, 2032.
suffrance, *sb.* patience, 38/9. Cf. **sufferance.**
sugetes, *sb. pl.* subjects, 389. Cf. **sogetes.**
suiftlike, *adv.* swiftly, quickly, 9/32.
suik, *adj.* such, 31/32 (perhaps a slip). **suilk,** 38/5, 42/2. *pron.* such a one, 42/9. **suilke,** *adj.* 5/29, 8/7, 19/33, 20/34, etc. "the same," *22/1. *pron. neut.* 21/30, 33/3. Cf. **sich, slik, swilk.**
suiþe, *adv.* much, quickly, 3/33.
suld, *vb. pt. and pt.-pr.* should; ought to, 57, 63, 76, 87, etc. **-e,** 5/20, 13/15, 16, 33/29, etc. Cf. **sal.**
sum, *rel.* See under **whar, what.**
sum, *pron.* some, 43/11, 255, 300, 473, etc. *adj.* 1253, etc. **summe,** *pron.* 5/20, 6/30, 20/20, etc. **al and sum,** all and every one, 1218. **sum tym,** sometimes, 752. **sum tyme,** 745. Cf. **sumþing.**
sumir, *sb.* summer, 17/5. **summir,** 29/7. Cf. **somer.**
sumþing, *pron.* something, 33/36. Cf. 33/22, 34/2.
sun, *sb.* son, 462. **sune,** 2/9, 27, 6/13, 22, etc. Cf. **son, sunis.**
sundais, *sb. pl.* Sundays, 17/4, 18, 33/18. **-day,** *sg.* 17/25, 27/16, 17. Cf. **sunendais, sunnday.**
sune, *sb.* sun, 9/15.
sune, *adv.* soon, at once. **sune when,** at once when, as soon as, 1309. Cf. **son.**
sunendais = sundais, 16/23.
sung, *pp.* 18/18. **-en,** 16/12, 18/15, 31/6, 33/2. Cf. **sing.**
sunis, *sb. pl.* sons, 15/20. **suns,** 81. Cf. **sun.**
sunnday, *sb.* Sunday, 1681. Cf. **sundais.**
supe, *vb.* sup, 28/7. Cf. **soup.**
super, *sb.* supper, 28/8. **-e,** 29/24. Cf. **sopper.**
supplant, *vb.* 1381.
surfait, *sb.* excess, extravagance, 26/31, 28/11, 40/28.

surfaitus, *adj.* excessive, extravagant, 40/34.
suspecius, *adj.* suspicious, 2292.
suspend, *pp.* suspended, 1249, 1258.
suth, *sb.* truth, 1548. *adj.* true, 781. Cf. **soth.**
suthfast, *adj.* truthful, 6.
suthfastnes, *sb.* truthfulness, 142. Cf. **sothfastnes.**
suthli, *adv.* truly, 708. **suthly,** 1647. Cf. **sothly.**
suuerainis, *sb. pl.* superiors, 47/9. Cf. **sufferaine.**
swa, *adv.* so, thus; then, 7/13, 149/35, 36. Cf. **sua.**
swer, *vb.* swear, 574, 593. Cf. **suere.**
swete, *vb.* sweat, 1709.
swete, *adj.* sweet, 1117. **swetest,** *sup.* 246. Cf. **suete.**
swetelike, *adv.* sweetly, 40/35.
swetnes, *sb.* sweetness, 245. Cf. **suetnes.**
swift, *adj.* quick, 987.
swilk, *adj.* such, 205, 231, 334, 514, etc. **swylke,** 43/1. Cf. **suik.**
swink, *vb.* toil, 1709.
syde, *sb.* side, 144/18. Cf. **side.**
syen, *adv.* then, further, 565. **syne,** afterwards, 10/28, 144/18, 282, 1251. Cf. **sine.**
syn, *sb.* sin, 58, 63, 140, 444, etc. Cf. **sin, synne.**
synful, *adj.* (*sb.*) sinful, 396, 1290, 1296, 1333. Cf. **sinful.**
synfully, *adv.* sinfully, 2505.
syng, *vb.* sing, 1127, 1165, 1561, 148/16, etc. *pl.* 16/24. Cf. **sing.**
synging, *sb.* singing, 1162.
syngne, *sb.* sign, 289. Cf. **singne.**
synne, *sb.* sin, 10/32, 22/29. **synnys,** *pl.* 15/10. **syns,** 1257, 2284. Cf. **syn.**
syþe, *sb. pl.* times, 17/31, 18/1. Cf. **siþe.**
sythen, *adv.* afterwards, then, 146/31. **syþin,** 16/3, 18/22, 33/7. Cf. **sithen.**

ta, *pron.* those, 15/30, 21/27, 23/21, 30/13, etc. Cf. **þa.**
ta, for **te** or **t',** *def. art.* in **ta apostil,** the apostle, 24/5. Cf. **ta-postil, þa.**
ta (after the def. art.), one, 143/26. Cf. **a, tane.**
ta, *vb.* take, 22/3, 24/31, 26/11, 27/15, etc. *pl.* 36/25. Cf. **tak** and **tan, tayn, ton.**
tabbes = **te abbes,** 24/13, 17, 25/10, 19, etc. **tabbesse,** 17/2, 20/4, 18, 24/30, etc.
tabels, *sb. pl.* tablets, 1623. Cf. **tabils.**
tabernakil, *sb.* tabernacle, 2/28, 3/2. **-ill,** 3/23.
tabes = **te abes,** 21/30, 43/32.
tabils = **tabels,** 25/8.
tai, *pron.* they, 37/23. Cf. **þa.**
taile, *sb.* tale, speech, 1606. Cf. **tale.**
taim, *pron.* them; those, 20/4, 5, 25/12, 33/10, etc. Cf. **þam.**
tair, *adj.* their, 25/10. **-e,** 26/9, 32, 27/10, 34/18, etc. Cf. **þair.**
tak, *vb.* take, 38, 77, 1419, etc. *pl.* 61, 619. *imp.* 23, 35. *imp. pl.* 71. **-and,** *ppr.* 2223. **-e,** 7/15, 20, 8/7, 2305, etc. *pl.* 335, 597, etc. *imp.* 1/3, 1523. **-es,** *sg.* 179, 374, 417, 467, etc. *pl.* 281, 334, 822, 1495. **-is,** *sg.* 1/7, 6/3, 142/21. *pl.* 43/13, 141/17. **-in,** *pp.* 2286. **-yn,** 1434. Cf. **ta** and **toke, tuke.**
takyn, *sb.* token, 290.
tald, *pp.* told, 764, 1107, 2040, 2110. Cf. **tel.**
tale, *sb.* tale, speech, 35. **tales,** *pl.* 1735. Cf. **taile.**
tam, *pron.* them, 13/33, 26/30, 31, etc. refl. 25/14. Cf. **þam.**
tan, *pp.* taken; caught, 6/4, 29/33. **tane,** 10/22, 22/32, 40/11, 142/26. Cf. **ta.**
tane (after the def. art.), one, 28/3. Cf. **ane, ta, ton.**
tanne, *adv.* then, 14/11, 39/8. Cf. **þanne.**
ta-postil = **te apostil,** 12/37, 37/33. **-s,** *pl.* 25/20, 32/35. Cf. **ta, þa-postil.**
tar, *adj.* their, 4/22. Cf. **þair.**
tarat, *adv.* thereat, 30/23.
tare, *adv.* there, 15/29, 21/1, *23/19, 30/1, etc. Cf. **þar.**
tare-eftir, *adv.* thereafter, 16/30. **-eftyr,** 16/3. Cf. **þareftir.**
tareyng, *sb.* tarrying, delay, 1216.
tary, *vb.* tarry, 723. Cf. **tery.**
tast, *vb.* taste, 1265, 1603, 1610, 1677.

tat, *dem. adj.* that, 42/8. *rel. pron.* what, 24/18. *conj.* that, 11/32, 15/11, 26/36. Cf. **þat.**
tay, *pron.* they, 3/22, 6/6, 7/32, 12/13, etc. such (.. as), 20/2. **taym,** them, 20/18. Cf. **þa, þam.**
tayn, *pp.* taken, 360, 2062, 2131, 2258, etc. **-e,** 90. Cf. **ta.**
te, *def. art.* the, 3/1, 15, 24, 7/28, 9/1, 26, etc. Cf. **þe.**
tech, *vb.* teach, 343, 378, 388, 406, etc. 3 *sg.* 1284. *pl.* 642. Cf. **teches.**
techers, *sb. pl.* teachers, 694.
teches, *vb. sg.* teaches, 120, 395, 636, 638, etc. **techis,** 191, 719, 970. Cf. **tech.**
teching, *sb.* teaching, 349, 400, 2483, 2496, etc. **techyng,** 347, 363, 397. **-es,** *pl.* 24.
tel, *vb.* tell, 315, 671, 880, 989. 1 *sg.* 1921. **teles,** *sg.* 1163. **tell,** 104, 363, 449, 2397. **telland,** *ppr.* 2341. **telle,** 9/21, 30/7, 45/5. **telles,** *sg.* 5/32, 15/13, 684, 736. *pl.* 285. **tellis,** *sg.* 2/24, 19/9. **tels,** 30, 178, 452, 694, etc. *pl.* 307, 801. Cf. **tald, told.**
telfete, *num.* = **twelft,** 15/5.
temper (-ir), *vb.* 42/32, 37.
tempil, *sb.* temple, 35/25.
temprance, *sb.* temperature, 36/20.
ten, *num.* 20/20.—**tende,** *num.* tenth, 14/29. **tent,** 1869.
tene, *sb.* injury, harm, 2399. **tenes,** *pl.* 978.
tent, *sb.* attention, heed, care, 23, 35, 671, 1449, etc. *vb.* be attentive, attend (to), 919, 2351. **-es,** *sg.* 1877.
teris, *sb. pl.* tears, 9/7, 33/34, 34/34. **terys,** 19/29.
tery, *vb.* tarry, 445. Cf. **tary.**
testament, *sb.* 16/9, 19, 42/17, 47/15, etc.

þa, *pron.* those, 3/5, 4/16, 23, 5/1, etc. **tha,** *adj.* 43/14. Cf. **day, ta, tai, tay, þai, þay, þo.**
þa, for **þe** or **þ',** *def. art.* in **þa apocalips,** the Apocalypse, 17/14, **þa apostils,** the apostles, 37/19, 20. Cf. **ta, þa-postil, to.**
þabbasse = þe abbasse, the abbess, 16/4. **þabbes,** 16/34, 36, 20/5, 21/35, etc. *gen.* 36/10. **þabbesse,** 8/1, 21/21, 22/20, etc. *gen.* 35/27. **þabes,** 7/20, 29, 30/20, 31/11, etc.
þabot = þe abot, 5/35, 6/26, 7/9.
þai, *pron.* they, those, 2/31, 4/11, 187, 212, 924, etc. **þaim,** them, 4/24, 33, 216, 2228, etc. **þaime,** refl. 271. Cf. **þa, þam.**
þaimselfe, *pron.* themselves, 13/37, 39/13. Cf. **thameselfe.**
þair, *adv.* there, 299, 307, 958, 1533, etc. Cf. **þar.**
þair, *adj.* their, 4/30, 3, 151, etc. **-e,** 2/35, 4/27, 5/21, 6/18, etc. of them, 20/26. Cf. **tair, tar, þar, þare, thayre, þeir, þer.**
þairbi, *adv.* thereof, 413. Cf. **þarby.**
þairefor, *adv.* therefore, 240. **þairfor,** 199, 312, 454, 475, etc. Cf. **þarfor.**
þairto, *adv.* thereto, 187, 558. Cf. **þarto.**
þalde = þe alde, 16/9, 19, 20/27, 28/15, etc.
þam, *pron.* them, 4/18, 20, 107, etc. refl. 1222, 1884, etc. **tham,** 2351. **þame,** 26/12, 38/23. **thame,** 43/26. refl. 43/13. Cf. **taim, tam, taym, þai(m), þay(m).**
thameselfe, *pron.* themselves, 43/12, 28. **þamself,** 4/28, 405, 2343, 2466, etc. **-e,** 21/26, 33/13. Cf. **þaimselfe.**
þan, *adv.* then, 2/13, 3/25, 9/33, 10/1, etc. *conj.* when, 2/30, 3/30, 7/12, 11/18, etc. than, 2/16, 4/32, 288, 636, etc. Cf. **þanne, þen.**
þanane, *adv.* for this reason, 4/21.
þanc, *sb.* thanks, 24/28. *vb.* thank, *40/31.
þanne, *adv.* then, 3/33, 5/22, 9/22, 15/24, etc. Cf. **tanne, þan.**
þa-postil = þe apostil, 22/10. **-s,** *pl.* 16/13. Cf. **ta-postil, þa.**
þar, *adj.* their, 4/21, 6/32, 14, 19, etc. Cf. **þair.**
þar, *vb. sg.* "needest," 6/32. Cf. **þarf.**
þar, *adv.* there, 28/10, 142/4. *rel.* where, 31/13. **þar es,** where, 8/3. Cf. **tare, þair, þare, þer.**
þarabowte, *adv.* about it, 39/8.
þaragain, *adv.* against it, 46/23.
þarby, *adv.* thereby, 11, 447. Cf. **þairbi, þerbi.**

þare, *adj.* their, 4/20, 6/7, 146, 151, etc. Cf. **þair.**

þare, *adv.* there, 3/26, 4/1, 5/34, 11/17, etc. *rel.* where, 2/25, 11/16. Cf. **þar.**

þarefor, *adv.* therefore, 170. Cf. **þarfor.**

þareftir, *adv.* thereafter, 21/11. Cf. **tare-eftir.**

þareof, *adv.* thereof, 14/23. Cf. **þarof.**

þarf, *vb.sg.* is needed, 29/16. Cf. **þar.**

þarfor, *adv.* therefore, 29, 57, 460, etc. **þarfore,** 13/4, 699, 1005. **tharfore,** 1/6. Cf. **þairefor, þarefor, þerfor.**

þarfra, *adv.* therefrom, 5/23.

þarinne, *adv.* therein, 21/6. Cf. **þerin.**

þaris, *pron.* theirs, 33/9.

þarne, *vb.* go without, 30/26.

þarof, *adv.* thereof, etc., 8/24, 10/24, 28/26, 37/30, etc. **-offe,** 34/9. Cf. **þareof, þerof.**

þarogain, *adv.* against it, 9/10.

þaron, *adv.* thereon, 37/17, 1032.

þarto, *adv.* thereto, 3/25, 7/24, 7, 17, etc. Cf. **þairto, þerto.**

þarþurz, *adv.* through that, 23/25.

þas, *dem. adj. pl.* these, those, 147/32. Cf. **þos.**

þat, *dem. adj.* that, 2/10, 148/18, 51, 99, etc. *dem. pron.* 1/21, 63, 89, etc. *rel. pron.* that, which, who, 1/7, 10, 2/31, 1, 7, 1892, etc. what, 141, 221, 223, 505, etc. he (she, those, ye) who, 2/4,32, 4/11, 6/12, 10/20, 36/12, etc. one whom, 42/3. *conj.* that, 1/4, 9, 190, 2296, 2472, etc.; cf. **so.** in case that, if, 38/25. after words expressive of time: that, when, 150/4, etc.; cf. **time, whilis.** pleonastic, 47, 120; after rel., see under **wha, whareþurz, who**; after adv. and conj., see under **bicaus, efter, how, if, or, wen, whan, why. that,** *conj.* 43/4. Cf. **tat.**

þaue, for **þai haue,** 446.

þauter = **þe auter,** 24/11, 26/18, 20, 27/17, etc.

þay, *pron.* they, those, 20/35, 5, 8, 11, etc. **thay,** 43/3, 26, 2003. **þaym,** them, 294. **thayme,** 43/28. Cf. **þa, þam.**

thayre, *adj.* their, 43/12, 25. Cf. **þair.**

þe, *def. art.* the, 1/2, 3, etc. **the,** 16/8, 46/27, 1597, etc. (for **þi,** 19/34; cf. 1968). Cf. **te, þa, to.**

þe, *instr. case of* **þat,** before comp.: the, 6/14, 7/13, 1154, 1397, etc.

þe, *pron.* thee, 2/7, 27, 30, 42, etc. refl. 2/12, 5/34. **the,** 1/7.

þeder, *adv.* thither, 2166. **þedir,** 1813. Cf. **þidir.**

þeir, *adj.* their, 262, 908, 918, 1620, etc. Cf. **þair.**

þeir, *adj.* these, 146/22. **þeis,** 142/23. Cf. **þer, þes.**

þelder = **þe elder,** 41/32, 46/14.

þen, *adv.* then, 145/13, 875, 1029, 1035, 1575, etc. *conj.* than, 2334. Cf. **þan.**

þending = **þe ending,** 14/20.

þeneke (for **þencke**?), *vb.* think, 15/10. Cf. **þincke.**

þentendement = **þe e-t,** 9/17.

þenticement = **þe e-t,** 35/11.

þenuius = **þe enuius,** 37/2.

þer, *adv.* there, 4/5, 43/11, 1152, 2133, etc. Cf. **þar.**

þer, *adj.* these, 657, 681, 696, 2150, etc. Cf. **þeir, þir, ȝer.**

þer, *adj.* their, 144/5, 509, 531, 538, 1139, etc. **þere,** 1936. Cf. **þair.**

þerbi, *adv.* thereby, thereof, 1080, 1264. **-by,** 864, 946, 1924, 2061, etc. Cf. **þarby.**

þerfor, *adv.* therefore, 163, 730, 791, 869, etc. **therfore,** 42/36. Cf. **þarfor.**

þerin, *adv.* therein, 945, 1916, 2126, 2489. Cf. **þarin.**

þerof, *adv.* thereof, etc., 32/18, 45/24, 46/1, 1549, 1641. Cf. **þarof.**

þertil, *adv.* thereto, 798, 2073, 2514. **-till,** 136, 711.

þerto, do., 40/7, 928, 1822, 2148, etc. Cf. **þarto.**

þerþe = **þe erþe,** 15/10, 46/16.

þerwith, *adv.* therewith, 2103.

þes, *adj.* these, 18/1, 150/3. Cf. **þeis, þis.**

thews, *sb. pl.* manners, 1425.

þi, *adj.* thy, 2/11, 28, 3/2. *19/34, 24, 26, 30, etc. Cf. **þin, ti, thy.**

þi, *instr. case of* **þat. for þi,** therefore, 3/15, 17, 10/1, 26, etc. Cf. **ty,** also **na-for-þi.**

þidir, *adv.* thither, 2/*27, 31. Cf. **þeder.**

þifte, *sb.* theft, 8/16, 36/31.

þin, *adj.* thy, 5/35, 8/18, 11/26, 15/1, 403, etc. Cf. **þi, þine.**

þinc, *vb. pl.* seem, 13/2. Cf. **think.**

þincke, *vb.* think, 24/5, 20. Cf. **þeneke, think.**

þine, *adj.* thy, 2/22, 14/13, 142/5, 25, 34. Cf. **þin, tine.**

þing, *sb. sg. and pl.* thing(s), 2/33, 4/3, 5/11, 7/6, 25/21, etc. a thing, anything, 39/10, 45/10. **thing**, 1/10, 24/4, 27/23, etc. **þinge**, 37/16, **þinges**, *pl.* 28/36, 38/9, 1749. **thinges**, 787, 830, 1099, etc. **þingis**, 13/2, 38, 24/13, 32, etc. **thingis**, 43/1, 4, 8. Cf. **thyng.**

think, *vb. sg.* seems, appears, 294, 296, 2510. *pl.* 853. **þinke**, *sg.* appears suitable, pleases, 36/11. Cf. **þinc, thynk.**

think, *vb.* think, 19/13, 608, 618, 842, etc. **-and**, *ppr.* 1371, 2278, 2345. **þinke**, 6/26, 9/2, 13/39, 15/12, etc. **thinke**, 821. *imp.* 1 *pl.* 863. **þinkes**, *sg.* 1903. *imp. pl.* 14/31. **thinkis**, *pl.* 43/12. Cf. **þincke, thynk.**

þir, *adj.* these, 9/23, 15/20, 858, 893, etc. **þire**, 15/18. Cf. **þer.**

third, *num.* 905, 1349, 1582, 1840, etc. **þirdde**, 20/9. Cf. **thrid.**

thirld, *pp.* thrilled, 1194.

þis, *adj.* this, 1/20, 2/20, 5, 21, etc. *pl.* these, 26/6, 742. *pron.* 146/33. **this**, *adj.* 25/29. *pron.* 141/1. **þise**, *adj. pl.* 47/7. Cf. **tis, þes.**

þiself, *pron.* thyself, 396. Cf. **tiself.**

þo, *adj. pl.* those, 130, 391, 500, etc. *pron.* 256, 585, etc. Cf. **þa.**

þoght, *sb.* thought, 11/38, 14/32. **thoght**, 143, 481, 607, etc. **-es**, *pl.* 619, 839. **-is**, *pl.* 43/20. **þoht**, 2/34, 3/1, 5/15, etc. **-es**, *pl.* 11/35, 12/2, 4, etc. **-is**, *pl.* 9/4.

þordir = **þe ordir**, 21/34, 37/32, 38/11, 39/24, etc.

thoro, *prep.* through, 1/16, 43/22. Cf. **þur.**

þos, *adj. pl.* these, those, 1712. Cf. **þas.**

þoþir = **þe oþir**, the other thing, 39/18. the others, 22/25, 41/11.

þou, *pron.* thou, 10/25, 29, 32, 43, etc. **þow**, 755. Cf. **þu.**

þoz, þoȝ, *conj.* although, 10/4, 22, 15/8, 41/14, etc. Cf. **als.**

þre, *num.* three, 16/5, 6, 11, etc. **thre**, 142/4, 675, 681, etc.

thrid, *num.* third, 279. **þridde**, 4/23, 12/35, 16/1, etc. Cf. **third.**

thrin, *num.* three, *428.

þris, *adv.* thrice, 15/34, 23/18, 26/18, 21, etc. **thris**, 1519, 147/37. **-e**, 143/19, 21, 1404, 2152.

thrugh, *prep.* through, 142/27, 249. **thruth**, 80. Cf. **þur.**

þu, *pron.* thou, 1/4, 5, 9, 395, 396, 397, etc. Cf. **þou, tu.**

þur, *prep.* through, 14/11. **thurgh**, 193, 198, 226, 267, etc. **thurth**, 34, 39, 159, 192, etc. **þurz, þurȝ**, 2/28, 6/33, 9/33, 22/27, etc. **þurȝe**, 38/40. Cf. **thoro, thrugh, ȝur.**

þus, *adv.* thus, 2/13, 3/16, 4/1, 79, 99, 111, etc.

þusgaite, *adv.* in this way, thus, 1032, 1098. **-gate**, 370. **-gayt**, 94, 164.

thy, *adj.* 1/3, 7. Cf. **þi, ty.**

thyng, *sb. sg. and pl.* thing(s), 86, 142, 166, 196, etc. **-es**, *pl.* 549, 675, 681, 761, etc. **-is**, 142/4. **thynk**, *sg.* 674. Cf. **þing.**

thynk, *vb. sbj.* seem, appear, 237. *pl.* 855. Cf. **think.**

thynk, *vb.* think, 241, 616, 664. **-and**, *ppr.* 830. **-yng**, *42/33. Cf. **think.**

ti, *adj.* thy, 2/12, 8/14, 35/24. Cf. **þi.**

tide, *sb.* time, season, 1890, 2158.

til, *prep.* to; till, 1/23, 2/14, 17, 147, 1794, etc. (postpos.) 887, 892, 1585, 1692. *conj.* until, 21/12, 148/20, 1546, 1800, etc. **till**, *prep.* 3/32, 5/28, 30, 7/14, etc. (postpos.) 684, 2136. **tille**, 37/13. Cf. **tyl.**

time, *sb.* 17/8, 24/26, 25/15, 1701, etc. hour, 15/24. **times**, *pl.* 18/1, 33/32, 1702, 1729, etc. adverbially: at times, 32/24. **timis**, *pl.* 27/1, 33/11, 17, 28, etc. **fro time**, from the time that (or when), 2201. **fro time þat**, do.,

1719. **in þe times,** at times, 32/24. Cf. **tym.**

tine, *adj.* thy, 2/11, 23. Cf. **þine.**

tine, *vb.* lose; forfeit, 41/19. **tines,** *pl.* 4/27. **tinis,** *sg.* 31/36. **tint,** *pp.* 22/13, 27.

tis, *adj.* this, 18/28. Cf. **þis.**

tiself, *pron.* thyself, 8/14. Cf. **þiself.**

tit, *adv.* soon. **als tit als,** 35/8. **als tite a(l)s,** 29/24, 30/4, 44/21. **titter,** *comp.* rather, 731.

to, *def. art.*, in the phr. **to whilis þat,** whilst, as long as, 40/29, 33. Cf. **do, þa.**

to ? 29/32.

to, *prep.* to; for, 1/4, 7, 26, 1669, etc. (postpos.) 43, 550, 576, 633, etc. before an inf., 1/8, 10, 12, 13, etc. till, 142/27. *conj.* till, 31/6, 141/11. *adv.* to, 1/2. too, 42/35, 604, 2024.

togeder, *adv.* together, 517, 704. **togidir,** 7/21, 35/10, 13.

toke, *vb. pt.* took, 10/10, 22/24. Cf. **tak.**

told, *pp.* 2136, 2204. Cf. **tel.**

ton (after the def. art.), one, 1569. **tone,** 1482. Cf. **on, tane.**

ton, *pp.* taken, 171, 2112. **tone,** 1350, 2200. refl. 2120. Cf. **ta.**

tong, *sb.* tongue, 144, 1052. Cf. **tung.**

tonsure, *sb.* 290.

toppyng, *sb.* topping, top, 146/34.

toqueme, *adv.* agreeably, 14/27.

torch-lyght, *sb.* torch-light, 150/7.

toþer (after the def. art.), other, 1570. others, 35/20. **tother,** others, 145/5. **toþir,** 26/20, 28/3, 143/26, 144/12, 18. second, 4/18, 12/26, 15/33. others, 16/20, 26/10 (the first), 33/19, 41/1, etc. others', 26/10 (the second). Cf. **oþer.**

touches, *vb. sg.* 1400.

toumbe, *sb.* tomb, 145/9.

toun, *sb.* town, 1987. **town,** 467, 596, 1091, 1182. **towne,** 345.

towel, *sb.* cloth, 147/28. Cf. **tuaile.**

toȝ-wheþir, *adv.* nevertheless, 39/29.

trauaile, *sb.* work, toil, labour; hardship, 28/9, 28, 29/8, 32/22, etc. **trauayle,** 556, 1538. **trauel,** 770, 1112, 1265, 1710, etc. *vb.* 410. *pl.* 1599.

trayne, *sb.* train, artifice, 989.

tres, *sb. pl.* beams, stalks, sides (of a ladder), 11/21, 24.

trespas, *sb.* trespass, 19/4. **-passe,** *vb. sg.* intr. 31/36. **-passis,** tr. breaks, infringes, 45/24. **tress-passis,** *pl.* intr. 45/31. Cf. **trispas.**

tresur, *sb.* treasure, 7/2. **-e,** 2034.

trete, *vb.* deal, 441.

tretes, *sb.* treaty, covenant, 2/24.

trew, *adj.* true, 592, 2322.

trewly, *adv.* truly, faithfully, 1538, 2326.

tribulacioun, *sb.* tribulation, 978.

tricherie, *sb.* treachery, deceit, 37/21.

trinite, *sb.* Trinity, 16/8.

trispas, *sb.* trespass, transgression, 1252, 1355, 1544, 2365, etc. *vb.* trespass, 1907. **-e,** *sb.* 1256. **-t,** *vb. pt.* 740. Cf. **trespas.**

trofils, *sb. pl.* trifles, 1735, 1877.

troht, *sb.* belief, faith; trust, 5/15. **trouht,** 4/8. **trouz,** 2/22, 7/4, 8/32, 9/16, etc. **trouȝe,** 45/19. **wrang trouȝ,** despair, 42/22.

trou, *vb.* believe, 2/8. **trow,** 1823. *pl.* 1143, 1149. **true,** 19/10.

trubellus, *adj.* turbulent, 42/28.

tu, *pron.* thou, 2/22, 4/10, 5/32, 6/30, etc. Cf. **þu.**

tua, *num.* two, 11/21, 28/3, 29/7, 10, etc. Cf. **twa, two.**

tuaile, *sb.* cloth, 39/8. **tuailis,** *pl.* towels, 26/8. Cf. **towel.**

tuelmonethes, *sb. gen.* twelve-month's, 38/16. Cf. **twelue-monez.**

tuelue, *num.* twelve, 16/21. Cf. **twelf.**

tuenty, *num.* twenty, 20/20.

tuinne, *num.* two, 36/26. Cf. **twine.**

tuis, *adv.* twice, 29/18. **-e,** 29/23. Cf. **twis.**

tuke, *vb. pt.* took, 270. Cf. **tak.**

tung, *sb.* tongue, 105, 740, 757, 2184. **-e,** 2/10, 33, 10/31, 35. **-es,** *pl.* 11/36. Cf. **tong.**

turmentes, *sb. pl.* torments, 1293.

turn, *vb.* often refl. 147/33, 32, 49,

208, etc. *imp.* 109, 848. *imp. pl.* 70. **-and,** *ppr.* 147/30. **-e,** 1/4, 3/22, 22/8, 34/10. *imp.* 2/12. *imp. pl.* 12/8. **-ed,** *pp.* 144/4. **-es,** *sg.* 14/32. **-id,** *pp.* 38/6.
turnyng, *sb.* 147/21.
twa, *num.* two, 142/32. Cf. **tua.**
twane, do., 27/33.
twelf, *num.* twelve, 1107. **twelue,** 1025. Cf. **tuelue.**
twelft, *num.* twelfth, 1085. Cf. **telfete.**
tweluemonez, *sb.* twelve-month, 28/1. Cf. **tuelmonethes.**
twine, *num.* two, 5/26. Cf. **tuinne.**
twins, *vb. sg.* separates, 2459, 2463.
twis, *adv.* twice, 453. **-e,** 29/4, 1227, 1579, 1628. Cf. **tuis.**
two, *num.* 809. Cf. **tua.**
ty, *adj.* thy, 10/24. Cf. **thy.**
ty, *instr. case of* **þat (tat)**; **for ty,** therefore, 10/25. Cf. **þi.**
tyl, *prep.* to, 12/38, 14/2, 23, 18/9, etc. **tyll,** 12/20, 141/21, 13, 44, etc. Cf. **til.**
tym, *sb.* time, 444, 752. **-e,** 1/12, 15/22, 739, 1121, etc. "place," 15/34. **-es,** *pl.* 515, 147/35. **fro tyme,** from the time that, 701. **al tyme þat,** each time that, whenever, 1250. **or tyme þat,** ere, before, 2286. Cf. 2076 and time.
tyranry, *sb.* tyranny, 43/13.

vaile, *sb.* veil, 144/6. **vales,** *pl.* 144/9. **valis,** *pl.* 144/11. Cf. **vayle.**
vanitè, *sb.* vanity, 34/10, 1196.
vassels, *sb. pl.* vessels, 24/9, 11, 26/11. Cf. **vessel.**
vayle, *sb.* veil, 146/10, 147/5, 12. Cf. **vaile.**
vayn, *adj.* vain, 649. **in vayn,** 573, 724.
veine, *sb.* **take hir veine,** take her pardon, make her supplication, 31/10, 13, 17, 21, 29, 32/2. **do taire veinis,** make their supplications, 34/18. **takis þare venyse,** 141/17. [O.F. *prendre se veine.*]
vengance, *sb.* vengeance, 8/26. **vengeance,** 590.
verce, *sb.* verse, 1966. **vers,** 15/32, 16/7, 1686, etc. **verse,** 18/11, 27/18, 1139, etc. **verses,** *pl.* 1530.
verrey, *adj.* true, 1/9.
verset, *sb.* versicle, 16/4, 32, 18/22, 25, etc. **uerset,** 17/15. Cf. **werset.**
uertu, *sb.* virtue; power, 8/14. **vertu,** 33/30, 47/26. **-es,** *pl.* 42/37. **-s,** 47/20. **-se,** 2502.
vessel, *sb.* 2276. *pl.* 1453, 1480. Cf. **vassels, wessell.**
vestmentes, *sb. pl.* vestments, 1477.
vice, *sb.* 18/32, 23/20, 25/14, 2284, etc. **vices,** *pl.* 25/6, 33/33, 2269, 2502, etc. **vicis,** 44/6.
vigil, *sb.* fast observed on the day preceding a holiday, 1959.
uil, *sb.* vile or bad thing, evil, 144. **vile,** *adj.* 859, 1011. **vilist,** *sup.* 2020. Cf. **uyl, wil.**
uiltez, accidental spelling of **uiltes,** *sb. pl.* "vilenesses," injuries (Lat. *iniurias*), 38/2. [O.F. *viltez.*]
vinemens (**v** is vowel), *sb. pl.* ointments, 23/3.
virgins, *sb. pl.* 2497.
viset, *vb.* visit, 583. **visit,** 12/20. *pt.* 26/28. Cf. **wisit.**
visioun, *sb.* vision, 799.
umbe-þinke, *vb.* refl. remember, consider, think, 37/2. **vmbe-,** 6/17, 18/33, 37/18, 41/16, etc.
unait, *adj.* useless, idle, 9/5. **vnait,** 11/37, 32/23, etc. *sb.* idle or vain thing, 29/28, 30/15, 33/12. **unat,** *sb.* 10/33.
vnbayne, *adj.* unwilling, disobedient, 1639.
vnbousumnes, *sb.* disobedience, 732. **vnbowsumnes,** 34.
vnbowsum, *adj.* unyielding, disobedient, 1223, 2447. **unbuxum,** 5/22. **vnbuxum,** 13/18, 40/1.
vnbun, *pp.* unbound, freed, 508.
vncleth, *vb.* uncloth, 145/18.
vncunyng, *adj.* unknown, strange, 40/25.
uncuþe, *adj.* unacquainted, 8/22.
under, *prep.* 6/31, 10/7. **vnder,** 11/24, 12/37, 318, 2273. Cf. **undir.**
vnderly, *vb.* be subject to, suffer, endure; undertake, 1012, 1273, 1534.

vnderlynges, *sb. pl.* underlings, inferiors, subjects, 762.
vndern, *sb.* divine office about 9 a.m. 18/5, 14, 33/2,3, etc. Cf. **vndirn.**
understand, *vb.* 10/37. **vn-,** 201, 340, 469, 1045, etc. *pl.* 1143. **understande,** 1/23, 7/9, 10/1. **vn-,** 22/18, 25, 33/25, 44/32, etc. **vnderstandis,** *pl.* 23/21, 23, 47/27.
vnderstandyng, *sb.* understanding, meaning, 802.
vndertake, *vb.* understand, 1651. **-tan,** *pp.* undertaken, 22/14. **-tayne,** 770.
vndinge, *adj.* unworthy, 13/40.
undir, *prep.* under, 6/33. **vndir,** 4/17, 40/10, 142/5.
vndirn, *sb.* = **vndern,** 32/26, 27. **vndrin,** 17/26, 33.
vnleel, *adj.* disloyal, 23/10. **vnlele,** unlawful, 2509.
vnlefful, *adj.* not permissible, 296.
vnmesurely, *adv.* immoderately, 2332.
vnryght, *adv.* wrongly, 362.
vnskilful, *adj.* irrational, senseless, 298.
vntil, *prep.* unto, to, 165, 392, 476, 686, etc. (postpos.) 910, 1466, 1960. before an inf. 1601. *conj.* until, till, 1275, 1812, 2362. **-till,** *prep.* 38. (postpos.) 216, 378, 491, etc. *conj.* 1238. **-tyl,** *prep.* 284, 1271. **-tyll** (postpos.) 30.
vnto, *prep.* unto, to, 4, 53, 59, 122, etc. (postpos.) 104. until, till, 1123, 150/3. *conj.* 1132, 149/36. Cf. **onto.**
unwise, *adj.* 4/28. **vnwise,** 878.
vnworthi, *adj.* unworthy, 1027, 1101.
voce, *sb.* voice, 71, 118, 1065, 1919. **uoice,** 1/23, 2/1, 16, 27/20, etc. **voice,** 19/19, 34/35. **vose,** 67, 69, 1068.
vochyd (*pp.*) **safe** (*adj.*), vouchsafed, 1/11. **vouches** (*sg.*) **safe,** 1016. **vowches saue,** 45. Cf. **wouches saue.**
vp, *adv.* up, 11/16, 18, 20, 786, 800, 808, etc.
upryse, *vb.* rise, begin, 21.
vpward, *adv.* upward, 804.
ure, *adj.* our, 1/21, 2/21, 3/12, 16, etc. **vre,** 11/21, 12/24, 13/15, etc. Cf. **our.**
ure, *sb.* hour, 30/6, 45/3. **vre,** 18/11, 31/6, 17, 35/10, etc. **vres,** *pl.* 18/17. **vris,** 17/32, 18/9, 23, 27, etc. Cf. **houre, our.**
uresun, *sb.* orison, prayer, 7/4, 9/6. **vresun,** 33/34, 34/34. **-s,** *pl.* 34/1, 8. **vrisun,** 19/29, 30, 32, 33, etc. Cf. **orison.**
us, *pron.* 1/20, 2/8, 17, etc. **vs,** 1/12, 14, 28, 38, etc. Cf. **hus.**
vsand, *ppr.* using, 2230. Cf. **vse.**
vse, *sb.* use, manner, method, 17/19. *vb.* use, make use of; practise, 141/11, 1084, 1221, 1356, etc. refl. accustom yourselves, 10/33, 14/22. *sg.* or *pl.* (*sbj.*) 751, 754, 1055. **vsed,** *pp.* 1801. **vsede,** *pp.* taken the Eucharist, 149/40. **uses,** *pl.* 860. **vses,** *pl.* 732. **vsid,** *pp.* 1596.
usself, *pron.* ourselves, 7/16. Cf. **oureself.**
vstilement, *sb.* utensil(s), 24/32.
ut, *adv.* out, 12/19, 20/10, 23/16, 26/9, etc. **vt,** 26/16. **vte,** 21/6, 45/2, 6, 46/23, etc. Cf. **out.**
utcastyng, *sb.* outcast, 14/10.
vtrage, *sb.* outrage, excess, 30/1, 42/21. Cf. **outrage.**
vt-takyn, *pp.* except(ed), 16/21.
vttermest, *adj.* outmost, 149/36.
vun, *pp.* come, 17. Cf. **win.**
uyl, *sb.* vile or bad thing, evil, 106. **vyl,** 19/11. Cf. **uil.**

waim, *rel. pron.* whom, 17/8. Cf. **wha(m).**
wais, *sb. pl.* ways, 738, 992, 1119. Cf. **way.**
waisse, *vb.* wash, 26/8, 10, 35/22, 36/27, etc. Cf. **wesch.**
waist, *vb.* waste, consume, destroy, 2284. Cf. **wast.**
wait, *vb.* wait for, 1805. **-es,** *sg.* watches, 863. Cf. **wayt.**
wakande, *ppr.* waking, 1/21. **wakid,** *pt.* 18/3. Cf. **wakis,** *pl.* 18/2.
wakin, *vb.* waken, 20/27.—**waking,** *sb.* **16/24.**
wald, *vb. pt.* would, 1/17, 783. **-e,** 8/17, 11/12, 30/34, 31/30, etc. Cf. **will.**

walk, *v*. 1893.
walkyng, *sb.* walking, 42/35.
wand, *sb.* rod, 6/22, 31, 463. **-e**, 31/32, 1357.
wane, *sb.* number, 22/22.
wane, *vb. pt.* won, 1306. Cf. **win.**
want, *adj.* missing, 22/23.
want, *sb.* be wanting or missing, 1796. **-and**, *ppr.* 1505.
wantunly, *adv.* wantonly, 2393.
wapyn, *sb.* weapon, 568.
war, *adj.* worse, 311. Cf. **wer.**
war, *vb. pt. pl. and sbj.* were, 576, 2488. **ware**, 2/2, 10/8, 16/10, 24/22, etc. Cf. **wer, whor, wor.**
warant, *sb.* warrant, 5/11.
warest, *vb. pt.* healed, cured, 1306. [O.F. *warir, wariss-*, F. *guérir.*]
warfore, *rel. adv.* for which, 23/15.
wark, *sb.* work, 377, 446, 470, 685, etc. **-es**, *pl.* 231, 561, 617, 743, etc. Cf. **werk.**
warli, *adv.* warily, cautiously, 453.
warmer, *adj. comp.* 36/21.
warn, *vb.* refuse, 1438. **-e**, protect, screen, 45/22. **-ed**, *pp.* warned, 1628. **-id**, 33/14, 16. **-yd**, 1404. Cf. **wernyd.**
warnyng, *sb.* warning, 1/4.
was, *vb. pt. sg.* 12/32, 14/10, 996, 1352, etc. Cf. **wos.**
wast, *vb.* waste, consume, 1266. **-ande**, *ppr.* wasting, wasteful, 23/31. **-e**, 24/12. 1 *sg.* 844. **-id**, *pp.* 1019. Cf. **waist.**
wat, *int. adj.* what, 5/4. *pron.* 2/4, 5, 3/12, 6/26, etc. Cf. **what.**
wate, *vb. sg.* knowest, 838. *pl.* 2003. Cf. **wit.**
water, *sb.* 3/15, 35/21, 44/26, 1963, etc. **watter**, 2427, 146/22.
waxe, *sb.* wax, 1478.
waxe, *vb.* wax, grow, 20/7.
way, *sb.* 88, 120, 138, 706, etc. **ways**, *pl.* 707. Cf. **wais.**
wayt, *vb.* watch, mind, 2471. Cf. **wait.**
wayue, *vb.* pass, 444.
we, *pron.* 1/20, 21, 36, 47, etc.
wede, *sb.* weed, habit, garment, 141/11, 1338, 2175. **wedes**, *pl.* clothes, 2169.
wedenisdai, *sb.* Wednesday, 29/8. **wedinsday**, 1708.
wel, *adv.* well, 5/7, 16, 11/32, 12/21, etc. much (before comp.), 4/29, 24/22. Cf. **wele.**
welcum, *vb.* welcome, 2411.
weld, *vb.* wield, possess, 1181.
welde, *sb.* power, possession, 501.
wele, *sb.* wealth, weal, prosperity, 570, 2316, 2325.
wele, *vb. sg.* will, 778. Cf. **will.**
wele, *adv.* well, 2/26, 12/18, 55, 89, etc. very, 181. **well**, 7/11, 46/7. **welle**, 15/3, 31/33, 32/17, 37/9, etc. Cf. **wel.**
wele-lifing, *sb.* happy life, 243.
welth, *sb.* weal, prosperity, 102.
wemen, *sb. pl.* women, 254, 280. Cf. **woman.**
wen, *conj.* when, 3/23, 4/9, 25, 5/21, etc. **wen þat**, when, 2/13. Cf. **when.**
wend, *vb. pt.* weened, 1019.
wend, *vb.* go; turn, 43, 55, 124, 800, etc. 1 *sg.* 313. *imp.* 873. **-e**, 143/16, 934, 2373. **-es**, *sg. or pl.* 1585. *pl.* 306. **went**, *inf.* 2027. *pt.* 1308, 1342, 1906, 2390.
wer, *adv.* worse, 635. Cf. **war, were, werre, wor.**
werangus, *adj.* wrongous, unjust, 43/23.
wer, *vb. pt. pl.* 2398. Cf. **war, were, where.**
wer, *vb.* wear, 2430. Cf. **were.**
were, *adj.* worse, 311. Cf. **wer.**
were, *vb. pt. sbj.* 1301. Cf. **wer.**
were, *vb.* defend, 613.
were, *vb.* wear, 2030, 2176. **weris**, *pl.* 13/21. Cf. **wer.**
werk, *sb.* work, deed, 43, 125, 371, 424, etc. **-e**, 3/14, 30/5, 37/12. **-is**, *pl.* 3/17, 24, 42/32. **-s**, 128. Cf. **wark.**
werld, *sb.* world, 4/26, 8/22, 37/27. **werld alwais**, world without end, 331. Cf. **world.**
wernyd, *pp.* warned, 2359. Cf. **warn.**
werre, *adj.* worse, 4/29. Cf. **wer.**
werset, *sb.* versicle, 16/29. Cf. **verset.**
wesch, *vb.* wash, 1964. Cf. **waisse.**
wessell, *sb. pl.* = **vessel**, 1502.
weterly, *adv.* evidently, surely, truly, 863. [Cf. O. Swed. *veterlig*, evident.] Cf. **witerli.**
wha, *int. pron.* who, 2/28, 29, 3/23.

wham, whom, 2259. *rel.* 484, 966, 1373, 1997. **whame,** *rel.* 1/5, 3/7. **wha sa euir,** *rel.* whosoever, 142/13. **wha sam,** 3/13, 10/1, 23/13, 47/6. **wha sua,** 7/7, 13/5, 24/5, 47/11. **whaim þat,** whom, 19/27. **wham þat,** 33. Cf. **waim, who.**

whaire, *rel. adv.* where, 206. Cf. **whar.**

whan þat, *conj.* when, 30/16. Cf. **when.**

whar, *rel. adv.* where, 1177, 1351. **-e,** 36/11, 141/16, 144/24. **whare sam,** wherever, 34/17. **whar so,** 326. **whare sua,** 35/32. **whare sum,** 31/17. Cf. **whaire, wher, whor.**

wharefore, *adv.* wherefore, 36/14. Cf. **wharfore.**

whareinne, *adv.* wherein, 38/12.

whareþurz þat, *adv.* wherethrough, 39/10, 17.

wharfore = **wharefore,** 27/22.

wharof, *adv.* whereof, 27/25, 28/4 ("de quoi," cf. Spec. of Early Engl., ed. Morris and Skeat, part ii, p. 166, l. 60), 2350. Cf. **whorof.**

wharto, *adv.* whereto, 38/16, 39/29, 295. **wharto so,** *rel.* wherever, 293. Cf. **wherto.**

whas, *rel. pron.* whose, 28, 770.

what, *int. adj.* 117, 242, 315, etc. *pron.* 5/5, 7/4, 477, 764, etc. *rel. pron.* 2094. **what sam,** whatever, 14/5. **what** (*adj.*) . . **sam,** 14/3, 15/7, 9, *28/1, 41/24, 46/17, 47/14. **what so,** 534, 910, 925, 969, etc. **what** (*adj.*) . . **so,** 43, 1262, 1717, 1895. **what sum,** 47/15. Cf. **quat, wat.**

whatkyn . . so, whatever kind of, 1625.

wheder, *rel. pron.* whichever (of the two), 2047. *conj.* whether, 868, 1579, 2295, etc. **wheder so euer,** *conj.* 1763. Cf. **wheþer.**

when, *conj.* 8/23, 11/7, 41, 115, etc. **when so,** whenever, 861, 1077, 2417. Cf. **qwen, wen, whan.**

wher, *rel. adv.* where, 1983. **where,** 43/15. Cf. **whar.**

where, *vb. pt. pl.* were, 41/20. Cf. **wer.**

wherein, *rel. adv.* 22/29.

wherto, *adv.* whereto, 2120. Cf. **wharto.**

wheþer, *int. pron.* which (of the two), 10/35. *conj.* whether, 2261, 2493. **whider,** *conj.* 254, 713, 980. Cf. **wheder, whyder.**

whi (*instr. case of* **what**), *adv.* why, 5/6, 32, 395, 852. **for whi,** wherefore, "and therefore," 711, 2037. Cf. **why.**

while, *sb.* 13/21. **whilis,** *pl.* see **to.** Cf. **qwil, whils, wilis.**

whilk, *int. adj.* what, 95. *pron.* who, 212. *rel. adj.* 43/16 (the second), 27. *pron.* which, 42/32, 43/6, 62, 236, etc. who, 43/16, 21. **whilke,** *int. pron.* 7/22. *rel. adj.* 17/31. **whilke sam,** whomsoever, 43/30. **whilk** (*adj.*) . . **sua,** whatever, 44/34. **þe whilk,** *adj.* which, 337, 807, 811. *pron.* 750, 1109, 1705. Cf. **wilke, whylk.**

whils, *conj.* whilst, 43/11, 230, 885, 1535, etc. Cf. **while, whyls.**

whit, *prep.* with, 45/15. Cf. **with.**

whitnes, *sb.* witness, 39/20. Cf. **witnes.**

who, *int. pron.* 94, 134, 354, etc. *rel.* whoever, 132, 153, 374, 671, 1443, 1565, 2007, etc. **whom,** *int.* 1506. **who so,** whoever, 175, 247, 333, 543, 901, 2005, etc. **who so euer,** 2447. **who þat,** 906. Cf. **wha.**

whor, *vb. pt. pl.* were, 1997. Cf. **war.**

whor, *rel. adv.* where, 1666, 1731, 2017. **whor so,** wherever, 2205. **whor so euer,** 2215. Cf. **whar.**

whorof, *adv.* whereof, 2194. Cf. **wharof.**

whreþid, *pp.* made angry, 46/17. Cf. **wreth.**

why, *adv.* 37/21. **why þat,** why, 1219. Cf. **whi.**

whyder, *adv.* whither, 12/3.

whyder, *conj.* whether, 92. Cf. **wheþer.**

whylk, *int. pron.* who, 130. *rel. adj.* which, 27, 183. *pron.* who, 1/17. **þe whylk,** who, 55. Cf. **whilk.**

whyls, *conj.* whilst, 87. Cf. **whils, wylys.**

wice, *adj.* wise, 42/30. Cf. **wise.**

wicke, *adj.* wicked, bad, 9/3, 12/12, 13, 17, etc. Cf. **wikke, wycke.**

wid, *prep.* with; by, 1/10, 2/21, 22, 33/29, etc. Cf. **with.**

widal, *prep.* (postpos.) with, 27/4. *adv.* at it, 29/33. Cf. **withal.**

widuten, *prep.* without, 2/10, 31, 9/26. out of, 17/25. **-vten,** 14/37, 16/2, 17/11, etc. outside, 31/6, 35. **-vtyn,** 29/12. Cf. **withoute.**

wife, *sb.* 37/18. woman, 229, 1892, 2179.

wightly, *adv.* quickly, 1765.

wikke, *adj.* wicked, bad, *37/1. Cf. **wicke.**

wikkid, *adj.* wicked, 43/11, 1337. Cf. **wykkyd.**

wikkidnes, *sb.* wickedness, 622, 996. Cf. **wykkydnes.**

wil, *sb.* vile or evil thing, 28/11. Cf. **uil, wils.**

wil, *sb.* will, wish, desire, 8/18, 24/25, 39/17, 703, etc. willingness, 1971. *vb. inf.* 2446. *sg.* 2/26, 4/2, 32, 207, etc. *pl.* 4/30, 10/2, 259, 291, etc. **wile,** *pl.* 11/33. Cf. **will.**

wilful, *adj.* 280. **-full,** willing, 142/8.

wilfully, *adv.* willingly, of free will, 259, 1804. **-fuly,** 983.

wilis, see **do,** *def. art.* Cf. **while, wylys.**

wilke, *int. pron.* which, who, 33/12. **wilke sam,** *rel.* whichsoever, who(m)soever, 35/16. **wilke . . sam,** 37/7. Cf. **whilk.**

will, *sb.* will, wish, desire, 10/4, 286, 540, etc. *vb. sg., pl.* 2/10, 3/22, 30, 153, 283, etc. wish to go, 4/1. wants to have, 6/2. **wille,** *sb.* 2/6, 3/33, 4/19, 31, 46/28, etc. *vb. sg., pl.* 27/26, 32/6, 34/7, 32, etc. **to will,** to His liking, 7/1. Cf. **wele, wil, wyl,** and **wald, wold.**

willy, *adj.* willing, 2093.

wils, *sb. pl.* vile things, evils, 28/18. Cf. **wil.**

wimpil, *sb.* wimple (worn round the chin, the sides of the face, and the top of the head), 146/38, 147/11.

win, *vb.* win, 427. go, repair; come, get, 243, 795, 1765. Cf. **wyn** and **wins, wane, vun.**

wind, *sb.* 2280. **-es,** *pl.* 185.

wind, *vb.* wind, wrap, 147/27. **-e,** 39/8. shroud, 8/21.

wine, *sb.* 1610. Cf. **wyne.**

wining, *sb.* earning, gain, profit, 2058. Cf. **winyng, wyning.**

wins, *vb. pl.* win, earn, 1444. Cf. **win.**

winter, *sb.* 17/5, 1121, 2014. *pl. gen.* 46/2. **wintir,** 15/22, 32.

winyng = **wining,** 2471.

wipe, *vb.* 26/9.

wirchep, *sb.* worship, honour, praise, 174, 427, 1141, 1165, etc. *vb.* 1186. **-e,** *sb.* 1950. **wirchip,** *vb.* 331.

wirk, *vb.* work, act, do, 33/25, 111, 194, 424, etc. *pl.* 641. **-e,** 9/17, 22/30, 32/26, 259, etc. *pl.* 34/17. **-is,** *sg. or pl.* 13/6. Cf. **workes, wyrk,** and **wrht, wroght.**

wirkyng, *sb.* work(ing), 637, 703.

wis, *adj.* wise, 5/13, 6/28. **wise,** 42/16, 522, 554, 745, etc. Cf. **wice, wyis, wyse.**

wisdom, *sb.* 5/10, 10/37, 42/5, 882. **-e,** 44/18.

wise, *sb.* 42/34, 142/26, 457, 755, etc. Cf. **wises, wyse.**

wise, *vb.* show, direct, guide, 1119, 1298, 2378. Cf. **wisses, wysand.**

wiselike, *adv.* wisely, 14/38. **wisely,** 194, 1159, 1475. Cf. **wyslike.**

wiseman, wise man, 462. Cf. **wisman.**

wises, *sb. pl.* ways, manners, 742. Cf. **wise.**

wisit, *vb.* visit, 8/20. Cf. **viset.**

wisman = **wiseman,** 753, 1080, 1606.

wisses, *vb. sg.* directs, 1073. Cf. **wise.**

wist, *vb. pt.* knew, 1545. Cf. **wit.**

wit, *sb.* sense, understanding, reason, 7/23, 14/34, 73, 1437, 1609, 2229.

wit, *vb.* know, 12/1, 351, 1252, 1484, 1549, 2245, etc. "say," 147/11, 36. *pl.* 701. **witand,** *ppr.* 1451, 1945, 2439. **wite,** 3/20, 5/5, 20/19, 465, etc. Cf. **witte, wyte,** and **wate, wote, wist.**

witerli, *adv.* evidently, surely, for

certain, 38/16. **-like,** 3/20. Cf. **weterly.**

with, *prep.* 11/3, 14/12, 40/35, 7, etc. Cf. **whit, wid, wyd.**

withal, *adv.* with it, also, 147/27. **-alle,** *prep.* (postpos.) with, 38/39, 39/15. Cf. **widal.**

within, *adv.* 41/34. *prep.* 44/28, 2402, 2430. (postpos.) 139.

withoute, *prep. or adv.* without, 325. **-outen,** *prep.* 46/4, 47/2, 142/14, 124, etc. **-outin,** 805, 1718. **-outyn,** 56, 102, 930, 989, etc. *adv.* 41/34. **-owtin,** 45/9. **-owtyn,** 38/26, 39/27, 142/9. **-uten,** 10/18. **-vten,** 46/18. Cf. **widuten.**

witnes, *sb.* witness, testimony, 8/16, 42/16, 466, 553, 571. *vb.* bear witness, 2142. *sg.* 554, 753, 1462, 1592, etc. Cf. **whitnes.**

witsundai, *sb.* Whitsunday, 17/21. **-day,** 17/23, 28, 29/5, 1707. **witsunnday,** 1703.

witte, *vb.* (*sbj.*) know, 12/18, 38/19, 25, 42/10, etc. Cf. **wit.**

wittely, *adj.* wise, sensible, 1079.

witti, *adj.* wise, 2410. **witty,** 1608. Cf. **wytty.**

witting, *sb.* knowledge, 142/14. **wittyng,** 142/9.

wne, *sb.* habit, 6/13. *vb.* dwell, 2/28, 29, 3/2, 40/26. refl. accustom yourselves, 10/8. **wnis,** *sg.* dwells, 2/35, 47/13. Cf. **won.**

wo, *sb.* woe, 750.

wold, *vb. pt.* would, 576, 950, 974, 1340, etc. Cf. **will.**

woman, *sb.* 497, 1010, 1031, 1553, etc. **women,** 567. *pl.* 13, 257, 471, 551, etc. Cf. **wemen, wymmen.**

won, *vb.* dwell, stay, 102, 130, 134, 213. **wone,** 3/23, 30, 4/10, 29, 30, etc. **wons,** *pl.* 1632, 1825, 2054. Cf. **wne.**

wor, *vb. pt. pl. and sbj.* were, 1365, 1367, 1372, 1855, etc. Cf. **war.**

wor, *adv.* worse, 1016, 1019. Cf. **wer.**

word, *sb.* 3/13, 19, 78, 123, etc. **-e,** 1/6, 43/5, 44/8, 724, etc. **-es,** *pl.* 38/31, 81, 179, 192, etc. **-is,** 5/34, 9/6, 33, 10/15.

wordly, *adj.* worldly, 286, 570, 622. Cf. **worldly.**

workes, *vb. imp. pl.* work, 639. Cf. **wirk.**

world, *sb.* 93, 139, 194, 831, etc. **-e,** 42/32. Cf. **werld.**

worldly, *adj.* 287, 2232, 2296. Cf. **wordly.**

worm, *sb.* 1031. Cf. **wrmis.**

worth, *adj.* 922. Cf. **wrz.**

worthi, *adj.* worthy, worth, 228, 750, 900, 1013, etc. **worthy,** 54, 125, 128, 434, etc.

wos, *vb. pt. sg.* was, 448, 913, 1114, 1311, etc. Cf. **was.**

wote, *vb. pl.* know, 875, 879, 1153. Cf. **wit.**

wouches saue = vouches safe, 1622.

wouk, *sb.* week, 1513. **-e,** 1492, 1499, 1682. Cf. **wuke.**

wrad, *adj.* angry, 9/15. Cf. **wrath.**

wrang, *sb.* wrong, 8/26, 27, 13/3, 567, etc. *adj.* 42/22 (see **trouȝ**), 926, 2248. *adv.* wrong, wrongly, 14/26, 641, 973, etc. **-e,** *adj.* 4/3. **-es,** *sb. pl.* 597.

wrang-doande, *adj.* unjust, 23/30.

wrath, *adj.* angry, 1/14, 980. **wraze,** 8/22. Cf. **wrad.**

wrathid, *pp.* made angry, 1/16. Cf. **wreth.**

wrechidnes, *sb.* wretchedness, 609.

wreke, *sb.* punishment, 750.

wreth, *vb.* make angry, 48. **-id,** *pt.* 2390. *pp.* *24/26. **wrez,** refl. be angry, 36/11, 13. **wrezis,** *sb. pl.* (feelings of) anger, 19/6. Cf. **whreþid, wrathid.**

wretyn, *pp.* written, 2492. Cf. **write.**

wrht, *pp.* wrought, built, 3/16. Cf. **wirk.**

wriches, *sb. pl.* wretches, 878.

writ, *sb.* Scripture, 2/3, 5, 413, 457, etc. **-e,** 19/16, 41/8, 46/5, 847, 851. Cf. **wrytt.**

write, *vb.* 38/27, 28. **writen,** *pp.* 1/22, 6/21, 10/34. **writin,** 39/28, 47/8, 25, etc. **writyn,** 47/6, 2368. Cf. **wretyn, wrytyn.**

wrmis, *sb. pl.* worms; probably for *sg.*, perhaps influenced through the Lat. *vermis,* 14/9. Cf. **worm.**

wroght, *vb. pt.* wrought, did, 831. *pp.* 144, 850, 2145, 2393, 2430. **wroht,** 2/26, 25/1. Cf. **wirk**

wrytt, *sb.* Scripture, 60, 74. Cf. **writ.**
wrytyn, *pp.* written, 12/10. Cf. **write.**
wrz, *adj.* worth, 37/17. Cf. **worth.**
wuke, *sb.* week, 26/7, 10, 16, 27/16, etc. **wukis,** *pl.* 29/7, 38/11. Cf. **wouk.**
wycke, *adj.* wicked, 23/9. Cf. **wicke.**
wyd, *prep.* with, 15/23, 19/12, 14, etc. Cf. **with.**
wyis, *adj.* wise, 3/14. Cf. **wise.**
wykkyd, *adj.* wicked, 1/17, 54, 143. Cf. **wikkid.**
wykkydnes, *sb.* wickedness, 47. Cf. **wikkidnes.**
wyl, *sb.* will, wish, desire, 11/34, 12/6, 27. *vb. sg.* 22/6, 95, 210, etc. *pl.* 11/13, 12/3, 36, 362, etc. **wyll,** *sb.* 28, 37, 492, 689. *vb. sg.* 94, 101, 112. *pl.* 1, 3, 79, 92, etc. **wylle,** *sb.* 11/37, 12/9, 13, 15, etc. *vb. sg.* 30/24. Cf. **will.**
wylys, *conj.* whilst, 21/11. Cf. **whyls, wilis.**
wymmen, *sb. pl.* women, 37/31. Cf. **woman.**
wyn, *vb.* win, 64, 438, 946, 2056. go, repair, 1915. *pl.* 510. Cf. **win.**
wyne, *sb.* wine, 28/24, 30, 1605, 1607. Cf. **wine.**
wyning, *sb.* earning, gain, profit, 2059, 2067. Cf. **wining.**
wyrk, *vb.* work, act, do, 11, 64. **-es,** *sg.* 141. Cf. **wirk.**
wysand, *ppr.* showing, 138. Cf. **wise.**
wyse, *sb.* wise, way, manner, 141/21, 22, 60, 74, 103, etc. Cf. **wise.**
wyse, *adj.* wise, 15/2, 22/6, 182. **wysest,** *sup.* 551. Cf. **wis.**
wyslike, *adv.* wisely, 19/16. Cf. **wiselike.**
wyte, *vb.* know, 22/13. **wytt,** 11. Cf. **wit.**
wytty, *adj.* wise, 22. Cf. **witti.**

yd, *pron.* it, 72, 78. Cf. **id, it.**
ydilnes, *sb.* idleness, 1829. Cf. **idilnes.**
ye, *pron.* ye, you, 2/1, 7, 22, 8/12, etc. (to God) 23/26. Cf. **ȝe.**
ye, *adv.* yea, 10/26. See Notes.
yede, *vb. pt.* went, 22/22.
yef, *conj.* if, 2/1, 10, 3/6, 39/11, etc. Cf. **giue, if.**
yelde, *vb.* give, yield, give up, 6/28, 7/3, 10, 36/25, etc. **yeldis,** *sg.* 26/13. Cf. **ȝeld.**
yeme, *sb.* care, 22/3, 23/32, 24/8, 31, etc. *vb.* keep; guard, protect, preserve; observe, 4/5, 6/33, 7/2, 10, etc. **yemis,** *sg.* 12/1. Cf. **ȝem.**
yeming, *sb.* care, 38/5.
yer, *sb.* year, 33/28. Cf. **ȝer.**
yet, *adv.* yet, further, 5/25, 11/1, 13/31, 14/6, etc. Cf. **ȝet.**
yf, *conj.* if, 55. Cf. **if.**
ymbrin-days, *sb. pl.* a certain fast, "jejunia quattuor temporum," 1959. [O.I. *imbrudagar.*]
yme, *sb.* hymn, 148/15, 17, *20. **ymne,** 16/3, 35, 17/15, 18/10, etc. **ymnis,** *pl.* 18/16. Cf. **hym.**
yn, *prep.* in, 450, 666, 1037, etc. Cf. **in.**
ynke, *sb.* ink, 143/15.
youre, *adj.* your, 46/32. Cf. **yure, ȝor.**
yow, *pron.* you, 47/2. **yu,** 2/5, 8/33, 9/3, 4, *12/3, etc. Cf. **ȝou.**
yt, *pron.* it, 20/18. Cf. **it, yd.**
yung, *adj.* (*sb.*) young, 6/3, 7/25, 30, 41/25, etc. **-e,** 7/26, 9/13, 23/23, 26, etc. **-er,** *comp.* 41/31, 32, 46/13. Cf. **ȝung.**
yure, *adj.* your, 1/22, 2/2, 8/13, 14, 28, 32, etc. (to God) 23/26. Cf. **youre, ȝor.**
yuþe, *sb.* youth, 14/27. Cf. **ȝouth.**
yuȝhed, do., 41/19.

(ȝ = gh, þ).

ȝapli, *adv.* keenly, 1674.
ȝarnyng, *sb.* yearning, desire, 867. **-es,** *pl.* 874. Cf. **ȝernyng.**
ȝate, *sb.* gate, 44/17, 19, 20, 2414, 2423, etc. **ȝates,** *pl.* 2409. **ȝatis,** 47/28.
ȝe, *pron.* ye, you, 1/23, 2/6, 69, 71, etc. Cf. **ye.**
ȝeld, *vb.* give, pay, 2259. **-e,** 44/18, 47/8, 468, 502, 595. Cf. **yelde.**
ȝem, *vb.* keep; guard, protect; care for, take care of; heed, observe, 1052. **ȝeme,** *sb.* care, 1429. *vb.* 47/30, 475, 738, 741, 1434, etc. Cf. **yeme.**

ȝemer, *sb.* keeper, 2244.
ȝer, *sb.* year, 1833, 145/6. Cf. **yer**, **ȝere**.
ȝer (= **þer**), *adj.* these, 340. Cf. **þer**.
ȝerd, *sb.* yard, 1092.
ȝere, *sb.* year, 39/14, 141/11, 1702, 1882. *gen.* 143/6, 2173. *pl.* 2362. Cf. **ȝer**.
ȝern, *vb.* tr. yearn for, desire, 485. *pl.* 861.
ȝerne, *adv.* eagerly, 39/23, 26. Cf. **gerne**.
ȝernyng, *sb.* yearning, desire, 630, 680, 1602. Cf. **ȝarnyng**.
ȝet, *adv.* yet, nevertheless, 928. **ȝit**, yet, further, 299, 373, 493, 509, etc. **ȝitte**, 143/5. Cf. **yet**.
ȝing, *adj.* (*sb.*) young, 519, 650, 658, 1355, etc. **ȝong**, 106, 526, 1051, 1209, etc. **-er**, *comp.* 2216. **-est**, *sup.* 2209. Cf. **ȝung**, **ȝyng**.
ȝor, *adj.* your, 1157, 1158. **ȝour**, 10/31, 114, 492, 1593, 1934. **ȝoure**, 4/4, 70, 204. **ȝoures**, *pron.* yours, 141/20. Cf. **youre**, **yure**, **ȝure**.
ȝou, *pron. obj.* you, 491, 642, 695. **ȝow**, 2/13, 4/6, 73, 82, etc. Cf. **yow**.
ȝouth, *sb.* youth, 14, 1092, 2260. Cf. **yuþe**.
ȝung, *adj.* (*sb.*) young, 739, 1354, 2183. Cf. **yung**, **ȝing**.
ȝur (= **þur**), *prep.* through, 3/19. **ȝurh**, 41/7. Cf. **þur**.
ȝure, *adj.* your, 2/14, 14/4, 142/27. Cf. **ȝor**.
ȝyng, *adj.* (*sb.*) young, 528, 691, 1596. Cf. **ȝing**.

INDEX OF NAMES.

SHORT GLOSSARY TO THE CAXTON TEXT.

abyte, *sb.* habit, 119/6.
accompte, *sb.* account, 120/36, 128/12.
accustome, *sb.* custom, 126/9.
aferd(e), *pp.*, *adj.* frightened, afraid, 124/21, 139/8.
al ; **though al**, even though, 138/35.
amonge, *adv.* in between, at intervals, 133/36.
aperte, *adj.* open, 130/32.
appropryed, *adj.* appropriate, 126/19.
arn, *vb. pl.* are, 120/5, 127/26, 133/24. Cf. **er**, **is**, and **be(n)**.
as, *conj.* "as to," 130/32.
ascryue, *vb. imp. pl.* ascribe, 122/11.
atte=**at te**, at the, 120/37, 128/13, 131/4, etc.
avoyde, *vb.* intr. keep away, 133/23.
awaye, *adv.* **maye awaye with**, can endure, 132/31.
awe, *sb.* (keeping in) order, discipline, 135/10, 139/10.
awter, *sb.* altar, 128/16, 136/24, 39, etc.
ayen(s), *adv.*, *prep.* again(st), 121/4, 127/26, etc.

be, *vb. pl.* are, 123/4, 10, etc. **ben**, 121/1, 122/31, 123/35, 124/29, etc. Cf. **arn**.
besy, *adj.* busy, 129/27.
bette, *pp.* beaten, 131/32.
bileue, *sb.* belief, 126/23.
boden, *pp.* bidden, commanded, 125/17.
by-cause ; **for by-cause**, because, in order that, 138/5. **for by-cause that**, because, 132/34. **for by-cause of**, on account of, 130/2, 131/3.

cace, *sb.* **yf cace be that (þat),** if it should happen that, in case, 128/1, 131/1, 135/14, 138/26.
celary, *sb.* cellarage, 131/34.
chap(i)tour(s), *sb.* chapter(s), 125/38, 126/16, 127/28.
charge, *sb.* weight, importance, 120/20.
chesith, *vb. sg.* choses, 119/13.
childern, *sb. pl.* children, 127/26.
clymme, *vb.* climb, 124/19.
commen, *vb. pl.* come, 133/30.
com(m)yn, *adj.* common, 123/9, 125/26, 129/12, etc.
condycyoned; well c-d, good-natured, 127/32.
correct(e), *pp.* corrected, 127/10, 18, 129/16, etc.
cours, *sb.* **by cours,** in succession, in their turn, 129/32.
cowde, *vb. pt.* could, 122/34.
crafte, *sb.* art, trade, 122/32.

declyne, *vb.* decline, deviate, *120/28.
defawte, *sb.* fault, 127/11.
discharged, *pp.* relieved, 127/8.
dissymyle, *vb.* make pretences, 119/27.
distribute, *pp.* distributed, 135/4.
dompe, *adj.* dumb, 123/29.
dronklew, *adj.* addicted to drink, 122/7.
dyden, *vb. pt. pl.* did, 132/14.
dyttee, *sb.* song, 126/33.

els, *adv.* else, otherwise, 130/35, 131/30, etc.
emonge, *prep.* among, 129/12.
emsample, *sb.* example, 119/8.
enduring, *prep.* (postpos.) throughout, 125/3.
enleuenth, *num.* eleventh, 125/33.
entree, *sb.* entry, admission, 135/12, 137/1, etc.
entretyth, *vb. sg.* treats, deals with, 129/1.
er, *vb. pl.* are, 139/10. Cf. **arn.**
euery, *pron.* every one, 120/14.

fawty, *adj.* faulty, 139/2.
feliship, *sb.* fellowship, 131/24.
felowyth, *vb. sg.* follows, 119/1. Perhaps an error; in all other instances: **fol-.**
ferefull, *adj.* impressing fear, 127/33.
folowyngly, *adv.* in the continuation, after, 137/11.
forthy. See **thy.**
foryeue, *vb.* forgive, 125/11.

god(e)ly, *adj.* goodly, 125/34, 131/17.
goone, *vb. pl.* go, 127/25.
gyrde, *pp.* girt, 127/14.

hem, *pron.* them, 119/18, 120/1, 7, 33, etc.
her, *pron.* their, 119/21, 123/9. Usually **their, theyr.**
hert(e), *sb.* heart, 120/16, 121/31, 39, etc.
heyth, *sb.* height, 124/15.
high, *adj.* "deep," 130/32. **on high,** aloud, 133/20.
him, *pron.* refl. 123/25, 136/10, etc.
how be it, however, 130/33. **how be it that,** although, 132/33.

Iapes, *sb. pl.* jests, 122/22, 132/21.
inwardes, *sb. pl.* inwards, inmost parts, 125/20.
Ionger, *sb.* junior, 137/19.
is, *vb. pl.* are, 128/27, 136/6, 138/11. Cf. **arn.**

knowleche, *vb.* acknowledge, 125/12, 132/1. **knowlechyng,** *ppr.* knowing, 136/8.

large, *adj.* extensive, comprehensive, 137/12. profuse, lavish, 127/33.
largelier, *adj. comp.* more extensive, 131/30.
lasse, *adj., adv.* less, 134/27. **lesse,** 120/20, 127/15.
last, *adj.* the last, 138/10.
le(e)full, *adj.* allowable, permissible, 129/7, 134/15, 139/4. loyal(ly), 122/25.
leseth, *vb. sg.* loses, 132/1.
let, *vb.* hinder, 133/18.
longe, *adv.* **so longe to the tyme,** ever until, 139/30.

mekyth, *vb. sg.* humbles, 124/12, 35.
mele, *sb.* meal, 134/1.

mete, *vb. pl.* meet, 134/12.
meuynge, *ppr.* moving, 123/34.
mixtum (Lat.), 131/3. Cf. **miste,** p. 189.
moche, *adv.* very, 121/26.
moreyne, *adj.* murrain, 127/23.

naprye, *sb.* napery, 129/37.
namely, *adv.* specially, 123/2, 129/4.
norisshe, *sb.* nourishment, nourisher, 121/29.
note, *sb.* notice, observation, 120/26.
nought, *pron.* **is nought,** will not do, 121/16.

obedience, *sb.* obeisance, 136/15.
obediencers (-dy-), *sb. pl.* obeyers, 123/2, 11.
of, *prep.* of, out of, 119/2, 137/3, etc. by, 123/3, 126/19, etc. *adv.* off, 136/33, 34.
one, *pron.* one, a person, 125/14, 139/36, 140/1.
ony, *adj., pron.* any, any one, 122/4, etc.
oo, one, some, 120/36.
other, *pron.* the other, 139/19. each other, 133/34. other things; "so forth," 130/29, 34, 132/20.
owe, *vb. sg. and pl.* ought, 120/7, 21, 31, etc. **owen,** 127/15. **owne,** 119/16.

partie, *sb.* **in p-e,** partly, 127/7.
pensy, *adj.* pensive, 128/28.
percels, *sb. pl.* articles, 128/35.
perfyte, *adj.* perfect, 122/29, 124/15.
portar, *sb.* porter, gate-keeper, 137/35.
premyses, *sb. pl.* limits, "regards," 124/8.
preued, *pp.* proved, tried, tested, 135/36.
processe, *sb.* proceeding, course, "account," 130/34, 137/12.
professid, *pp.* **be p-d,** make the vow, 136/13.
promytte, *vb.* promise, 136/13.
propre, *adj.* "as property," 129/7.

rad, *pp.* read, 130/34. Usually **red(e).**
religion, *sb.*, cf. p. 197.
repreef, *sb.* reproof, 125/22.
riȝtwys, *adj.* just, 122/6.

saaf, *adj.* safe, 131/14. Cf. **sauff.**
sacrate, *adj.* sacred, 128/15.
sadder, *adj. comp.* (*sb.*) graver, more serious or sensible, 119/13, 120/22.
sadnes(se), *sb.* seriousness, etc., 124/5, 125/33, 131/8.
sauff, *adj.* safe, saved, 125/5. Cf. **saaf.**
sauter, *sb.* Psalter, 123/27.
selfe, *adj.* same, 137/11.
sentence, *sb.* sense, 126/32. opinion, judgment, 138/29.
set, *vb.* **be set lytill by,** be thought little of, 125/15.
seyenges, *sb. pl.* sayings, 120/14.
shrewde, *adj.* wicked, malicious, 122/20.
shulde, *vb. pt.* would, 138/3.
sith, *conj.* since, as, 126/23.
skale, *sb.* ladder, steps, 124/17.
som, *rel.* **whan someuer,** whenever, 121/12, 24, 137/31. **what som euer,** whatever, 120/10. **who som euer,** whoever, 126/4.
sore, *adv.* sorely, greatly, 135/32.
souereyn, *sb.* superior, 119/10, etc.
spirituell, *adj.* spiritual, 122/32. special, 134/1. **spiritually,** *adv.* specially, 132/36, 133/2. **spyrituelly,** 124/2.
state, *sb.* person of high rank, dignitary, 126/34.
streyt(e), *adj.* strict, 119/6, 120/33, etc. **streytly,** *adv.* strictly, 120/27, etc.
stuff, *sb.* articles, things, 128/29, 34, 134/20, etc.
subgette(s), *sb.* subject(s), 119/28, 139/22.
suspect, *sb.* fear, 126/1. **-e,** *pp.* feared, 122/14.
synguler, *adj.* particular, 120/25.

take, *pp.* taken, 125/15. Usually **taken.**
that, *rel.* what; who, 122/33, 127/25, etc. *conj.* when, if, 137/32. **in that,** that, when, if, 134/22. **in that aswell,** so well, 128/15. **after that, how that, leest þat,**

etc., *conj.* after, how, lest, etc., 120/32, 122/9, 127/11, 132/34, 133/15, 134/22, etc. **how . . that,** 127/17 (19). **whan . . þat,** 125/6 (8).

theim, *pron.* themselves, 121/15, 133/2.

theis, *adj.* these, 124/8. Cf. **theys.**

therfro, *adv.* therefrom, 120/29, 130/22.

theyrself(e), *pron.* themselves, 121/34, 129/7, 131/27, etc.

theys, *pron.* these, 128/12. *adj.* 132/36. **thise,** *adj.* 126/5. Cf. **theis, thyes.**

thought, *conj.* though, 138/20. Usually **though.**

thy, *instr. case of* **þat. not for thy,** nevertheless, 130/14, 136/4. **not forthy,** 134/19.

thyes, *pron.* these, 122/31. **thys,** these things, 127/27. Cf. **theys.**

to, *prep.* from, 120/19.

towell, *sb.* cloth, 137/8.

translate, *pp.* translated, 119/1.

trowbelous, *adj.* troublesome, turbulent, 127/32.

visely, *adv.* wisely, 120/19. Usually **w-.** Cf. **vysely.**

vnryȝtwysly, *adv.* unjustly, 121/2.

vnwytty, *adj.* unwise, 120/16.

vtterly, *adv.* altogether, entirely, 132/37, 136/6.

vysely = visely, 135/24.

welle, *sb.* weal, 119/7.

wertues, *sb. pl.* vertues, 121/22. Usually **v-.**

wertuous, *adj.* vertuous, 121/9.

whan soo euer, *conj.* whenever, 119/14. Cf. under **som.**

whiche, *rel. pron.* which, 121/21. **the (þe) which(e),** do., 119/3, 120/7, 122/32, etc. *rel. adj.* 127/37.

who þat, *rel.* whoever, 139/1. **who that euer,** 131/33. Cf. under **som.**

without, *conj.* unless, 123/25. Cf. **wythout.**

wittely, *adv.* wisely, 137/27.

woll, *vb. sg.* will, wishes, 133/17, 137/28, 138/4, etc.

worthe, *sb.* **in w-e,** in good part, 134/22.

wythout, *conj.* = **without,** 129/29, 134/1.

yeft(es), *sb.* gift(s), 128/23, 134/17.

yeue(n), *vb.* give(n), 120/36, 126/12, etc. Also **gyue(n),** 124/3, 133/2, etc. **gaue,** *pt.* 133/27.

ȝele, *sb.* zeal, 139/34, 36.